# LEARNING DISABILITIES

This book is printed on recycled paper. ⊕

# LEARNING DISABILITIES

## *Lifelong Issues*

edited by
Shirley C. Cramer
& William Ellis

·P·A·U·L·H·
BROOKES
PUBLISHING CO

Baltimore • London • Toronto • Sydney

**Paul H. Brookes Publishing Co.**
Post Office Box 10624
Baltimore, Maryland 21285-0624

Typeset by Signature Typesetting & Design, Inc., Baltimore, Maryland.
Manufactured in the United States of America by
The Maple Press Company, York, Pennsylvania.

**Library of Congress Cataloging-in-Publication Data**

Learning disabilities : lifelong issues / edited by Shirley C. Cramer and William
Ellis.
    p.  cm.
    Includes bibliographical references and index.
    ISBN 1-55766-240-1
    1.  Learning disabilities—United States.  2.  Learning disabled—
Education—United States.  3.  Learning disabled—Services for—
United States.  4.  Learning disabled—Employment—United States.
I.  Cramer, Shirley C.  II.  Ellis, William, 1940–1995.
LC4705.L365  1996
371.91—dc20
                              96-5887
                              CIP

British Library Cataloguing-in-Publication data are available from the British
Library.

# Contents

# Contributors

## The Editors

**Shirley C. Cramer, M.S.,** 2235 Harcourt Drive, Cleveland Heights, OH 44106, is currently coordinating a national public awareness campaign on learning disabilities. She was the executive director of the National Center for Learning Disabilities (NCLD) (1992–1995) and the executive director of the Heart Research Foundation of New York. She grew up in the United Kingdom, where she trained as a social worker. She was appointed Director of Fundraising for the Muscular Dystrophy Group of Great Britain in 1987. Cofounder and former Chair of Women in Fundraising Development in London, Ms. Cramer consulted in fundraising for a number of national groups in the United Kingdom. She has organized special events and, among other interests, has been an active supporter of the American Field Service youth exchange program, in which she personally participated in her high school years. She has served on the board of the Lenox Hill Neighborhood House in New York City. During her tenure at NCLD, she solidified a number of NCLD's initiatives and was instrumental in establishing a series of summits in various parts of the country.

**William Ellis, M.S.,** joined the staff of NCLD in 1990 in the position of director of professional services, serving in that capacity until his death in October 1995. A teacher in general education, he became interested in learning disabilities because of experiences in the late 1960s with students who were clearly very able, but did not perform in school at anticipated levels. Nothing in his training had prepared him to respond to such occurrences. He became an active member of the Orton Dyslexia Society and was its national president from 1980 to 1984. He maintained a participatory interest in learning disabilities as he became an administrator in independent schools. He advocated the need for services for people with learning disabilities in independent presentations at the conferences of many organizations in the learning disabilities field. Known for his efforts to forge coalitions, he spearheaded a national effort to enhance understanding of effective teaching for individuals with learning disabilities and served several times on the National Joint Committee on Learning Disabilities. Among his duties at NCLD was serving as executive editor of *Their World,* NCLD's annual publication.

## The Chapter Authors

**Pasquale J. Accardo, M.D.,** Professor of Pediatrics, St. Louis University School of Medicine, 1465 South Grand Boulevard, St. Louis, MO 63104. Pasquale Accardo has a distinguished record of accomplishment in support of children and adults with special needs, including learning disabilities (LD), attention deficit disorders, mental retardation, cerebral palsy, and substance abuse. He has written and lectured widely, serves as editor of several professional journals, is on the editorial board of the *Journal of Pediatrics*, and is a co-author of the *Dictionary of Developmental Disabilities Terminology* (Paul H. Brookes Publishing Co., 1996). Dr. Accardo is well known in his community for the personal interest he takes in the school-based problems of his patients.

**Duane Alexander, M.D.**, Director, National Institute of Child Health and Human Development, Building 31, Room 2A04, 9000 Rockville Pike, Bethesda, MD 20892. Duane Alexander is the director of the National Institute of Child Health and Human Development (NICHD) at the National Institutes of Health. He oversees programs relating to the reproductive, developmental, rehabilitative, and behavioral processes that determine the health of children, adults, families, and populations. Dr. Alexander is listed in *Who's Who in America* and is the recipient of numerous awards and honors, including the Public Health Service Commendation Award and the Surgeon General's Exemplary Service Medal. He is a diplomate of the American Board of Pediatrics (1973) and an Assistant Surgeon General (Rear Admiral) in the U.S. Public Health Service. He is a member of the American Academy of Pediatrics, the Society for Developmental Pediatrics, the Association for Retarded Citizens, and the American Pediatric Society.

**Gary F. Beasley, Ph.D.**, Training Manager, Crossett Paper Operations, P.O. Box 3333, Crossett, AR 71635. Gary Beasley is the training manager for Georgia-Pacific. He was formerly a management consultant and training manager for Weyerhauser and a member of the faculty of Mississippi State University. He is a member of several professional organizations and has written numerous articles related to vocational and career education.

**Benita A. Blachman, Ph.D.**, Professor and Chair, Graduate Program in Learning Disabilities, 200 Huntington Hall, Syracuse University, Syracuse, NY 13244-2280. Benita Blachman is a professor in the Reading and Language Arts Department at Syracuse University, where she directs the Graduate Program in Learning Disabilities. Her research interests focus on the early literacy acquisition of students at risk for school failure and the language factors important in reading development, especially the importance of phonological processing. Dr. Blachman is widely sought as a speaker at major conferences, and her research has appeared in numerous journals, including *Reading Research Quarterly, The Journal of Learning Disabilities,* and *Reading and Writing: An Interdisciplinary Journal*. A member of NCLD's Professional Advisory Board, she is on the editorial boards of several professional journals, including *The Journal of Learning Disabilities*.

**Douglas Carnine, Ph.D.**, Director, National Center to Improve the Tools of Educators, 805 Lincoln Avenue, Eugene, OR 97401. Douglas Carnine is the director of the National Center to Improve the Tools of Educators (NCITE), which was established by a grant from the U.S. Department of Education to "improve the quality of instructional technology, media, and materials for students with diverse learning needs." Dr. Carnine has participated in the development of Connecting Math Concepts basal series; Corrective Math, a computer networking system; nine CAI programs; and six video disc programs. He has served as consulting editor or editorial board member for eight journals and has more than 100 scholarly publications, including six books.

**Dorothy Crawford, M.Ed.,** Executive Administrator, Life Development Institute, 1720 East Monte Vista, Phoenix, AZ 85006. Dorothy Crawford, a past president of the Association for Children and Adults with Learning Disabilities (ACLD) (now known as the Learning Disabilities Association of America), was the national project director, ACLD–Research and Development Project, funded by the National Institute for Juvenile Justice and Delinquency Prevention, Department of Justice. This 5-year study investigated the link between learning disabilities and juvenile delinquency. She is the president of the Life Development Institute in Phoenix, Arizona, with particular oversight of the Independent Residential and Living Center/Program. She consults widely, is active in a number of organizations and sororities, and has received a substantial number of awards. She has written and presented widely on a variety of topics related to LD.

**G. Emerson Dickman, Esq.,** 178 Westervelt Avenue, Tenafly, NJ 07670. Emerson Dickman is an attorney who since 1980 has specialized in the representation of children with disabilities and their families, including advocacy and special needs planning. Among the cases he has handled are New Jersey's leading precedent protecting the due process rights of pupils in special education in 1989 and the leading precedent declaring and protecting the constitutional rights of adults with developmental disabilities in 1993. He is a member of the national board of directors of the Orton Dyslexia Society, the Government Affairs Committee chairman of the New Jersey Arc, and a board member of the NJP&A, Inc., which has been designated by Governor Christine Todd Whitman as the protection and advocacy system for the state of New Jersey. He has authored a number of articles and has been the recipient of several awards for his work in the disabilities field.

**Carolyn R. Eggleston, Ph.D.,** Assistant Professor of Special Education, Director of the Center for the Study of Correctional Education, California State University San Bernardino, 5500 University Parkway, San Bernardino, CA 92407-2397. Carolyn Eggleston is the director of the Center for the Study of Correctional Education. She is developing a master's degree program that will train educators to teach in prisons, juvenile facilities, and alternative schools. She is also teaching an undergraduate course for the prison education program at several local prisons. She has been closely involved in the development of special education services for the incarcerated population with disabilities. She is spearheading an effort to develop a correctional special education network within the Correctional Education Association (CEA). She has authored several articles on correctional education and formerly edited the *Journal of Correctional Education.*

**Jack M. Fletcher, Ph.D.,** Professor, Department of Pediatrics, University of Texas Medical School at Houston, 6431 Fannin, MSB 7.142, Houston, TX 77030. Jack Fletcher is a professor of pediatrics and a researcher. He has focused on the classification of reading disabilities and on the development of children with different types of brain injuries. He has authored innumerable papers and chapters, demonstrating his widespread interest in children's learning issues, including the effects of cancer treatments on childhood learning. He is a proponent of early intervention in learning disabilities and is a major contributor to the continuing discussion of reliable assessment tools. Dr. Fletcher is a member of the editorial boards of several professional journals, including *The Journal of Learning Disabilities.*

**Paul J. Gerber, Ph.D.,** Professor of Special Education, Division of Education Studies, School of Education, Virginia Commonwealth University, Richmond, VA 23284-2020. Paul Gerber holds a dual appointment as professor of special education at the Virginia Commonwealth University and in the Department of Psychiatry at VCU's Medical College of Virginia. He has written extensively in the area of LD, particularly on adults with learning disabilities and employment issues, and serves on several editorial boards, including *The Journal of Learning Disabilities*. He served for 4 years as vice president of the International Academy for Research in Learning Disabilities. In 1990, he served as the chairperson of the "Pathways to Employment" Consensus Conference for the Employment of People with Learning Disabilities sponsored by the President's Committee for the Employment of People with Disabilities. He serves on several national boards.

**Patricia Glatz, M.Ed.,** Special Education Teacher, 3804 West 80th Place, Chicago, IL 60652. Patricia Glatz is the president of the Learning Disabilities Association of Illinois. She has served on its board of directors in various capacities since 1987. She has also served as the president of her local chapter and continues to be actively involved as the school liaison and treasurer. She is a special education teacher for the Chicago board of education and has facilitated an inclusion program since 1987. She serves on an advisory council at the Cook County Juvenile Detention Center School. She has completed required coursework and applied for an administrative certificate with a supervisory endorsement in special education.

**Noel Gregg, Ph.D.,** Director, Learning Disabilities Center, University of Georgia, 534 Aderhold Hall, Athens, GA 30602. Noel Gregg is also the director of the Learning Disability Research and Training Center, funded by the National Institute on Disability and Rehabilitation Research. The center serves as a national clearinghouse of research and training information for adults with specific learning disabilities, will generate avenues of research, will provide training activities and products pertaining to adults with learning disabilities, and will provide for frequent dissemination of research data, training manuals, and teleconferencing on adults with LD. Dr. Gregg has written and presented widely on topics related to adults with learning disabilities, particularly in the area of nonverbal learning disabilities and women's issues.

**Mark J. Griffin, Ph.D.,** Headmaster, Eagle Hill School, 45 Glenville Road, Greenwich, CT 06830. Mark Griffin is the founding headmaster of Eagle Hill School in Greenwich, Connecticut. Eagle Hill serves the population of children with learning disabilities. Dr. Griffin is the current chair of the professional advisory board of the National Center for Learning Disabilities. He has a private practice in psychology and focuses on psychotherapeutic intervention for children and adolescents. Active in many professional and community-based organizations, he was the program chairman for the International Conference on Learning Disabilities (LDA) in March 1995. He has presented widely on a variety of issues pertaining to children and adults with learning disabilities.

**Judith E. Heumann,** Assistant Secretary, Office of Special Education and Rehabilitative Services, U.S. Department of Education, Room 306, 330 C Street, S.W., Washington, DC 20202. Judy Heumann was the cofounder of the World Institute on Disability (WID) in 1983 and served at its Vice President for 10 years. WID is the world's first independent living center and the world's first disability think tank. Ms. Heumann has served as the special assistant to the executive director of the California State Department of Rehabilitation, a position to which she was appointed by former Governor Jerry Brown. Personal experience led her to recognize that discrimination against disabled people was a civil rights issue, and she has championed the cause for equality for disabled people around the United States and the world. She participated in the development of the Education for All Handicapped Children Act of 1975 (PL 94-142) and worked on the regulations for Section 504 of the Rehabilitation Act (PL 93-112).

**Barbara K. Keogh, Ph.D.,** Professor Emerita of Educational Psychology, Graduate School of Education and Professor of Psychiatry, University of California, Los Angeles, 405 Hilgard Street, Moore Hall, Los Angeles, CA 90024. Barbara Keogh's research activities include the study of developmental problems in young children, temperament, and learning disabilities. She has written numerous articles and chapters and has edited or coauthored nine books. Dr. Keogh serves on the advisory boards of a number of national organizations and has held consultancies at the federal and state government levels. She has been particularly concerned with bridging the gap between policy and practice.

**Rolf Loeber, Ph.D.,** Psychologist and Professor, School of Medicine, University of Pittsburgh, Western Psychiatric Institute & Clinic, 3811 O'Hara Street, Pittsburgh, PA 15213. Rolf Loeber is a clinical psychologist as well as a professor of psychiatry, psychology, and epidemiology at the University of Pittsburgh. He is codirector of the Life History Studies Program and directs two longitudinal studies. The largest one, the Pittsburgh Youth Study, is a study of the development of delinquency, substance use, and mental health problems in a sample of 1,517 inner-city boys. At the beginning of the study, the boys were in first, fourth, or seventh grade. The boys are being followed up on for 9 years ending in 1996. The second longitudinal study, the Development Trends Study, concerns the study of conduct-disordered boys with and without attention-deficit hyperactivity disorder. The study examines which boys recover and which become boys who develop multiple problems and eventually become psychopaths.

**G. Reid Lyon, Ph.D.,** Psychologist, Human Learning and Behavior Branch, National Institute of Child Health and Human Development, 6100 Executive Boulevard, Room 4B05D, National Institutes of Health, Bethesda, MD 20892. G. Reid Lyon is the director for Extramural Research Programs on Learning Disabilities at the National Institute of Child Health and Human Development (NICHD). Dr. Lyon is responsible for the development and management of research programs in learning disabilities, language development and disorders, and disorders of attention in children. His background is in developmental neuropsychology and special education, and he has served as a classroom teacher, special education teacher, research neuropsychologist, school psychologist, and university professor before joining the National Institutes of Health. His current research interests include biobehavioral mechanisms related to language and learning and intervention practices with children with learning and language disorders. Among his many publications, Dr. Lyon is a coeditor of *Neuroimaging: A Window to the Neurological Foundations of Learning and Behavior in Children* (Paul H. Brookes Publishing Co., 1996), *Attention, Memory, and Executive Function* (Paul H. Brookes Publishing Co., 1996), and *Better Understanding Learning Disabilities: New Views from Research and Their Implications for Education* *and Public Policies* (Paul H. Brookes Publishing Co., 1993), and is editor of *Frames of Reference for the Assessment of Learning Disabilities: New Views on Measurement Issues* (Paul H. Brookes Publishing Co., 1994).

**Eugene Maguin, Ph.D.,** Research Institute on Addictions, 1021 Main Street, Buffalo, NY 14203. Eugene Maguin is with the Research Institute on Addictions in Buffalo, New York. He was the research analyst for the Social Development Research Group, Department of Social Work, University of Washington, until 1995. The author of a variety of articles and technical reports, he has been interested in a number of social, mental health, and health issues, including delinquency, alcohol use and driving, school performance as a predictor of the onset of delinquency, temperament and antisocial behavior, family violence, and the impact of Huntington disease. Dr. Maguin has held a number of consultancies and research positions.

**Edwin W. Martin, Ph.D.,** President Emeritus, National Center for Disability Services, 201 I.U. Willets Road, Albertson, NY 11507-1599. Edwin Martin is president emeritus of the National Center for Disability Services in Albertson, New York. The center provides a wide range of services to children and adults with disabilities and is a consultant to more than 175 of the nation's largest companies and labor organizations. Dr. Martin served under four presidents, both as the director of the U.S. Bureau of Education of the Handicapped and as the nation's first Assistant Secretary of Education and Rehabilitative Services. A former member of NCLD's Professional Advisory Board, Dr. Martin has written widely and is professor of education (adjunct) at Teacher's College, Columbia University, and has been a lecturer in education at the Harvard Graduate School of Education.

**Thomas P. McGee, J.D.,** Chief Judge, Jefferson Parish Juvenile Court, P.O. Box 1900, Harvey, LA 70059. Thomas McGee is the chief judge of the Juvenile Court in Jefferson Parish, Louisiana. He has been particularly active in bringing up-to-date information about learning disabilities to family court judges in presentations around the country and as a lecturer at the National College of Juvenile and Family Court Judges, Reno, Nevada. Known for the personal interest he takes in the young people he encounters, Judge McGee devotes time to preventive approaches, including mentoring programs, scuba diving, and pottery. He is a member of NCLD's Professional Advisory Board and serves on innumerable boards in the state of Louisiana.

**Louisa Cook Moats, Ed.D.,** Psychologist, Upper Valley Associates in Psychology, Assistant Professor of Clinical Psychiatry (Adjunct), Dartmouth Medical School, P.O. Box 253, East Thetford, VT 05043. Louisa Cook Moats has a long-standing commitment to teacher education. In addition to holding several teaching posts at the University of Vermont and Dartmouth College, she is involved in diagnosis of individuals with learning disabilities and is a counselor to individuals and families as well as a consultant to many school districts and other agencies. She coauthored a much-acclaimed 1993 article with G. Reid Lyon entitled "Learning Disabilities in the United States: Advocacy, Science, and the Future of the Field," in *The Journal of Learning Disabilities.* She is also the author of *Spelling Disabilities* (York Press, 1996). Dr. Moats is a member of the board of directors of the Orton Dyslexia Society.

**Melinda Parrill, Ph.D.,** Director, Child and Family Institute, 5775-A Glenridge Drive, Suite 110, Atlanta, GA 30328. Melinda Parrill is the director of the Institute for Child and Family Development and Research, Atlanta, Georgia. Additionally, she has a clinical appointment in the Department of Psychiatry in the Emory University School of Medicine. She has been particularly interested in assessment issues, both for learning disabilities and attention deficit disorders. She has been an active participant in innumerable professional meetings and symposia, as well as a member of a number of professional organizations, including the LDA and the Division of Learning Disabilities of the Council for Exceptional Children.

**Marcia B. Reback,** President, Rhode Island Federation of Teachers, 356 Smith Street, Providence, RI 02908. Marcia Reback is the chair of the American Federation of Teachers' Task Force on Special Education. She has served on a number of boards and commissions, both nationally and for the state of Rhode Island, related to issues as diverse as property tax, public libraries, drug abuse, and leadership. She is a former elementary school teacher specializing in reading, science, and social studies.

**Waldemar Rojas, M.A.,** Superintendent of Schools, San Francisco Unified School District, 135 Van Ness Avenue, San Francisco, CA 94102. Waldemar Rojas is the superintendent of the San Francisco Unified School District, a diverse urban school district serving 63,000 students. Before his appointment in San Francisco, he served as the executive director of special education for the New York City public school system and worked in various capacities within the New York City school system. As superintendent of Citywide Programs, he supervised 53 schools in more than 243 sites serving students with severe disabilities. A strategic plan was developed, with initiatives focused on the integration of services, technological improvements, language acquisition, augmentative communication, and multicultural infusions. He has been a teacher, assistant principal, and high school principal, and his experiences with the private sector have resulted in positive school–corporate linkages.

**Joseph P. Shapiro, M.A.,** Senior Editor, *U.S. News & World Report,* 2400 N Street, N.W., Washington, DC 20037. As a senior editor of *U.S. News & World Report,* Joseph Shapiro has covered social policy issues since 1987. He is the author of the award-winning *No Pity: People with Disabilities Forging a New Civil Rights Movement* (Times Books/Random House, 1993), the first popular history of the disability rights movement. Since he joined the magazine in 1982, he has served as its Rome bureau chief, White House correspondent, and congressional reporter. He has written on a variety of topics, including a widely discussed article on special education. He has contributed chapters to four books on disabilities and is a frequent speaker on the subject.

**Bennett A. Shaywitz, M.D.,** Professor of Pediatrics and Neurology, Codirector, Yale Center for the Study of Learning and Attention, Yale University School of Medicine, P.O. Box 333B, New Haven, CT 06510. Bennett Shaywitz is a graduate of Washington University (A.B. 1960, M.D. 1963). He trained first in pediatrics and then child neurology at the Albert Einstein College of Medicine and served as Lieutenant Colonel in the Air Force before joining the Yale University faculty in 1972. He has served as the chief of pediatric neurology since 1975, and is currently a professor of pediatrics and neurology, at the Yale University School of Medicine. Dr. Shaywitz's primary and long-standing research interest is in the neurobiological influences in learning and attention disorders, and he has authored more than 200 articles and chapters focused on learning and attention. Dr. Shaywitz heads a team that is using functional magnetic resonance imaging to study neurobiological influences underlying reading disability and attention disorders. He is codirector of the first federally funded Center for the Study of Learning and Attention Disorders, and he serves on the advisory boards of the National Institute of Neurological and Communicative Disorders and Stroke and the National Academy of Sciences, and on the Professional Advisory Board of NCLD.

**Sally E. Shaywitz, M.D.,** Professor of Pediatrics, Codirector, Yale Center for the Study of Learning and Attention, Yale University School of Medicine, P.O. Box 333B, New Haven, CT 06510. Sally Shaywitz is the founder and codirector with her husband, Dr. Bennett A. Shaywitz, of the Yale Center for Learning and Attention at the Yale University School of Medicine. She is particularly interested in using epidemiological and biological strategies to more clearly elucidate the nature of learning and attention disorders. She has addressed issues relating to gender, measurement, and conceptual models for, and the emergence of, learning and attention disorders. A member of NCLD's Professional Advisory Board, Dr. Shaywitz has contributed innumerable articles and chapters to the literature and serves on the editorial advisory board of *The Journal of Learning Disabilities* and as Editorial Consultant to the National Institute of Child Health and Human Development and the U.S. Department of Education.

**Delos R. Smith, B.A.,** Senior Business Analyst, The Conference Board, 845 Third Avenue, New York, NY 10022. Delos Smith is The Conference Board's senior business analyst. The former Chairman of the New York Downtown Economists, Mr. Smith directs The Conference Board's widely watched Business and Financial Outlook Conferences, which are held annually in New York City. He is a specialist in fiscal policy, taxation, the federal budget process, and leading economic indicators. He appears regularly on the CNBC cable television network and is an advisor to the CBS television network. Mr. Smith addresses a wide variety of business audiences throughout the United States and abroad, and his commentaries are also frequently heard on radio networks, including the BBC, Business Radio Network, CBS Radio Network, and The Wall Street Journal Radio Network.

**Sally L. Smith, M.A.,** Founder/Director, The Lab School of Washington, 4759 Reservoir Road, N.W., Washington, DC 20007, and Professor, The American University, Head/Graduate Program in Special Education/Learning Disabilities. Sally Smith has a long and distinguished history of substantive and creative activity in all phases of the learning disabilities experience. Tenured at The American University, she has been at the forefront of efforts to bring about improved public awareness of learning disabilities through audiotapes and videotapes, presentations, television shows, and print media. Her books, *No Easy Answers: The Learning Disabled Child at Home and at School* and *Succeeding Against the Odds: Strategies and Insights from the Learning Disabled,* have received wide acclaim and provide a broad base of accessible information for parents and individuals with learning disabilities. She is a much-sought-after lecturer throughout the United States and internationally. She has written two books for children with learning disabilities: *Different Is Not Bad, Different Is the Word* and *Color Me Successful.*

**Shelley Mosley Stanzel, A.B.,** CEO, Archiped Classics, 315 Cole Street, Dallas, TX 75207. Shelley Mosley Stanzel entered the world of learning disabilities while a student at Dartmouth College. Noted for her numerous academic and extracurricular achievements, she was overwhelmed when diagnosed with auditory learning disabilities during her sophomore year. Unable to meet the requirement imposed by the rapid-fire auditory Rassias language method developed at Dartmouth College, Ms. Stanzel challenged the college. Her lobbying and organizational activities resulted in a Department of Education decision in favor of the students. The first federal case affirming the rights of college students with learning disabilities set a compliance precedent that has spread throughout the educational establishment. A member of NCLD's board of directors, Ms. Stanzel continues to speak out and work on behalf of the rights of individuals with learning disabilities.

**Richard C. Strauss,** Chairman and Chief Executive Officer, RCS Investments, 8440 Walnut Hill Lane, Suite 800, L. Box 4, Dallas, TX 75231. Richard Strauss is chairman and chief executive officer of RCS Investments in Dallas, Texas. RCS Investments and its affiliates have been active in real estate development and management throughout the United States. Mr. Strauss also serves on innumerable boards and is the founder of a number of banks in the Dallas–Fort Worth area. He was appointed by Governor Mark White as chairman of the State Purchasing and General Services Commission. He served on the commission from 1984 to 1987. He was also a member of the board of directors and executive committee of the Capitol Committee Inc., established to renovate the Capitol Building and Grounds in Austin, Texas. He is a recipient of the Outstanding Learning Disabled Achiever Award from the Lab School of Washington, D.C., for which he serves as a member of the board of directors.

**Neil A. Sturomski, M.S.,** Director, National Adult Literacy and Learning Disabilities Center, Academy for Educational Development, 1875 Connecticut Avenue, N.W., Washington, DC 20009-1202. Neil Sturomski is the director of the National Adult Literacy and Learning Disabilities Center, established by the National Institute for Literacy. To this role he brings considerable experience related to individuals with learning disabilities in a variety of capacities, including direct service, diagnostics, administration, curriculum design, research, information management, and graduate-level teaching. From 1987 to 1993, he served as the Director of the Night School program at the Lab School of Washington, D.C., the only comprehensive, community-based adult education program serving the needs of adults with learning disabilities in the nation. He has served as a consultant to several agencies, including the state of Maryland, the U.S. Department of Education, and the Central Intelligence Agency.

**Helen Taylor,** Associate Commissioner, Head Start Bureau, 2050 Switzer Building, 330 C Street, S.W., Washington, DC 20201. Sworn in as the associate commissioner of the Head Start Bureau on March 14, 1994, Helen Taylor was formerly the executive director of the National Child Day Care Association in Washington, D.C. She is known nationally for her work in early childhood education, having worked for more than 25 years in designing, implementing, and managing effective early childhood education programs. She serves on a number of commissions and boards, including Secretary of Health and Human Services Donna Shalala's Advisory Committee on Head Start Quality and Expansion and the National Academy of Early Childhood Education. She is active locally as a member of the Washington Child Development Council and of the Bright Beginning Program for Homeless Children. She is the recipient of many awards and honors.

**Susan A. Vogel, Ph.D.,** Professor of Special Education, Department of Educational Psychology, Counseling, and Special Education, Northern Illinois University, DeKalb, IL 60115. Susan Vogel is a professor and the chair, Department of Educational Psychology, Counseling, and Special Education, Northern Illinois University, DeKalb, Illinois. She has written extensively on the issues of adults with learning disabilities, including the assessment of adults, factors contributing to their success, and the development of postsecondary programs for students with learning disabilities. She serves or has served on the boards of many national organizations in the field of learning disabilities and sits on the advisory board of the National Institute for Literacy in Washington, D.C.

**John L. Wodatch, Esq.,** Chief, Public Access Section, Civil Rights Division, U.S. Department of Justice, P.O. Box 66738, Washington, DC 20035-6738. John Wodatch is a civil rights attorney with more than 24 years of experience with the federal government, specializing in the rights of persons with disabilities. He is the chief of the Public Access Section in the Civil Rights Division of the U.S. Department of Justice, which is responsible for enforcement of Titles II and III of the Americans with Disabilities Act (ADA). He plays a key role in developing administration policy on the ADA and is the chief author of the Department of Justice's ADA regulations and of the federal regulations implementing Section 504 of the Rehabilitation Act of 1973.

**Glenn Young, M.P.A.,** Program Specialist, U.S. Department of Health and Human Services, Administration for Children and Families, Pacific Region, 2201 Sixth Avenue, Suite 600, Seattle, WA 98121-1827. Glenn Young is a program specialist for the U.S. Department of Health and Human Services, Administration for Children and Families, in Washington State. From 1991 to 1993, he was a presidential management intern with the same department. He is directly involved in the incorporation of disabilities policies into service delivery programs and development of regional policy and programs on the impact of learning disabilities on employment and training programs. Among many achievements, he provided lead staff support to the National Institute on Literacy in the creation of the National Adult Literacy and Learning Disabilities Center. He was diagnosed as learning disabled when he was in his thirties, when he was finally taught how to read. His story, "The Passage of a Tough Man," appears in the 1994 issue of NCLD's magazine, *Their World.*

# For the Reader

This book is intended for a diverse readership—those seeking a snapshot of the state of the field of learning disabilities in the mid-1990s and for those parents and professionals concerned about the future of individuals with learning disabilities. Many edited books are written for a specific audience and feature chapters with a similar style and level of expertise. The chapters in this book are of necessity very different and reflect the diversity of the contributors, their disciplines, and their perspectives on the subject of learning disabilities. The reader will discover some chapters written in an academic vein and others in a more colloquial style. All of the chapters, however, are understandable to the general reader. Professionals in the learning disabilities field believe that all voices are vital to represent the entire picture of learning disabilities. The challenge is to synthesize the information and to develop a coherent plan that can be implemented to improve services.

# Tribute to William Ellis

On October 19, 1995, William Ellis lost his long and valiant struggle against cancer. For all of us who knew and loved Bill, it was not surprising that he worked until the end. Bill was steadfast and outspoken in his advocacy for individuals with learning disabilities. In his distinguished career as a teacher and school administrator, he championed those children who needed his special encouragement, attention, and expertise. As former President of the Orton Dyslexia Society and as Director of Professional Services with the National Center for Learning Disabilities, he inspired everyone with his deep understanding of learning disabilities and his well-articulated solutions to many complex issues. Bill always had a clear vision of what needed to be done to help those with LD, and his clear thinking led to a successful national summit on LD in 1994, which is captured herein.

Bill was also the consummate diplomat: able to understand all points of view, but strong enough to bring about consensus. His commitment was rare, his caring deep, and his contributions to those with LD extraordinary. Bill was exceptionally happy with the title of this book, because he believed too few people understand the lifelong nature of learning disabilities and the issues related to adults. Bill has left many legacies, but two that are unique are the masterful way that he brought the national summit on LD to fruition and his creation of the first-of-its-kind national training program on the warning signs of LD for professionals and parents of preschool children. This farsighted program is due to be launched in 1996.

Bill was a wonderful friend, advisor, and colleague. We will miss him very much.

# Acknowledgments

We wish to extend our heartfelt appreciation to all those whose active participation in the National Center for Learning Disabilities (NCLD) 1994 summit on learning disabilities made this volume possible. Our particular thanks go to Anne Ford, NCLD Chairman, and to U.S. Senator Christopher J. Dodd for the superb job they did in cochairing the summit. The program cochairs worked long and hard to ensure a well-balanced program and a superb group of speakers. Many thanks for guidance, expertise, and good humor go to Tom Hehir, Director of the Office of Special Education Programs, U.S. Department of Education; Andrew Hartman, Director of the National Institute for Literacy; Ann Kornblet, President of The Learning Disabilities Association of America (LDA); and G. Reid Lyon, Director for Programs on Learning Disabilities at the National Institute of Child Health and Human Development. You made a first-class team.

Likewise, we were delighted to have excellent moderators for our four panels, who exceeded all expectations in their ability to preside over the proceedings. Thank you all very much indeed to Stevan Kukic, Director of At-Risk and Special Education Services, Utah State Office of Education; Judy Woodruff, Anchor and Senior Correspondent, Cable News Network (CNN); Carol Jenkins, News Anchor, WNBC-TV, New York City; and Drake Duane, Director of The Institute for Developmental Behavioral Neurology, Arizona.

We deeply appreciate the presence and eloquence of the political leaders who showed their dedication and commitment to all those with learning disabilities. Thanks to all the members of Congress, cabinet secretaries, and First Lady Hillary Rodham Clinton. We were privileged to have an exceptional group of summit presenters, who gave generously of their time and considerable talents to the summit and in contributing chapters to this book.

As always, the NCLD staff worked hard and long hours to ensure the success of the summit, and it is in no small measure due to their enthusiasm and efficiency that the 2-day event ran so smoothly. Christine Lord, Janet Weinstein, Marcia Griffith, John Thompson, Bernadette Colas, and David Fleishman are due an enormous vote of thanks. We are especially grateful to John Thompson and Bernadette Colas, who helped to coordinate the book with the editors.

Finally, the production, editorial, and marketing staff at Paul H. Brookes Publishing Co. were exceptionally supportive and creative every step of the way. We owe them a great debt of gratitude, particularly Theresa Donnelly, Elaine Niefeld, and Paul Klemt for all their encouragement and understanding.

*To Anne Ford, whose charismatic and committed leadership
of the National Center for Learning Disabilities and concerned,
persistent advocacy for those with learning disabilities
are a constant inspiration to us all*

# INTRODUCTION

*William Ellis*
*Shirley C. Cramer*

This book is based on the varied presentations made at the Summit on Learning Disabilities: A National Responsibility, which was developed and sponsored by the National Center for Learning Disabilities (NCLD), a nonprofit organization dedicated to improving the lives of the millions of Americans with learning disabilities (LD). The 2-day summit was held in September 1994 in the Dirksen Auditorium of the U.S. Senate with an invited audience and was jointly chaired by NCLD Chairman Anne Ford and U.S. Senator Christopher J. Dodd. The aim of this book is ambitious, and the book has an agenda different from the usual volumes on the subject of LD.

This book examines current thinking in the field of LD from different but crucial perspectives to delineate where the field should be headed by 2000. The editors believe that developing a consensus around the next steps in the field would add a much-needed direction to all the parties involved in helping children and adults with LD, their families, and the professionals who serve them. This introduction explains why this book is needed and the rationale behind its structure and the hoped-for outcomes. NCLD conceived of the summit as a strategic planning process for the field of LD, with the end result being a set of recommendations (Cramer & Ellis, 1995) that will take the field of learning disabilities into the 21st century and the enactment of which will substantially improve the services for and lives of individuals with LD.

## THE ISSUE OF LEARNING DISABILITIES

Learning disabilities are referred to as the hidden handicap with good reason. Although approximately 15% of the U.S. population are affected by LD, their disabilities frequently go undetected because of a lack of awareness by teachers, physicians, and parents. The term *learning disabilities* covers a variety of disorders in the domains of listening, speaking, basic reading skills, reading comprehension, and mathematical calculation and reasoning. These disabilities interfere with an individual's ability to store, process, or produce information and are unexpected, given the individual's general level of ability. Among the array of LD, deficits in basic reading skills are the most prevalent and often the most debilitating to children and adults. Learning disabilities can co-occur with and be complicated by problems in attention and social skills. Individuals with LD suffer from what one expert referred to as the myth of mildness (Martin, 1993). LD are not considered serious, despite all the evidence to the contrary. Issues of stigma and a lack of awareness and understanding of LD by the general public have contributed to the confusion about their existence and impact. Universally adapted definitions do not yet exist in the LD field, despite improved scientific knowledge.

## Plethora of Interventions

Although LD are known to be biological in origin, the interventions are more often educational. Parents and teachers alike are bemused by the array of treatments or therapies purporting to cure those with LD. Many of these interventions lack any validating evidence, and if evidence exists, it often has not been successfully replicated. For the concerned parent and teacher, the cottage industry of interventions for those with LD can be confusing, often expensive, sometimes contradictory, and very frustrating. This book summarizes all of the research, policy, and practice to provide a core base of information that both parents and professionals can rely upon and an objective picture of what is known and scientifically validated about LD.

## Scientific Progress: Bridging the Gap

Scientific discoveries about LD have exciting and positive implications for helping all those with LD, but these discoveries have not been quickly translated into appropriate interventions for students with learning disabilities, particularly in the education system, where they would be the most efficacious. Research progress has not received the widespread attention in the popular press that it deserves, given the large numbers of individuals affected. Research findings have not been disseminated effectively to parents and, particularly, to professionals. This book is a significant step in bridging the gap between research and its practical applications to LD.

## Fragmentation in the Field

The field of LD is fragmented across a number of academic and professional disciplines. Each of these groups has focused on different aspects of LD, which has led to disagreements and differences in priorities. Often one group is unaware of the findings and practices of other groups because there are few formal communication channels. The scope and purpose of many agencies that are important in the learning disabilities field have been too narrowly defined. As a consequence, many agencies and organizations that *need* to know more about LD to effect change have been left out of the dialogue or have been uninformed. This book brings together a broad range of people from a variety of backgrounds, experience, and expertise to widen the discussion about LD and to include many government departments and private agencies. It also emphasizes the critical role of collaboration between public and private agencies in creating an exchange of information and ideas.

## Precedents

A National Summit on Learning Disabilities was convened in 1987 following a mandate by the Health Research Extension Act of 1985 (PL 99-158) to establish an Interagency Committee on Learning Disabilities (ICLD). The major impetus for this congressional mandate was provided by a number of LD advocacy groups. The ICLD was charged by Congress to review and assess federal research priorities, activities, and findings regarding LD. The ICLD recommended that several multidisciplinary learning disability research centers be established under the leadership of the National Institute of Child Health and Human Development to discover, codify, and disseminate new knowledge relevant to the definition, prevention, diagnosis of and intervention with LD. Since that summit, researchers have achieved a number of significant discoveries that bear directly on the understanding of LD. A major purpose of this summit was to ensure that these critical discoveries were heard by those who effect policy and by those responsible for the identification and education of youngsters and adults with LD.

## No Vehicle for Looking to the Future

There has been a pervasive view that the LD field has been stagnant and mired in internal strife regarding definition, research methods, and interventions. This book seeks to bring a sense of purpose and direction to *all* the voices in the field and to help delineate and develop consensus on what we need to do to improve outcomes for the millions of people with LD. It is hoped that this book will be a valuable asset in helping to plan for the future.

## Evidence of Failure for Individuals with Learning Disabilities

An overriding reason for publishing this book is that the outcomes for far too many individuals with LD are unfavorable. Despite the substantial gains that have been made via federal legislation for those with LD since the passage of Public Law 94-142, the Education for All Handicapped

Children Act of 1975, reauthorized and amended several times and reenacted as the Individuals with Disabilities Education Act of 1990 (IDEA) (PL 101-476), and the Americans with Disabilities Act of 1990 (ADA) (PL 101-336), uneven and uninformed implementation of these laws has led to many individuals failing in the education system and in the world of work. The following statistics indicate the extent of the problem of LD nationally and clearly show that early identification and intervention are vital for individuals with LD. There will continue to be an enormous cost to pay, both for the individual with LD and for society, if we do not provide better solutions.

- Fifty-two percent of all students in special education in public school have LD. This equates to approximately 2.25 million children (U.S. Department of Education, 1994).
- Seventy-five percent to eighty percent of these special education students identified as having LD have basic deficits in language and reading (Lyon, 1994).
- Thirty-five percent of students identified as having LD drop out of high school. This is twice the rate of their peers without disabilities. This figure does not include students who are not identified and drop out (Wagner, 1991).
- Estimates suggest that 30%–50% of illiterate adults in Adult Basic Education and literacy programs may be learning disabled (National Adult Literacy and Learning Disabilities Center, 1995).
- Fifty percent of juvenile delinquents tested were found to have undetected learning disabilities.
- Up to 60% of adolescents in treatment for substance abuse have learning disabilities.
- Sixty-two percent of students with LD were unemployed 1 year after graduating from high school (Wagner, 1991).
- Fifty percent of females with learning disabilities will be mothers (many of them single) within 3–5 years of leaving high school (Wagner, 1991).
- Thirty-one percent of adolescents with learning disabilities will be arrested 3–5 years after leaving high school (Wagner, 1991).
- Learning disabilities and substance abuse are the most common impediments to the employment of welfare clients (Office of the Inspector General, 1992).

These findings highlight many of the negative outcomes and the extent of the problems that need to be addressed.

## Informing Decisions Makers

This book, as an outgrowth of the summit, provides invaluable information to those involved with policy implementation and reauthorization of legislation, including IDEA and the Carl D. Perkins Vocational and Applied Technology Education Act of 1990 (PL 101-392). With this as background, this book serves as a vehicle to ensure that everyone understands that LD are lifelong issues that do not disappear with age, but that, with intervention, individuals with LD can be successful and productive members of society.

## REFERENCES

Americans with Disabilities Act of 1990 (ADA), PL 101-336. (July 26, 1990). Title 42, U.S.C. §§ 12101 et seq.: *U.S. Statutes at Large, 104,* 327–378.

Carl D. Perkins Vocational and Applied Technology Education Act of 1990, PL 101-392. (September 25, 1990). Title 20, U.S.C. §§ 2301 et seq.: *U.S. Statutes at Large, 104,* 753–843.

Cramer, S.C., & Ellis, W. (1995, February). *Learning disabilities: A national responsibility* (pp. 11–22). Report of the Summit on Learning Disabilities. New York: National Center for Learning Disabilities.

Education for All Handicapped Children Act of 1975, PL 94-142. (August 23, 1977). Title 20, U.S.C. §§ 1401 et seq.: *U.S. Statutes at Large, 104,* 1103–1151.

Health Research Extension Act of 1985, PL 99-158. (November 20, 1985). Title 42, U.S.C. §§ 201 et seq.: *U.S. Statutes at Large, 99,* 820–886.

Individuals with Disabilities Education Act of 1990 (IDEA), PL 101-476. (October 30, 1990). Title 20, U.S.C. §§ 1401 et seq.: *U.S. Statutes at Large, 104,* 1103–1151.

Lyon, G.R. (Ed.). (1994). *Frames of reference for the assessment of learning disabilities: New views on measurement issues.* Baltimore: Paul H. Brookes Publishing Co.

Martin, E.W. (1993). Learning disabilities and public policy: Myths and outcomes. In G.R. Lyon, D.B. Gray, J.F. Kavanagh, & N.A. Krasnegor (Eds.), *Better understanding learning disabilities: New views from research and their implications for education and public policies* (pp. 325–342). Baltimore: Paul H. Brookes Publishing Co.

National Adult Literacy and Learning Disabilities Center. (1995, Spring). From the director. *Linkages, 2*(1), 1.

Nightingale, D., Yudd, R., Anderson, S., & Barnow, B. (1991). *The learning disabled in employment and training programs* (Research and Evaluation Rep. Series 91-E). Washington, DC: U.S. Government Printing Office.

Office of the Inspector General. (1992). *Functional impairments of AFDC clients.* Washington, DC: U.S. Government Printing Office.

Office of Special Education Programs, U.S. Department of Education. (1995). *17th annual report to Congress on implementation of the Individuals with Disabilities Education Act.* Washington, DC: U.S. Government Printing Office.

Wagner, M., Newman, L. et al. (1991). Youth with disabilities: How are they doing? Report from the *National Longitudinal Transition Study of Special Education Students.* Menlo Park, CA: SRI International.

# SECTION I

## OVERVIEW

# Chapter 1

# The State of Research

*G. Reid Lyon*

Recognized as a federally designated handicapping condition in 1968, learning disabilities (LD) represents approximately one half of all children receiving special education services nationally (U.S. Department of Education, 1989). At the same time, LD remains one of the least understood and most debated of the disabling conditions that affect children. Indeed, even a cursory perusal of the literature relevant to the status of LD reveals that the field has been, and continues to be, beset by pervasive and at times contentious disagreements about the definition of the disorder, diagnostic criteria, assessment practices, intervention procedures, and educational policies (Lyon, 1987, 1995a; Lyon, Gray, Kavanagh, & Krasnegor, 1993; Lyon & Moats, 1988, 1993; Moats & Lyon, 1993).

A number of influences have contributed to these disagreements, which, in turn, have produced difficulties in building a generalizable body of scientific and clinical knowledge relevant to LD and in establishing reliable and valid diagnostic criteria (Lyon, 1985a, 1987). Although some progress has been made since the mid-1980s in establishing more precise definitions and a theoretically based classification system for LD (see Lyon et al., 1993), a number of factors have impeded the development of a valid scientific basis for the study of learning disabilities and their interrelationships with other developmental disorders.

In this context, the next section of this chapter reviews briefly the impediments to research efforts in the field of LD. Subsequent sections in this chapter address in detail the core features of specific types of LD and the available research literature relevant to each type. The reader should note at this point that LD are not homogenous disorders. In fact, learning disabilities, by definition, refer to deficits in one or more of several domains that include reading disorders, mathematics disorders, disorders of written expression, and receptive (listening) and expressive (speaking) language disorders. Because each of these types of LD is characterized by its own distinct definitional and diagnostic issues, as well as issues associated with heterogeneity, each type is reviewed separately in the following sections. Thus, for each type of LD, a review of critical background information, constructs, and research and clinical trends is provided. More specifically, the review of the major learning disabilities addresses: 1) particular historical issues related to each disability; 2) a review of current definitional and diagnostic issues concerning the specific type of disability; 3) the developmental course, prognosis, and epidemiology of the disability; 4) the major theoretical frameworks that are guiding research and practice in each area of disability; and 5) a review of the etiological mechanisms and comorbidities hypothesized to cause or contribute to the specific type of LD. The chapter then concludes with a brief review of current issues and a look toward the future.

## SPECIFIC IMPEDIMENTS TO RESEARCH IN LEARNING DISABILITIES

It has been only since 1980 that serious and systematic research efforts have been deployed toward understanding the causes, developmental course, intervention conditions, and long-term outcomes of LD from a scientific perspective. Still, many of these efforts have not yet led to precise definitions and a scientific understanding of learning disabilities and their educational, linguistic, genetic, physiological, and neurophysiological correlates. On the positive side, we have begun to identify specific influences and reasons why research in LD has not produced knowledge fundamental to definition, diagnosis, developmental course, and intervention. A brief overview of these influences can serve as a reminder that unless we understand and address these historical and methodological issues our ability to define, classify, and intervene with LD effectively will be limited.

### Youth of the Field

The limitations of the field as a clinical science can be related to its brief tenure as a recognized category of disability (Lyon, 1987, 1994a). LD as a federally designated condition has existed only since 1968 (Moats & Lyon, 1993). Thus, there has not been sufficient time to collect and consolidate the necessary observations under experimental conditions that could lead to a better understanding of the critical diagnostic markers and interventions that have a known probability of success.

### Theoretical and Conceptual Heterogeneity

Many different theoretical and conceptual views have been offered to explain LD, and these views clearly reflect the multidisciplinary nature of the field (Lyon, 1996; Moats & Lyon, 1993; Torgesen, 1993). Learning disabilities are considered the legitimate concern of many disciplines and professions including psychology, education, neurology, neuropsychology, psychiatry, speech-language pathology, and optometry. Each of these disciplines has focused on different aspects of the child or adult with LD so that there exist highly divergent ideas and frequent disagreements about the importance of etiology, diagnostic methods, intervention methods, and professional roles and responsibilities (Torgesen, 1991, 1993). Unfortunately, from the perspective of developing a valid definition and classification system of LD, such variations in views and beliefs result in differences in the numbers of children (and adults) identified as having learning disabilities and differences in how phenotypic characteristics are measured and described. In turn, conducting research on samples of individuals with putative LD who vary widely in diagnostic and demographic characteristics provides little opportunity for the replication and generalization of clinical and empirical findings—the cornerstones of scientific inquiry.

## Limitations in Measurement Practices

Many diagnostic and intervention decisions about individuals with LD have been based on technically inadequate tests and measures. Recent comprehensive reviews of instruments used to diagnose oral language, reading, mathematics, and written language deficits do not meet criteria for adequate norms, reliability, and validity (Lyon, 1994b). As important, the valid assessment of change over time, and change as a function of intervention, is very difficult to accomplish because few instruments have the scaling properties necessary to satisfy conditions for the measurement of individual growth curves (Francis, Shaywitz, Steubing, Shaywitz, & Fletcher, 1994; Shaywitz & Shaywitz, 1994).

## Limitations in Experimental Design and Criteria for Diagnosis

The study of individuals identified with LD by school or clinic criteria from "single-shot" investigations or cross-sectional designs has significantly hampered efforts to develop a valid definition and classification system for LD (an issue that is discussed in detail later). It has been observed that schools and clinics lack consistency in the way LD is diagnosed. A child can literally be "cured" of an LD condition or have a diagnosis changed from mental retardation to LD simply by moving across state boundaries or even by changing schools within the same community (Lyon, 1994b, 1996; Lyon et al., 1993; Moats & Lyon, 1993). Such variability in sample characteristics prohibits replication and generalization of findings—a severe impediment to the development of any clinical science. Moreover, single-shot investigations that compare typically achieving children with children with LD on one or more dependent variables of interest at one point in time ignore the developmental nature of learning and change over time and how such change interacts with information-processing characteristics, teacher characteristics, particular interventions, and classroom settings and climates (Lyon, 1987, 1996). As such, information relevant to the developmental course of LD and how children may display different characteristics at different points in time remains limited.

## Problems in Establishing a Valid Definition and Classification System

By far the most significant and persistent problem impeding progress in the field of LD has been the difficulty in establishing a precise *inclusionary* definition and *theoretically based classification system* that can provide 1) a framework for the identification of different types of LD and 2) a framework for recognizing distinctions and interrelationships (comorbidities) between LD and other learning and behavioral disorders to include attention-deficit/hyperactivity disorder (ADHD), mental retardation, general academic underachievement, and the psychopathologies (Fletcher & Morris, 1986; Lyon & Moats, 1993; Lyon et al., 1993; Morris, 1988, 1993). At present, the field continues to construct and utilize vague, ambiguous, *exclusionary*, and nonvalidated definitions of LD that attempt to cluster extremely heterogeneous subgroups of disorders. Consider the past and current *general* definitions, which serve to frame diagnostic and eligibility criteria.

The Education for All Handicapped Children Act of 1975 (PL 94-142) incorporated the following definition of LD, originally proposed by the National Advisory Committee on Handicapped Children in 1968:

> The term specific learning disability means a disorder in one or more of the basic psychological processes involved in understanding or in using language, spoken or written, which may manifest itself in an imperfect ability to listen, speak, read, write, spell, or do mathematical calculations. The term includes such conditions as perceptual handicaps, brain injury, minimal brain dysfunction, dyslexia, and developmental aphasia. Such terms do not include children who have learning difficulties which are primarily the result of visual, hearing, or motor handicaps, of mental retardation, of emotional disturbance, or of environmental, cultural, or economic disadvantage. (U.S. Office of Special Education, 1977, p. 65,083)

Unfortunately, this definition is virtually useless with respect to providing clinicians and researchers with objective guidelines and criteria for distinguishing individuals with LD from those with other primary disabilities or generalized learning difficulties. Indeed, many papers have been written criticizing the use of this vague definition in driving diagnostic and educational practices (e.g., Fletcher & Morris, 1986; Kavale & Forness, 1985; Kavale & Nye, 1986; Lyon, 1987, 1994b; Lyon et al., 1993; Moats & Lyon, 1993; Senf, 1981, 1986, 1987).

As Torgesen (1991) has pointed out, the 1968 definition has at least four major problems that render it ineffective:

1. The definition does not indicate clearly that learning disabilities are a heterogeneous group of disorders.
2. It fails to recognize that learning disabilities frequently persist and are manifested in adults as well as children.
3. It does not clearly specify that, whatever the cause of the learning disabilities, the final common path involves inherent alterations in the way information is processed.
4. It does not adequately recognize that people with other disabilities or environmental limitations may have a learning disability *concurrently* with these conditions.

Formal attempts to refine the general definition of LD have not fared appreciably better (Moats & Lyon, 1993), as can be seen in the revised definition produced by the National Joint Committee on Learning Disabilities (NJCLD) (see Hammill, 1993; Hammill, Leigh, McNutt, & Larsen, 1981). This revised definition states:

> *Learning disabilities* is a general term that refers to a heterogeneous group of disorders manifested by significant difficulty in the acquisition and use of listening, speaking, reading, writing, reasoning, or mathematical abilities. These disorders are intrinsic to the individual, presumed to be due to central nervous system dysfunction, and may occur across the life span. Problems in self-regulatory behavior, social perception, and social interaction may exist with learning disabilities but do not by themselves constitute a learning disability. Although learning disabilities may occur concomitantly with other handicapping conditions (sensory impairment, mental retardation, social and emotional disturbance) or with extrinsic influences (cultural differences, insufficient or inappropriate instruction) they are not the result of these conditions. (Hammill et al., 1981, p. 10)

Although this revised definition addresses the issues of heterogeneity, persistence, intrinsic etiology, and comorbidity discussed by Torgesen (1991), it continues to offer a vague and ambiguous description of multiple and heterogeneous disorders. In essence, this definition cannot be easily operationalized and empirically validated. Thus, to date, most definitions of LD still do not provide clinicians, teachers, and researchers with useful information to enhance communication or improve predictions. Given this state in the field, many scholars have called for a moratorium on the development of broad definitions (at least for research purposes) and advocate a definition that addresses learning disabilities defined only in terms of coherent and operational domains.

For example, Stanovich (1993) argued the following point:

> Scientific investigations of some generically defined entity called "learning disability" simply make little sense given what we already know about heterogeneity across various learning domains. Research investigations must define groups specifically in terms of the domain of deficit (reading disability, arithmetic disability). The extent of co-occurrence of these dysfunctions then becomes an empirical question, not something decided a priori by definition practices. (p. 273)

It should be noted that both the *Diagnostic and Statistical Manual of Mental Disorders* (DSM-IV) (American Psychiatric Association, 1994) and the *ICD-10 Classification of Mental and Behavioural Disorders* (ICD-10) (World Health Organization, 1992) have, in fact, defined, classified, and coded learning disorders and specific developmental disorders of scholastic skills into specific domains of deficit. For example, DSM-IV subdivides communication disorders (listening and speaking in the language of educational definitions) into expressive language disorder, mixed receptive-expressive language disorder, and phonological disorder (American Psychiatric Association, 1994). DSM-IV provides criteria for the diagnosis of reading disorder while ICD-10 provides identification criteria under the term *specific reading disorder*. DSM-IV and ICD-10 refer to disabilities in mathematics as *mathematics disorder* and *specific disorder of arithmetical skills*, respectively. Finally, disabilities involving written language skills are classified and coded in DSM-IV as a *disorder of written expression* and in ICD-10 as a *specific spelling disorder*.

However, regardless of whether one approaches the task of defining learning disabilities generally, as has been traditional at the federal level, or seeks to define domain-specific learning disabilities such as reading disability, as advocated by Stanovich (1993), the American Psychiatric Association (1994), and the World Health Organization (1992), the definitional process must be informed by, and constructed within, a classification system that ultimately has communicative and predictive power. The logic underlying the development of such a classification system is that identification, diagnosis, intervention, and prognosis for learning disabilities cannot be addressed effectively until the heterogeneity across and within domain-specific learning disabilities is accounted for and subgroups and subtypes are delineated that are theoretically meaningful, reliable, and valid.

More specifically, in developing such a classification system, the resulting nosology must be 1) theory driven (Fletcher & Morris, 1986; Kavale & Forness, 1985; Lyon, 1985b, 1987; Skinner, 1981); 2) based on variables that have theoretical relevance and adequate psychometric properties (Blashfield, 1993; Fletcher et al., 1993; Lyon & Risucci, 1989; Morris, 1993); 3) developed on nonreferred samples within the context of prospective, longitudinal studies (Fletcher, Francis, Rourke, Shaywitz, & Shaywitz, 1993; Francis et al., 1994; Lyon, 1987, 1994a; Shaywitz & Shaywitz, 1994); 4) replicable and internally valid (Blashfield & Draguns, 1976; Morris, 1993; Skinner, 1981); and 5) externally valid and useful for precise description of subject attributes, prediction, and clinical practice (Lyon, 1985b; Lyon & Flynn, 1991; Lyon & Moats, 1988; Lyon, Moats, & Flynn, 1989).

As Shaywitz and Shaywitz (1994) have eloquently pointed out, "The decisions emanating from a classification influence how an entity is defined, and consequently, who is selected and identified as having a particular disorder" (p. 2). If the factors guiding classification decisions do not adhere to the criteria cited above and are not stated explicitly, heterogeneity will continue to confuse the definitional and diagnostic process in the field of learning disabilities. As a result, children with LD will continue to be defined in different ways and identified by different sets of criteria. Thus, generalization and replication of research and clinical findings is impossible.

## Problems with the Concept of Discrepancy

As pointed out earlier, a fundamental historical assumption underlying the construct of LD is that the academic difficulties manifested by individuals with learning disabilities are *unexpected* given the discrepancy between their relatively robust intellectual capabilities, opportunities to learn, and freedom from social disadvantage or emotional disability (as specified in the exclusionary criteria of most definitions) and their reading, written language, and math performance. The assumption of "unexpected underachievement" as reflected in an aptitude–achievement discrepancy typically assessed by intelligence tests is based on the premise that individuals who display such a discrepancy are indeed different from individuals who do not (i.e., "slow learners") with respect to phenotypic variables such as information-processing characteristics or response to intervention and genotypic variables such as differences in the heritability of the disorder or its neurophysiological signature (Lyon, 1988).

Studies published in the mid-1990s of reading development and disorders among children with LD and among pervasively underachieving children cast doubt on the utility and validity of the notion of discrepancy, however. More specifically, Fletcher et al. (1994) and Stanovich and Siegel (1994) have clearly demonstrated, at least in the area of dyslexia, that discrepancies between IQ and reading achievement are meaningless in that discrepant and nondiscrepant poor readers *do not* differ on measures of information processing, genetic variables, response to instruction, or neurophysiological markers. These particular findings, which are addressed in detail in the section in this chapter devoted to learning disabilities in reading, do not obviate the possibility that unexpected underachievement is, in fact, a cardinal sign of LD, but the data clearly demonstrate that the practice of assessing IQ in relation to achievement in order to determine unexpected underachievement (at least in reading) is invalid. It is possible that comparisons between intellectual functioning and performance in different achievement domains may have relevance as a secondary characteristic that predicts response to intervention, level of self-concept, or long-term outcomes (Lyon, 1989).

## Limited Knowledge About Cultural and Ethnic Factors

Although all current definitions of learning disabilities state that learning deficits encompassed by the disorder *cannot* be attributed to cultural factors (including race and ethnicity), limited information exists regarding how race, ethnicity, and cultural background might influence school learning in general and the expression of different types of LD in particular. However, it is encouraging to note that work conducted by Wood and colleagues (1991) has begun to shed light on these issues. In a longitudinal study of specific learning (reading) disabilities in a random sample of 485 children selected in the first grade and followed through the third grade (55% Caucasian, 45% African American), Wood et al. (1991) found that the effects of race were, in fact, important as well as highly complicated. For example, at the first-grade level, race did not appear to be an influential variable in reading development when vocabulary was accounted for. That is, once the child's age and level of vocabulary development were known, race did not provide any additional predictive power to forecasting first-grade reading scores. However, by the end of the third grade, race had become a significant predictive factor ($p = .001$) even when the most powerful predictor—first-grade reading scores—was included in the prediction equation. Specifically, by the end of the third grade, African American youngsters were having significantly greater difficulties learning to read.

In an attempt to understand this race effect, Wood et al. (1991) assessed a number of additional demographic factors including parental marital status, parental education, parental status as a welfare recipient, socioeconomic status, the number of books in the home, and occupational status. Their findings were clear: The presence of any or all of these demographic variables in the prediction equation "did not remove the race effect from its potency as an independent predictor of third-grade reading" (Wood et al., 1991, p. 9).

In continuing to explore this systematic bias of race vis-á-vis the development of reading abilities, Frank Wood (personal communication, March 26, 1993) has hypothesized that African American youngsters may be penalized by the particular teaching methods used to develop reading skills. More specifically, during this longitudinal study, the majority of children (Caucasian and African American) were taught reading via a whole language curriculum that deemphasized decoding and word recognition strategies and emphasized the use of context to infer meaning from text. Unfortunately, as Wood noted, the nature of the dialect of the African American children may interact negatively with any reading approach that does not explicitly emphasize specific sound–symbol relationships. Wood continued this longitudinal study with the children into the fifth grade and found that African American children's reading difficulties became more severe with age. Because of these findings, the National Institute of Child Health and Human Development (NICHD) within the National Institutes of Health has provided support for these studies to be continued through the high school years *and* to be replicated with a new sample of first-grade children.

It is clear from these emerging data that some aspects of race and culture can influence the development of reading abilities, even if such a bias or disadvantage is not reflected in referral patterns. Obviously, continued systematic study is required to fully understand these phenomena.

In summary, a number of factors have impeded the efforts of the general field of LD to establish a valid definition and classification system. However, substantial progress is being made in a number of domain-specific areas such as reading and language with less progress in the areas of mathematics and written language. With this as background, the next sections of this chapter address learning disabilities in oral language (primarily phonology), reading, written language, and mathematics. For each specific type of learning disability, findings concerning definition, developmental course, prognosis, epidemiology, theoretical frameworks, and etiologies are presented.

## SPECIFIC LEARNING DISABILITIES IN ORAL LANGUAGE

### Historical Underpinnings

Deficits in oral language (broadly termed *listening* and *speaking*) and their relationship to the field of learning disabilities were mentioned briefly in the first section of this chapter. Keeping in mind that the fundamental clinical manifestations of learning disabilities have been *unexpected under-achievements*, recall that in the 1800s (see Wiederholt, 1974) patients were observed who could produce thoughts in writing but who could not pro-duce expressive language, thus demonstrating an unexpected dissocia-tion between listening, speaking, and writing (Hammill, 1993; Torgesen, 1991). More recently, the work of Kirk and associates (Kirk, McCarthy, & Kirk, 1968) stands out as a major contribution to the realization that lan-guage development and disorders were not only critical to learning but could negatively affect the development of specific academic abilities. In this context, Kirk et al. (1968) developed the Illinois Test of Psycholinguis-tic Abilities to assess relative strengths and weaknesses in receptive and expressive language and to use the resulting data in designing prescrip-tive education programs. Although Kirk et al.'s diagnostic and interven-tion concepts have not stood the test of time (Newcomer & Hammill, 1976), these researchers made explicit the fact that children could display unexpected patterns of strengths and weaknesses in linguistic abilities as well as the need to consider oral language development as a significant prerequisite to academic learning. Similar contributions in this regard were made by Berry and Eisenson (1956), de Hirsch, Jansky, and Lang-ford (1966), Johnson and Myklebust (1967), and Myklebust (1955). For comprehensive reviews of the early history in the area of oral language and learning disabilities, the reader is referred to Gerber (1993).

## Definitions and Diagnostic Criteria

Both the National Advisory Committee on Handicapped Children (NACHC) definition of *learning disabilities* (1968) and the NJCLD (letter to member organizations, 1988) definition reference the terms *listening* and *speaking disorders*. Moreover, the NACHC definition states that "spe-cific learning disability means a disorder in one or more of the basic psychological processes involved in using language" (p. 65,083). Unfor-tunately, neither the NACHC nor NJCLD definition provides specific inclusionary criteria for diagnosis.

DSM-IV addresses oral language disorders under the major heading Communication Disorders, which are identified as expressive language disorder, mixed receptive/expressive language disorder, phonological disorder (articulation disorder), stuttering, and communication disorder not otherwise specified. Stuttering and nonspecified communication dis-orders are not covered in this chapter as they are not routinely considered as part of the diagnostic net of LD. Table 1 displays the DSM-IV diagnos-tic criteria for expressive language disorder, mixed receptive-expressive language disorder, and phonological disorder.

Table 1. Diagnostic criteria for the diagnosis of language disorders related to learning disabilities

### Diagnostic Criteria for Expressive Language Disorder

A. The scores obtained from standardized individually administered measures of expressive language development are substantially below those obtained from standardized measures of both nonverbal intellectual capacity and receptive language development. The disturbance may be manifest clinically by symptoms that include having a markedly limited vocabulary, making errors in tense, or having difficulty recalling words or producing sentences with developmentally appropriate length or complexity.

B. The difficulties with expressive language with academic or occupational achievement or with social communication.

C. Criteria are not met for Mixed Receptive-Expressive Language Disorder or a Pervasive Developmental Disorder.

D. If Mental Retardation, a speech-motor or sensory deficit, or environmental deprivation is present, the language difficulties are in excess of those usually associated with these problems.

### Diagnostic Criteria for Mixed Receptive-Expressive Language Disorder

A. The scores obtained from a battery of standardized individually administered measures of both receptive and expressive language development are substantially below those obtained from standardized measures of nonverbal intellectual capacity. Symptoms include those for Expressive Language Disorder as well as difficulty understanding words, sentences, or specific types of words, such as spatial terms.

B. The difficulties with receptive and expressive language significantly interfere with academic or occupational achievement or with social communication.

C. Criteria are not met for a Pervasive Developmental Disorder.

D. If Mental Retardation, a speech-motor or sensory deficit, or environmental deprivation is present, the language difficulties are in excess of those usually associated with these problems.

### Diagnostic Criteria for Phonological Disorder

A. Failure to use developmentally expected speech sounds that are appropriate for age and dialect (e.g., errors in sound production, use, representation, or organization such as, but not limited to, substitutions of one sound for another [use of /t/ for target /k/ sound] or omissions of sounds such as final consonants).

B. The difficulties in speech sound production interfere with academic or occupational achievement or with social communication.

C. If Mental Retardation, a speech-motor or sensory deficit, or environmental deprivation is present, the speech difficulties are in excess of those usually associated with these problems.

Adapted from American Psychiatric Association (1994).

As is true of the majority of definitions used to describe specific types of LD, the NACHC, NJCLD, and DSM-IV definitions for expressive, receptive, and phonological language disorders have not been internally or externally validated. Although the DSM-IV definitions provide inclusionary criteria (Table 1), it is not yet known whether such criteria (i.e., discrepancy between nonverbal IQ and expressive or receptive language test scores) differentiate among different disorders or differentiate between different types within a specific disorder.

## Relationship of Developmental
## Language Disorders to Learning Disabilities

Several issues must be addressed when analyzing the place of oral language disorders in a discussion of learning disabilities. First, it should be noted that the terms used in the NACHC, NJCLD, and DSM-IV definitions to describe subsets or components of language (with the exception of phonology) are vague, ambiguous, and typically lead to multiple interpretations by clinicians and researchers. Clearly, the terms *listening* and *speaking*, as noted in the NACHC and NJCLD definitions, reflect conceptualizations of language that are far too broad and imprecise to provide a foundation for the measurement and assessment of linguistic capabilities (Moats, 1994). To do justice to the complex area of oral language development and its relation to the learning of other symbol systems (i.e., reading, spelling, and written language), the domain itself should, at the least, be subdivided into linguistic competence, which refers to a child's knowledge of phonological rules, morphological rules, semantic rules, syntactic rules, and pragmatic language functions (Moats, 1994) and into linguistic performance, which refers to how the individual deploys the component rule systems in communication and thought (Gerber, 1993).

Second, disorders of receptive and expressive language, which are also ambiguous and imprecise terms, clearly vary in severity and presentation. In general, children who display language delays, severe language comprehension deficits, and marked deficits in the use of syntactic and morphosyntactic rules are seen first by speech-language pathologists, who usually formulate the diagnosis and intervention plans. The point is that developmental language disorders constitute an extremely complex and large domain of study that are distinct from learning disabilities. Some subtle linguistic deficits do, however, co-occur with different types of LD. For example, the one major area of oral language competence and performance that is clearly related to learning disabilities and particularly to reading is phonology, which is discussed in detail in this section and in the section devoted to developmental reading disorders. The decision to focus on the relationship between phonological development and learning disabilities should not imply that semantics, syntax, morphology, and pragmatics are not also critically related to some types of LD—they are. However, space limitations do not allow for an in-depth discussion of these rule systems, how and when they develop, and how they influence cognitive and academic development. As such, the reader is referred to Gerber (1993), Tallal (1988), and Wiig and Semmel (1976) for comprehensive reviews of these issues.

***Phonological Processing and Learning Disabilities*** It is clear that the majority of children and adults with LD manifest their greatest difficulties in language-based activities related to learning to read and spell (Lyon, 1985b). Although developmental reading disorders are addressed in greater detail in the next section, it is important to point out that deficits in phonology appear to be the major culprit impeding reading development in children with learning disabilities (Catts, 1986; Kamhi & Catts, 1989). By definition, phonology refers to the linguistic rule system containing the inventory of speech sounds that occur in the language and the rules for combining the sounds into meaningful units. Phonological processing refers to the use of phonological information, especially the sound structure of oral language, in processing written and oral information (Jorm & Share, 1983; Wagner & Torgesen, 1987). Speech sounds, or phonemes, are described by their phonetic properties such as the manner or place of articulation and their acoustic features or the patterns of sound waves (Gerber, 1993).

***Phonology and Learning to Read and Spell*** In English, an alphabetic language containing 44 phonemes, the unit characters (letters) that children learn to read and spell are keyed to the phonological structure of words (Liberman & Shankweiler, 1979). Thus, the child's primary task in the early development of reading and spelling is to become aware that speech can be segmented into phonemes and that these phonemes represent printed forms (Blachman, 1991; Liberman, 1971). However, as Blachman (1991) has pointed out, this awareness that words can be divided into the smallest discernible segments of sound is very difficult for many children to realize. The difficulty lies in large part in that fact that speech, unlike writing, "does not consist of separate phonemes" produced one after another "in a row over time" (Gleitman & Rosen, 1973, p. 406; see also Blachman, 1991). Instead, the sounds are coarticulated (overlapped with one another) to permit rapid communication of speech rather than sound-by-sound pronunciation. This property of coarticulation, critical for speech but possibly difficult for the beginning reader and speller, is explained by Liberman and Shankweiler (1991) as follows:

> The advantageous result of ... coarticulation of speech sounds is that speech can proceed at a satisfactory pace—at a pace indeed at which it can be understood (Liberman, Cooper, Shankweiler, & Studdert-Kennedy, 1967). Can you imagine trying to understand speech if it were spelled out to you letter by painful letter? So coarticulation is certainly advantageous for the perception of speech. But a further result of coarticulation, and a much less advantageous one for the would-be reader, is that there is, inevitably, no neat correspondence between the underlying phonological structure and the sound that comes to the ears. Thus, though the word "bag," for example, has three

phonological units, and correspondingly three letters in print, it has only one pulse of sound: The three elements of the underlying phonological structure—the three phonemes (/b/ /a/ /g/)—have been thoroughly overlapped (coarticulated) into the one beginning sound - "bag.". . .

[Beginning readers] can understand, and properly take advantage of, the fact that the printed word *bag* has three letters, only if they are aware that the spoken word "*bag*," with which they are already quite familiar, is divisible into three segments. They will probably not know that spontaneously, because as we have said, there is only one segment of sound, not three, and because the processes of speech perception that recover the phonological structure are automatic and quite unconscious. (pp. 5–6)

Thus, the awareness of the phonological structure of the English language, the way in which phonological awareness makes possible the reading of new words, and the automatic and fluent recognition of known words are language skills critical for basic reading, reading comprehension, spelling, and written expression (Shankweiler & Liberman, 1989). In addition to serving as a prerequisite for basic reading skills, phonological processing also appears highly related to expressive language development. For example, Kamhi, Catts, Mauer, Apel, and Gentry (1988) attempted to identify whether different types of phonological processing deficits were related to deficits in oral and written language (reading). In essence, Kamhi and colleagues found similar phonological deficits in both oral and written language with the only difference being that the group with expressive language disorders manifested more severe phonological processing difficulties. Kamhi et al. (1988) speculated that the greater severity of phonological deficits observed in children with expressive language disorders could be attributed to a more specific deficit in speech programming abilities.

The development of phonological awareness in the young child is reviewed now, and the relationship of phonological processing to written language domains is explicated in the section addressing developmental reading disabilities. In addition, diagnostic tasks useful in the assessment of phonological awareness are addressed.

**Development of Phonological Awareness** Liberman, Shankweiler, Fischer, and Carter (1974) conducted a number of studies to determine the developmental trajectories of young children's ability to identify the number of segments in spoken utterances and syllables. Using a game-like procedure, Liberman and associates (1974) required 4-, 5-, and 6-year-old children to indicate the number of syllables and phonemes in a series of test utterances by tapping a wooden dowel on a table. At age 4, none of the children could segment by phoneme, although nearly half of them could segment by syllable. The ability to segment syllables into their respective phonemes did not appear until age 5, and even then only one fifth of the children could accomplish the task. However, approximately one half of the 5-year-olds could segment multisyllabic words into syllables. By age 6, 70% of the children succeeded in the phoneme segmentation task and 90% were successful in the syllable task.

More recent studies by Ball and Blachman (1988), Blachman (1991), and Bradley and Bryant (1983) have suggested that approximately 80% of children have mastered the ability to segment words and syllables into constituent phonemes by the time they reach 7 years of age. Unfortunately, studies conducted by Fletcher et al. (1994), Francis et al. (1994), and Shaywitz and Shaywitz (1994) strongly indicate that at least 15%–20% of young children have difficulty understanding the alphabetic principle underlying the ability to segment words and syllables into phonemes, and, not surprisingly, approximately the same percentage of children manifest difficulties in learning to read.

**Epidemiology of Phonological Disorders**   Phonological disorders are common among children with LD and particularly among those children who display reading and spelling difficulties. Approximately 20% of children in the United States manifest difficulties in the development of basic reading skills (Shaywitz, Escobar, Shaywitz, Fletcher, & Makuch, 1992), and approximately 80%–90% of these readers with difficulties have deficits in phonological processing (Fletcher et al., 1994). As is noted in the discussion of developmental reading disorders, the gender ratio among individuals with phonological deficits does not differ from the gender ratio of the population as a whole (DeFries & Gillis, 1991; Felton & Brown, 1991; Shaywitz, Shaywitz, Fletcher, & Escobar, 1990; Wood & Felton, 1994), although more males than females have been reported to display a greater frequency of syntactic and pragmatic language deficits and more severe impairments of general language development (Montgomery, Windsor, & Stark, 1991).

### Etiological Bases for Phonological Deficits

*Neurobiological Factors*   There is converging evidence from anatomical microstructure studies, gross morphology studies, and neuroimaging studies that deficits in phonology, particularly deficits in phonological awareness and segmentation that interfere with reading development, are related to anomalous organization of neural tissue and processing systems subserved within the posterior left hemisphere, particularly in the region of the perisylvian fissure (Lyon, 1991, 1996). For example, regional blood flow studies indicate that poor performance on tasks demanding phonological awareness is associated with less than normal activation in the left temporal region and with atypically increased activation in the region of the angular gyrus (Wood, 1990; Wood et al., 1991). Neuroimaging studies employing positron emission

tomography (Gross-Glenn et al., 1986) and structural magnetic resonance imaging (Filipek & Kennedy, 1991; Lubs et al., 1991) have led to
similar findings. These neuroimaging data should be interpreted with
caution, given that the majority of studies have been conducted with heterogeneous groups of adults whose developmental histories are typically unknown. Nevertheless, the data strongly suggest a neurobiological
correlate for phonological deficits that involves aberrant processing in
posterior left hemisphere systems, an observation that agrees with clinical observations and lesion studies (Lyon, 1996; Lyon & Rumsey, 1996).

*Genetic Factors* There is increasing evidence from behavioral
genetic studies that deficits in phonological processing abilities are
heritable. For example, Lewis (1990) found that siblings of children with
severe phonological disorders manifested significantly poorer performance than siblings of children without phonological disorders on several
measures of phonological abilities (rhyming, elision, segmentation). Of
20 families of children with severe phonological disorders, 4 families
demonstrated a high incidence of speech-language problems over three
consecutive generations. Not surprisingly, given the previous discussion
of the critical role phonology plays in learning to read, those family
members displaying linguistic phonological deficits manifested a significantly higher rate of reading disorders.

In a series of twin studies designed to assess the relative contributions of phonological and orthographic processes to word-recognition
skill, Olson and colleagues (DeFries, Olson, Pennington, & Smith, 1991;
Olson, 1985; Olson, Forsberg, Wise, & Rack, 1994; Olson, Wise, Conners,
& Rack, 1990; Olson, Wise, Conners, Rack, & Fulker, 1989) have reported
that deficits on phonological coding tasks are significantly heritable
while deficits in orthographic skills are more highly related to environmental factors.

*Common Comorbidities* Comorbidities are a frequently encountered problem in learning disabilities, and understanding the causal
bases that link two or more co-occurring disorders in the same individual is critical because different explanations may have different implications for developmental theory and clinical practice (Pennington,
Groisser, & Welsh, 1993). In a broad sense, there are compelling data that
indicate that learning disabilities, no matter what specific type, manifest
social adjustment problems in addition to academic deficits (Hazel &
Schumaker, 1988). Bruck (1986), in a review of the literature related to
social and emotional adjustment, concluded that children with LD were
more likely to exhibit increased levels of anxiety, withdrawal, depression, and low self-esteem compared with their peers without LD. Social
skills deficits have been found to exist at significantly high rates among
children with LD (see Gresham, 1986, and Hazel & Schumaker, 1988, for

comprehensive reviews). In general, social skills deficits include difficulties interacting with people in an appropriate fashion (e.g., lack of knowledge of how to greet people, how to make friends, how to engage in playground games, a failure to use such skills in these situations). Although all children with LD do not exhibit social skills deficits, there are certain common characteristics among those who do. For example, Bruck (1986) reported that the severity of the learning disability is positively related to the number and severity of social skills deficits that are manifested by the child. Moreover, the sex of the child appears to be another factor with evidence suggesting that female children with LD are more likely to have social adjustment problems than males (see also Bruck, 1986).

Comorbidities between specific language disorders and social-emotional disorders have also been identified. For example, Cantwell, Baker, and Mattison (1980) reported the results of a comprehensive psychiatric evaluation of 100 consecutive cases of children with speech and language disorders seen in a community clinic. Psychiatric assessment of this cohort indicated the presence of a psychiatric disorder, according to DSM-III criteria, in at least 50% of the group. It should be noted that included in the types of psychiatric disorder were deficits in reading and mathematics as well as attention-deficit disorder. It was reported that children with speech articulation problems, without co-occurring language deficits, had the lowest prevalence of psychiatric morbidity, and youngsters with speech and language disorders or language disorders alone were most at risk for DSM-III diagnoses.

In a more specific vein, there is a wealth of evidence that deficits in phonology clearly co-occur with deficits in reading, decoding, and word recognition skills (Vellutino & Scanlon, 1987) and that the relationship is, in fact, causal, with phonological deficits impeding the acquisition of reading skills (Wagner, 1988; Wagner & Torgesen, 1987). As previously addressed, English orthography and its alphabetic characteristics place heavy demands on those linguistic abilities that allow the reader to parse words into their constituent sounds (phonemes). A lack of awareness of this alphabetic principle leads to slow and inaccurate decoding and word recognition (Liberman, Shankweiler, & Liberman, 1989; Lundberg, Olofsson, & Wall, 1980; Mann, 1984).

## Summary

The preceding sections addressing oral language deficits and LD focused on the nature of phonological disorders with an emphasis on their theoretical underpinnings, their developmental course, their assessment, their epidemiology, their etiology, and their co-occurrence and causal role in reading and spelling disabilities. Clearly, deficits in other language domains, including semantics, syntax, and pragmatics, are also influential in the phenotypic expression of learning disabilities. Readers interested in a comprehensive review of these linguistic areas and how they influence reading comprehension, written expression, mathematics, and social behavior are referred to Gerber (1993).

## SPECIFIC LEARNING DISABILITIES IN READING

### Historical Underpinnings

Of all the learning disabilities, reading disability has the richest clinical and experimental history. Many sources are available that provide fine-grained analyses of the history of reading disability (Coles, 1987; Doris, 1993; Kavale & Forness, 1985; Wiederholt, 1974), and these sources should be consulted for a comprehensive review. For the purposes of this chapter, however, it is important to point out that difficulties in learning to read in the presence of intellectual strength and integrity in other academic skills have been observed and recorded for at least a century. Consider the following observations of a 14-year-old boy made by Morgan in 1896:

> I then asked him to read me a sentence out of an easy child's book without spelling the words. The result was curious. He did not read a single word correctly, with the exception of "and", "the", "of", "that", etc.; the other words seemed to be quite unknown to him, and he could not even make an attempt to pronounce them.... He multiplied 749 by 876 quickly and easily.... I may add that the boy is bright and of average intelligence in conversation.... The schoolmaster who has taught him for some years says that he would be the smartest lad in school if the instruction were entirely oral. (p. 1378)

A critically important historical figure in the development of research and clinical interest in reading disability was Samuel Orton, who studied children with unexpected reading failure over a 10-year period. In 1937, Orton published an explanation for reading disability that stressed that the disorder was not due to localized brain damage, as proposed by Hinshelwood (1917), but could be attributed to a failure or a delay in establishing dominance for language in the left hemisphere of the brain. Orton's theory of reading disability also predicted that children's inefficient reading was related to the tendency to reverse and transpose letters and words, prompting him to coin the term "strepho-symbolia" (twisted symbols) (Orton, 1937). Although Orton's specific neurological theories were never validated (Liberman, Shankweiler, Orlando, Harris, & Bell-Berti, 1971; Torgesen, 1991), his work stimulated much research and clinical activity in the development of remediation and intervention methods for reading disability. Orton's contributions to the intervention area eventually led to the founding in 1949 of the Orton

Dyslexia Society. Of some importance here is that the term *dyslexia* began to be used frequently in clinical and educational communities and, to this date, is frequently used synonymously with the terms *reading disability, reading disorder,* and *LD in reading.*

## Definitions and Diagnostic Criteria

Both the NACHC definition and the NJCLD definition of LD discussed earlier make only passing reference to learning disabilities in reading. The U.S. Office of Education (USOE) (1977) helped to operationalize the identification of learning disabilities in reading by developing criteria (Section 121a.541) that delineate the reading domain into 1) basic reading skills that include decoding and word recognition abilities and 2) reading comprehension skills that include the ability to derive meaning from print. The USOE criteria also specified that learning disabilities in basic reading skills or reading comprehension skills could be identified only if a severe discrepancy existed between a child's intellectual ability and his or her reading abilities as assessed by standardized intelligence and achievement measures (USOE, 1977).

The DSM-IV (American Psychiatric Association, 1994) definition and criteria for reading disorder specify that the condition is marked by subaverage reading ability in the presence of average to above-average intelligence. In addition, a diagnosis of reading disorder should adhere to the three major criteria cited in DSM-IV and listed in Table 2.

The criteria presented in Table 2 show that the core issue in the diagnosis of reading disability is the degree to which an individual's reading accuracy or reading comprehension differs from that expected given chronological age or measured intelligence. It is important for the reader to note again that the concept of discrepancy reflected in these criteria is problematic and is not validated (Lyon, 1995a; Lyon et al., 1993). This issue is explored in detail in the next section.

In contrast to the definitions and criteria discussed thus far, the *ICD-10 Classification of Mental and Behavioural Disorders* (World Health Organization, 1992) provides diagnostic criteria for research with individuals with specific reading disorder (Table 3) and a separate set of guidelines

Table 2.　Diagnostic criteria for the diagnosis of reading disorder

| | |
|---|---|
| A. | Reading Achievement, as measured by individually administered standardized tests of reading accuracy or comprehension, is substantially below that expected given the person's chronological age, measured intelligence, and age-appropriate education. |
| B. | The disturbance in Criterion A significantly interferes with academic achievement or activities of daily living that require reading skills. |
| C. | If a sensory deficit is present, the reading difficulties are in excess of those usually associated with it. |

Adapted from American Psychiatric Association (1994).

Table 3. Diagnostic criteria for the diagnosis of specific reading disorder

A. Either of the following must be present:
  (1) a score on reading accuracy and/or comprehension that is at least 2 standard errors of prediction below the level expected on the basis of the child's chronological age and general intelligence, with both reading skills and IQ assessed on an individually administered test standardized for the child's culture and educational system;
  (2) a history of serious reading difficulties, or test scores that met criterion A(1) at an earlier age, plus a score on a spelling test that is at least 2 standard errors of prediction below the level expected on the basis of the child's chronological age and IQ.

B. The disturbance described in Criterion A significantly interferes with academic achievement or with activities of daily living that require reading skills.

C. The disorder is not the direct result of a defect in visual or hearing acuity, or of a neurological disorder.

D. School experiences are within the average expectable range (i.e., there have been no extreme inadequacies in educational experiences).

E. Most commonly used exclusion clause: IQ is below 70 on an individually administered standardized test.

Adapted from World Health Organization (1992).

for clinical descriptions and clinical guidelines for diagnoses. Table 3 depicts the major diagnostic criteria for specific reading disorder for research with individuals who display deficits in this area. Readers are encouraged to peruse the ICD-10 clinical descriptions for an elaboration of the characteristics of reading disorders.

The publication of diagnostic criteria for research purposes coupled with an extended discussion of clinical characteristics and manifestations across different developmental epochs reflects an impressive attempt to aid in the standardization of sampling procedures for the study of individuals with LD (Morris et al., 1994). In addition, the ICD-10 clinical descriptions and diagnostic guidelines provide information related to possible predictors of reading disorder as well as commonly observed comorbidities.

By comparison, the definition of reading disorder by the World Federation of Neurology is general to the point of being vague. This definition refers to learning disabilities in reading as "specific developmental dyslexia" and defines it as "a disorder manifested by difficulty in learning to read despite conventional instruction, adequate intelligence, and sociocultural opportunity. It is dependent upon fundamental cognitive disabilities which are frequently of constitutional origin" (Rutter, 1978, p. 12).

**Validity of Discrepancy as a Diagnostic Criterion** As alluded to earlier in the section identifying specific impediments to research in LD, a basic assumption underlying current definitions and diagnostic practices for LD in reading (reading disability, dyslexia) is that readers with LD manifest a significant discrepancy between their potential, as reflected in IQ scores, and their reading abilities, as assessed by achievement measures (Lyon, 1987). Tacitly ingrained in this assumption are the notions that 1) poor readers with average or above-average IQs are cognitively and neurologically different from poor readers with low IQs (i.e., IQ scores that matched their reading scores); 2) readers with LD can be reliably differentiated from readers without LD and "slow-learning" or nondiscrepant children on a variety of nonreading cognitive tasks; and 3) readers with LD, in contrast to slow learners, can attain levels of achievement commensurate with their IQs if they are assessed and taught appropriately (Lyon, 1987; Lyon & Moats, 1988). However, the concept of discrepancy as a diagnostic marker and the assumptions that derive from it stand on shaky empirical, conceptual, and logical ground.

All professional and legal definitions of LD in reading highlight the same salient features: that is, the child with a reading disability manifests an unexpected difficulty in decoding, word recognition, or comprehension that is not predicted by general intellectual competence. However, as authorities have noted (Fletcher at al., 1994; Stanovich & Siegel, 1994), the concept of discrepancy and the definitions that employ it as a diagnostic criterion have never been empirically validated. To do this, one would have to demonstrate that the reading difficulties of children with LD in reading and with high IQ (discrepant readers) are different from those characterizing children with reading disabilities and low aptitude (nondiscrepant readers) (Pennington, Gilger, Olson, & DeFries, 1992). It has been only since 1989 that studies designed to assess differences between discrepant and nondiscrepant readers have been carried out. Unfortunately, without exception, such studies do not support the use of IQ–reading achievement discrepancy criteria in the identification of reading disabilities (see Fletcher, 1992, for comprehensive coverage of these studies).

For example, a series of studies by Shaywitz and associates (Fletcher et al., 1994; Fletcher, Francis, Rourke, Shaywitz, & Shaywitz, 1992; Shaywitz, Fletcher, Holahan, & Shaywitz, 1992) have not supported the use of discrepancy-based definitions for LD in reading. In 1992, Shaywitz and colleagues reported the results of a longitudinal study in which a group of poor readers diagnosed according to a discrepancy criterion was compared with a group of poor readers matched for level of reading deficit without discrepancy with IQ. Given that the investigation had followed a longitudinal cohort from kindergarten through fifth grade, a number of comparisons could be made over time between the two poor-reader groups as well as a typical-reader group. B.A. Shaywitz et al. (1992) found no differences between the poor-reader groups on measures of tests of linguistic function, dexterity, visual perception, and teacher assessment of learning and behavior at any time within the developmental trajectory. The investigation also indicated that as many as 75% of children meeting criteria for discrepancy were also identified as low achieving.

In a more recent study, Fletcher et al. (1994) compared children with LD in reading identified according to a discrepancy criterion with a group of nondiscrepant poor readers on nine cognitive variables related to reading proficiency. The groups did not differ with respect to performance on visual, vocabulary, memory, or phonological measures. In addition, measures of phonological awareness were the most robust indicators of differences between children with impaired reading and children without impaired reading, *regardless* of how reading disability was defined. Finally, Stanovich and colleagues (Stanovich, 1993; Stanovich & Siegel, 1994) have obtained compelling data that show no differences between discrepant LD readers and nondiscrepant, "garden-variety" poor readers on measures of word recognition skills, phonology, and orthography. The discrepant and nondiscrepant groups were found to differ on tasks assessing memory and arithmetic. In summarizing their findings, Stanovich and Siegel (1994) stated:

> Neither the phenotypic nor genotypic indicators of poor reading are correlated in any reliable way with IQ discrepancy. If there is a special group of children with reading disabilities who are behaviorally, cognitively, genetically, or neurologically different, it is becoming increasingly unlikely that they can be easily identified by using IQ discrepancy as a proxy for the genetic and neurological differences themselves. Thus, the basic assumption that underlies decades of classification in research and educational practice regarding reading difficulties (LD in reading) is becoming increasingly untenable. (p. 48)

**Some Caveats with Respect to Discrepancy** The converging evidence reviewed here indicates clearly that IQ–achievement discrepancies are invalid diagnostic markers for LD in basic reading skills. Such a discrepancy simply does not differentiate a poor reader with average to above-average intelligence from a poor reader whose intelligence is commensurate with his or her low reading ability. It is also important to keep in mind that all the studies reviewed used single-word reading or word recognition as the measure of reading disability and ability. It remains to be seen whether differences exist between discrepant and nondiscrepant readers on measures of reading comprehension or response to instruction (Lyon, 1989; Moats & Lyon, 1993). Moreover, as Stanovich (1993) has pointed out, the lack of validity demonstrated for IQ–achievement discrepancies in the diagnosis of LD in reading does not obviate the conceptual notion that the poor academic performance of individuals with LD in reading can be characterized as unexpected. The critical task is to identify the most valid predictor of an individual's potential to read. Although the best predictor does not appear to be IQ, preliminary data suggest measures of listening comprehension as a possible predictor (Stanovich, 1991).

## Categorical versus Dimensional Definitions and Models of Learning Disabilities in Reading

As Shaywitz, Fletcher, and Shaywitz (1994) have pointed out, LD in reading, dyslexia, or specific reading retardation (used synonymously) have been viewed as a "specific *categorical* entity that affects a small, circumscribed group of children, that is invariable over time" (p. 3). Moreover, the categorical view holds that more males than females are affected with the disorder, that the specific type of reading deficits observed is qualitatively different from that of other poor readers with lower aptitudes for reading, and that a discontinuity exists between the distribution for specific reading disability and the reading disabilities associated with lower cognitive potential (the hypothesized "hump" at the tail of the reading distribution) (Yule & Rutter, 1976).

However, a number of studies have been conducted that do not support the Rutter and Yule (1975) hypothesis of a bimodally distinct reading distribution characterized by a hump at the tail of the reading distribution (Fletcher & Morris, 1986; Olson et al., 1985; Share, Jorm, MacLean, & Matthews, 1984; Silva, McGee, & Williams, 1985; Stanovich, 1988). In the most convincing study to date to refute the bimodality hypothesis, S.E. Shaywitz and colleagues (1992) used data from their Connecticut Longitudinal Study to ascertain whether a categorical or dimensional definition and model best described LD in reading (or dyslexia). The Shaywitz group hypothesized that reading ability follows a normal distribution with reading disability at the lower end of the continuum. Using Rutter's and Yule's (1975) criteria, reading disability was defined in terms of a discrepancy score representing the difference between the actual reading achievement and the achievement predicted on the basis of intelligence. S.E. Shaywitz and colleagues (1992) obtained empirical evidence to support Stanovich's (1988) findings that LD in reading (or dyslexia) occurs along a continuum that blends imperceptibly with normal reading ability. The results clearly indicated that no distinct cutoff point is available to clearly distinguish readers with LD from slow learners or from normal readers. These findings support a revision in the definitional model for LD in reading (dyslexia) in that the data support a shift from a categorical model to one that considers LD in reading to be similar to hypertension and other biological disorders that occur along a continuum (Shaywitz et al., 1994). Moreover, these findings indicate that LD in reading is not an all-or-nothing phenomenon but occurs in degrees. These results are in line with the data showing no differences between discrepant and nondiscrepant poor readers and suggest that many more children may be affected with LD in reading than previously thought. The impact of these findings on clinical diagnostic practices and public policy could be substantial. For example, although limited resources may necessitate imposition of cutoff points for the provision of special education services, it must be recognized that such cutpoints are arbitrary and that many children in need of specialized interventions may be denied the help they need (Shaywitz et al., 1994).

## Characteristics, Theories, and Proposed Etiologies

*Characteristics* As could be expected given the continuous and heterogeneous distribution of reading behaviors associated with reading ability and disability (Shaywitz, Shaywitz, Schnell, & Towle, 1988), both single-causal and multiple-causal theories have been advanced to represent the nature and etiologies of reading disorders. In the area of LD in reading, the phenotypic characteristics of the disorder are intimately interwoven with known and hypothesized causes of such characteristics. As such, the following section reviews the most frequent types of reading deficits observed in LD readers. Etiological theories and models that have the greatest amount of empirical support are also presented and analyzed.

*Core Reading Deficits Manifested by Readers with LD* The major academic deficits characterizing children with LD in reading are difficulties in decoding and in the ability to read single words (Olson et al., 1994; Perfetti, 1985; Stanovich, 1986). Although this statement may appear to be at odds with those who argue that reading comprehension skills reflect the most salient abilities in reading development (Goodman, 1986; Smith, 1971), consider that comprehension is dependent on the ability to rapidly decode and recognize single words in an automatic and fluent manner. Stanovich (1994) places the substantial importance of word recognition to reading comprehension in the following perspective: "Reading for meaning [comprehension] is greatly hindered when children are having too much trouble with word recognition. When word recognition processes demand too much cognitive capacity, fewer cognitive resources are left to allocate to higher-level processes of text integration and comprehension" (p. 281).

In essence, then, the core academic deficit in reading disability involves a failure to rapidly, accurately, and automatically read single words. The paramount importance given to single-word reading is based on the finding that word recognition is a prerequisite to understanding what is read (Olson et al., 1994; Vellutino, Scanlon, & Tanzman, 1994). This is primarily because slow and labored decoding and recognition of single words requires substantial effort and detracts from the child's ability to retain what has been communicated in a sentence, much less a paragraph or a passage (Lyon, 1995a).

The relatively greater importance of word recognition skills over reading comprehension flies in the face of theories and models of reading that hold that the ability to use contextual information to predict upcoming words is the cornerstone of fluent reading (Goodman, 1986; Smith, 1971). However, work conducted by a number of investigators (Bruck, 1988; Leu, DeGroff, & Simmons, 1986; Nicholson, 1991; Perfetti, 1985; Stanovich, 1980; Stanovich, West, & Feeman, 1981; West & Stanovich, 1978) have demonstrated that less skilled readers were more likely to depend on text for word recognition; highly skilled readers did not rely on contextual information for decoding or single-word reading because their word recognition processes were so rapid and automatic (Stanovich, 1994).

Given the converging evidence documenting the importance of word recognition, it is not surprising that the ability to read single words accurately and fluently has been the most frequently selected research target in the study of LD in reading (dyslexia). Again, this is not to diminish the role of reading comprehension as an academic and cognitive skill to be taught and acquired. However, word recognition is not only a prerequisite behavior for comprehension; it is a more narrowly circumscribed behavior and is not related to numerous nonreading factors typically associated with comprehension (Wood et al., 1991). Therefore, it offers a more precise developmental variable for study. With the dependent variable thus identified, there continues to be some debate about the nonreading factors (i.e., linguistic, perceptual, temporal processing speed) that account for deficits in single-word reading. Two different perspectives continue to exist. One school of thought is that deficits in the ability to read single words rapidly and automatically are referable to multiple factors, thus giving rise to hypothesized subtypes of reading disabilities. The second and more influential school of thought proposes that deficits in word recognition are primarily associated with, or caused by, one primary nonreading factor (i.e., phonological awareness). Each view is now discussed in turn.

### Multiple Etiologies and Subtypes of Reading Disabilities

It has been increasingly recognized since the early 1970s that learning disabilities in general are composed of multiple *subgroups*, reflecting that some children with LD manifest reading deficits while others have difficulties in oral language, written expression, and/or mathematics (Blashfield, 1993; Feagans, Short, & Meltzer, 1991; Fletcher et al., 1993; Fletcher & Morris, 1986; Hooper & Willis, 1989; Lyon & Risucci, 1989; Morris, 1993; Newby & Lyon, 1991; Rourke, 1985; Speece, 1993). Obviously, comorbidities can exist between and among these general conditions.

It has also been hypothesized that a number of *subtypes* exist within the population of readers with LD and can be identified on the basis of how individuals perform on measures of cognitive-linguistic, perceptual, memory span, and achievement skills (Bakker, 1988; Boder, 1973; Doehring & Hoshko, 1977; Fisk & Rourke, 1979; Lovett, 1984; Lyon, 1985a, 1985b, 1987; Lyon & Flynn, 1989, 1991; Lyon, Rietta, Watson, Porch, & Rhodes, 1981; Lyon, Stewart, & Freedman, 1982; Lyon & Watson, 1981; Mattis, French, & Rapin, 1975; Petrauskas & Rourke, 1979; Satz & Morris, 1981).

The argument for the existence of subtypes in the population of readers with LD has been based on the practical observation that, even though readers with LD may appear very similar with respect to their reading deficits (i.e., word recognition deficits), they may differ significantly in the development of skills that are correlated with basic reading development (Lyon, 1985a). Thus, even within well-defined samples of readers with LD, there is large within-sample variance. This degree of heterogeneity suggests that not all children read poorly for the same reason or respond equally well to the same interventions (Newby & Lyon, 1991). This observation may explain, in part, why readers with LD have been reported to differ from controls on so many variables related to reading (Rourke, 1978).

The literature on subtyping reading disabilities is voluminous, comprising more than 100 classification studies since 1963, and the reader is referred to Hooper and Willis (1989) and Newby and Lyon (1991) for comprehensive reviews of this literature. For the purposes of this chapter, two subtype research programs are reviewed. The first subtype research program focuses on rational (clinical) grouping of readers with LD into subtypes on the basis of clinical observations, theories, or both related to LD (Lovett, 1984, 1987; Lovett, Ransby, & Baron, 1988). The second approach exemplifies the use of empirical multivariate statistical methods to identify homogeneous subtypes of LD readers (Lyon, 1983, 1985a, 1985b; Lyon & Flynn, 1991).

***Rational (Clinical) Subtyping***   As an example of a rational (clinical) subtyping research program, Lovett (1984, 1987) proposed two subtypes of reading disability based on the theory that word recognition develops in three successive phases. The three phases are related to response accuracy in identifying printed words, automatic recognition without the need to sound-out words, followed by developmentally appropriate maximum speed as components of the reading process become consolidated in memory. Children who fail at the first phase are identified as *accuracy disabled,* and those who achieve age-appropriate word recognition but are markedly deficient in the second or third phases are termed *rate disabled.* The greatest strength of the Lovett subtype research program has been its extensive external validation (Newby & Lyon, 1991). In a study of the two subtypes (rate disabled and accuracy disabled) and a typical sample matched on word recognition ability to the rate-disabled group, accuracy-disabled readers were deficient in a wide array of oral and written language areas external to the specific reading behaviors used to identify subtype members. However, the deficiencies of rate-disabled readers were more restricted to deficient contextual reading and spelling (Lovett, 1987). Reading comprehension was impaired on all measures for the accuracy-disabled group and was highly correlated with word recognition skills, but the rate-disabled group was impaired on only some comprehension measures. In two additional subtype-intervention interaction studies (Lovett et al., 1988; Lovett, Ransby, Hardwick, & Johns, 1989), some differences were found between accuracy- and rate-disabled groups on contextual reading while word recognition improved for both groups.

Lovett's program is founded on explicit developmental reading theory; illustrates methodological robustness; and offers detailed, thoughtful alternative explanations for the complex external validation findings (Newby & Lyon, 1991). Important intervention-outcome findings are muted somewhat by clinically minimal reading gains on standardized measures despite statistically significant results and by the lack of significant subtype and treatment interactions (Lyon & Flynn, 1989).

**Empirical Subtyping** In a series of studies employing multivariate cluster analytic methods, Lyon and colleagues (Lyon, 1983, 1985a, 1985b; Lyon, Rietta, Watson, Porch, & Rhodes, 1981; Lyon et al., 1982; Lyon & Watson, 1981) identified six subtypes of older readers with LD (11- to 12-year-old children) and five subtypes of younger LD readers (6- to 9-year-old children) on measures assessing linguistic skills, visual-perception skills, and memory span abilities. The theoretical viewpoint guiding this subtype research was based on Luria's (1966, 1973) observations that reading is a complex behavior effected by means of a complex functional system of cooperating zones of the cerebral cortex and subcortical structures. In the context of this theoretical framework, it was hypothesized that a deficit in any one of several zones of the functional system could impede the acquisition of fluent reading behavior. The identification of multiple subtypes within both age cohorts suggested the possibility that several different types of readers with LD exist, each characterized by different patterns of neuropsychological subskills relevant to reading acquisition.

Follow-up subtype-by-intervention interaction studies using both age samples (Lyon, 1985a, 1985b) only partially supported the independence of the subtypes with respect to response to intervention. It was, however, found that the subtypes characterized at both age levels by significant deficits in blending sounds, rapid naming, and memory span did not respond to intervention methods employing synthetic phonics procedures. Rather, members of this linguistic-deficit subtype first had to learn phonetically regular words by sight and then learn the internal phonological structure using the whole word as a meaningful semantic context. Again, this was true for both younger and older readers within the linguistic-deficit subtype.

In summary, multiple causal models of LD in reading have been tested primarily through the use of rational/clinical inferential methods or through the application of multivariate statistical approaches. Since the mid-1980s, criteria for the reliability and validity of these complex subtype models have been proposed (Lyon & Flynn, 1989, 1991) and applied with some success (Newby & Lyon, 1991). An integrated analysis of several prominent reading disability subtype systems that have been intensively investigated suggests some areas of convergence in the literature (Hooper & Willis, 1989). In particular, memory span and phonological and orthographic processing in reading appear to be central in defining subtypes. Although a dichotomy of auditory-linguistic versus visuospatial reading disability subtypes has been commonly proposed, this differentiation has not been effectively validated (Newby & Lyon, 1991) The field has been moving from a search for discrete subtypes toward a dimensional view of individual differences in reading development (S.E. Shaywitz et al., 1992).

### Single Causal Theories and Models of Reading Disabilities

In contrast to the view that word recognition deficits can have multiple independent causes, a substantial body of evidence has accrued since the mid-1980s that suggests that phonological processing deficits are the single, core etiological factor in reading disability (Stanovich, 1993) (see earlier discussion on phonological development and processing). The theoretical and experimental evidence for a phonological processing deficit as an explanation for LD in reading derives centrally from the work of Liberman and associates (Brady & Shankweiler, 1991; Shankweiler & Liberman, 1989). According to the phonological deficit theory, children with LD in reading display particular difficulties in acquiring fluent word identification skills. Such children have great difficulty in learning to apply the alphabetic principle to take advantage of grapheme-phoneme correspondences in the reading of unfamiliar words (Torgesen, 1993). As Frith (1985) has pointed out, children with LD in reading with this key phonological deficit are often unable to attain alphabetic reading skills.

A review of the literature shows that children with LD in reading with core deficits in phonological processing have difficulty segmenting phonemes, retrieving the names for common objects and letters, storing phonological codes in short-term memory, categorizing phonemes, and producing some speech sounds (Bruck & Treimar, 1990; Fletcher et al., 1994; Kamhi & Catts, 1989; Liberman & Shankweiler, 1985; Liberman,

Meskill, Chatillion, & Shupack, 1985; Mann, 1986; Pennington, 1986; Perfetti, 1985; Pratt & Brady, 1988; Snowling, 1987; Stanovich, 1993; Stanovich & Siegel, 1994; Torgesen, 1993; Vellutino et al., 1994; Wagner & Torgesen, 1987). As Stanovich (1993) has also pointed out, there is increasing evidence that the linkage between phonological processing ability and reading development is a causal one, and this view is supported by a number of studies (Adams, 1990; Ball & Blachman, 1991; Blachman, 1991; Bradley & Bryant, 1985; Lundberg, Frost, & Peterson, 1988; Stanovich, 1986, 1988; Treiman & Baron, 1983; Wagner & Torgesen, 1987; Vellutino & Scanlon, 1987).

Although substantial support exists for the causal role of deficient phonological processing in reading disabilities, the unitary nature of the phonological deficit is challenged by data that suggest that some readers with LD have difficulties gaining access to the lexicon on a visual/ orthographic basis (Stanovich, 1992, 1993; Stanovich & West, 1989). Furthermore, Lovegrove and associates (Lovegrove, Martin, & Slaghuis, 1986; Martin & Lovegrove, 1988) have adduced evidence that suggests a visually based reading disability, although the data remain somewhat controversial (Hulme, 1988).

However, the evidence indicates that the ability to read and comprehend depends on rapid and automatic recognition and decoding of single words and that slow and inaccurate decoding are the best predictors of difficulties in reading comprehension. In turn, the ability to decode single words accurately and fluently is dependent on the ability to segment words and syllables into abstract constituent sound units (phonemes). Based on the extant data, one can conclude that, for the majority of children with LD in reading, deficits in phonological processing reflect the core deficit in reading disabilities.

**Developmental Course of LD in Reading**    Reading disabilities reflect a persistent deficit rather than a developmental lag in linguistic and reading skills (Francis et al., 1994; Lyon, 1994b). Longitudinal studies show that, of children with reading disabilities in the third grade, 74% still have disabilities in the ninth grade (Fletcher et al., 1993; Francis et al., 1994; S.E. Shaywitz et al., 1992). Clearly, these data reflect a pessimistic outcome for youngsters with LD who have difficulties learning to read. However, at least three factors could be responsible for the lack of progress made by children with LD in reading. First, because most diagnostic criteria continue to require a discrepancy between IQ and reading achievement for eligibility, many children are not identified as having a reading disorder until the third grade—the point at which their achievement has suffered sufficiently to demonstrate the required discrepancy between the ostensible predictor (IQ) and reading skills. As Fletcher (1992) has pointed out, initiating intervention after a child has failed for 2 or 3 years does not bode favorably for realistic gains in reading. Second, it has not yet been established which teaching interventions are most efficacious for children with LD in reading. In addition, many of the children followed in the longitudinal studies described above were provided several different types of interventions without the researcher's knowing how each intervention interacted with the next. Given this lack of systematic program planning and teaching, it is not surprising that only 20%–25% of children made gains in reading. In addition, those who did improve their reading ability were children with the least severe forms of reading disability (S.E. Shaywitz et al., 1992). Third, it is quite possible that the motivation to learn to read diminishes with time, given the extreme effort that many children with reading disabilities put into the learning process without success and that results in protracted periods of failure.

**Epidemiology**  Reading disabilities affect at least 10 million children, or approximately 1 child in 5 (S.E. Shaywitz et al., 1992). This figure indicates an increase over previous estimates primarily because it reflects the finding that children with and without IQ–achievement discrepancies (see the earlier section on the validity of IQ–achievement discrepancies) are similar with respect to severity levels, etiology, and language characteristics. Although schools identify approximately four times as many boys as girls as having reading disabilities, longitudinal and epidemiological studies show that approximately as many girls are affected as boys (DeFries et al., 1991; Lubs et al., 1991; Shaywitz et al., 1990). In the Shaywitz et al. (1990) epidemiological study of reading disabilities, the male–female ratio was found to be 1.2:1.

**Etiology of Phonologically Based Reading Disability**  The same neurobiological and genetic factors noted in the earlier section devoted to the etiological bases of phonological disorders are linked to reading deficiency as well. This would be expected given the substantial role played by phonological abilities in the developmental reading process. To briefly review, the locus of brain dysfunction hypothesized to be responsible for phonologically based reading disorders is in the left temporal region of the brain. One research team has hypothesized that the particular anomalies in this area of the cortex arise early in development and most likely cause the phonological processing deficit leading to LD in reading (Galaburda, 1988).

Substantial evidence derived from studies of twins with reading disabilities indicates that the brain anomalies described above are related to genetic transmission. DeFries and colleagues (Cardon, DeFries, Fulker, Kimberling, Pennington, & Smith, 1994; DeFries et al., 1991; Olson et al., 1989; Pennington, 1995) have further found that deficits in phonological awareness are highly heritable and that there appears to be a quantitative trait locus on chromosome 6 predisposing children to LD in reading.

**Common Morbidities** Disorders of reading often co-occur with disorders of attention (attention-deficit/hyperactivity disorder [ADHD]) (Barkley, 1990; Shelton & Barkley, 1994), but the two disorders are distinct and separable (Lyon, 1994a; Wood et al., 1991). As pointed out earlier, reading disabilities are consistently associated with deficits in phonological awareness, but the effects of ADHD on cognitive functioning are variable with primary deficits noted in rote verbal learning and memory. Furthermore, ADHD appears relatively unrelated to phonological awareness tasks (Wood et al., 1991).

A number of authors have reported that children with LD in reading present with co-occurring social-emotional difficulties (Bryan & Bryan, 1978; Tallal, 1988). A majority of such social-emotional difficulties appear in some clinical studies to be secondary to difficulties in learning to read. For example, of the 93 adults in a learning disabilities clinic population, the majority of whom displayed reading problems, 36% had received counseling or psychotherapy for low self-esteem, social isolation, anxiety, depression, and frustration (Johnson & Blalock, 1987). Likewise, others (Bruck, 1986; Cooley & Ayers, 1988; Paris & Oka, 1989) have reported that many of the emotional problems displayed by individuals with LD in reading reflect adjustment difficulties resulting from labeling or from academic failure. These findings point out the significant need to identify and intervene early with those children who are at risk for reading failure given the substantial social and emotional consequences that can occur if the disability is not addressed.

## LD in Reading

A number of significant new findings relevant to LD in reading have been discussed in this section. Given the importance of these findings, selected discoveries critical to diagnosis, research, and clinical practices are now summarized. For an in-depth review of these findings, the reader is referred to Lyon (1995a).

- One in five children is affected by deficits in reading.
- Reading disability reflects a persistent deficit rather than a developmental lag.
- Individuals with LD in reading differ from one another and from typical readers along a continuous distribution and do not aggregate together in a distinct hump at the tail of the distribution as previously thought.

- The gender ratio in individuals with reading disability is no different from the gender ratio in the population as a whole.
- Accurate and fluent reading ability is dependent on rapid and automatic recognition and decoding of words. Therefore, reading disability is best studied at the single-word level.
- Slow and inaccurate decoding and recognition of single words is a robust predictor of deficient reading comprehension.
- The etiological basis for the deficient word recognition and decoding skills of individuals with LD in reading appears to be a specific deficit in phonological processing. This deficit appears to be heritable and is further characterized by a distinct neurophysiological signature in the left posterior regions of the brain.
- Phonological deficits appear to impede the development of basic reading abilities (decoding and word recognition) regardless of the level of general intelligence. Poor readers, with and without IQ–achievement discrepancies, demonstrate impairments in the ability to segment words and syllables into abstract constituent phonemes.
- Disorders of attention and reading disability often co-occur, but the two disorders are distinct and separable.
- Intervention programs that capitalize on code emphasis methodologies are superior to meaning-based whole language approaches.

Given the reliability of these findings across research programs (see Lyon, 1995a, 1995b), the Orton Dyslexia Society Research Committee (Lyon, 1995b) constructed a new definition of dyslexia that reduces the exclusionary language in previous definitions of LD and dyslexia and defines dyslexia using current and valid research data. The definition is as follows:

> Dyslexia is one of several distinct learning disabilities. It is a specific language-based disorder of constitutional origin characterized by difficulties in single word decoding, usually reflecting insufficient phonological processing abilities. These difficulties in single word decoding are often unexpected in relation to age and other cognitive and academic abilities; they are not the result of generalized developmental disability or sensory impairment. Dyslexia is manifest by variable difficulty with different forms of language, often including, in addition to problems reading, a conspicuous problem with acquiring proficiency in writing and spelling. (Lyon, 1995b, p. 10)

This new definition provides a good example of how research can inform both policy and practice. Note that, in contrast to the definitions of learning disabilities, developmental reading disorder, and dyslexia previously discussed, the Orton Research Committee definition is composed of specific data-based inclusionary statements that can be operationalized.

# SPECIFIC LEARNING DISABILITIES IN WRITTEN EXPRESSION

## Historical Underpinnings

Disorders in the writing process have been discussed since the 1960s (Hooper et al., 1994), and over a century ago Ogle (1867) used the term *agraphia* to describe the relationship between aphasia and agraphia, although he noted that the two disorders were dissociable. Later Goldstein (1948) and Head (1926) applied clinical observation and case study methodology to explore the association and dissociation between written and oral expression. According to Hooper et al. (1994), much of the research related to disorders of written expression and agraphia continues to employ case study methodology and, in the main, continues to rely on the study of individuals with acquired brain damage.

It has been only since the mid-1980s that the study of disorders of written expression has risen from its status as "a poor relative of aphasia" (Shallice, 1988). For example, Wong (1991) argued that deficits in written expression are clinically important because they are frequently associated with reading disorders and/or are governed by similar metacognitive processes that include planning, self-monitoring, self-evaluation, and self-modification. As Hooper et al. (1994) have pointed out, these more recent perspectives have contributed to an understanding that written expression and its disorders are multidimensional in nature and require detailed definition. Hooper et al. (1994) have also reported that, in research, writing has been conceptualized as a complex problem-solving process reflecting the writer's declarative knowledge, procedural knowledge, and conditional knowledge, all of which is subserved by a network of neuropsychological factors, personality factors, and other conditions that include teacher–student relationships, amount of writing instruction, and the teacher's knowledge of the writing process. In this context, declarative knowledge refers to the specific writing and spelling subskills that the learner has acquired, and procedural knowledge refers to the learner's competence in using such knowledge in writing.

## Definitions and Diagnostic Criteria

A review of the available definitions of disorders of written expression reveals that the complexity and multidimensionality of the disorders are not reflected appropriately in any formal characterization or definition. This statement is based on the observation that there are literally no clear operational definitions of written language expression that address all components of the written language domain (see Berninger, 1994a, for a discussion of these issues). Emergent research on written language indicates that most, if not all, children with learning disabilities have problems with at least one component of writing, whether it is handwriting, spelling, written syntax, vocabulary, or written discourse (Hooper et al., 1994). As of 1996, no definition identifies and defines these components in any objective or operational manner.

Perusal of the NACHC, NJCLD, and DSM-IV definitions of LD indicates that none of them provide comprehensive and operational coverage for the diagnosis of disorders of written expression. For example, both the NACHC and NJCLD definitions discussed earlier refer to writing and spelling in vague and ambiguous terms that are not useful to researchers, clinicians, and teachers. In addition, even though the NACHC definition of LD, which was codified into PL 94-142, includes *spelling* in the definition, most guidelines for learning disabilities (with the exception of ICD-10) do not include spelling as a recognized area of disability (Moats, 1994). DSM-IV conceptualizes developmental expressive writing disorders using vague terms that cannot be operationalized and regards the disorders as the unitary construct, disorder of written expression (see Table 4).

Given the criteria presented in Table 4, one would be hard pressed to accurately characterize a group of children diagnosed using this highly ambiguous definition. In fact, research with samples of children identified on the basis of criteria in the NACHC, NJCLD, and DSM-IV definitions would result in substantially heterogeneous groups and in difficulty in replicating and generalizing results.

In contrast to providing criteria for the diagnosis of written language disorders, ICD-10 limits identification of writing disorders to deficits in spelling by the term specific spelling disorder. The diagnostic guidelines are presented in Table 5.

Perusal of ICD-10 indicates that the main feature of specific spelling disorder is an impairment in the development of spelling skills in the *absence* of a history of reading problems. By dissociating spelling and reading deficits, ICD-10 provides the most circumscribed description of

Table 4.    Criteria for the diagnosis of a disorder of written expression

A.    Writing skills, as measured by individually administered standardized tests (or functional assessments of writing skills), are substantially below those expected given the person's chronological age, measured intelligence, and age-appropriate education.

B.    The disturbance in Criterion A significantly interferes with academic achievement or activities of daily living that require the composition of written texts (e.g., writing grammatically correct sentences and organized paragraphs).

C.    If a sensory deficit is present, the difficulties in writing skills are in excess of those usually associated with it.

Adapted from American Psychiatric Association (1994).

Table 5. Diagnostic criteria for the diagnosis of specific spelling disorder

A.  The score on a standardized spelling test is at least 2 standard errors of prediction below the level expected on the basis of the child's chronological age and general intelligence.

B.  Scores on reading accuracy and comprehension and on arithmetic are within the normal range (−/+ 2 standard deviations from the mean).

C.  There is no history of significant reading difficulties.

D.  School experience is within the average expectable range (i.e., there have been no extreme inadequacies in educational experiences).

E.  Spelling difficulties have been present from the early stages of learning to spell.

F.  The disturbance described in Criterion A significantly interferes with academic achievement or with activities of daily living that require spelling skills.

G.  Most commonly used exclusion clause: IQ is below 70 on an individually administered standardized test.

Adapted from World Health Organization (1992).

a writing deficit of all the definitions and guidelines reviewed thus far. Unfortunately, the isolation of spelling as a major disorder leaves unconsidered the critical aspects of writing that are as or more important than spelling, such as written language formulation, organization, and thematic maturity (Berninger, 1994b).

Although a number of authorities in this area have offered strategies to refine definitions of disorders in written language (Graham, Harris, & MacArthur, 1990; Graham, Harris, MacArthur, & Schwartz, 1991; Gregg, 1991), the major criterion for this category continues to depend on the use of IQ–achievement discrepancy models (Hooper et al., 1994). As pointed out in this chapter and elsewhere (Kavale, 1987), discrepancy models are most likely to be invalid and serve more to confuse diagnostic issues than to clarify them.

## Characteristics, Theories, and Proposed Etiologies

*Characteristics*  Despite continued difficulties in establishing exact criteria for disorders of written expression and in developing reliable and valid measures of the multiple processes involved in writing, much work has been completed describing the characteristics of good and poor writers. For example, several investigators (Bereiter, 1980; Berninger, 1994a, 1994b; Hayes & Flower, 1980; Hooper et al., 1994) reported that good writers are goal directed, understand the purpose of the writing assignment, have or develop a good knowledge of the topic before writing, generate more ideas and use significant numbers of transitional ties, produce a more cohesive text and flow of ideas, and continuously monitor their written products for correctness of spelling and grammar.

In contrast, Hooper et al. (1994) and others (Englert, 1990; Graham & Harris, 1987) reported that individuals with LD in writing demonstrate deficits in deploying strategies during production of written text and also have problems in actually generating text. When compared to good writers, individuals with LD in writing produce shorter and less interesting essays; produce poorly organized text at the sentence and paragraph levels; and are less likely to review spelling, punctuation, grammar, or the body of their text to increase clarity (Hooper et al., 1994).

**Theoretical Models of Written Language Expression** A comprehensive review of several theoretical models of written language expression is presented by Hooper and colleagues (Hooper et al., 1994) and by Berninger (1994b). Because of space constraints, only the theoretical model proposed by Ellis (1982) is reviewed here.

According to Ellis (1982), the writing process is a series of transformations between different types of representations, and the representations are stored in temporary form in a series of memory buffers. Ellis's framework is dependent on a recall hierarchy that distinguishes between graphemes (abstract letters), allographs (concrete letter formations), and graphic-motor patterns. When content information reaches the last stage of the hierarchy, neuromotor execution can occur. In this theoretical model, different types of written language difficulties are hypothesized to correspond to deficits in different memory buffers. For example, letter transformations are assumed to occur when information is retrieved from the graphic buffer, and letter substitutions are attributed to deficits in the graphic–motor buffer. As Hooper et al. (1994) pointed out, although the Ellis model makes a comprehensive case for different types of memory necessary for written language, other variables (e.g., neuropsychological variables) are excluded. Alternative theoretical models have been proposed by Abbott and Berninger (1993), Berninger (1994b), Hayes and Flower (1980), and Roeltgen (1985).

**Developmental Predictors of Written Expression** Johnson and Myklebust (1967) presented a developmental model of language learning that posited that the ability to write is dependent on adequate development of listening, speaking, and reading abilities. In a series of more current studies, Berninger and associates (Berninger, 1994a, 1994b; Berninger & Hart, 1993; Berninger, Yates, Cartwright, Rutberg, Remy, & Abbott, 1992) have reported that automaticity in the production of alphabet letters, rapid coding of orthographic information, and speed of sequential finger movements were the best predictors of handwriting and composition skills. Spelling abilities were predicted by orthographic-phonological mappings and visual-motor integration (although see Lindamood, 1994, and Moats, 1994, for alternative predictions). Berninger, Mizokawa, and Bragg (1991) have also suggested that neuropsychological, linguistic, and higher cognitive constraints may operate together throughout the development of the writing process but that each of these constraints may exert relatively more influence at different points in the developmental process (Hooper et al., 1994).

**Epidemiology**   As Hooper et al. (1994) have pointed out, few epidemiological studies of disorders of written expression have been carried out. Likewise, the American Psychiatric Association (1994) concluded that the prevalence of disorders of written language is difficult to establish because "many studies focus on the prevalence of Learning Disorders in general without careful separation into specific disorders of reading, mathematics, or written expression. Disorder of Written Expression is rare when not associated with other Learning Disorders" (p. 26).

Basso, Taborelli, and Vignolo (1978) reported that acquired disorders of written expression occurred infrequently at a rate of approximately 1 in every 250 subjects. However, given the high rate of developmental language disorders in the general population (8%–15%) and the significantly high rate of disorders in basic reading skills (15%–20% of the general population), written language disorders could be predicted to affect at least 10% of the school-age population.

Berninger and Fuller (1992) reported that more boys than girls display written language deficits when level of achievement was used as the comparison variable, but there were no gender differences when IQ–achievement criteria were used. Hooper et al. (1994) studied 30% of a middle school population that included an equal number of boys and girls as well as an equal number of whites and nonwhites. Of the children studied, approximately 34%–47% fell greater than 1 *SD* below the mean on subtests of the Test of Written Language–2 (Hammill & Larsen, 1988). Non-Caucasians evidenced spontaneous writing problems at a ratio of almost 2:1, and boys showed a greater rate of impairment at a ratio of approximately 1.5:1. Clearly, the amount and accuracy of epidemiological data are lacking, particularly in comparison to studies of oral language and reading. However, with the development of objective criteria for the assessment of the components of written language, this situation should improve in the future (see Berninger, 1994b).

**Etiology of Written Language Disorders**   The multivariate nature of the writing process suggests that disorders in written language can be referable to multiple etiologies spanning biological, genetic, psychosocial, and environmental causes. Indeed, to express thoughts in writing, one must first formulate an idea; sequence relevant points in appropriate order; ensure that the written output is syntactically and grammatically correct; spell individual words correctly; and express the words, sentences, and passages in a legible manner via the graphic-motor system.

Given this multidimensional nature of the writing process, multiple causal models for deficits in writing are the rule. For example, Gregg

(1991) reported that a variety of language-based deficits in phonology and word retrieval could impair several aspects of the writing task as could deficits in visual-spatial skills and executive functions including organization, planning, and evaluating. Similarly, Roeltgen (1985) proposed that deficits in linguistic, visual-spatial, and motor systems can interfere with the developmental writing process in distinct ways.

In addition to cognitive, linguistic, and neuropsychological etiologies, it is clear that the way in which children are taught (or not taught) to write can influence their development of writing skills (Lyon, Vaasen, & Toomey, 1989; Nolen, McCutchen, & Berninger, 1990). The complexity of written language expression and its dependence on multiple correlated factors (e.g., language ability, reading ability, visual-motor skills) require that teachers not only understand the developmental abilities necessary for writing but also the content and the declarative and procedural aspects of the writing process itself. In many cases, teachers have simply not been provided with in-depth instruction in these areas.

**Common Morbidities**   Because of the complexity of the writing process and because written expression is the last language domain to develop in children (Hooper et al., 1994; Johnson & Myklebust, 1967), it should not be surprising that deficits in written expression can co-occur with deficits in oral language, reading, and mathematics. As Berninger (1994a) has pointed out, however, the relation between these symbol systems is by no means invariant. For example, Abbott and Berninger (1993) found that written expression could not be explained simply by oral expression; receptive written language ability always contributed specifically to expressive written language ability. In addition, the widely held view that deficits in written expression invariably co-occur with reading disorders is not substantiated. More specifically, Berninger, Mizokawa, and Bragg (1991) and Berninger and Hart (1992, 1993) have demonstrated that reading and writing systems can be dissociated. Some children have reading problems but not writing problems, and other children have writing problems but not reading problems. As expected, many, but not all, individuals with writing disabilities manifest deficits in reading.

Berninger and Abbott (1994) have found that children with LD in writing frequently also present with deficits in attention, executive functions, and motivation. Hooper et al. (1994) also reported that impaired writing can lead to a lack of motivation, conduct problems, or a tendency to withdraw. Hooper's group hypothesized that difficulties in producing appropriate written material in the classroom have the potential to result in daily embarrassment or humiliation in school. To cope with these negative factors, children with LD in writing may attempt to avoid writing tasks by engaging in inappropriate behavior.

## Summary

In contrast to the current understanding of oral language and reading disorders among children with LD, little is known about the etiology, developmental course, prognosis, and intervention for disorders of written expression. As Hooper et al. (1994) pointed out, the area of written expression requires systematic longitudinal study to increase the knowledge of possible predictors and precursors of written language competence. In addition, an emphasis must be placed on the design of multivariate studies and the use of growth curve analyses to develop comprehensive models of written language expression, map developmental trajectories, conduct syndrome analyses, and design efficacious intervention programs (Berninger, 1994b).

## SPECIFIC LEARNING DISABILITIES IN MATHEMATICS

### Historical Underpinnings

Deficits in mathematics among individuals with learning disabilities have not been extensively reported in the literature. In general, clinicians and researchers have paid less attention to children and adults with math difficulties, possibly because illiteracy has been considered to be more of a problem to society than problems in math proficiency (Fleishner, 1994). Given this limited knowledge base, Keller and Sutton (1991) argued for a research emphasis on the mathematical abilities and performance of individuals with LD. Clearly, this suggestion is warranted given that achievement in mathematics of students in the United States has declined steadily since 1970 (Alexander & James, 1987). Although this downward trend cannot be fully attributed to learning disabilities, LD is certainly a large source of the underachievement.

### Definitions and Diagnostic Criteria

All current definitions of learning disabilities acknowledge that impairment in the ability to learn math should be considered as a major disorder in the category of LD, if certain inclusionary and exclusionary conditions are met. The NACHC (1968) definition adopted by the USOE (1977) refers to disabilities in mathematical calculations, and the NJCLD (1988) definition of LD refers to significant difficulties in mathematical abilities (see earlier discussion of the NACHC and NJCLD definitions).

DSM-IV refers to deficits in mathematics with the term *mathematics disorder* and provides criteria to be used in the diagnostic process (see Table 6).

As with specific spelling disorder, the *ICD-10 Classification of Mental and Behavioural Disorders* (World Health Organization, 1992) provides

Table 6. Diagnostic criteria for the diagnosis of a mathematics disorder

| | |
|---|---|
| A. | Mathematical ability, as measured by individually administered standardized tests, is substantially below that expected given the person's chronological age, measured intelligence, and age-appropriate education. |
| B. | The disturbance in Criterion A significantly interferes with academic achievement or activities of daily living that require mathematical ability. |
| C. | If a sensory deficit is present, the difficulties in mathematical ability are in excess of those usually associated with it. |

Adapted from American Psychiatric Association (1994).

research criteria for the identification of individuals with deficits in a highly specific domain termed *specific disorder of arithmetical skills* (see Table 7).

Similar to the criteria presented for disorders of spelling, Table 7 indicates that the diagnosis of a specific disorder of arithmetical skills is appropriate when such disorders occur against a background of normal reading and spelling development. Again, this level of specificity via dissociation with other commonly occurring learning disorders has both positive and negative implications. Although this definition is circumscribed sufficiently to permit replication and generalization of research findings, limiting the mathematics domain to basic computational skills ignores the very important aspects of arithmetic reasoning and problem solving.

Thus, definitions of LD in mathematics, like definitions of LD in oral language, reading, and written expression, are based on assumptions of normal or above average ability to learn (as assessed by IQ measures), normal sensory function, adequate educational opportunity, and absence of developmental disorders and emotional disturbance.

Because of the persistent vagueness and parochial nature of the LD definitions, no clear objective standards have been established by which

Table 7. Diagnostic criteria for the diagnosis of a specific disorder of arithmetical skills

| | |
|---|---|
| A. | The score on a standardized arithmetic test is at least 2 standard errors of prediction below the level expected on the basis of the child's chronological age and general intelligence. |
| B. | Scores on reading accuracy and comprehension and on spelling are within the normal range (−/+ 2 standard deviations from the mean). |
| C. | There is no history of significant reading or spelling difficulties. |
| D. | School experience is within the average expectable range (i.e., there have been no extreme inadequacies in educational experiences). |
| E. | Arithmetical difficulties have been present from the early stages of learning arithmetic. |
| F. | The disturbance described in Criterion A significantly interferes with academic achievement or with activities of daily living that require arithmetical skills. |
| G. | Most commonly used exclusion clause: IQ is below 70 on an individually administered standardized test. |

Adapted from World Health Organization (1992).

to determine the presence or absence of a learning disability in mathematics. Adding to this dilemma is the fact that learning disabilities in mathematics, developmental arithmetic disorder, math disabilities, and specific math disabilities are broad terms used typically for a variety of impairments in mathematics skills. In addition, as Fleishner (1994) has pointed out, in some cases the term *math learning disability* has been used synonymously with the term *dyscalculia*, to denote *specific* (as opposed to generalized) deficits in calculation or mathematical thinking. In such situations, there is often the assumption that oral language, reading, and writing are intact (i.e., see the ICD-10 definitions in Table 7, and Strang & Rourke, 1985). However, as is discussed in the section on common morbidities, math deficits are frequently associated with other learning disabilities (Fleishner, 1994).

## Characteristics, Theories, and Proposed Etiologies

*Characteristics*   In general, children who manifest LD in mathematics typically display deficits in arithmetic calculation and/or mathematics reasoning abilities. Historically, characteristics in mathematics were described by the term *developmental dyscalculia*, which refers to the failure to develop arithmetic competence (Novick & Arnold, 1988, p. 132). Classification of the characteristics of LD in math or of dyscalculia was initiated by Kosc (1974), who identified the following six subtypes:

1.  Verbal dyscalculia: an inability to name mathematical amounts, numbers, terms, symbols, and relationships
2.  Practognostic dyscalculia: an inability to enumerate, compare, and mathematically manipulate objects, either pictured or real
3.  Lexical dyscalculia: a disorder in reading mathematical symbols
4.  Graphical dyscalculia: a disability in writing mathematical symbols
5.  Ideognostical dyscalculia: a disorder in understanding mathematical concepts and in performing calculations mentally
6.  Operational dyscalculia: a disability in performing computational operations

Kosc (1974) hypothesized that these variants of mathematics disability were a function of a congenital structural disorder of the cortical regions of the brain involved in mathematical abilities. To date, however, there has been no evidence to suggest that these subtypes are either distinct or that their deficiencies are associated with specific cortical regions. It is clear from Kosc's (1974) description of the characteristics of each type that children diagnosed with LD in mathematics today would most likely manifest difficulties similar to those observed in ideognostical dyscalculia and/or operational dyscalculia.

More recent attempts to characterize the population of children who manifest LD in mathematics have been made by Rourke and associates. For example, Ozols and Rourke (1988), Rourke and Finlayson (1978), and Rourke and Strang (1978) identified different patterns of performance on verbal-auditory and visual-spatial skills of children with LD who either 1) had low achievement scores on all subtests of the Wide Range Achievement Test (WRAT) (Jastak & Wilkinson, 1984), 2) had low achievement scores in reading and spelling but not in arithmetic, or 3) had low achievement scores in arithmetic relative to reading and spelling scores. In the main, those children with low arithmetic performance relative to reading and spelling demonstrated high scores on auditory-verbal measures and low scores on visual-perceptual and visual-spatial measures. These same patterns of performance have now been identified in children ranging in age from 7 to 14 (Keller & Sutton, 1991). Rourke's data clearly support the long-held belief that deficits in arithmetic calculation tasks or mathematics reasoning tasks are highly associated with deficiencies in visual-perceptual and visual-spatial domains (Novick & Arnold, 1988; Rourke, 1985).

Other subtyping schemes have been proposed by Ackerman, Anhalt, and Dykman (1986); Nolan, Hammeke, and Barkley (1983); and Spreen and Haaf (1986). The Nolan et al. (1983) and Ackerman et al. (1986) investigations did not show subtype differences in shape or severity of patterns of performance. However, Spreen and Haaf (1986) adduced data supporting a distinct arithmetic subtype, thus lending some support to Rourke's (1985) hypothesis.

In a more general vein, it is known that achievement in math is related to other attributes in addition to visual-spatial and visual-perceptual ability. For example, Aiken (1971) found clear relationships between math achievement and general intelligence and verbal ability. In addition, Kulm (1980) reported strong correlations between math performance and affective characteristics such as attitude, interest, and anxiety.

**Theories and Etiologies of LD in Math**    A number of neuropsychological theories of math disabilities are directly tied to an etiological focus. For example, Novick and Arnold (1988) hypothesized that neuropsychological deficits in posterior right hemisphere regions of the brain are highly associated with deficits in comprehension and production of written mathematics because of the high loading on visual-spatial capabilities. Conversely, the performance of mathematics reasoning tasks appears more related to those posterior secondary and tertiary cortical regions that subserve linguistic comprehension and analysis of relationships among ideas. This particular set of theoretical hypotheses does not differ notably from that proposed by Luria (1973).

Gaddes (1985) and Novick and Arnold (1988) have argued that children who display difficulties in doing rapid calculations, conceptualizing abstract information, and solving problems have neuropsychological deficits that are referable to deficiencies in the frontal lobes. Gaddes (1985) implicated deficits in the temporal lobes of children who display poor auditory-verbal memory for math. The reader is referred to Gaddes (1985), Keller and Sutton (1991), and Novick and Arnold (1988) for comprehensive reviews of the literature related to neuropsychological theories and proposed etiologies. It would be safe to say at this time, however, that both neuropsychological and cognitive theories of mathematics performance are in emerging stages.

Many clinicians and researchers believe that the most significant etiological factor in disabilities in math relates to poor teaching. Russell and Ginsburg (1984) found that teachers were not adequately prepared in mathematics principles, much less in how to teach them. This finding was replicated by Lyon, Vaasen, and Toomey (1989) in studies of both general education and special education teachers. Carnine (1991) and Russell and Ginsburg (1984) have also found that mathematics textbooks are frequently confusing for typical students and students with LD alike. In an evaluation of math textbooks, Carnine (1991) concluded that textbook organization and coverage almost ensured that teachers had to teach too many math concepts in a rapid and superficial manner. Because of this, students do not have the time or practice to attain mastery of the concepts, procedures, or algorithms that are introduced.

**Epidemiology**   As Fleishner (1994) has pointed out, efforts to establish the prevalence of math learning disabilities have produced similar estimates. For example, Badian and Ghublikian (1983), Kosc (1974), and Norman and Zigmond (1980) have all reported that approximately 6% of school-age children have some form of LD in math. Children with LD in mathematics can be identified early in their schooling, and their difficulties tend to persist through adolescence (Cawley & Miller, 1989). A number of studies have also found gender differences in math performance and achievement (see Stanley, Brody, Dauber, Lupkowski, & Benbow, 1987), although the direction and source of the differences are not clear (Fleishner, 1994).

**Common Comorbidities**   Fleishner (1994) has reported that math learning disabilities often co-occur with deficits in reading, writing, and/or spoken language. Fleishner and others made the point, however, that when comorbidity occurs to this degree LD in math should not be construed to be a selective impairment but rather a feature of a generalized problem in learning (Fleishner & Frank, 1979). However, Shaywitz and Shaywitz (1994) have found in their classification studies that children who manifest specific LD in math are more likely to also display disorders of attention than children with reading or writing deficits.

For some time, Rourke and colleagues (Casey, Rourke, & Picard, 1991; Rourke, 1987, 1988, 1989, 1995) have been attempting to identify features of the syndrome of nonverbal learning disabilities (NLD). Through this process these investigators have uncovered a replicable set of features that appear to co-occur with deficiencies in mechanical arithmetic (addition, subtraction, multiplication, and division). Specifically, the NLD syndrome, in addition to being characterized by math deficiencies, is marked by bilateral tactile deficits (more observable on the left side of the body); bilateral psychomotor coordination deficiencies (more observable on the left side); deficiencies in visual-spatial-organizational abilities; deficits in nonverbal problem solving and concept formation; well-developed verbal capabilities; difficulties in adapting to novel and complex situations; significant deficits in social perception and social interaction skills; and a tendency to communicate in a rote, repetitive manner. (See Rourke, 1995, for a comprehensive discussion of these features.) Although still in an early stage of development, the NLD syndrome model has significant implications for addressing the neuropsychological basis for deficits in math and comorbidities, which may be useful in predicting accuracy of diagnosis and response to intervention.

## Summary

As was seen in the review of learning disabilities in written language, solid research in LD in math is just beginning to emerge. A major difficulty in diagnosing math learning disabilities is that learning mathematics concepts is, more than any other content area, tied closely to the teacher's knowledge and to the way the concepts are presented. It is clear, however, that approximately 6% of school-age children demonstrate some form of math deficit that cannot be attributed to sociocultural factors, poor instruction, low intelligence, or substantial comorbidity. Some late 1980s research applied to pure math disabilities (Rourke, 1989) holds promise in explicating neuropsychological and cognitive factors associated with this type of learning disability.

## CONCLUSIONS

This chapter has attempted to provide a review of recent research related to learning disabilities in children. In this context, it can be clearly noted that the most productive research in LD has been carried out in the areas of language and reading, particularly in the study of the relationship between specific linguistic skills such as phonological processing and word recognition abilities. Substantial gaps continue to exist in our knowledge of written language and mathematics disabilities, particularly with respect to etiologies, developmental course, and intervention.

A major advance that has occurred in learning disabilities research has been the emphasis on conducting prospective, longitudinal studies to develop valid classification systems and definitions. This approach to classification and definition does not assume an a priori identification of children with LD but rather requires the identification of large representative cohorts of preschool children who are then followed for a period of at least 5 years. During this period, the children are administered a number of theoretically and conceptually grounded measures of cognitive, linguistic, academic, neurophysiological, and attentional skills at intervals of 6 months or 1 year. By conducting studies of these unselected samples, problems associated with school-identified and clinic-referred samples are controlled, and the emergence of abilities, disabilities, and comorbidities can be operationally defined and classified. Clearly, with this type of methodology, substantial progress has been made in the classification and definition of LD in reading. These findings should provide a stable base for additional epidemiological studies of various learning disabilities (written language, math) and allow better data to be gathered on their prevalence, developmental course, and response to various interventions.

Certainly one research direction for the future lies in the design and conduct of intervention studies for all types of LD. Historically, little emphasis has been placed on understanding which specific types of interventions or combination of interventions is most efficacious for well-defined groups of children with LD. This trend is changing with major new treatment initiatives sponsored by the NICHD (Lyon, 1995a). As the data from these and new studies accrue, relationships between cognitive, neuropsychological, linguistic, and behavioral attributes and responses to intervention will be able to be discerned. Given these data, the selection of specific intervention methodologies for individual children will become possible.

## REFERENCES

Abbott, R.D., & Berninger, V.W. (1993). Structural equation modelling of relationships among developmental skills and writing skills in primary- and intermediate-grade writers. *Journal of Educational Psychology, 85,* 478–508.

Ackerman, P.T., Anhalt, J.M., & Dykman, R.A. (1986). Arithmetic automatization failure in children with attention and reading disorders: Associations and sequela. *Journal of Learning Disabilities, 19,* 222–232.

Adams, M.J. (1990). *Beginning to read: Thinking and learning about print.* Cambridge, MA: MIT Press.

Aiken, L.R. (1971). Intellective variables and mathematics achievement: Directions for research. *Journal of School Psychology, 9,* 201–212.

Alexander, L., & James, H.T. (1987). *The nation's report card*. Cambridge, MA: National Academy of Education.

American Psychiatric Association. (1980). *Diagnostic and statistical manual of mental disorders* (3rd ed.). Washingtion, DC: Author.

American Psychiatric Association. (1994). *Diagnostic and statistical manual of mental disorders* (4th ed. rev.). Washington, DC: American Psychiatric Press.

Badian, N.A., & Ghublikian, M. (1983). The personal-social characteristics of children with poor mathematical computation skills. *Journal of Learning Disabilities, 16*, 154–157.

Bakker, D.J. (1988, July). *Neuropsychological treatment of dyslexia subtypes*. Paper presented as part of the Symposium Subtyping in Developmental Dyslexia at the Eleventh European Conference of the International Neuropsychological Society, Lahti, Finland.

Ball, E.W., & Blachman, B.A. (1988). Phoneme segmentation training: Effect on reading readiness. *Annals of Dyslexia, 38*, 208–225.

Ball, E.W., & Blachman, B.A. (1991). Does phoneme awareness training in kindergarten make a difference in early word recognition and developmental spelling? *Reading Research Quarterly, 26*, 49–66.

Barkley, R.A. (1990). *Attention-deficit hyperactivity disorder: A handbook for diagnosis and treatment*. New York: Guilford Press.

Basso, A., Taborelli, A.M., & Vignolo, L.A. (1978). Dissociated disorders of speaking and writing in aphasia. *Journal of Neurology, Neurosurgery, and Psychiatry, 41*, 556–563.

Bereiter, C. (1980). Toward a developmental theory of writing. In L.W. Gregg & E.R. Steinberg (Eds.), *Cognitive processes in writing* (pp. 73–93). Hillsdale, NJ: Lawrence Erlbaum Associates.

Berninger, V.W. (1994a). Future directions for research on writing disabilities: Integrating endogenous and exogenous variables. In G.R. Lyon (Ed.), *Frames of reference for the assessment of learning disabilities: New views on measurement issues* (pp. 419–439). Baltimore: Paul H. Brookes Publishing Co.

Berninger, V.W. (1994b). *Reading and writing acquisition: A developmental neuropsychological perspective*. Madison, WI: Brown and Benchmark.

Berninger, V.W., & Abbott, R.D. (1994). Redefining learning disabilities: Moving beyond aptitude-achievement discrepancies to failure to respond to validated treatment protocols. In G.R. Lyon (Ed.), *Frames of reference for the assessment of learning disabilities: New views on measurement issues* (pp. 163–184). Baltimore: Paul H. Brookes Publishing Co.

Berninger, V.W., & Fuller, F. (1992). Gender differences in orthographic, verbal, and compositional fluency: Implications for assessing writing disabilities in primary grade children. *Journal of School Psychology, 30*, 363–382.

Berninger, V., & Hart, T. (1992). A developmental neuropsychological perspective for reading and writing acquisition. *Educational Psychologist, 27*, 415–434.

Berninger, V.W., & Hart, T. (1993). From research to clinical assessment of reading and writing disorders: The unit of analysis problem. In R.M. Joshi & C.K. Leong (Eds.), *Reading disabilities: Diagnosis and component processes* (pp. 33-61). Amsterdam: Kluwer Academic Publishers.

Berninger, V.W., Mizokawa, D.T., & Bragg, R. (1991). Theory-based diagnosis and remediation of writing disabilities. *Journal of School Psychiatry, 29*, 257–280.

Berninger, V.W., Yates, C., Cartwright, A., Rutberg, J., Remy, E., & Abbott, R. (1992). Lower-level developmental skills in beginning writing. *Reading and Writing: An Interdisciplinary Journal, 4*, 257–280.

Berry, M.F., & Eisenson, J. (1956). *Speech disorders: Principles and practices of therapy.* New York: Appleton-Century-Crofts.

Blachman, B.A. (1991). Getting ready to read. In J.F. Kavanagh (Ed.), *The language continuum: From infancy to literacy* (pp. 41–62). Parkton, MD: York Press.

Blashfield, R.K. (1993). Models of classification as related to a taxonomy of learning disabilities. In G.R. Lyon, D.B. Gray, J.F. Kavanagh, & N.A. Krasnegor (Eds.), *Better understanding learning disabilities: New views from research and their implications for education and public policies* (pp. 17–26). Baltimore: Paul H. Brookes Publishing Co.

Blashfield, R.K., & Draguns, J.G. (1976). Towards a taxonomy of psychopathology: The purposes of psychiatric classification. *British Journal of Psychiatry, 129,* 574–583.

Boder, E. (1973). Developmental dyslexia: A diagnostic approach based on three atypical reading-spelling patterns. *Developmental Medicine and Child Neurology, 15,* 663–687.

Bradley, L., & Bryant, P. (1983). Categorizing sounds and learning to read. *Nature, 30,* 419–421.

Bradley, L., & Bryant, P. (1985). *Rhyme and reason in reading and spelling.* Ann Arbor: University of Michigan Press.

Brady, S.A., & Shankweiler, D.P. (Eds.). (1991). *Phonological processes in literacy.* Hillsdale, NJ: Lawrence Erlbaum Associates.

Bruck, M. (1986). Social and emotional adjustments of learning disabled children. In S. Ceci (Ed.), *Handbook of cognitive, social, neuropsychological aspects of learning disabilities* (Vol. 1, pp. 361–380). Hillsdale, NJ: Lawrence Erlbaum Associates.

Bruck, M. (1988). The word-recognition and spelling of dyslexic children. *Reading Research Quarterly, 23,* 51–69.

Bruck, M., & Treimar, R. (1990). Phonological awareness and spelling in normal children and dyslexics: The case of initial consonant clusters. *Journal of Experimental Child Psychology, 50,* 156–178

Bryan, T.H., & Bryan, J.H. (1978). Social interactions of learning disabled children. *Learning Disability Quarterly, 1,* 33–38.

Cantwell, D.P., Baker, L., & Mattison, R.E. (1980). Factors associated with the development of psychiatric disorders in children with speech and language retardation. *Archives of General Psychiatry, 37,* 547–553.

Cardon, L.R., Smith, S.D., Fulker, D.W., Kimberling, W., Pennington, B.F., & DeFries, J.C. (1994). Quantitative trait locus for reading disability on chromosome 6. *Science, 226,* 276–279.

Carnine, D. (1991). Reforming mathematics instruction: The role of curriculum materials. *Journal of Behavioral Education, 1,* 37–57.

Casey, J.E., Rourke, B.P., & Picard, E.M. (1991). Syndrome of nonverbal learning disabilities: Age differences in neuropsychological, academic, and socioemotional function. *Development and Psychopathology, 3,* 331–347.

Catts, H.W. (1986). Speech production/phonological deficits in reading-disordered children. *Journal of Learning Disabilities, 19,* 504–508.

Cawley, J.F., & Miller, J.H. (1989). Cross-sectional comparisons of the mathematical performance of children with learning disabilities: Are we on the right track toward comprehensive programming? *Journal of Learning Disabilities, 22,* 250–259.

Coles, G. (1987). *The learning mystique: A critical look at learning disabilities.* New York: Pantheon Press.

Cooley, E.J., & Ayers, R.R. (1988). Self-concept and success-failure attributions of nonhandicapped students and students with learning disabilities. *Journal of Learning Disabilities, 21*, 174–178.

DeFries, J.C., & Gillis, J.J. (1991). Etiology of reading deficits in learning disabilities: Quantitative genetic analyses. In J.E. Obrzut & G.W. Hynd (Eds.), *Neuropsychological foundations of learning disabilities: A handbook of issues, methods, and practice* (pp. 29–48). New York: Academic Press.

DeFries, J.C., Olson, R.K., Pennington, B.F., & Smith, S.D. (1991). Colorado Reading Project: An update. In D. Duane & D. Gray (Eds.), *The reading brain: The biological basis of dyslexia* (pp. 53–87). Parkton, MD: York Press.

de Hirsch, K., Jansky, J., & Langford, W. (1966). *Predicting reading failure.* New York: Harper & Row.

Denckla, M.B. (1977). Minimal brain dysfunction and dyslexia: Beyond diagnosis by exclusion. In M.E. Blaw, I. Rapin, & M. Kinsbourne (Eds.), *Topics in child neurology* (pp. 22–36). New York: Spectrum Publications.

Doehring, D.G., & Hoshko, I.M. (1977). Classification of reading problems by the Q-technique for factor analysis. *Cortex, 13*, 281–294.

Doris, J.L. (1993). Defining learning disabilities: A history of the search for consensus. In G.R. Lyon, D.B. Gray, J.F. Kavanagh, & N.A. Krasnegor (Eds.), *Better understanding learning disabilities: New views from research and their implications for education and public policies* (pp. 97–116). Baltimore: Paul H. Brookes Publishing Co.

Education for All Handicapped Children Act of 1975, PL 94-142. (August 23, 1977). Title 20, U.S.C. §§ 1400 et seq.: *U.S. Statutes at Large, 89*, 773–796.

Ellis, A.W. (1982). Spelling and writing (and reading and speaking). In W.W. Ellis (Ed.), *Normality and pathology in cognitive functions* (pp. 113–146). New York: Academic Press.

Englert, C.S. (1990). Unraveling the mysteries of writing through strategy instruction. In T.E. Scruggs & B.Y.L. Wong (Eds.), *Intervention research in learning disabilities* (pp. 220–262). New York: Springer-Verlag.

Feagans, L., Short, E., & Meltzer, L. (1991). *Subtypes of learning disabilities.* Hillsdale, NJ: Lawrence Erlbaum Associates.

Felton, R.H., & Brown, I.S. (1991). Neuropsychological prediction of reading disabilities. In J.E. Obrzut & G.W. Hynd (Eds.), *Neuropsychological foundations of learning disabilities: A handbook of issues, methods, and practice* (pp. 387–410). New York: Academic Press.

Filipek, P., & Kennedy, D. (1991). Magnetic resonance imaging: Its role in developmental disorders. In D.D. Duane & D.B. Gray (Eds.), *The reading brain: The biological basis of dyslexia* (pp. 133–160). Parkton, MD: York Press.

Fisk, J.L., & Rourke, B.P. (1979). Identification of subtypes of learning disabled children at three age levels: A neuropsychological multivariate approach. *Journal of Clinical Neuropsychology, 1*, 289–310.

Fleishner, J.E. (1994). Diagnosis and assessment of mathematics learning disabilities. In G.R. Lyon (Ed.), *Frames of reference for the assessment of learning disabilities: New views on measurement issues* (pp. 441–458). Baltimore: Paul H. Brookes Publishing Co.

Fleishner, J.E., & Frank, B. (1979). Visual-spatial ability and mathematics achievement in learning disabled and normal boys. *Focus on Learning Problems in Mathematics, 1*, 7–22.

Fletcher, J.M. (1992). The validity of distinguishing children with language and learning disabilities according to discrepancies with IQ: Introduction to the special series. *Journal of Learning Disabilities, 25*, 546–548.

Fletcher, J.M., Francis, D.J., Rourke, B.P., Shaywitz, S.E., & Shaywitz, B.A. (1992). The validity of discrepancy-based definitions of reading disabilities. *Journal of Learning Disabilities, 25,* 555–561.

Fletcher, J.M., Francis, D.J., Rourke, B.P., Shaywitz, S.E., & Shaywitz, B.A. (1993). Classification of learning disabilities: Relationships with other childhood disorders. In G.R. Lyon, D.B. Gray, J.F. Kavanagh, & N.A. Krasnegor (Eds.), *Better understanding learning disabilities: New views from research and their implications for education and public policies* (pp. 27–55). Baltimore: Paul H. Brookes Publishing Co.

Fletcher et al. (1994). Cognitive profiles of reading disability: Comparisons of discrepancy and low achievement definitions. *Journal of Educational Psychology, 86,* 6–23.

Fletcher, J.M., & Morris, R. (1986). Classification of disabled learners: Beyond exclusionary definitions. In S.J. Cici (Ed.), *Handbook of cognitive, social, and neuropsychological aspects of learning disabilities* (pp. 55–80). Hillsdale, NJ: Lawrence Erlbaum Associates.

Francis, D.J., Shaywitz, S.E., Steubing, K.K., Shaywitz, B.A., & Fletcher, J.M. (1994). Measurement of change: Assessing behavior over time and within a developmental context. In G.R. Lyon (Ed.), *Frames of reference for the assessment of learning disabilities: New views on measurement issues* (pp. 29-58). Baltimore: Paul H. Brookes Publishing Co.

Frith, U. (1985). Beneath the surface of developmental dyslexia. In K. Patterson, J. Marshall, & M. Colheart (Eds.), *Surface dyslexia* (pp. 301–330). London: Lawrence Erlbaum Associates.

Gaddes, W.H. (1985). *Learning disabilities and brain function: A neuropsychological approach.* New York: Springer-Verlag.

Galaburda, A.M. (1988). The pathogenesis of childhood dyslexia. In F. Plum (Ed.), *Language, communication, and the brain* (pp. 22–64). New York: Raven Press.

Gerber, A. (1993). *Language-related learning disabilities: Their nature and treatment.* Baltimore: Paul H. Brookes Publishing Co.

Gleitman, L.R., & Rosen, P. (1973). Teaching reading by use of a syllabary. *Reading Research Quarterly, 8,* 447–483.

Goldstein, K. (1948). *Language and language disorders.* New York: Grune & Stratton.

Goodman, K. (1986). *What's whole about whole language?* Portsmouth, NH: Heinemann.

Graham, S., & Harris, K. (1987). Improving composition skills of inefficient learners with self-instructional strategy training. *Topics in Language Disorders, 7,* 67–77.

Graham, S., Harris, K., & MacArthur, C. (1990). [Learning disabled and normally achieving students' knowledge of the writing process.] Unpublished raw data.

Graham, S., Harris, K., MacArthur, C., & Schwartz, S. (1991). Writing and writing instruction with students with learning disabilities: A review of a program of research. *Learning Disability Quarterly, 14,* 89–114.

Gregg, N. (1991). Disorders of written expression. In A. Bain, L.L. Bailet, & L.C. Moats (Eds.), *Written language disorders: Theory into practice* (pp. 65–97). Austin, TX: PRO-ED.

Gresham, F.M. (1986). The assessment of social behavior/competence in children. In P. Strain, M. Guralnick, & H. Walker (Eds.), *Children's social behavior: Development, assessment, and modification* (pp. 143–179). New York: Academic Press.

Gross-Glenn, K., Duara, R., Yoshii, F., Baker, W., Chen, Y., Apicella, A., Boothe, T., & Lubs, H. (1986). PET-scan studies during reading in dyslexic and non-dyslexic adults. *Society of Neuroscience, Abstracts, 12*, 1364.

Hammill, D.D. (1993). A brief look at the learning disabilities movement in the United States. *Journal of Learning Disabilities, 26*, 295–310.

Hammill, D.D., & Larsen, S. (1988). *Test of Written Language—Revised.* Austin, TX: PRO-ED.

Hammill, D.D., Leigh, J., McNutt, G., & Larsen, S. (1981). A new definition of learning disabilities. *Journal of Learning Disabilities, 4*, 336–342.

Hayes, J.R., & Flower, L.S. (1980). Identifying the organization of the writing process. In L.W. Gregg & E.R. Steinberg (Eds.), *Cognitive processes in writing* (pp. 3–30). Hillsdale, NJ: Lawrence Erlbaum Associates.

Hazel, S.J., & Schumaker, J.B. (1988). Social skills and learning disabilities: Current issues and recommendations for future research. In J.F. Kavanagh & T. Truss (Eds.), *Learning disabilities: Proceedings of the national conference* (pp. 293–344). Parkton, MD: York Press.

Head, H. (1926). *Aphasia and kindred disorders of speech.* London: Cambridge University Press.

Hinshelwood, J. (1917). *Congenital word-blindness.* London: H.K. Lewis.

Hooper, S.R., Montgomery, J., Scwartz, C., Reed, M., Sandler, A., Levine, M., & Watson, T. (1994). Measurement of written language expression. In G.R. Lyon (Ed.), *Frames of reference for the assessment of learning disabilities: New views on measurement issues* (pp. 375–418). Baltimore: Paul H. Brookes Publishing Co.

Hooper, S.R., & Willis, W.G. (1989). *Learning disability subtyping: Neuropsychological foundations, conceptual models, and issues in clinical differentiation.* New York: Springer-Verlag.

Hulme, C. (1988). The implausibility of low-level visual deficits as a cause of children's reading difficulties. *Cognitive Neuropsychology, 5*, 369–374.

Jastak, S., & Wilkinson, G.S. (1984). *Wide Range Achievement Test (WRAT–R), Revised Edition.* Wilmington, DE: Jastak Associates.

Johnson, D.J., & Blalock, J. (Eds.). (1987). *Adults with learning disabilities.* Orlando, FL: Grune & Stratton.

Johnson, D.J., & Myklebust, H. (1967). *Learning disabilities: Educational principles and practices.* New York: Grune & Stratton.

Jorm, A.F., & Share, D.L. (1983). Phonological reading and acquisition. *Applied Psycholinguistics, 4*, 103–147.

Kamhi, A.G., & Catts, H.W. (1989). *Reading disabilities: A developmental practice perspective.* Boston: College-Hill Press.

Kamhi, A.G., Catts, H.W., Mauer, D., Apel, K., & Gentry, B.F. (1988). Phonological and spatial processing abilities in language- and reading-impaired children. *Journal of Learning Disabilities, 53*, 316–327.

Kavale, K. (1987). Theoretical issues surrounding severe discrepancy. *Learning Disabilities Research, 3*, 12–20.

Kavale, K., & Forness, S. (1985). *The science of learning disabilities.* San Diego, CA: College-Hill Press.

Kavale, K., & Nye, C. (1981). Identification criteria for learning disabilities: A survey of the research literature. *Learning Disability Quarterly, 4*, 383–388.

Kavale, K.A., & Nye, C. (1986). Parameters of learning disabilities in achievement linguistics, neuropsychological, and socio-behavioral domains. *Journal of Special Education, 19*, 443–458.

Keller, C.E., & Sutton, J.P. (1991). Specific mathematics disorders. In J.E. Obrzut & G.W. Hynd (Eds.), *Neuropsychological foundations of learning disabilities: A handbook of issues, methods, and practice* (pp. 549–572). New York: Academic Press.

Kirk, S.A., & Kirk, W.D. (1975). *Psycholinguistic learning disabilities: Diagnosis and remediation.* Urbana: University of Illinois Press.

Kirk, S.A., McCarthy, J.J., & Kirk, W.D. (1968). *Illinois Test of Psycholinguistic Ability.* Urbana: University of Illinois Press.

Kosc, L. (1974). Developmental dyscalculia. *Journal of Learning Disabilities, 7,* 164–177.

Kulm, G. (1980). Research on mathematics attitudes. In R.J. Shumway (Ed.), *Research in mathematics education* (pp. 356–387). Reston, VA: National Council of Teachers of Mathematics.

Leu, D.J., DeGroff, L., & Simmons, H.D. (1986). Predictable texts and interactive-compensatory hypotheses: Evaluating individual differences in reading ability, context use, and comprehension. *Journal of Educational Psychology, 78,* 347–352.

Lewis, B.A. (1990). Familial phonological disorders: Four pedigrees. *Journal of Speech and Hearing Disorders, 55,* 160–170.

Liberman, I.Y. (1971). Basic research in speech and lateralization of language: Some implications for reading disability. *Bulletin of the Orton Society, 21,* 71–87.

Liberman, I.Y., & Shankweiler, D. (1979). Speech, the alphabet, and teaching to read. In L.B. Resnick & P.A. Weaver (Eds.), *Theory and practice in early reading* (Vol. 2, pp. 109–134). Hillsdale, NJ: Lawrence Erlbaum Associates.

Liberman, I.Y., & Shankweiler, D. (1985). Phonology and the problems of learning to read and write. *Remedial and Special Education, 6,* 8–17.

Liberman, I.Y., & Shankweiler, D. (1991). Phonology and beginning reading: A tutorial. In L. Rieben & C.A. Perfetti (Eds.), *Learning to read: Basic research and its implications* (pp. 22–76). Hillsdale, NJ: Lawrence Erlbaum Associates.

Liberman, I.Y., Shankweiler, D., Fischer, F.W., & Carter, B. (1974). Explicit syllable and phoneme segmentation in the young child. *Journal of Experimental Child Psychology, 18,* 201–212.

Liberman, I.Y., Shankweiler, D., & Liberman, A. (1989). The alphabetic principle and learning to read. In D. Shankweiler & I.Y. Liberman (Eds.), *Phonology and reading disability: Solving the reading puzzle* (pp. 1–34). Ann Arbor: University of Michigan Press.

Liberman, I.Y., Shankweiler, D., Orlando, C., Harris, K.S., & Bell-Berti, F. (1971). Letter confusions and reversals of sequence in the beginning reader: Implications for Orton's theory of developmental dyslexia. *Cortex, 7,* 127–142.

Liberman, P., Meskill, R.H., Chatillon, M., & Schupack, H. (1985). Phonetic speech perception deficits in dyslexia. *Journal of Speech and Hearing Research, 28,* 480–486.

Lindamood, P.C. (1994). Issues in researching the link between phonological awareness, learning disabilities, and spelling. In G.R. Lyon (Ed.), *Frames of reference for the assessment of learning disabilities: New views on measurement issues* (pp. 351–374). Baltimore: Paul H. Brookes Publishing Co.

Lovegrove, W., Martin, F., & Slaghuis, W. (1986). A theoretical and experimental case of a visual deficit in specific reading disability. *Cognitive Neuropsychology, 3,* 225–267.

Lovett, M.W. (1984). A developmental perspective on reading dysfunction: Accuracy and rate criteria in the subtyping of dyslexic children. *Brain and Language, 22,* 67–91.

Lovett, M.W. (1987). A developmental approach to reading disability: Accuracy and speed criteria for normal and deficient reading skill. *Child Development, 58,* 234–260.

Lovett, M.W., Ransby, M.J., & Baron, R.W. (1988). Treatment, subtype, and word type effects on dyslexic children's response to remediation. *Brain and Language, 34*, 328–349.

Lovett, M.W., Ransby, M.J, Hardwick, N., & Johns, M.S. (1989). Can dyslexia be treated? Treatment specific and generalized treatment effects in dyslexic children's response to remediation. *Brain and Language, 37*, 90–121.

Lubs, H., Duara, R., Levin, B., Jallad, B., Lubs, M.L., Rabin, M., Kushch, A., & Gross-Glenn, K. (1991). Dyslexia subtypes: Genetics, behavior, and brain imaging. In D.D. Duane & D.B. Gray (Eds.), *The reading brain: The biological basis of dyslexia* (pp. 89–118). Parkton, MD: York Press.

Lundberg, I., Frost, J., & Peterson, O. (1988). Effects of an extensive program for stimulating phonological awareness in preschool children. *Reading Research Quarterly, 23*, 263–284.

Lundberg, I., Olofsson, A., & Wall, S. (1980). Reading and spelling skills in the first school years, predicted from phoneme awareness skills in kindergarten. *Scandinavian Journal of Psychology, 21*, 159–173.

Luria, A.R. (1966). *Higher cortical functions in man.* New York: Basic Books.

Luria, A.R. (1973). *The working brain: An introduction to neuropsychology.* New York: Basic Books.

Lyon, G.R. (1983). Learning-disabled readers: Identification of subgroups. In H.R. Myklebust (Ed.), *Progress in learning disabilities* (Vol. 5, pp. 103–134). New York: Grune & Stratton.

Lyon, G.R. (1985a). Educational validation studies of learning disability subtypes. In B.P. Rourke (Ed.), *Neuropsychology of learning disabilities: Essentials of subtype analysis* (pp. 228–256). New York: Guilford Press.

Lyon, G.R. (1985b). Identification and remediation of learning disability subtypes: Preliminary findings. *Learning Disability Focus, 1*, 21–35.

Lyon, G.R. (1987). Learning disabilities research: False starts and broken promises. In S. Vaughn & C. Bos (Eds.), *Research in learning disabilities: Issues and future directions* (pp. 69–85). San Diego, CA: College-Hill Press.

Lyon, G.R. (1988). The concept of severe discrepancy in the diagnosis of learning disabilities: Theoretical, developmental, psychometric, and educational implications. *Learning Disabilities Research, 3*(1), 9–11.

Lyon, G.R. (1989). IQ is irrelevant to the definition of learning disabilities: A position in search of logic and data. *Journal of Learning Disabilities, 22*, 504–512.

Lyon, G.R. (1994a). Critical issues in the measurement of learning disabilities. In G.R. Lyon (Ed.), *Frames of reference for the assessment of learning disabilities: New views on measurement issues* (pp. 3–13). Baltimore: Paul H. Brookes Publishing Co.

Lyon, G.R. (Ed.). (1994b). *Frames of reference for the assessment of learning disabilities: New views on measurement issues.* Baltimore: Paul H. Brookes Publishing Co.

Lyon, G.R. (1995a). Research initiatives in learning disabilities: Contributions from scientists supported by the National Institute of Child Health and Human Development. *Journal of Child Neurology, 10*, 120–126.

Lyon, G.R. (1995b). Toward a definition of dyslexia. *Annals of Dyslexia, 45*, 3–26.

Lyon, G.R. (1996). Foundations of neuroanotomy and neuropsychology. In G.R. Lyon & J.M. Rumsey (Eds.), *Neuroimaging: A window to the neurological foundations of learning and behavior in children* (pp. 3–23). Baltimore: Paul H. Brookes Publishing Co.

Lyon, G.R., & Flynn, J.M. (1989). Educational validation studies with subtypes of learning disabled readers. In B.P. Rourke (Ed.), *Neuropsychology validation of learning disability subtypes* (pp. 233–242). New York: Guilford Press.

Lyon, G.R., & Flynn, J.M. (1991). Assessing subtypes of learning disabilities. In H.L. Swanson (Ed.), *Handbook on the assessment of learning disabilities: Theory, research, and practice* (pp. 59–74). Austin, TX: PRO-ED.

Lyon, G.R., Gray, D.B., Kavanagh, J.F., & Krasnegor, N.A. (Eds.). (1993). *Better understanding learning disabilities: New views from research and their implications for education and public policies.* Baltimore: Paul H. Brookes Publishing Co.

Lyon, G.R., & Moats, L.C. (1988). Critical issues in the instruction of the learning disabled. *Journal of Consulting and Clinical Psychology, 56,* 830–835.

Lyon, G.R., & Moats, L.C. (1993). An examination of research in learning disabilities: Past practices and future directions. In G.R. Lyon, D.B. Gray, J.F. Kavanagh, & N.A. Krasnegor (Eds.), *Better understanding learning disabilities: New views from research and their implications for education and public policies* (pp. 1–14). Baltimore: Paul H. Brookes Publishing Co.

Lyon, G.R., Moats, L.C., & Flynn, J.M. (1989). From assessment to treatment: Linkages to interventions with children. In M. Tramontana & S. Hooper (Eds.), *Issues in child neuropsychology: From assessment to treatment* (pp. 133–144). New York: Plenum Press.

Lyon, G.R., Rietta, S., Watson, B., Porch, B., & Rhodes, J. (1981). Selected linguistic and perceptual abilities of empirically derived subgroups of learning disabled readers. *Journal of School Psychology, 19,* 152–166.

Lyon, G.R., & Risucci, D. (1989). Classification of learning disabilities. In K.A. Kavale (Ed.), *Learning disabilities: State of the art and practice* (pp. 40–70). San Diego, CA: College-Hill Press.

Lyon, G.R., & Rumsey, J. (Eds.). (1996). *Neuroimaging: A window to the neurological foundations of learning and behavior.* Baltimore: Paul H. Brookes Publishing Co.

Lyon, G.R., Stewart, N., & Freedman, D. (1982). Neuropsychological characteristics of empirically derived subgroups of learning disabled readers. *Journal of Clinical Neuropsychology, 4,* 343–365.

Lyon, G.R., Vaasen, M., & Toomey, F. (1989). Teachers' perceptions of their undergraduate and graduate preparation. *Teacher Education and Special Education, 12,* 164–169.

Lyon, G.R., & Watson, B. (1981). Empirically derived subgroups of learning disabled readers: Diagnostic characteristics. *Journal of Learning Disabilities, 14,* 256–261.

Mann, V. (1984). Longitudinal prediction and prevention of early reading difficulties. *Annals of Dyslexia, 34,* 117–136.

Mann, V.A. (1986). Why some children encounter reading problems: The contribution and linguistic sophistication to early reading disability. In J.K. Torgesen & B.Y. Wong (Eds.), *Psychological and educational perspectives on learning disabilities* (pp. 133–159). New York: Academic Press.

Martin, F., & Lovegrove, W. (1988). Uniform and field flicker in control and specifically-disabled readers. *Perception, 17,* 203–214.

Mattis, S., French, J.H., & Rapin, I. (1975). Dyslexia in children and adults: Three independent neuropsychological syndromes. *Developmental Medicine and Child Neurology, 17,* 150–163.

Moats, L.C. (1994). The missing foundation in teacher education: Knowledge of the structure of spoken and written language. *Annals of Dyslexia, 44,* 81–102.

Moats, L.C., & Lyon, G.R. (1993). Learning disabilities in the United States: Advocacy, science, and the future of the field. *Journal of Learning Disabilities, 26,* 282–294.

Montgomery, J.W., Windsor, J., & Stark, R.E. (1991). Specific speech and language disorders. In J.E. Obrzut & G.W. Hynd (Eds.), *Neuropsychological foundations of learning disabilities: A handbook of issues, methods, and practice* (pp. 573–601). New York: Academic Press.

Morgan, W.P. (1896). A case of congenital word blindness. *British Medical Journal, 2,* 1378.

Morris, R. (1988). Classification of learning disabilities: Old problems and new approaches. *Journal of Clinical Neuropsychology, 3,* 79–99.

Morris, R. (1993). Issues in empirical versus clinical identification of learning disabilities. In G.R. Lyon, D.B. Gray, J.F. Kavanagh, & N.A. Krasnegor (Eds.), *Better understanding learning disabilities: New views from research and their implications for education and public policies* (pp. 73–94). Baltimore: Paul H. Brookes Publishing Co.

Morris et al. (1994). Proposed guidelines and criteria for describing samples of persons with learning disabilities. *Learning Disability Quarterly, 17,* 106–109.

Morrison, S.R., & Siegel, L.S. (1991). Learning disabilities: A critical review of definitional and assessment issues. In J.E. Obrzut & G.W. Hynd (Eds.), *Neuropsychological foundations of learning disabilities: A handbook of issues, methods, and practice* (pp. 79–98). New York: Academic Press.

Myklebust, H. (1955). *Auditory disorders in children: A manual for differential diagnosis.* New York: Grune & Stratton.

National Advisory Committee on Handicapped Children. (1968). *Special education for handicapped children* (first annual report). Washington, DC: Department of Health, Education, & Welfare.

Newby, R.F., & Lyon, G.R. (1991). Neuropsychological subtypes of learning disabilities. In J.E. Obrzut & G.W. Hynd (Eds.), *Neuropsychological foundations of learning disabilities: A handbook of issues, methods, and practice* (pp. 355–385). New York: Academic Press.

Newcomer, P., & Hammill, D.D. (1976). *Psycholinguistics in the school.* Columbus, OH: Charles E. Merrill.

Nicholson, T. (1991). Do children read words better in contexts or in lists? A classic study revisited. *Journal of Educational Psychology, 83,* 444–450.

Nolan, D.R., Hammeke, T.A., & Barkley, R.A. (1983). A comparison of the patterns of the neuropsychological performance in two groups of learning disabled children. *Journal of Clinical Child Psychology, 12,* 22–27.

Nolen, P., McCutchen, D., & Berninger, V. (1990). Ensuring tomorrow's literacy: A shared responsibility. *Journal of Teacher Education, 41,* 63–72.

Norman, C.A., & Zigmond, N. (1980). Characteristics of children labeled and served as learning disabled in school systems affiliated with Child Service Demonstration Center. *Journal of Learning Disabilities, 13,* 542–547.

Novick, B.Z., & Arnold, M.M. (1988). *Fundamentals of clinical child neuropsychology.* New York: Grune & Stratton.

Ogle, J.W. (1867). Aphasia and agraphia. *Report of the Medical Research Council of Saint George's Hospital, 2,* 83–122.

Olson, R.K. (1985). Disabled reading processes and cognitive profiles. In D.B. Gray & J.F. Kavanagh (Eds.), *Biobehavioral measures of dyslexia* (pp. 215–244). Parkton, MD: York Press.

Olson, R., Forsberg, H., Wise, B., & Rack, J. (1994). Measurement of word recognition, orthographic, and phonological skills. In G.R. Lyon (Ed.), *Frames of reference for the assessment of learning disabilities: New views on measurement issues* (pp. 243–278). Baltimore: Paul H. Brookes Publishing Co.

Olson, R.K., Kliegel, R., Davidson, B.J., & Foltz, G. (1985). Individual and developmental differences in reading disability. In G.E. MacKinnon & T.G. Waller (Eds.), *Reading research: Advances in theory and practice* (Vol. 4, pp. 1–64). New York: Academic Press.

Olson, R.K., Wise, B., Conners, F., & Rack, J. (1990). Organization, heritability, and remediation of component word recognition and language skills in disabled readers. In T.H. Carr & B.A. Levy (Eds.), *Reading and its development: Component skills approaches* (pp. 261–322). New York: Academic Press.

Olson, R., Wise, B., Conners, F., Rack, J., & Fulker, D. (1989). Specific deficits in component reading and language skills: Genetic and environmental influences. *Journal of Learning Disabilities, 22,* 339–348.

Orton, S. (1937). *Reading, writing and speech problems in children: A presentation of certain types of disorders in the development of the language faculty.* New York: W.W. Norton.

Ozols, E.J., & Rourke, B.P. (1988). Characteristics of young learning-disabled children classified according to patterns of academic achievement: Auditory-perceptual and visual-perceptual abilities. *Journal of Clinical Child Psychology, 17,* 44–52.

Paris, S., & Oka, E.R. (1989). Strategies for comprehending text and coping with reading difficulties. *Learning Disability Quarterly, 12,* 32–42.

Pennington, B.F. (1986). Issues in the diagnosis and phenotype analysis of dyslexia: Implications for family studies. In S.D. Smith (Ed.), *Genetics and learning disabilities* (pp. 69–96). Bristol, PA: College-Hill Press.

Pennington, B.F. (1995). Genetics of learning disabilities. *Journal of Child Neurology, 10,* 69–77.

Pennington, B.F., Gilger, J.W., Olson, R.K., & DeFries, J.C. (1992). The external validity of age versus IQ-discrepancy definitions of reading disability: Lessons from a twin study. *Journal of Learning Disability, 25,* 562–573.

Pennington, B.F., Groisser, D., & Welsh, M. (1993). Contrasting cognitive deficits in attention deficit hyperactivity disorder versus reading disability. *Developmental Psychology, 29,* 511–523.

Perfetti, C.A. (1985). *Reading ability.* New York: Oxford University Press.

Petrauskas, R., & Rourke, B.P. (1979). Identification of subgroups of retarded readers: A neuropsychological multivariate approach. *Journal of Clinical Neuropsychology, 1,* 17–37

Pratt, A.C., & Brady, S. (1988). Relation of phonological awareness to reading disability in children and adults. *Journal of Educational Psychology, 80,* 319–323.

Roeltgen, D. (1985). Agraphia. In K.M. Heilman & E. Valenstein (Eds.), *Clinical neuropsychology* (pp. 75–96). New York: Oxford University Press.

Rourke, B.P. (1978). Neuropsychological research in reading retardation: A review. In A.L. Benton & D. Pearl (Eds.), *Dyslexia: An appraisal of current knowledge* (pp. 240–278). New York: Oxford University Press.

Rourke, B.P. (1985). *Neuropsychology of learning disabilities: Essentials of subtype analysis.* New York: Guilford Press.

Rourke, B.P. (1987). Syndrome of nonverbal learning disabilites: The final common pathway of white-matter disease/dysfunction? *The Clinical Neuropsychologist, 1,* 209–234.

Rourke, B.P. (1988). The syndrome of nonverbal learning disabilities: Developmental manifestations in neurological disease, disorder, and dysfunction. *The Clinical Neuropsychologist, 2,* 293–330.

Rourke, B.P. (1989). *Nonverbal learning disabilities: The syndrome and the model.* New York: Guilford Press.

Rourke, B.P. (1995). *Syndrome of nonverbal learning disabilities: Neurodevelopmental manifestations.* New York: Guilford Press.

Rourke, B.P., & Finlayson, M.A.J. (1978). Neuropsychological significance of variations in patterns of academic performance: Verbal and visual-spatial abilities. *Journal of Pediatric Psychology, 3,* 62–66.

Rourke, B.P., & Strang, J.D. (1978). Neuropsychological significance of variations in patterns of academic performance: Motor, psychomotor, and tactile perception abilities. *Journal of Pediatric Psychology, 3*, 212–225.

Russell, R., & Ginsburg, H.P. (1984). Cognitive analysis of children's mathematics difficulties. *Cognition Instruction, 1*, 217–247.

Rutter, M. (1978). Dyslexia. In A.L. Benton & D. Pearl (Eds.), *Dyslexia: An appraisal of current knowledge* (pp. 3–26). New York: Oxford University Press.

Rutter, M., & Yule, W. (1975). The concept of specific reading retardation. *Journal of Child Psychology and Psychiatry, 16*, 181–197.

Satz, P., & Morris, R. (1981). Learning disability subtypes: A review. In F.J. Pirozzolo & M.C. Wittrock (Eds.), *Neuropsychological and cognitive processes in reading* (pp. 109–141). New York: Academic Press.

Senf, G.M. (1981). Issues surrounding the diagnosis of learning disabilities: Child handicap versus failure of the child-school interaction. In T.R. Kratochwill (Ed.), *Advances in school psychology* (Vol. 1, pp. 88–131). Hillsdale, NJ: Lawrence Erlbaum Associates.

Senf, G.M. (1986). LD research in sociological and scientific perspective. In J.K. Torgesen & B.Y.L. Wong (Eds.), *Psychological and educational perspectives on learning disabilities* (pp. 27–53). New York: Academic Press.

Senf, G.M. (1987). Learning disabilities as a sociologic sponge: Wiping up life's spills. In S. Vaughn & C. Cos (Eds.), *Research in learning disabilities: Issues and future directions* (pp. 87–104). Boston: College-Hill Press.

Shallice, T. (1988). *From neuropsychology to mental structure.* New York: Cambridge University Press.

Shankweiler, D., & Liberman, I.Y. (Eds.). (1989). *Phonology and reading disability: Solving the reading puzzle.* Ann Arbor: University of Michigan Press.

Share, D.J., Jorm, A.F., MacLean, R., & Matthews, R. (1984). Sources of individual differences in reading achievement. *Journal of Educational Psychology, 76*, 466–477.

Shaywitz, B.A., Fletcher, J.M., Holahan, J.M., & Shaywitz, S.E. (1992). Discrepancy compared to low achievement definitions of reading disability: Results of the Connecticut longitudinal study. *Journal of Learning Disabilities, 25*, 639–648.

Shaywitz, B.A., & Shaywitz, S.E. (1994). Measuring and analyzing change. In G.R. Lyon (Ed.), *Frames of reference for the assessment of learning disabilities: New views on measurement issues* (pp. 29–58). Baltimore: Paul H. Brookes Publishing Co.

Shaywitz, S.E., Escobar, M.D., Shaywitz, B.A., Fletcher, J.M., & Makuch, R. (1992). Evidence that dyslexia may represent the lower tail of a normal distribution of reading ability. *New England Journal of Medicine, 326*, 145–150.

Shaywitz, S.E., Fletcher, J.M., & Shaywitz, B.A. (1994). Issues in the definition and classification of attention deficit disorder. *Topics in Language Disorders, 14*, 1–25.

Shaywitz, S.E., Shaywitz, B.A., Fletcher, J.M., & Escobar, M.D. (1990). Prevalence of reading disability in boys and girls: Results of the Connecticut longitudinal study. *Journal of the American Medical Association, 264*, 998–1001.

Shaywitz, S.E., Shaywitz, B.A., Schnell, C., & Towle, V.R. (1988). Concurrent and predictive validity of the Yale Children's Inventory: An instrument to assess children with attentional deficits and learning disabilities. *Pediatrics, 81*, 562–571.

Shelton, T.L., & Barkley, R.A. (1994). Critical issues in the assessment of attention deficit disorders in children. *Topics in Language Disorders, 14*, 26–41.

Silva, P.A., McGee, R., & Williams, S. (1985). Some characteristics of 9-year-old boys with general reading backwardness or specific reading retardation. *Journal of Child Psychology and Psychiatry, 26*, 407–421.

Skinner, H.A. (1981). Toward the integration of classification theory and methods. *Journal of Abnormal Psychology, 90*, 68–87.

Smith, F. (1971). *Understanding reading: A psycholinguistic analysis of reading and learning to read*. New York: Holt, Rinehart & Winston.

Snowling, M.J. (1987). *Dyslexia*. Oxford, England: Basil Blackwell.

Speece, D.L. (1993). Broadening the scope of classification research. In G.R. Lyon, D.B. Gray, J.F. Kavanagh, & N.A. Krasnegor (Eds.), *Better understanding learning disabilities: New views from research and their implications for education and public policies* (pp. 57–72). Baltimore: Paul H. Brookes Publishing Co.

Spreen, O., & Haaf, R.G. (1986). Empirically derived learning disability subtypes: A replication attempt and longitudinal patterns over 15 years. *Journal of Learning Disabilities, 19*, 170–180.

Stanley, J.C., Brody, L.E., Dauber, S.L., Lupowski, A.E., & Benbow, C.P. (1987). *Sex differences in cognitive abilities and achievements*. A symposium presentation at the annual meeting of the American Educational Research Association, Washington, DC.

Stanovich, K.E. (1980). Toward an interactive-compensatory model of individual differences in the development of reading fluency. *Reading Research Quarterly, 16*, 32–71.

Stanovich, K.E. (1986). Matthew effects in reading: Some consequences of individuals' differences in the acquisition of literacy. *Reading Research Quarterly, 21*, 360–407.

Stanovich, K.E. (1988). Explaining the differences between the dyslexic and the garden-variety poor reader: The phonological-core variable difference model. *Journal of Learning Disabilities, 21*, 590–612.

Stanovich, K.E. (1991). Word recognition: Changing perspectives. In M.L. Kamil, P. Mosenthal, & P.D. Pearson (Eds.), *Handbook of reading research* (Vol. 2, pp. 418–452). New York: Longman.

Stanovich, K.E. (1992). Speculations on the causes and consequences of individual differences in early reading acquisitions. In P.B. Gough, L.C. Ehri, & R. Treiman (Eds.), *Reading acquisition* (pp. 307–342). Hillsdale, NJ: Lawrence Erlbaum Associates.

Stanovich, K.E. (1993). The construct validity of discrepancy definitions of reading disability. In G.R. Lyon, D.B. Gray, J.F. Kavanagh, & N.A. Krasnegor (Eds.), *Better understanding learning disabilities: New views from research and their implications for education and public policies* (pp. 273–307). Baltimore: Paul H. Brookes Publishing Co.

Stanovich, K.E. (1994). Romance and reality. *The Reading Teacher, 47*, 280–291.

Stanovich, K.E., & Siegel, L.S. (1994). Phenotypic performance profile of children with reading disabilities: A regression-based test of the phonological-core variable-difference model. *Journal of Educational Psychology, 86*, 24–53.

Stanovich, K.E., & West, R.F. (1989). Exposure to print and orthographic processing. *Reading Research Quarterly, 24*, 402–433.

Stanovich, K.E., West, R.F., & Feeman, D.J. (1981). A longitudinal study of sentence context effects in second-grade children: Tests of an interactive-compensatory model. *Journal of Experimental Child Psychology, 32*, 185–199.

Strang, J.D., & Rourke, B.P. (1985). Arithmetic disability subtypes: The neuropsychological significance of specific arithmetic impairment in childhood.

In B. P. Rourke (Ed.), *Neuropsychology of learning disabilities: Essentials of sub-type analysis.* New York: Guilford Press.

Tallal, P. (1988). Developmental language disorders. In J.F. Kavanagh & T. Truss (Eds.), *Learning disabilities: Proceedings of the national conference.* Parkton, MD: York Press.

Torgesen, J.K. (1991). Learning disabilities: Historical and conceptual issues. In B.Y.L. Wong (Ed.), *Learning about learning disabilities* (pp. 3–39). New York: Academic Press.

Torgesen, J.K. (1993). Variations on theory in learning disability. In G.R. Lyon, D.B. Gray, J.F. Kavanagh, & N.A. Krasnegor (Eds.), *Better understanding learning disabilities: New views from research and their implications for education and public policies* (pp. 153–170). Baltimore: Paul H. Brookes Publishing Co.

Treiman, R., & Baron, J. (1983). Phonemic-analysis training helps children benefit from spelling-sound rules. *Memory and Cognition, 11,* 382–389.

U.S. Department of Education. (1989). *To assure the free appropriate public education of all handicapped children: Eleventh report to Congress on the implementation of the Education of the Handicapped Act.* Washington, DC: Department of Education.

U.S. Office of Education. (1977). Definition and criteria for defining students as learning disabled. 42 Fed. Reg. 65,083. Washington, DC: U.S. Government Printing Office.

Vellutino, F.R., & Scanlon, D.M. (1987). Linguistic coding and reading ability. In S. Rosenberg (Ed.), *Advances in applied psycholinguistics* (pp. 33–197). Hillsdale, NJ: Lawrence Erlbaum Associates.

Vellutino, F.R., Scanlon, D.M., & Tanzman, M.S. (1994). Components of reading ability: Issues and problems in operationalizing word identification, phonological coding, and orthographic coding. In G.R. Lyon (Ed.), *Frames of reference for the assessment of learning disabilities: New views on measurement issues* (pp. 279–329). Baltimore: Paul H. Brookes Publishing Co.

Wagner, R.K. (1988). Causal relationships between the development of phonological-processing abilities and the acquisition of reading skills: A meta-analysis. *Merrill-Palmer Quarterly, 34,* 261–279.

Wagner, R.K., & Torgesen, J.K. (1987). The nature of phonological processing and its causal role in the acquisition of reading skills. *Psychological Bulletin, 101,* 192–212.

West, R.F., & Stanovich, K.E. (1978). Automatic contextual facilitation in readers of three ages. *Child Development, 49,* 717–727.

Wiederholt, J.L. (1974). Historical perspectives on the education of the learning disabled. In L. Mann & D.A. Sabatino (Eds.), *The second review of special education* (pp. 103–152). Austin, TX: PRO-ED.

Wiig, E.H., & Semmel, E.M. (1976). *Language disabilities in children and adolescents.* Columbus, OH: Charles E. Merrill.

Wong, B.Y.L. (1991). *Learning about learning disabilities.* New York: Academic Press.

Wood, F.B. (1990). Functional neuroimaging in neurobehavioral research. In A.A. Boulton, G.B. Baker, & M. Hiscock (Eds.), *Neuromethods: Vol. 17. Neuropsychology* (pp. 65–89). Clifton, NJ: Humana Press.

Wood, F.B., & Felton, R.H. (1994). Separate linguistic and attentional factors in the development of reading. *Topics in Language Disorders, 14,* 42–57.

Wood, F.B., Felton, R., Flowers, L., & Naylor, C. (1991). Neurobehavioral definition of dyslexia. In D.D. Duane & D.B. Gray (Eds.), *The reading brain: The biological basis of dyslexia* (pp. 1–26). Parkton, MD: York Press.

World Health Organization (1992). *International statistical classification of diseases and related health problems (ICD-10)*. Geneva, Switzerland: Author.

Yule, W., & Rutter, M. (1976). Epidemiology and social implications of specific reading retardation. In R.M. Knights & D.J. Bakker (Eds.), *The neuropsychology of learning disorders* (pp. 76–102). Baltimore: University Park Press.

# SECTION II

## EDUCATION

# Chapter 2

# Preventing Early Reading Failure

*Benita A. Blachman*

Among the millions of Americans who have learning disabilities, at least 75% have their primary disability in the area of reading (National Institute of Child Health and Human Development [NICHD], 1994). Consequently, research in early intervention to prevent reading failure has critical importance. In this chapter, I briefly address four questions: 1) What do we know about the consequences of early reading failure? 2) what do we know about preventing early reading failure? 3) why is information about early reading failure not being used? and 4) what can we do to change the situation?

## WHAT DO WE KNOW ABOUT THE CONSEQUENCES OF EARLY READING FAILURE?

The tragic consequences of early reading failure are well documented. From research supported by NICHD (Lyon, 1995), we know that 74% of the students who are unsuccessful readers in third grade are still unsuccessful readers in ninth grade. These early literacy problems lead not only to low literacy rates among adults but also to a host of devastating problems including high dropout rates in schools and unemployment.

Perhaps the most eloquent description of the disastrous consequences of early reading failure has been provided by Stanovich (1986). Children who do not learn to decode, or read words, in first grade will read less and dislike it more than children who are successful readers—not a surprising scenario. With less practice, the poor readers become seriously delayed in the development of automatic word recognition strategies. When you do not learn to recognize words quickly, you have to focus considerable attention on sounding out each new word. This limits the cognitive resources available to focus on the meaning of what you are reading. Reading also increases vocabulary and general knowledge about the world and exposes readers to new ideas and concepts. As might be imagined, children with reading disabilities are less likely to acquire either the vocabulary or the general knowledge acquired by their peers. Consequently, the gap between good and poor readers grows wider as children move through school.

It is a vicious cycle: If you cannot read, you do not practice; if you don't practice, you don't become automatic and fluent in your ability to recognize words. Without fluency in word recognition, you use your energy trying to read individual words and comprehension suffers. Vocabulary is limited and knowledge about the world is compromised. In addition, the children who experience this cycle of failure often suffer traumatic emotional consequences from which they never fully recover.

## WHAT DO WE KNOW ABOUT PREVENTING EARLY READING FAILURE?

The good news is that there have been scientific breakthroughs in our knowledge about the development of literacy. We know a great deal about how to address reading problems even before they begin. Converging research evidence from numerous disciplines, including education, psychology, and the neurosciences, indicates that problems in early reading acquisition occur at the level of the word (Adams, 1990; Chall, 1989; Ehri, 1991; Gough & Tunmer, 1986; Stanovich, 1986; Vellutino, 1991). What this means is that many children with learning disabilities or reading disabilities are less likely to learn how to read or decode individual words accurately and fluently.

Why is it that learning to read even simple words is so difficult for so many? Again, the research findings appear incontrovertible. Numerous studies have found that both children and adults with reading problems have deficits in the language skills related to reading (Brady & Shankweiler, 1991; Liberman & Shankweiler, 1979, 1985; Wagner & Torgesen, 1987). For example, one language skill that we have learned a great deal about is phonological awareness (for a review of the literature, see Blachman, 1994). This is an awareness of and the ability to manipulate the sounds in spoken words. Simple oral language activities, such as producing words that rhyme, knowing that there are two sounds in a spoken word such as *up,* or producing the word that remains when *fat* is said without the *f,* indicate an awareness that words have parts. These parts of words or sound segments are more or less represented by the letters of the alphabet.

Why is this knowledge important? If you do not know that spoken words have parts, it will be very hard to understand how alphabetic transcription works. If you are not aware that a spoken word such as *sun* has three segments, you will be less likely to understand why the word is written with three letters. Research from all over the world is unequivocal on this point: Children who lack this awareness are likely to be among our poorest readers (e.g., Bradley & Bryant, 1983; Iversen & Tunmer, 1993; Juel, 1988; Share, Jorm, Maclean, & Matthews, 1984; Vellutino & Scanlon, 1987). These are the children who cannot unlock words they have never seen before. Reading unfamiliar words is something most of us do effortlessly every day of our lives.

However, the research findings also suggest that we have the tools to break the cycle of early failure. One exciting discovery from recent research is that phonological awareness, for example, can be taught to young children before failure has occurred (Byrne & Fielding-Barnsley, 1991, 1993; Lundberg, Frost, & Peterson, 1988). When phonological awareness is taught in conjunction with instruction in how the alphabet works—that is, how letters and strings of letters represent sounds—children improve significantly in both reading and spelling (Ball & Blachman, 1991; Blachman, Ball, Black, & Tangel, 1994; Bradley, 1988; Bradley & Bryant, 1983; Iversen & Tunmer, 1993).

## WHY IS INFORMATION ABOUT EARLY READING FAILURE NOT BEING USED?

The tragedy is that we are not exploiting what is known about reducing the incidence of reading failure. Specifically, the instruction currently being provided to our children does not reflect what is known from research. Direct, systematic instruction about the alphabetic code is not routinely provided in kindergarten and first grade, despite the fact that, given what we know at the moment, this may be the most powerful weapon in the fight against illiteracy.

If it is known that children with reading and learning disabilities have trouble learning to read words, then it makes sense to focus instruction, at least initially, on that task. Unfortunately for many children with reading disabilities, the politically correct methodology for teaching reading today, called whole language, deemphasizes the structure of words and breaking words into parts (Goodman, 1986). The idea is that children will go directly to meaning by immersion in literature. Unfortunately, however, there can be no meaning for the child who cannot read the words on the page.

Now, no one can be reasonably against immersion in good literature. For many lucky children it works quite well. But for literally millions of children who need very focused, direct instruction to learn to read words, what is currently in vogue ignores what has been learned from research. As Isabelle Liberman (personal communication, November 11,

1988) often said, "If you can't read the words on the page, it doesn't matter if you give children Dickens or Dick and Jane, they still won't be able to read."

As is discussed in other chapters of this book, teachers are not being trained to provide the type of instruction that we know can make a difference (Moats, 1994). The fact that we know how to identify reading problems early and how to begin to intervene before the devastation sets in, and yet are not training teachers to do this, is a travesty.

## WHAT CAN WE DO TO CHANGE THE SITUATION?

We need to renew our commitment to research and training. Research dollars *are* making a difference. Not only do we know from medical, psychological, and educational research that a variety of phonological deficits (or problems in using the sounds of one's language) are at the core of most cases of reading failure, we are learning how to identify and treat these problems early. In addition, groundbreaking medical research has begun to uncover the biological bases for learning and reading disabilities. Without a commitment to both basic and applied research, however, it will not be possible to ascertain which specific interventions work best for which children in which settings. Without a commitment to instruct teachers in research-based strategies for the prevention of reading failure, the knowledge already gained will not be put into practice. As a society, we cannot afford to let substantial numbers of children fail to become literate.

This is not a story just about children of low-income families. Although poor children may come to school with more risk factors, reading disabilities and the larger problem of learning disabilities affect children and adults from every walk of life in every school district in the country—urban, rural, rich, and poor. No segment of society is immune. There are millions of American children and adults with learning disabilities and we have a responsibility not to let them down.

## REFERENCES

Adams, M.J. (1990). *Beginning to read: Thinking and learning about print.* Cambridge, MA: MIT Press.

Ball, E.W., & Blachman, B.A. (1991). Does phoneme awareness training in kindergarten make a difference in early word recognition and developmental spelling? *Reading Research Quarterly, 26*(1), 49–66.

Blachman, B.A. (1994). Early literacy acquisition: The role of phonological awareness. In G. Wallach & K. Butler (Eds.), *Language learning disabilities in school-age children and adolescents: Some underlying principles and applications* (pp. 253–274). Columbus, OH: Merrill/Macmillan.

Blachman, B.A., Ball, E.W., Black, R.S., & Tangel, D.M. (1994). Kindergarten teachers develop phoneme awareness in low-income, inner-city classrooms: Does it make a difference? *Reading and Writing: An Interdisciplinary Journal, 6,* 1–18.

Bradley, L. (1988). Making connections in learning to read and spell. *Applied Cognitive Psychology, 2,* 3–18.

Bradley, L., & Bryant, P. (1983). Categorizing sounds and learning to read: A causal connection. *Nature, 30,* 419–421.

Brady, S., & Shankweiler, D. (Eds.). (1991). *Phonological processes in literacy: A tribute to Isabelle Y. Liberman.* Hillsdale, NJ: Lawrence Erlbaum Associates.

Byrne, B., & Fielding-Barnsley, R. (1991). Evaluation of a program to teach phonemic awareness to young children. *Journal of Educational Psychology, 83,* 451–455.

Byrne, B., & Fielding-Barnsley, R. (1993). Evaluation of a program to teach phonemic awareness to young children: A 1-year follow-up. *Journal of Educational Psychology, 85,* 104–111.

Chall, J.S. (1989). Learning to read: The great debate 20 years later: A response to "Debunking the great phonics myth." *Phi Delta Kappan, 70,* 521–538.

Ehri, L. (1991). Learning to read and spell words. In L. Rieben & C.A. Perfetti (Eds.), *Learning to read: Basic research and its implications* (pp. 57–73). Hillsdale, NJ: Lawrence Erlbaum Associates.

Goodman, K.S. (1986). *What's whole in whole language: A parent-teacher guide.* Portsmouth, NH: Heinemann.

Gough, P., & Tunmer, W. (1986). Decoding, reading, and reading disability. *Remedial and Special Education, 7,* 6–10.

Iversen, S., & Tunmer, W. (1993). Phonological processing skills and the Reading Recovery Program. *Journal of Educational Psychology, 85,* 112–126.

Juel, C. (1988). Learning to read and write: A longitudinal study of 54 children from first through fourth grades. *Journal of Educational Psychology, 80,* 437–447.

Liberman, I.Y., & Shankweiler, D. (1979). Speech, the alphabet, and teaching children to read. In L. Resnick & P. Weaver (Eds.), *Theory and practice of early reading* (Vol. 2, pp. 109–132). Hillsdale, NJ: Lawrence Erlbaum Associates.

Liberman, I.Y., & Shankweiler, D. (1985). Phonology and the problems of learning to read and write. *Remedial and Special Education, 6,* 8–17.

Lundberg, I., Frost, J., & Peterson, O. (1988). Effects of an extensive program for stimulating phonological awareness in preschool children. *Reading Research Quarterly, 23*(3), 263–284.

Lyon, G.R. (1995). Research initiatives and discoveries in learning disabilities: Contributions from scientists supported by the National Institute of Child Health and Human Development. *Journal of Child Neurology, 10*(Suppl. 1), S120–S126.

Moats, L.C. (1994). The missing foundation in teacher education: Knowledge of the structure of spoken and written language. *Annals of Dyslexia, 44,* 81–102.

National Institute of Child Health and Human Development (NICHD). (1994, August). National Institute of Child Health and Human Development Conference on Intervention Programs for Children with Reading and Related Language Disorders, Washington, DC.

Share, D.J., Jorm, A.F., Maclean, R., & Matthews, R. (1984). Sources of individual differences in reading achievement. *Journal of Educational Psychology, 76*(6), 466–477.

Stanovich, K.E. (1986). Matthew effects in reading: Some consequences of individual differences in the acquisition of literacy. *Reading Research Quarterly, 21,* 360–407.

Vellutino, F.R. (1991). Introduction to three studies on reading acquisition: Convergent findings on theoretical foundations of code-oriented versus whole-language approaches to reading instruction. *Journal of Educational Psychology, 83,* 437–443.

Vellutino, F.R., & Scanlon, D.M. (1987). Phonological coding, phonological awareness, and reading ability: Evidence from a longitudinal and experimental study. *Merrill-Palmer Quarterly, 33,* 321–363.

Wagner, R., & Torgesen, J. (1987). The nature of phonological processing and its causal role in the acquisition of reading skills. *Psychological Bulletin, 101*(2), 192–212.

# Chapter 3

# Public Policy

## An Agenda for the Future

*Edwin W. Martin*

For many years, programming for children and youth with learning disabilities (LD) has suffered from what I termed the "myth of mildness" (Martin, 1993). Essentially, I and many other professionals learned from earlier literature in this field to anticipate that some, perhaps most, children with LD would "outgrow" their problems during their elementary school years or perhaps would learn to "compensate" for their problems and be able to succeed relatively well in general education settings. There was also a tendency among early researchers to focus on language and, to some extent, related cognitive skills as the root of the problems we call learning disabilities. More recently, there has been greater focus on more global organizational and social and behavioral difficulties faced by some children and youth, but traditional educational interventions have not necessarily focused on these broader dimensions of human behavior. Evidence substantiating this observation comes from a national survey (Wagner, 1992–1993) in which investigators found that only a minority of secondary school children in special education received any of the "related services" called for under the Individuals with Disabilities Education Act of 1990 (IDEA) (PL 101-476). This was true, for example, of counseling services not only for children with LD but also for children the schools had identified as "emotionally or behaviorally disabled." Approximately only one third of the students enrolled in special education programs for children with emotional or behavioral problems were receiving any counseling.

Assumptions about mildness have influenced state and federal policies not only linked to the provision of related services but also to such characteristics of special education as the grouping of children with varying disabilities; general certification of teachers that allowed them to teach any assortment of so-called mildly disabled children; enrolling virtually all children with LD in some classes with typically achieving children; and, in some instances, increasing class size. In part, these policies were fueled by research that pointed out the difficulty of differential diagnosis of children with language and learning problems using the standard procedures widely employed by schools. What is open to question, however, is whether the difficulties faced in differential diagnosis imply that similar or identical interventions will serve all children with so-called generic mild disabilities. Increasingly, I doubt that these interventions are effective and the assumptions accurate.

## PUBLIC POLICY SHOULD BE DRIVEN BY RESEARCH

Although it is a recommendation that is almost universally poorly received, public policy in learning disabilities needs to be driven much more completely by research and demonstration findings. This recommendation is poorly received by various audiences for several reasons. For parents and those involved in direct services, the wait for research findings seems too long, and there is not always the confidence that the research is relevant. Policy makers also tend to wish for quicker solutions—and sometimes more economical ones—and so the field frequently moves in directions based on what might be called "sound-good theories," the most recent of which is called inclusion. In fairness, my wish is not to attack the concept of inclusion, which is the logical extension of the concepts of integration, mainstreaming, and normalization, that are each based on the wish to include persons with disabilities more fully in society. My point, for now, is simply that public policy moves forward based primarily on belief systems and not on documented success in the classroom for large samples of children.

It is important that research be focused on the identification and nature of learning disabilities. In this area, the National Institute of Child Health and Human Development has been leading the way, and a critical mass of information is gradually accumulating. Although I have read in newspapers, sometimes in the editorial and news columns, more frequently in letters to the editor, statements that learning disabilities are a figment of the imagination of educators, serious scholars, reviewing the works in neurology, physiology, genetics, psychology, linguistics, and education among other fields, have accumulated volumes of information validating various variations in learning behaviors and abilities.

It is my feeling that the U.S. Department of Education should develop a more consistent and comprehensive approach to its research in learning disabilities. Too many of the studies, while legitimate in their own right, do not help to form a coherent and cohesive understanding of educational interventions and their outcomes.

On the positive side, however, the Department of Education has placed increasing emphasis on the development of outcome measures and the application of those outcome measures. A center at the University of Minnesota is dedicated to this purpose, and the Department of Education, at the direction of Congress, has supported a landmark study of outcomes of education for high school and post–high school age youth with disabilities (Wagner, 1992–1993). This study is now completed, and I am not certain that the Department of Education intends to fund similar longitudinal outcome studies, but I have recommended that it does so as I am sure many others also have. Let me use some data from that study to make my final points.

When I served as Assistant Secretary for Special Education and Rehabilitative Services in the U.S. Department of Education and, earlier, as Director of the U.S. Bureau of Education for the Handicapped in the former Department of Health, Education, and Welfare, we helped design and implement the law known as IDEA, originally the Education for All Handicapped Children Act of 1975 (PL 94-142). During that period, we also helped Congress design other legislation, including the authorization of model programs for children with specific learning disabilities in 1970 and a similar early childhood education program in 1968.

During those years, we were faced with the public policy task of attempting to define learning disabilities in such a way that children with these problems would be eligible to receive special educational assistance. It was not an easy task academically or politically, and, in fact, several times efforts to include children with LD in the original Education of the Handicapped Act (PL 89-750) were defeated. On the academic side, the definition, really a kind of description of what behaviors were and were not considered learning disabilities, was seen, at best, as a pragmatic way to allow children to be assisted and not as a validly determined, scientifically based definition. Although the definition has served its broad societal purpose for the large part, it has also allowed many problems and inconsistencies to occur. It is telling that this definition with its dramatic weaknesses, is still in the law (IDEA). What better argument is there for my recommendation that we must use science to help us develop a more effective way to identify the learning disabilities that children demonstrate and to base intervention efforts on the understanding of that population?

Throughout the development of PL 94-142 and in the years it has been implemented and amended, the federal government and, I believe, state and local governments have based much of their programming on the assumption that integration or mainstreaming of children was the preferred course, and this was not only required by state and federal law in many instances and consistent with social policy but assumed to be educationally valid as well.

I doubt there are many who would not subscribe at least generally to that proposition. I know that we considered in our annual reports to Congress as positive findings that the overwhelming number of children with learning disabilities (approximately 90%) were enrolled in general education classes with children without disabilities for at least part of each day. If integration was the goal of PL 94-142, it was being met to some substantial degree, at least for children identified as having learning disabilities.

While we were congratulating ourselves on this attainment and expressing disappointment at less significant enrollments in other areas of disability or in states and communities with variant records, a study of the outcomes of high school–age children identified as having learning disabilities was begun (Wagner, 1992–1993).

In the briefest of summations, Wagner found that children with LD got lower grades in general education classes than peers without disabilities; in fact, two out of three children with LD failed at least one general education class over their 4 years, and, not surprising, their dropout rate was greater than that of children without LD (Table 1). The numbers of high school students with LD who went on to 4-year colleges was infinitesimal, approximately only 4% (Table 2). Among the post–high school findings that also caused alarm was that approximately 25% of the school leavers reported being arrested in the first 5 years after leaving school. Only children identified as seriously emotionally or behaviorally disturbed had a higher arrest rate.

I see these outcomes as terribly shocking and disappointing. As a special educator, I had no idea that so many children were having so

Table 1. Percentage of youth with disabilities failing at least one general education high school course

| Disability | Percentage |
| --- | --- |
| Learning disability | 65.1% |
| Emotional disturbance | 77.4 |
| Speech impairment | 56.4 |
| Mental retardation | 48.5 |
| Visual impairment | 53.5 |
| Hard of hearing | 54.2 |
| Deaf | 44.1 |
| Orthopedic impairment | 50.7 |
| Other health impairment | 65.7 |
| Multiple disabilities | 50.0 |
| All conditions | 62.2 |

Adapted from Wagner et al. (1993).

Table 2. Attendance at postsecondary schools by youth with disabilities

| Disability | Percentage attending | | |
| --- | --- | --- | --- |
| | Vocational school | 2-year college | 4-year college |
| Learning disability | 19.0% | 13.7% | 4.4% |
| Emotional disturbance | 15.4 | 10.1 | 4.2 |
| Speech impairment | 16.4 | 25.4 | 13.3 |
| Mental retardation | 9.6 | 3.6 | — |
| Visual impairment | 15.6 | 27.5 | 33.4 |
| Hard of hearing | 16.0 | 40.4 | 15.7 |
| Deaf | 22.5 | 33.2 | 22.1 |
| Orthopedic impairment | 12.6 | 32.3 | 12.9 |
| Other health impairment | 33.9 | 28.4 | 21.9 |
| Multiple disabilities | 0.7 | 7.9 | 2.2 |
| Deaf/blind | 13.4 | 8.9 | 8.9 |
| All conditions | 15.9 | 11.8 | 4.2 |

Adapted from Wagner et al. (1993).

much difficulty and doing so poorly. Clearly, our educational interventions are not sufficiently effective. The critical point about public policy and human services ethics that I am attempting to make is that we must not allow such an absence of information to continue. We must understand what happens to the students we serve. Granted, such measures may be scientifically crude, particularly at first, and will necessarily have to be tailored to various types and degrees of disability, but a public policy that blithely moves ahead while two out of three children are failing even one course is not acceptable.

## CONCLUSIONS

We must create and evaluate public policy for students with LD, not on the basis of deeply held convictions, but on the basis of a reasonable record of measured achievement. In addition to formal outcome research studies, which I believe are of critical importance, we should also have a federally funded major demonstration program that would support a range of various service delivery models—from those designed to be inclusive to those targeting special services for groups of children with similar learning needs (Martin, 1994).

I mentioned earlier the successful demonstration programs that created new knowledge and practices in early childhood services and in services for children with learning disabilities and with severe disabilities. This approach, although time consuming, is much more professionally and ethically responsible than radically modifying service programs for millions of youngsters based on deeply held beliefs, however philosophically attractive. We should not accept rhetoric in place of data.

## REFERENCES

Education for All Handicapped Children Act of 1975, PL 94-142. (August 23, 1977). 20 USC §§ 1400 et seq.: *U.S. Statutes at Large, 89,* 773–796.

Education of the Handicapped Act, PL 89-750. (November 3, 1966). Title VI of the Elementary and Secondary Education Act, PL 103-382. (1994). Title 20, U.S.C. §§ 6301 et seq.: *U.S. Statutes at Large, 108,* 3518–4062.

Handicapped Children's Early Education Assistance Act of 1968, PL 90-538. (September 30, 1968). Title 20, U.S.C. §§ 621 et seq.: *U.S. Statutes at Large, 82,* 901–902.

Individuals with Disabilities Education Act of 1990 (IDEA), PL 101-476. (October 30, 1990). 20 U.S.C. §§ 1400 et seq.: *U.S. Statutes at Large, 104,* 1103–1151.

Martin, E.W. (1993). Learning disabilities and public policy: Myths and outcomes. In G.R. Lyon, D.B. Gray, J.F. Kavanagh, & N.A. Krasnegor (Eds.), *Better understanding learning disabilities: New views from research and their implications for education and public policies* (pp. 325–342). Baltimore: Paul H. Brookes Publishing Co.

Martin, E.W. (1994). Inclusion: Rhetoric and reality. *Exceptional Parent, 24*(4), 39–42.

Wagner, M. (1992–1993). *National longitudinal transition study of special education students.* Menlo Park, CA: SRI International.

Wagner, M., Newman, L., D'Amico, R., Jay, E.D., Butler-Nalin, P., Marder, C., & Cox, R. (1991). *Youth with disabilities: How are they doing?* Report from the National Longitudinal Transition Study of Special Education Students. Menlo Park, CA: SRI International.

Wagner, M., D'Amilo, R., et al. (1993). *What happens next? Trends in postschool outcomes of youth with disabilities.* Report from the National Longitudinal Transition Study of Special Education Students. Menlo Park, CA: SRI International.

# Chapter 4

# Strategies for Implementing Policies

*Barbara K. Keogh*

The discussion in this chapter is based on two assumptions: 1) education policies reflect social values, and 2) the implementation of policy is a function of sociopolitical conditions and influences. An implication of the first assumption is that we should expect that policies will change as social values change. Examples of such changes are the landmark Education for All Handicapped Children Act of 1975 (PL 94-142), reauthorized as the Individuals with Disabilities Education Act of 1990 (IDEA) and subsequent amendments, and PL 101-336, the Americans with Disabilities Act of 1990 (ADA). These laws grew out of a strong commitment to equal opportunity for all citizens, including those with disabilities.

An implication of the second assumption is that the implementation of policy is affected by advocacy, by economics, and by politics, which sometimes lead to inconsistencies and even conflicts in practices. An example is the potential conflict between policies such as Goals 2000: Educate America Act of 1994 (PL 103-227), which calls for more academic curricula, higher achievement, and national standards and policies that call for full inclusion of all students into general education programs, regardless of the nature or severity of their learning problems.

Federal policies provide focus and direction to education reform and spur changes in practices at state and local levels. Federal policies also ensure educational opportunity for all learners, including those with learning disabilities (LD). The landscape of American education would be markedly different were it not for major policy directives at the federal level. What is missing in the current call for education reform and improved services, however, is a comprehensive and coherent strategy or plan for implementation. Unfortunately, in the absence of such a plan, it is too often advocacy and political expediency that determine what is implemented and how it is implemented. Furthermore, the "one plan fits all" assumption characteristic of many advocacy positions ignores the reality of individual differences in educational needs and aptitudes and often places unreasonable burden on students and on education professionals. I ask, then, what should be the federal role in implementing policies calling for improved educational programs for students with LD? In response, I focus on two major topics, research and professional preparation, and propose an emphasis on prevention as an overarching goal for federal policies aimed at improving educational practice.

## RESEARCH

Examination of funding patterns makes clear that the support for research and development by the U.S. Department of Education is small compared to that afforded other federal agencies. In a 1994 report, the American Association for the Advancement of Science summarized the pattern for fiscal 1994 of federal support for research and development conducted by colleges and universities. Of all federal funding for research, 52% was through the National Institutes of Health (NIH), 14% was through the National Science Foundation, 13% was through the Department of Defense, 6% was through the National Aeronautics and Space Administration, and 1% was through the Department of Education.

As an educator, I do not question the importance of support for the research efforts of other agencies, because researchers in those agencies address a range of important and timely questions and needs. Examination of the activities of NIH, for example, indicates that many of its research projects have direct relevance to the understanding of LD. (See the Interagency Committee on Learning Disabilities, 1987, and Lyon, 1995, for summary reviews.) Solid and generalizable developmental data describing the course of learning and language disabilities over time, emerging from research supported by the National Institute of Child Health and Human Development, are essential. Basic research on neurobiological and psychological processes carried out at the National Institute of Neurological and Communicative Disorders and the National Institute of Mental Health is another example of research central to this effort.

Given the importance of education in American society, however, the disparity in support for education research, compared to support for other federal agencies, is striking. The limited funding for education research is especially troubling when considered in relation to the current demand for education reform. It is clear that the quality of public school education in the United States must be improved. However, the lack of consistent support for education research does not allow us to address relevant implementation questions that affect education in general and LD in particular. I emphasize that only a fraction of the 1% of the 1994 funding for research in the Department of Education went to research on LD, despite the fact that LD is the single largest category of special education need.

Although there are continuing disagreements about specifics of definition and prevalence, there is a consensus that students with LD represent a significant subgroup of learners. In the 1991–1992 school year, more than 5% of all students ages 6–17 received special services under the designation of LD (Office of Special Education Programs, 1993). We cannot assume that research aimed at typical learners will provide necessary insights about LD or that research on basic neurological or psychological processes will lead to effective interventions for these individuals. Thus, research on LD is critical.

Education research focused on the particular problems of students with LD is especially important as the policy of inclusion becomes the educational placement of choice. The vast majority of students with LD spend their school years in general education programs and are taught by general education teachers; the continuum of services as we know it is being phased out. Thus, we must know considerably more about the ways in which classroom contexts, instructional programs, and teaching methods affect the achievement, performance, and adjustment of students with LD. It is also important to note that the world of learning disabilities contains a broad range of intervention approaches, many of which have not been well tested but have strong advocates. Advocacy and good intentions are not enough. It is time to take a critical look at programs and interventions and to make clear which programs work and which do not.

## PROFESSIONAL PREPARATION

Research-based evidence about LD is necessary but not sufficient in itself for successful implementation of policy. The effectiveness of intervention programs is also strongly tied to the quality and expertise of the personnel who plan and carry out policy directives. Thus, a critical area of federal influence is in the area of training. Teachers are, of course, key people in the delivery of educational services for students with LD. Yet, according to Haselkorn and Calkins (1993), LD is one of the four special education areas in which a teacher shortage is greatest. I suggest, in addition, that the need for improved professional preparation is limited not only to teachers, but also includes the training of clinicians and educational practitioners at all levels, such as school psychologists and administrators. The successful implementation of policy requires reconsideration of the roles and the training needs of all professionals associated with students with LD.

The issue of personnel quality is especially acute, given the recognition that LD are not limited to school-age children, but rather are expressed across a broad age range: preschool through adulthood. A major impetus for change in services to younger children came from the Education of the Handicapped Act Amendments of 1986 (PL 99-457), which established services for infants and toddlers through Part H and expanded services to preschoolers through Section 619 in Part B, the Preschool Grants Program. To receive federal funds under the Preschool Grants Program, states are required to make early intervention services available to all eligible children from birth through age 2 and to provide older children, ages 3–5, with free, appropriate public education and related services as needed.

The individualized family service plan (IFSP) is a central component of the programs of Part H and, in addition to specification of the child's characteristics and needs, requires consideration of the child in the context of the strengths and needs of the family. The policy mandating family involvement in intervention means that professionals must have expertise in family as well as educational matters. Successful implementation requires understanding valid approaches for involving families, for planning and implementing interventions, and for assessing outcomes. Clearly these requirements imply major changes in the preparation of professional personnel.

Similar concerns may be expressed about the preparation of professionals who work with adolescents and young adults. An increasing awareness of the continuing needs of older youths with LD means that professionals with specialized knowledge of vocational and personal–social problems are essential. The particular difficulties faced by adolescents and young adults and their families are different from and often not relevant to issues involving younger children and their families. Thus, a major area of professional preparation must focus on LD in older individuals. The recognition that LD may be expressed across a broad age spectrum and that both individuals and families are affected represents a major step forward. The corollary is that more comprehensive and more effective programs to prepare personnel are essential if policies addressing LD in all age groups are to be implemented successfully. Support for professional preparation should entail a major federal effort.

## EMPHASIS ON PREVENTION

From both human and economic perspectives, I argue vigorously for the implementation of policies that focus on prevention. If only from a fiscal standpoint, the importance of prevention is clear. The average cost of educating a student with a disability is 2.3 times that of educating a student without a disability. (Council for Exceptional Children, 1994). Preventive programs have the potential for cutting education costs as well as for reducing the stress and misery associated with school failure. Few would argue with the goal of prevention, but to date only a limited number of programs have a preventive focus; the bulk of our efforts are still in the area of remediation.

Prevention has traditionally been conceptualized by an immunization model in the medical tradition: for example, DPT shots or the polio vaccine. Given the nature of social and educational problems prevalent today, I argue that we must expand our definition of *prevention* to include education programs and to place prevention in a larger time frame. Head Start is, of course, a prime example of a large-scale program that has had widespread impact, and there are other well-documented programs that have been effective in reducing the development of problems (see Ramey & Ramey, 1992, for a review). Effective reading readiness programs reduce the rate of reading failure in elementary school; early identification of and intervention with young children with LD lead to better school adjustment and performance in the primary grades. I have proposed elsewhere that prevention and intervention are inextricably linked and that both must be placed within a developmental perspective (Keogh, 1994). From this perspective, prevention is not a one-shot effort, but rather must be reconsidered as children enter each new developmental period.

## CONCLUSIONS

If we take seriously the federal commitment to improve education for students with LD, we must ensure adequate and stable support for research on educational practices as well as on biological and psychological processes that underlie LD. We must also improve the quality of the personnel who provide services through more effective professional preparation programs. Research and training are closely linked, and both require commitment and support at the federal level. They also require consistent priorities and support over time; fragmented and changing priorities lead to fragmented efforts and outcomes. Coherent research and evaluation plans and stable support are necessary if we are to improve services for individuals with LD. A focus on prevention provides a coherent way to focus medical and educational efforts, to bridge the gap between the efforts of different agencies, and to address a range of learning and developmental disorders. There is widespread support for policies aimed at improving services for students with LD. What is needed are policies for implementing the policies.

## REFERENCES

American Association for the Advancement of Science Committee on Science, Engineering, and Public Policy. (1994). *AAAS Report XIX Research and Development FY 1995*. Washington, DC: American Association for the Advancement of Science.

Americans with Disabilities Act of 1990 (ADA), PL 101-336. (July 26, 1990). Title 42, U.S.C. §§ 12101 et seq.: *U.S. Statutes at Large, 104*, 327–378.

Council for Exceptional Children. (1994). Statistical profile of special education in the United States, 1994. *Teaching Exceptional Children, 26*(3)(Suppl.), 1–3.

Education for All Handicapped Children Act of 1975, PL 94-142. (August 23, 1977). Title 20, U.S.C. 1401 §§ et seq.: *U.S. Statutes at Large, 89*, 773–796.

Education of the Handicapped Act Amendments of 1986, PL 99-457. (October 8, 1986). Title 20, U.S.C. §§ 1400 et seq.: *U.S. Statutes at Large, 100*, 1145–1177.

Goals 2000: Educate America Act of 1994, PL 103-227. (March, 1994). Title 20, U.S.C. §§ 5801 et seq.: *U.S. Statutes at Large, 108*, 125–280.

Haselkorn, D., & Calkins, A. (1993). *Careers in teaching*. Belmont, MA: Recruiting New Teachers, Inc.

Individuals with Disabilities Education Act of 1990 (IDEA), PL 101-476. (October 30, 1990). Title 20, U.S.C. §§ 1400 et seq.: *U.S. Statutes at Large, 104*, 1103–1151.

Interagency Committee on Learning Disabilities. (1987). *Learning disabilities: A report to the U.S. Congress*. Bethesda, MD: National Institutes of Health.

Keogh, B.K. (1994). What the special education research agenda should look like in the year 2000. *Learning Disabilities Research and Practice, 9*(2), 62–69.

Lyon, G.R. (1995). Research initiatives in learning disabilities: Contributions of scientists supported by the National Institute of Child Health and Human Development. *Journal of Child Neurology, 10*(Suppl. 1), S120–S126.

Office of Special Education Programs, U.S. Department of Education. (1993). *15th Annual Report to Congress on the Implementation of the Individuals with Disabilities Education Act*. Washington, DC: Author.

Ramey, S.L., & Ramey, C.T. (1992). Early educational intervention with disadvantaged children to what effect? *Applied and Preventive Psychology, 1*, 131–140.

Chapter 5

# Head Start and Young Children with Learning Disabilities

*Helen Taylor*

In her wisdom, and because of her great interest in children and families, Secretary of Health and Human Services Donna Shalala in 1993 appointed the Advisory Committee on Head Start Quality and Expansion to take an in-depth look at the Head Start program and to make recommendations for creating an improved Head Start program for the 21st century. The advisory committee consisted of a cross-section of people from a variety of disciplines, and it was bipartisan. The committee organized and developed three main goals to create a 21st-century Head Start. In January 1994, Secretary Shalala introduced to the public the recommendations of the advisory committee.

## GOALS FOR HEAD START

The goals are, first, to improve the quality of every Head Start program in America and to strive for excellence. Specific recommendations to improve the quality and range of individual Head Start programs in local communities include staff development for those who work directly with children and families and reengineering federal oversight of the Head Start program. We need to examine the training of federal employees to improve stewardship and oversight of the Head Start program.

The second broad goal is to make Head Start programs more responsive to the needs of children and families in local communities. We are not talking about a cookie-cutter kind of Head Start program where everybody follows the same kind of model with children and

---

This chapter is in the public domain.

families, but about programs that conduct in-depth community needs assessments to meet the needs of families in local communities. A responsive program in Dallas, Texas, would look very different from a program in Twin Falls, Idaho, or one in Washington, D.C., because the environments are different and the children and families are different.

Head Start really wants to become more responsive and more flexible in its approach to providing services. This includes being more responsive to the needs of families with children with disabilities or, in the case of many families, to the needs of parents with disabilities.

The third important goal for Head Start is to develop better linkages and to form better partnerships in local communities and also at the state and federal levels so that Head Start can coordinate services for families more effectively and utilize available resources at the federal, state, and local levels in more targeted ways.

As part of this effort, we are delighted to have formed a partnership with the National Center for Learning Disabilities (NCLD). NCLD will help educate Head Start directors, teachers, and parents about the warning signs of learning disabilities (LD). Head Start staff will be instructed in interventions to help children with LD and to ensure that their transition into kindergarten is smooth.

Head Start has been the most successful program in America for low-income children and families since the turn of the 20th century. Head Start is a comprehensive program, and it is locally based. Head Start provides educational, health, mental health, dental, nutritional, parent involvement, and social services for children and families. In the 1990s, a buzzword has been "two-generation family support." Head Start is the original two-generation family support program. Head Start has always been a program designed not only for children, but for children *and* families. Head Start recognizes that it is not possible to work effectively with children out of the context of their family members, the most significant people in their lives.

Head Start has a long tradition of serving children with disabilities. We continue to be the largest provider in the country of integrated placements for preschool children with disabilities. Each Head Start program reserves at least 10% of its slots for children with disabilities. So, we have considerable experience in including children with disabilities in our program and over the years have developed a training and technical assistance network to support that effort.

Head Start works with children with disabilities by joining with agencies in the local community to provide the specialized services that a child may need to address a specific disability as well as by including the child and family in the full Head Start program.

About one third of the children with disabilities in Head Start programs have been identified as having a disability at the time of enrollment. The remaining two thirds of the children with disabilities have their needs identified as a result of participating in a Head Start program. Only 6% of children in Head Start who have disabilities have been professionally assessed as having LD.

The developmental needs of children in Head Start most likely to be identified by observations, screenings, and assessments are predominantly in speech, language, and social domains. There tends to be a reluctance in Head Start programs, and among the professionals who provide assessments for the children, to use the term *learning disabilities* with preschool-age children. From the perspective of a practitioner, I believe there is a need for more research and training on the precision and stability of the diagnosis of LD in preschool children.

## CONCLUSIONS

The overall goal for children with disabilities in Head Start is the same as the goals for all children in Head Start. We want to help children develop social competence so that they can function effectively in their current environments and in the environments they will encounter, including school. We accomplish this overall goal by providing comprehensive Head Start services for the children who have identified disabilities and by working with community agencies to provide additional services.

# Chapter 6

# Implementing Effective Instruction

*Louisa Cook Moats*

Since the 1970s, our understanding of many specific learning disabilities (LD) has grown significantly. Among the various learning disabilities, disorders of language comprehension, language expression, reading, and writing are the most numerous. As many as 85% of the children categorized as having LD in fact have disorders of language (Kamhi, 1989; Kavale & Forness, 1985; Tallal, 1988).

Through research, we know that listening, speaking, reading, and writing are interdependent language skills. For example, children with disorders of oral language (listening and speaking) in preschool usually develop difficulties learning to read and write (Scarborough, 1990; Tallal, 1988). Conversely, most children who experience reading failure demonstrate a basic deficit in speech perception and speech-sound processing (Ball, 1993; Blachman, 1991; Liberman & Shankweiler, 1985). These children have trouble detecting the speech sounds in words and associating them with letter patterns. To illustrate, young children with reading disability usually can recognize that spoken words such as *moats* and *most* are different but cannot identify which sounds are different or how many sounds there are in each word. They may also have difficulty with rhyming activities, word games such as pig Latin, and activities requiring them to count or change the sounds in words. Because of their underlying insensitivity to word structure at the level of speech sounds, they may not easily learn the differences between words such as *goal* and *gold*, *boost* and *boast*, *unanimous* and *anonymous*. Their weak sense of word structure undermines their ability to learn the code of written English (Stanovich, 1991; Vellutino, 1991; Wagner, 1988). As time goes on, this core problem in turn compromises the learning of word meanings, comprehension of text, spelling, written expression, and motivation for language-based learning (Juel, 1994; Stanovich, 1986). Obviously, students with language-based reading disabilities are at high risk for school failure.

Do we know how to teach these students? Yes: Education researchers have agreed on many essential components of effective teaching for those with LD (Adams, 1990; Anderson, Heibert, Scott, & Wilkinson, 1985; Williams, 1987), and successful intervention programs have been validated by controlled studies (e.g., Blachman, 1991; Felton, 1993; Pikulski, 1994; Tunmer & Hoover, 1993; Williams, 1987).

Do we practice what we know? Unfortunately, we do not employ research-based practices broadly enough to prevent or ameliorate many learning disabilities. *Why* we do not employ the lessons of research is worthy of study in itself as well as why educational policy makers are often oblivious to the scientific basis of their choices or lack thereof (Moats & Lyon, 1993). But clearly, three major goals can be addressed on the basis of what we already know about good practices: 1) prevention of reading failure in the early grades, 2) retention of a broad range of service options for students with learning disabilities, and 3) changes in teacher training and support.

## PREVENTION OF READING FAILURE

Reading failure can be prevented or ameliorated for all but a small percentage of children. Intervention, however, must begin early, in kindergarten and first grade. The longer intervention is delayed, the more likely it is that reading failure will be entrenched (Fletcher & Foorman, 1994). Programs that reduce reading failure in public school classrooms involve individual or small-group instruction carried out by a well-trained teacher over a period ranging from many months to several years. Such programs include Project Read in Bloomington, Minnesota (Enfield & Greene, 1983); Success for All in Baltimore and Philadelphia (Slavin, Madden, Karweit, Dolan, & Wasik, 1991); Reading Recovery in New Zealand and Ohio (Clay, 1985); the Winston-Salem Project in North Carolina (Pikulski, 1994); and Blachman's projects in New York City and Syracuse, New York (Blachman, 1991). Effective prevention of reading failure includes structured, systematic reading and writing practice with a wide variety of worthwhile material. Most important, however, effective prevention includes direct teaching of speech-sound awareness, alphabet knowledge, the links between sounds and symbols, and fluent decoding of print. In reading disability, the nature of the problem dictates the nature of intervention: Children who are not able to break the print code can usually learn it when word structure is taught to them explicitly and directly. This type of instruction should be available in every school for those who need it.

## SERVICES FOR STUDENTS WITH LEARNING DISABILITIES

Students with LD are best served by a range of placement and program options and not by the ideology of "full inclusion" (Kaufman & Hallahan, 1995; National Joint Committee on Learning Disabilities, 1993; Zigmond, 1994). Although it is important to educate students with disabilities with their peers without disabilities to the extent that such inclusion is *beneficial* and *appropriate*, students with LD often need special tutorials, special classes, or even self-contained settings where children with similar needs are educated together. Whether instruction for children with reading disabilities takes place in class or out of class has been shown to be irrelevant to the children's progress (Gelzheiser, Meyers, & Pruzek, 1992), and there is no guarantee that the student who is educated primarily in general education classes derives social benefit simply from being in that setting (Bear, Clever, & Proctor, 1991; Fuchs & Fuchs, 1994–1995; Zigmond et al., in press). Academic progress depends on what and how teachers teach and whether instruction is tailored to the individual's needs for pacing, concept representation, corrective feedback, and reinforcement (Lyon & Moats, 1988). A sense of social well-being arises not from inclusion but from genuine social acceptance and academic success.

Unfortunately, in practice, inclusion often means that students with LD receive little or no special instruction in large general education classes. Those who learn differently often are not taught differently. Classroom teachers are often unable to instruct children with LD effectively, even though they are willing, because they do not have the time, resources, collaborative working conditions, expertise, or energy to be all things to all students (Baker & Zigmond, 1990; Houck & Rogers, 1994; Zigmond et al., in press). Students with learning disabilities in general education classes may be able to pass courses because their assignments are modified, they are read to, or someone writes for them, but often they are not learning *how* to read, write, calculate, solve problems, and study. It is not simply where instruction takes place but the quality, duration, and focus of the instruction that ultimately determines the success of students with LD. As Zigmond (1994) concluded, school districts should maintain a full range of service options for students with LD and decide which to use on a case-by-case basis.

## TEACHER TRAINING AND SUPPORT

So, who will implement these good practices? Most teachers, general and special education alike, are poorly prepared to teach students with language-related learning disabilities (Lyon, Vaasen, & Toomey, 1989). Only two thirds of the states even require coursework in understanding reading acquisition and in how to teach reading; these states typically require 6–12 course hours of instruction (Nolen, McCutchen, & Berninger, 1990). Usually no courses are required in written language, oral language, or study skills. In addition, the content of the courses may not include what teachers need to know. Many courses are superficial and method oriented. Teachers certified as learning specialists generally are not taught the language system itself—how it is structured, how it is learned, and why learning it is not natural for some children. My own surveys of experienced, certified teachers in graduate courses show that 10%–20% at most are proficient when tested on their knowledge of language structure and how to teach it to students with LD (Moats, 1994).

Why are so few teachers well prepared? This is a complex social, economic, and political issue that bears more study. Certainly teachers are willing to learn, and they express both resentment and dismay when they are not given the tools necessary to achieve their goals. One factor in the underpreparation of teachers is probably the difficulty of the content itself: The concepts are challenging and competence in language intervention requires disciplined study over several semesters. Another factor is the misdirection of the whole language movement, which has resulted in a generation of professionals trained *not to teach* what is most important for students with reading and writing disabilities: the structure of language.

But there is good news and hope. Teachers can be taught and relatively inexpensively. When teachers learn what they need to know and are able to practice under good supervision, they get results in the classroom. Almost all those whom I have taught language and how to teach it express gratitude for the information and for renewed confidence in their effectiveness.

Standards for teacher training in reading and LD must be upgraded nationwide. Kindergarten and primary-grade teachers should be required to learn about the importance of phonemic awareness and beginning decoding strategies for high-risk children. Both general and special education teachers should be asked to study in depth the structure of spoken and written language and how these can be taught to students with LD. Coursework for educators should emphasize language content and how to teach it using a variety of programs and methods. Teachers should be certified only when they are competent, and perhaps a more extensive internship is needed than is now required. Competent teachers should then be able to apply their skills in an atmosphere of professional advancement and peer collaboration. Untrained teaching assistants should never be given full responsibility for instruction.

## CONCLUSIONS

Information about the nature of learning disabilities and about programs that work must be disseminated among teacher educators, policy makers, and school administrators. The scientific basis for designing reading, writing, and language instruction, both preventive and remedial, is still a well-kept secret held from those most able to influence educational outcomes. Let us share the knowledge we have; in it lies our hope that good practice will become common practice.

## REFERENCES

Adams, M.J. (1990). *Beginning to read: Thinking and learning about print*. Cambridge, MA: MIT Press.

Anderson, R.C., Heibert, E.H., Scott, J.A., & Wilkinson, I.A.G. (1985). *Becoming a nation of readers: The report of the Commission on Reading*. Washington, DC: National Institute of Education, U.S. Department of Education.

Baker, J.M., & Zigmond, N. (1990). Are regular education classes equipped to accommodate students with learning disabilities? *Exceptional Children, 56*, 515–526.

Ball, E. (1993). Phonological awareness: What's important and to whom? *Reading and Writing: An Interdisciplinary Journal, 5*, 141–159.

Bear, G., Clever, A., & Proctor, W. (1991). Self-perceptions of nonhandicapped children and children with learning disabilities in integrated classes. *Journal of Special Education, 24*, 409–426.

Blachman, B.A. (1991). Getting ready to read: Learning how print maps to speech. In J.F. Kavanagh (Ed.), *The language continuum: From infancy to literacy* (pp. 41–62). Timonium, MD: York Press.

Clay, M. (1985). *The early detection of reading difficulties*. Portsmouth, NH: Heinemann.

Enfield, M.L., & Greene, V.E. (1983). *An evaluation of the results of standardized testing of elementary Project Read and SLD students based on district-wide tests administered in October, 1983*. Bloomington, MN: Bloomington Public Schools.

Felton, R.H. (1993). Effects of instruction on the decoding skills of children with phonological processing problems. *Journal of Learning Disabilities, 26*, 583–589.

Fletcher, J.M., & Foorman, B. (1994). Issues in definition and measurement of learning disabilities: The need for early intervention. In G.R. Lyon (Ed.), *Frames of reference for the assessment of learning disabilities: New views on measurement issues* (pp. 185–200). Baltimore: Paul H. Brookes Publishing Co.

Fuchs, D., & Fuchs, L.S. (1994–1995). Sometimes separate is better. *Educational Leadership, 52*, 22–26.

Gelzheiser, L.M., Meyers, J., & Pruzek, R.M. (1992). Effects of pull-in and pull-out approaches to reading instruction for special education and remedial reading students. *Journal of Educational and Psychological Consultation, 3*, 133–149.

Houck, C.K., & Rogers, C.J. (1994). The special/general education integration intiative for students with specific learning disabilities: A "snapshot" of program change. *Journal of Learning Disabilities, 27*, 435–453.

Juel, C. (1994). *Learning to read and write in one elementary school.* New York: Springer-Verlag.

Kamhi, A.G. (1989). Causes and consequences of reading disabilities. In A.G. Kamhi & H. Catts (Eds.), *Reading disabilities: A developmental language perspective* (pp. 67–99). San Diego: College-Hill Press.

Kaufman, J.M., & Hallahan, D.P. (Eds.). (1995). *The illusion of full inclusion: A comprehensive critique of a current special education bandwagon.* Austin, TX: PRO-ED.

Kavale, K.A., & Forness, S.R. (1985). *The science of learning disabilities.* San Diego: College-Hill Press.

Liberman, I.Y., & Shankweiler, D. (1985). Phonology and the problems of learning to read and write. *Remedial and Special Education, 6*, 8–17.

Lyon, G.R., & Moats, L.C. (1988). Critical issues in the instruction of the learning disabled. *Journal of Consulting and Clinical Psychology, 56*, 830–835.

Lyon, G.R., Vaasen, M., & Toomey, F. (1989). Teachers' perceptions of their undergraduate and graduate preparation. *Teacher Education and Special Education, 12*, 164–169.

Moats, L.C. (1994). The missing foundation in teacher education: Knowledge of the structure of spoken and written language. *Annals of Dyslexia, 44*, 81–102.

Moats, L.C., & Lyon, G.R. (1993). Learning disabilities in the United States: Advocacy, science, and future of the field. *Journal of Learning Disabilities, 26*, 282–294.

National Joint Committee on Learning Disabilities. (1993). A reaction to "full inclusion": A reaffirmation of the right of students with learning disabilities to a continuum of services. *LDA Newsbriefs, 28*(2), 3.

Nolen, P.A., McCutchen, D., & Berninger, V. (1990). Ensuring tomorrow's literacy: A shared responsibility. *Journal of Teacher Education, 41*, 63–72.

Pikulski, J.J. (1994). Preventing reading failure: A review of five effective programs. *The Reading Teacher, 48*, 30–39.

Scarborough, H. (1990). Very early language deficits in dyslexic children. *Child Development, 61*, 1728–1743.

Slavin, R., Madden, N., Karweit, N., Dolan, L., & Wasik, B. (1991). Research directions; Success for all: Ending reading failure from the beginning. *Language Arts, 68*, 404–409.

Stanovich, K.E. (1986). Matthew effects in reading: Some consequences of individual differences in the acquisition of literacy. *Reading Research Quarterly, 21*, 360–407.

Stanovich, K.E. (1991). Cognitive science meets beginning reading. *Psychological Science, 2*(70), 77–81.

Tallal, P. (1988). Developmental language disorders. In J.F. Kavanagh & T.J. Truss (Eds.), *Learning disabilities: Proceedings of the national conference* (pp. 181–272). Timonium, MD: York Press.

Tunmer, W.E., & Hoover, W.A. (1993). Phonological recoding skill and beginning reading. *Reading and Writing: An Interdisciplinary Journal, 5*, 161–179.

Vellutino, F.R. (1991). Has basic research in reading increased our understanding of the development of reading and how to teach reading? *Psychological Science, 2*(70), 81–83.

Wagner, R. (1988). Causal relations between the development of phonological processing abilities and the acquisition of reading skills: A meta-analysis. *Merrill-Palmer Quarterly, 34*, 261–279.

Williams, J. (1987). Educational treatments for dyslexia at the elementary and secondary levels. In R. Bowler (Ed.), *Intimacy with language: A forgotten basic in teacher education* (pp. 24–32). Baltimore: Orton Dyslexia Society.

Zigmond, N. (1994). Delivering special education services to students with learning disabilities in public schools: Out or in? [Special issue]. *Perspectives on Inclusion, 20*(4), 12–14.

Zigmond, N., Jenkins, J., Fuchs, L., Deno, S., Fuchs, D., Baker, J.N., Jenkins, L., & Couthino, M. (in press). Special education in restructured schools: Findings from three multi-year studies. *Phi Delta Kappan.*

# Chapter 7

# Academic Accommodations

## A Personal View

*Shelley Mosley Stanzel*

Academic accommodations are guaranteed by federal law, yet the majority of students with learning disabilities (LD) do not receive them, especially those classified as gifted students with learning disabilities. Section 504 of the Rehabilitation Act of 1973 (PL 93-112) (later reauthorized as PL 99-506 [1986] and PL 102-569 [1992]), the Individuals with Disabilities Education Act of 1990 (IDEA) (PL 101-476) and amendments, and the Americans with Disabilities Act of 1990 (ADA) (PL 101-336) are useless to students unless they are vigilantly enforced, and I regret to report that they rarely are.

My LD odyssey began when I attempted to participate in an introductory Spanish class to fulfill Dartmouth College's foreign language requirement. After 12 weeks of classes, language labs, and daily drills, I could not repeat a word in Spanish, much less conjugate a verb. After miserably failing the class, my professor suggested that I be tested for a learning disability, and I was shocked to discover at age 20 that I had an auditory language problem, which made second language acquisition through the Dartmouth-developed Rassias method impossible.

My diagnosis stated that I would be able to fulfill the requirement in a traditional classroom setting or through one of Dartmouth's existing advanced total immersion programs in Europe. However, I was denied academic accommodations and was not allowed to transfer credits from other Ivy League schools that offered traditional teaching of foreign languages.

## GIFTED STUDENTS WITH LD

Gifted students with LD fight a special battle in the accommodations war. Educators often have difficulty believing that gifted students with LD actually need alternative testing, untimed testing, or other accommodations because they do not exhibit the classic symptoms of dyslexia. The gifted student with LD is often met with skepticism and is denied accommodations because he or she is accused of trying to cheat the system. Administrators forget that academic testing was designed to test student knowledge, not the ability to master testing formats.

It is extremely difficult to wrench accommodations from an unwilling institution. The song "Impossible Dream" expresses how I felt while fighting the academic system: overcome with pervasive self-doubt. The song describes Don Quixote's fruitless quest for honor, truth, and justice. No one believed that I have a learning disability. I was constantly accused by teachers, administrators, and relatives of being lazy, stupid, and too overqualified to have a learning disability.

It is ironic that I was penalized because I wanted to learn the language rather than accept a waiver. I became obsessed with proving that I could overcome my disability, which meant scraping my way into the total immersion program recommended by my diagnostician. I spent 6 months memorizing a 360-page Spanish textbook and was able to pass Spanish 1 the second time by developing photographic memory. Although I had no understanding of context and could not read or write in the language, fulfilling the first leg of the language requirement allowed me to participate in the total immersion program in which I became semifluent in Spanish.

I soon discovered that I was not the only student at Dartmouth with a learning disability as I had been told by the administration. In fact, almost 3% of all students had the same auditory problem that I had, and all were experiencing difficulty with the auditory Rassias method (N. Pompian, personal communication, 1995). Some students were denied waivers whereas others were forced to take waivers to graduate. The college was in blatant violation of Section 504.

## A FEDERAL CASE

I filed a complaint with the U.S. Department of Education, Office for Civil Rights, when I was denied academic accommodations—the first federal case involving learning disabilities to be resolved in favor of a student with LD. I had spent 2 fruitless years lobbying the college administration, I organized a group of students with LD, and I filed the federal complaint as a last resort.

Since the case was settled in 1986, I have volunteered to help numerous people receive accommodations at the local and federal level, walking them through the complex processes and political nuances found in each case.

## OBTAINING ACCOMMODATIONS

Accommodations should be easy to obtain because the legal mandate has been set by federal laws. However, the reality is that those who receive accommodations have to fight for them. If you are a child, you must have a confident, knowledgeable parent who will tackle the academic authorities—a rare situation indeed! The framework for success exists, but the problem lies in the sheer number of cases pending before the U.S. Department of Education. You cannot run to the U.S. Department of Education and expect to get help unless you have organized a significant group complaint or have a case so unusual that the federal government would gain politically by pursuing it.

I advise parents to start with their child's teacher and then work their way up the power ladder until they get results. Many times it takes years to get accommodations—if they are granted at all. One has to be a politician of sorts, able to write well and speak well in public—the kind of abilities that most people with LD do not have. It is only by the grace of God that my disabilities are centered in auditory learning and primarily affect second language acquisition. If I had classic dyslexia, I would never have been able to even complete the federal complaint process, much less research and lobby for 2 years to ensure that my case received adequate attention.

## CONCLUSIONS

Academic accommodations are rarely discussed at conferences because most professionals do not realize how difficult it is for the average student to receive them. Each time a Summit on Learning Disabilities is held, general awareness trickles down to the public. Articles start appearing in newspapers, and as our country's leaders start to recognize the importance of academic accommodations, so too, eventually, will our nation's populace.

Those of us who are fighting for academic accommodations are not on a quixotic journey, questing for an impossible dream. Education and perseverance can make the dream of academic accommodations for every student with LD a reality.

## REFERENCES

Americans with Disabilities Act of 1990 (ADA), PL 101-336. (July 26, 1990). Title 42, U.S.C. §§ 12101 et seq.: *U.S. Statutes at Large, 104*, 327–378.

Individuals with Disabilities Education Act of 1990 (IDEA), PL 101-476. (October 30, 1990). Title 20, U.S.C. §§ 1400 et seq.: *U.S. Statutes at Large, 104*, 1103–1151.

Individuals with Disabilities Education Act Amendments of 1991, PL 102-119. (October 7, 1991). Title 20, U.S.C. §§ 1400 et seq.: *U.S. Statutes at Large, 105*, 587–608.

Rehabilitation Act of 1973, PL 93-112. (September 26, 1973). Title 29, U.S.C. §§ 701 et seq.: *U.S. Statutes at Large, 87*, 355–394.

Rehabilitation Act Amendments of 1986, PL 99-506. Title 29, U.S.C. §§ 701 et seq.: *U.S. Statutes at Large, 100*, 1807–1846.

Rehabilitation Act Amendments of 1992, PL 102-569. (October 29, 1992). Title 29, U.S.C. §§ 701 et seq.: *U.S. Statutes at Large, 100*, 4344–4488.

# Chapter 8

# Education Reform

## A Child-Centered Perspective

*Waldemar Rojas*

The education of the student with a learning disability requires a fundamental review at each level of the organizational culture of schooling: the deeply held attitudes and beliefs that lead to behavioral norms. Issues of research and issues of practice are frequently discussed, but we also need to review organizational culture. The stated missions and premises of each bureaucracy, from the federal to the state to the county to the district to the school level, all would benefit from the consideration of fundamental questions about culture. What is the predominant belief system of the people who deliver services to our children?

This is not a rhetorical question. It is posited to explore the fundamental beliefs that shape the expectations that we hold for ourselves and the children who are in our charge. Educational literature is replete with wonderful, carefully constructed missions, goals, and objectives. Surface artifacts of educational culture and stated values abound. There is no shyness about talking the talk and plastering much of that talk on reams of paper.

Children with learning disabilities (LD) are really calling for us to take their issues and concerns to a different level, a much deeper level. They implore us to examine our fundamental assumptions or our genuine belief system. They are shouting to us not only to talk the talk but also to walk the walk. They question whether it is really our deepest belief that all children can learn, and they question whether the commitment is there that all children will learn. Is the student the central focus of instructional services? Is he or she a customer receiving these services? Do his or her needs and concerns constitute our primary focus?

Our children are aware that many but not all are learning and overcoming numerous challenges and barriers. Children keenly perceive what researchers have also indicated: that those in the mainstream of the school are more likely to meet success than are those who are in ancillary programs in an orbit that rarely intersects with the mainstream. Children with challenges are asking—they are demanding—that the business of schooling be conducted in child-centered environments and not in adult-centered bureaucratic organizations.

## EDUCATIONAL OPPORTUNITY

Children come to school with varying life and educational experiences. Children vary in ethnicity and in socioeconomic and residential status. They come from literature-rich or literature-deprived environments. Some are monolingual, some are multilingual, and some are deaf; there is a multitude of diversity. Their common ground, however, is the search for educational opportunity.

"All students" means just that: It includes students with severe disabilities; those categorized, perhaps incorrectly, as having mild disabilities; students living in poverty who are eligible under chapter 1; students with limited English proficiency; and general education students. Children with learning disabilities cross all issues of diversity. The educational opportunity for which they ask would provide them with enriched experiences leading to competence in reading, mathematics, science, writing, listening, and speaking. The search is for the opportunity for total integration into the education environment, complete with access to college and careers.

What has separated students is not their desire to learn or their lifelong goals, but their differing learning styles. Students need to be recognized for their individuality, for the individuality of their learning styles, and for how they process and cognitively map the information provided to them. Ensuring the success of each student requires us to look at who they are and how they learn. The deficit model, which tells us simply what students with disabilities do not have, has for too long motivated a separatist, segregationist system of education that has not raised their level of competency and has not challenged them with high standards and a rich curriculum.

The function of this system is to be sure that no child is lost and that each and every child is provided with the opportunity to maximize his or her resources. Learners with challenges need support; they need modifications. Unfortunately, what is often provided is tender loving care and a curriculum with almost no accountability attached to it.

## EDUCATIONAL SOLUTIONS

We have heard very many solutions, ranging from one end of the continuum to the other, coming from great zealots of one or another approach. We hear from the whole language folks, and we hear, at the other extreme, from those whose view of language teaching is entirely phonetically based. It is a pity that they have such great arguments when neither faction has the complete answer. Somewhere in the middle of these arguments lies the child.

Educational solutions need to be complex, fluid responses, which are found only through the time-consuming process of search and invention. Too often, however, the educational community seems to be looking for the silver bullet: the one simple answer or process that will fix everything. As panaceas are hailed, we hear a loud thump as people jump on the bandwagon. After a few years, however, we hear another thump as the disillusioned abandon that bandwagon for another. This cycle of running from one fix-it philosophy to the next has characterized educational reform for far too long. Worse still, it has masked the fact that we are still dealing with the same stagnant adult-centered organizations.

I cannot overemphasize the importance of organizational culture. The beliefs and assumptions of the organization affect everything, right down to the class unit. Many people can remember some of the great myths of education reform. Perhaps it was individually guided education. Maybe it was SRA (Science Research Associates, a comprehension-based system), maybe it was DISTAR (a phonetics approach that incorporates hand signals), or maybe it was pull-out compensatory programs. All of them require us to rethink the services that we have been providing. The potential for successfully challenging students with LD is increased when the characteristics of the classroom and school reflect an approach that centers on the child, an approach that looks at services from several standpoints. What is instruction? What does it mean to learn? What does it mean to work? How is the school organized? Is it organized for adults, or is it organized for the students in cooperative groups? How is the school governed around issues of power? What is the accountability system?

Very often constructivists and traditionalists place themselves at opposite ends of a continuum. We often throw out very positive activities as well as maintain some negative activities when we jump on and off of these educational bandwagons. There are characteristics from both perspectives that must be incorporated for us to succeed. Teachers have to allow students to learn and discover at their own pace. School materials have to be focused around the needs of the individual. Students with disabilities must be given the opportunities traditionally reserved for only high-performing students.

Students need to be active participants. They need to be engaged and involved with their peers. Instruction needs to be meaningful and authentic, rich in language and literature, with an emphasis on what it takes to allow understanding by each and every student, not just by some. We need to invent a new, inclusive process that is geared for each student. We need to be willing to search for those complex fluid solutions. But whatever solutions are found through research and the data that support it, it is fundamental for us to review what we believe.

## CONCLUSIONS

Do we believe that all children will learn? Our financial priorities do not indicate this. Our social policies do not indicate this. Look at the children who have great needs. Look at the children with LD in public housing projects. What value is work training for low-income jobs for their parents? Perhaps what is needed is an America Corps for Parents in which parents would have an opportunity to participate in their children's schools. Such a corps would infuse schools with adults who believe in their children. Perhaps that would be the needed catalyst to change the school culture to one that truly challenges and supports children with LD.

# Chapter 9

# A Developmental Pediatric Perspective on Neurologically Based Specific Learning Disabilities

*Pasquale J. Accardo*

PL 94-142, the Education for All Handicapped Children Act of 1975, provided both a mandate and a procedure to ensure that all children with disabilities receive an appropriate education. Within the constraints of that and later federal directives, each state's department of education develops its own special education plan with targeted (or estimated) identification goals, specific diagnostic procedures, criteria and cutoffs, and intervention modalities to be used with each category of disability. It is easy to imagine some hypothetical unfairness because different states use different diagnostic criteria and cutoffs so that, for example, a child who meets the quantitative discrepancy formula cutoff for diagnosis with a learning disability (LD) in one state might then move to another state where the same ability and achievement scores would lead to a diagnosis of no LD. Although the variation in state criteria is a cause of some concern, the continued misclassification of children with special needs results much more from an attitudinal problem within state boundaries than from a definitional issue across state boundaries. Almost all states do allow professionals sufficient leeway to get around problematic test score numbers through the use of clinical judgment. The problem is often more the extent to which such individualization is encouraged or countenanced.

## THE ATTITUDINAL PROBLEM

The fundamental attitude that essentially undercuts many attempts to educationally address the special needs of children with LD might best be described as the "he or she could do better if he or she tried" philosophy. The idea that it is only effort that separates academic superstars from underachievers is patently false but remarkably resilient. Commonsense experience universal to everyone who has ever attended school testifies that it is simply untrue that the students who get A's are those who worked the hardest and that the students who barely squeak by with D's are those who worked the least. Indeed, a very strong case could be made for the opposite. Although most report card systems allow separate gradings for effort and achievement in each subject area, teachers and parents persist in interpreting the two as one. The classic composite scenario that I use to describe, if not diagnose, a learning disability to the medical students whom I teach is as follows:

---

Before he started school, Billy seemed just the smartest little boy to his proud mother, who anticipated absolutely no problems. His kindergarten teacher noted what appeared to be some signs of immaturity, but he nevertheless seemed to have mastered enough to go on to first grade—and he was so enthusiastic about school. In first grade, he struggled with the alphabet, phonics, and counting; he brought home unfinished papers to work on while the rest of the class had no homework. He was passed into second grade with some reservations. He would spend several hours a night on homework that took the other children less than 15 minutes, and he would lose recess because of incomplete classwork. His attitude toward school was definitely changing for the worse, and the social reward of being with his peers was being undercut by his miserable academic performance. There were one or two subjects in which he would at least occasionally do well enough to document to the significant adults in his life that he was intelligent and could learn. Outside of school, he seemed like a normal child, able to associate with his peers, and quite happy during summer vacations that were free from the pressures of schoolwork. In third grade, despite no recess, detention after school, 3–4 hours of homework a night, which was driving his mother crazy, and several hours of tutoring a week, his grades were consistently failing. Stomachaches and headaches reflected his psychosomatic response to the stress of schoolwork. At this point, when his parents or his teacher were questioned as to what they saw as the fundamental cause of his academic difficulties, the almost universal answer was that he was not trying hard enough! No recess, hours of homework each night, private tutoring, parents driven to distraction—and he was not trying hard enough!

---

The problem here is attitudinal. The school—in the person of the elementary school teachers—needs to be a lot more sensitive to the possibility of learning disabilities. I often joke that it would be very easy for a speaker to stand up at any regional or national meeting of general education teachers and receive a standing ovation for the statement that special education is a fraud; that all these spoiled children need is firmer discipline, higher standards, and more paddling both at home and at school. The loud applause that followed would typically not represent the overwhelming majority of the teachers present, but it would certainly reflect, at the least, a simple majority of the attendees. The seriousness of this failure to understand the reality of LD (School Attitudinal Disorder [SAD], the attitude of schoolteachers that LD is not real) (Accardo, 1991) is magnified by the fact that those children who are finally diagnosed with LD will continue to receive most of their education from these same skeptical general education teachers. The most difficult accommodation to have included in each child's individualized education program (IEP) is a sufficiently detailed list of general education classroom modifications. An adequate technical vocabulary exists for the interventions needed, but there does not appear to be any shortcut to remedy the ignorance of many general education teachers. More and more states are requiring newly certified teachers to be more knowledgeable about learning disabilities, but, for the most part, these efforts have had only a limited impact to date.

Although it is true that teachers may justifiably have been confused by a variety of conflicting recommendations and theories, this remains totally irrelevant to SAD. Many general education teachers work with children with disabilities in private and parochial schools and have no specialized support services available to them. Often, special education teachers working in sparsely populated regions of the country encounter students with rare and complicated learning problems that these teachers have not been adequately prepared to address. In circumstances such as these, where, for whatever reason, the most appropriate educational interventions are not available (regardless of legislation that mandates their existence), it is almost impossible to begin to imagine the positive impact on the child's self-image for the teacher to simply recognize that the child is intelligent and is trying his or her best. The absence of the ability to accept the child's LD is SAD (Accardo, 1991). This almost willful ignorance affects such important areas as incidence, inclusion, and professional abuse.

## PREVALENCE RATE AND THE INDIVIDUAL

First, many educational administrators focus on the fact that the incidence of LD seems to be rising at an exponential rate. They use an overall prevalence rate rather than looking at an individual case to identify a specific problem with the state-mandated diagnostic process. This is particularly true in inner-city schools where principals may be heard to complain, "If every child whose reading scores were this low were categorized as having a learning disability, we would have to give special education help to 80% of the class." There are many problems with the American public education system, there are many factors affecting the learning experiences of children in inner cities, and there are many budgetary constraints on the availability of special services in most school districts. But the one argument that is not applicable to any individual child is this indefensible statistical argument. For any number of reasons, the rate of diagnosis of LD may be too high, but that says nothing about an individual child. (In truth, most clinicians in the field would estimate that schools generally underdiagnose and underserve children with LD.) When such a theoretical concern is inappropriately applied to an individual, it unfortunately says something very negative about the educators supposedly committed to the appropriate education of children as individuals.

## INCLUSION

Second, the debate over inclusion is being interpreted by different parties according to very different underlying assumptions. If one starts from the assumption that some children exhibit significant differences in learning, then one might suspect that some of these children with LD might not be appropriate for inclusion, except under the most heroic of scholastic circumstances. This is not very different from the situation in medicine where we might really like to treat everyone as an outpatient, but I suspect that we will still need hospitals for those whose conditions are serious or complicated enough to warrant inpatient treatment. I very much fear that the enthusiastic commitment to inclusion represents a masked loyalty on the part of many educational administrators to the philosophy that children with LD do not really have any problems that could not be handled by their trying harder. The publicly stated promise of providing whatever special services might be needed for success in the general education classroom is belied by the private statements of these same administrators who see inclusion as a money-saving device when even the simplest arithmetic demonstrates that it might very well be more costly. The commitment should be not to a single theoretical model, but rather to a full continuum of services needed to match the wide range of different needs of children with LD.

## COMPONENT OF CHILD ABUSE

Finally, there is the component of child abuse in this continued attitudinal deficit on the part of the educational establishment. Emotional abuse, in terms of repeated assault on a child's self-image, probably has a more damaging long-term impact on adult outcomes than the actual failure to provide appropriate classroom interventions. Professional insult is often then added to this emotional injury by the further addition of such behavioral diagnoses as "oppositional defiant disorder" and "conduct disorder" (Accardo, 1994). The behavioral symptomatology that is interpreted as consistent with such diagnoses most often simply reflects a typical response on the part of the child to the school's inappropriate handling of the child's educational needs.

## CONCLUSIONS

"People who live in glass houses shouldn't throw stones." I teach in a medical school that has enrolled a number of students with LD. The graduate medical education system in the United States—from the Medical College Admission Test (MCAT) entrance examination, through the special modifications needed to teach and assess students' and residents' performance, and all the way through to the national boards for licensure and to other certification examinations—is unclear about the requirements of the Americans with Disabilities Act of 1990 (ADA) (PL 101-336) regarding appropriate modifications for adults with LD. Are there patterns of LD that cannot be accommodated in the medical school curriculum? Are there persons whose LD prevents them from becoming successful physicians? Are certain LD profiles incompatible with certain medical practice subspecialities (Accardo, Haake, & Whitman, 1989)?

At my level, the level of the teacher who teaches the professionals of the future, the existence of the problem is recognized, but the attempts at solutions remain chaotic. The very conceptualization of the *gifted* adult with a persisting LD represents a totally new challenge to our understanding of human differences. The reauthorization of the Individuals with Disabilities Education Act of 1990 (IDEA) (PL 101-476) and the Individuals with Disabilities Education Act Amendments of 1991 (PL 102-119) will continue to provide the needed framework within which we can continue to expand our understanding and management of children and adults with LD.

## REFERENCES

Accardo, P.J. (1991, Fall). SAD statistics on the rise. *Learning Disabilities Association of Missouri, St. Louis Council Newsletter*, 6–7.

Accardo, P.J. (1994). Conduct disorder versus oppositional defiant disorder: End point of learning disabilities. In A.J. Capute, P.J. Accardo, & B.K. Shapiro (Eds.), *Learning disability spectrum: ADD, AD/HD, and LD* (pp. 199–209). Timonium, MD: York Press.

Accardo, P.J., Haake, C., & Whitman, B.Y. (1989). The learning disabled medical student. *Journal of Developmental and Behavioral Pediatrics, 10*, 253–258.

Americans with Disabilities Act of 1990 (ADA), PL 101-336. (July 26, 1990). Title 42, U.S.C. §§ 12101 et seq.: *U.S. Statutes at Large, 79*, 1158–1162.

Education for All Handicapped Children Act of 1975, PL 94-142. (August 23, 1977). 20 USC §§ 1401 et seq.: *U.S. Statutes at Large, 89*, 773–796.

Education of the Handicapped Act Amendments of 1986, PL 99-457. (October 8, 1986). 20 USC §§ 1400 et seq.: *U.S. Statutes at Large, 100*, 1145–1177.

Individuals with Disabilities Education Act of 1990 (IDEA), PL 101-476. (October 30, 1990). 20 USC §§ 1400 et seq.: *U.S. Statutes at Large, 104*, 1103–1151.

Individuals with Disabilities Education Act Amendments of 1991, PL 102-119. (October 7, 1991). 20 USC §§ 1400 et seq.: *U.S. Statutes at Large, 105*, 587–608.

# Chapter 10

# A Separate and Unequal Education for Minorities with Learning Disabilities

*Joseph P. Shapiro*

As Americans, we have marked the 40th anniversary of *Brown v. Board of Education* (1954). As you know, it took another 21 years after the *Brown* decision before students with disabilities were guaranteed the right to any education at all. Students with disabilities, of all colors, did not even have a separate and unequal education. Many had to fight to get through the schoolhouse door at all. By the time Public Law 94-142 (the Education for All Handicapped Children Act of 1975) was passed, there were some 1 million children with disabilities outside the schoolhouse door.

## SEPARATE AND UNEQUAL EDUCATION

In the 1990s, the Individuals with Disabilities Education Act of 1990 (IDEA) (PL 101-476) protects the rights of children with disabilities in school, and the Americans with Disabilities Act of 1990 (ADA) (PL 101-336) protects their rights when they leave school. Yet I think it must be noted that for many students, particularly students from minority groups, special education has been a ticket to resegregation and isolation. It has been a track to dropping out without the skills necessary to work and live independently. For too many students, special education has become what *U.S. News & World Report* termed "a separate and unequal system of education" (Shapiro et al., 1993). This analysis found that African American students are twice as likely as Caucasian students to be placed in special education. Students from minority groups are also more likely to get stigmatizing labels. They are more likely to be labeled mentally retarded or emotionally disturbed. Once in special education, a student from a minority group is more likely to be segregated. At a time when the trend is toward integrating special education students into general education schools and classrooms, it is Caucasian students who are the first to benefit from inclusion. Students from minority groups are more likely to remain in separate classes or separate schools where academics are sometimes not stressed and academic failure becomes predictable.

## WHO GETS LABELED?

The trends described in the preceding section are clear in a study based on the records of more than 65,000 students in special education in Connecticut (Nerney, 1993). In Stamford, Connecticut, for example, 57% of Caucasian males in special education have a learning disability classification, but only 40% of African American males do. Males from minority groups, meanwhile, are more than twice as likely to be labeled as having a serious emotional disturbance (Nerney, 1993).

Even when students from minority groups are diagnosed as having learning disabilities, they are more than twice as likely in Connecticut to remain in separate classes. Only 15% of Caucasian students with learning disabilities spend their days in separate classes (Nerney, 1993). For males with learning disabilities from minority groups, 36% are educated in segregated classes; for females from minority groups, the number is 34% (Nerney, 1993). So, African American students in Connecticut are half as likely as Caucasian students to be labeled as having a learning disability, and, when they are, they are twice as likely to be separated from other students.

Who is diagnosed as having a learning disability can differ from state to state and from school district to school district. One study of students with learning disabilities found that in New York City they had an average IQ of 81, but in Westchester County, a largely white suburb, students who were classified as having a learning disability had an average IQ of 103 (Gottlieb, Alter, Gottlieb, & Wishner, 1994). In fact, according to the same study, 85% of inner-city students classified as having learning disabilities did not have any identifiable learning disability at all (Gottlieb et al., 1994). Rather, the study contends, these were students who not long ago would have been called "disadvantaged." They are the children of poor families. They come to school far behind. They are unprepared to learn. Some come not knowing how to spell their own names. The deficits of these students are greater than ever and speak to the importance of prevention and early intervention.

This study (Gottlieb et al., 1994) found that 90% of special education students in New York City come from families who receive some form of public assistance. Most live with a single parent, almost always their mother. Many are immigrants, too. Of the students labeled as having learning disabilities, 44% come from households where English is not the first language, and 19% of these students were born outside the United States. These are the children who need individual attention the most, and they are referred to special education because their teachers realize they need one-to-one help or to be in a small group and not in a classroom with 35 or more students. Classes are so big that many teachers do not have time to spend with individual students. Some teachers simply do not want children with special needs in their classes. They simply do not or cannot take the time necessary to reach students who are harder to teach. Most of these students could succeed in general education classes if the classes were small enough (Gottlieb et al., 1994). But special education is not set up to reach these children. For most students in New York City, special education is a road to failure (Gottlieb et al., 1994).

One solution may be smaller classes, but it is a difficult solution for schools in a time of tight resources. Smaller classes could be achieved by hiring more teachers or by putting competent aides in each classroom to reduce student–teacher ratios. Integrating these students into general classrooms could also be achieved with better teacher preparation and by preparing *all* teachers (special and general education teachers) to teach children who learn differently. We know from the NCLD study that the teachers want this preparation.

There is a successful school in East Harlem, New York City, where teachers, aides, and guidance counselors are taught to teach reading. Instead of five teachers teaching reading to all the third graders, there are eight teachers. The class size is smaller, the children receive more attention, and reading scores have improved.

Another important issue is the backlash to students and adults with disabilities. ADA and IDEA have led to a profound change in the way Americans look at disability. We see disability as an issue of rights, not as a medical problem. But any time a group gains rights, there is inevitably a backlash. It is the process of taking a few steps forward and then one back. Despite the ADA, the Department of Justice had to force the Educational Testing Service to offer equal access to SATs to students with learning and other disabilities. The Department of Justice had to force a state board of examiners to give a woman with a learning disability extra time to complete the test for licensure as a clinical social worker. These accommodations should have been automatic under the ADA. When we talk about the importance of lifetime learning for people with learning disabilities, these types of actions by the Justice Department are important.

Yesterday's poster children are not asking for pity today, they are asking for rights. In South Carolina, a young woman and her family asked to be reimbursed for the cost of sending her to a private school for students with learning disabilities. Her local school did not diagnose her learning disability until she was in high school, and then it failed to provide an adequate program to compensate. She was criticized for being so bold, but last year the U.S. Supreme Court ruled in favor of her and her family. In Virginia, a private school returned all the federal funding it received during the past 17 years rather than enroll and include a first grader with a learning disability. The school has returned thousands of dollars it used for a school lunch program and has stripped its library shelves of reference books paid for with federal dollars.

## CONCLUSIONS

Part of the backlash against people with LD is tied to the belief that special education is too expensive. Part of it is tied to a belief that people with disabilities are asking for too much, that they are asking for special rights. Part of it is tied to the general lack of sympathy in the 1990s for civil rights movements. But I think there is a real danger in this new trend, in this new readiness to scapegoat children and adults with disabilities. The backlash is dangerous because it undermines choices, and these are what people with disabilities and their parents want. Choices are what they need. They need choices about education. They need educational environments where they are challenged, where children are believed to be able to learn, and where they are not doomed by the low expectations of others.

## REFERENCES

Americans with Disabilities Act of 1990 (ADA), PL 101-336. (July 26, 1990). Title 42, U.S.C. §§ 12101 et seq.: *U.S. Statutes at Large, 104*, 327–378.

Brown v. Board of Education, 347 US 483 (1954).

Gottlieb, J., Alter, M., Gottlieb, B., & Wishner, J. (1994). Special education in urban America: It's not justifiable for many. *Journal of Special Education, 27*(4), 453–465.

Individuals with Disabilities Education Act of 1990 (IDEA), PL 101-476. (October 30, 1990). Title 20, U.S.C. §§ 1400 et seq.: *U.S. Statutes at Large, 104*, 1103–1151.

Nerney, T. (1993). *Special education in Connecticut: A fiscal and policy analysis.* Danbury, CT: Western Connecticut Association for Human Rights.

Shapiro, J.P., Loeb, P., Bowermaster, D., Wright, A., Headden, S., & Toch, T. (1993, December 13). Separate and unequal. *U.S. News & World Report,* 46–60.

# Chapter 11

# Strengthening the Profession

*Douglas Carnine*

Although those of us who attended the Summit on Learning Disabilities have become increasingly concerned and sophisticated about the educational environment for students with learning disabilities (LD), we seem to be naïve about the importance of the professional environment for teachers. Teachers experience dissemination overload, usually of contradictory information. Educational leaders tell them that every new initiative is research-based, that there are model demonstration projects to show its success, and that they need more training—the exact claims that the authors are making in this book.

## TEACHERS LACK PROFESSIONAL SUPPORTS

Why should teachers believe them? This is a very serious question. I submit that teachers lack the professional supports and controls enjoyed by other professionals. As we pursue the goals that other authors have identified in early reading intervention and professional development, we must also acknowledge that the underlying problem is strengthening the profession itself.

I think we can look at strengthening the profession in a very concrete way by examining other professions (Worrell & Carnine, 1994), although the differences between education and other professions are enormous. But we need some models as a starting point for strengthening the profession. At the core of every profession are rational methods that dismiss dogma, faith, and faddism for a knowledge base that grows from the accumulation of research and validated experience.

In looking at professions such as medicine and engineering, there are three sources of support and control: from the profession itself, from government, and from independent external groups. The American

Medical Association and the American Society of Mechanical Engineers publish journals, promote standards, and conduct reviews concerning complaints of malpractice. In general education, where rational methods play a relatively small role, professional organizations promote popular approaches such as whole language. Schools that go against these popular approaches are often punished, especially if they are successful. Wesley Elementary School in Houston, which has an early reading intervention program, is such a school. Of a population of 1,100 low-income inner-city students, I found only 18 who had been identified for special education. Every child who started in kindergarten was reading by the end of first grade.

ABC's *Prime Time Live* reported that because Wesley Elementary School went against the district curriculum, central administrators became increasingly antagonistic toward the school. Finally, they burst unannounced into classrooms to gather proof that teachers were cheating by giving students answers to test questions, which they were not. These attempts by a district to destroy its greatest success propelled it into television network news. Instead of depriving teachers of effective curriculum approaches, we must strengthen the profession by being more scientific.

At present, the teaching profession fails to provide teachers with a coherent, viable idea of how to carry out their role as teachers. The public slides so easily into criticizing schools because teachers and administrators are expected to solve the problems. But, in fact, the problems are ours. People such as the authors in this book influence the profession, and it is the profession that teachers rely on for the knowledge, skills, and beliefs that guide them in their work. The profession is what supports teachers and what, in turn, controls them.

The second source of professional support and control comes from government. An important example of government control is the use of litigation. Litigation shapes professional standards. Malpractice litigation is not possible in education, because the courts have ruled that there is not a professional body of knowledge to define acceptable standards of practice. We must change this. Without the support of a professional body of knowledge, there cannot be accountability and controls.

Government agencies also control licensure, but too often educational licensure creates expectations and explanations for failure. Alessi (1988) reviewed the files of school psychologists on 5,000 students with learning problems. In all 5,000 cases, the problems were attributed to the student or family. Medicine has a field, iatrogenics, devoted to the study of problems caused by the profession. Alessi's findings (1988) have led me to conclude that teaching is possibly the perfect profession, because school psychologists did not note the consequence of one professional shortcoming in 5,000 cases!

Data dissemination is another government activity. In medicine, data are disseminated through an online computer service called Medline. Medline provides relatively user-friendly, trustworthy syntheses of research findings for physicians. What do teachers get? Through a library, they can get a list of research articles in print or electronic form. The Educational Resource Information Center (ERIC) is not user-friendly for many teachers, and some articles may very well be untrustworthy.

The Food and Drug Administration, the Federal Aviation Administration, and the Department of Transportation all set standards for safety and efficacy. In education, submitting effectiveness data on educational approaches to the U.S. Department of Education's Program Effectiveness Panel is voluntary. Moreover, staff at the National Center to Improve the Tools of Educators (NCITE), funded by the Office of Special Education Programs, U.S. Department of Education, classified validated programs in the National Diffusion Network as supplemental or core academic, that is, a complete program of reading, mathematics, science, and other subjects. Fewer than 5% of the validated programs used in academic subjects in this country are from core curriculum areas.

The third source of professional support and control comes from external groups. In medicine, third-party entities such as hospitals, health maintenance organizations (HMOs), and insurance companies audit patient records and convene review committees. Special interest groups such as the American Cancer Society and the American Automobile Association provide consumer education and promote and fund research relevant to their aims. Independent organizations such as Consumers Union and Underwriters Laboratory provide consumer information. Better Business Bureaus and the National Council Against Fraud respond to consumer complaints. Education needs groups such as the National Center for Learning Disabilities (NCLD) and The Learning Disabilities Association of America (LDA) to take a more active role in areas involving instructional practices.

The professional, governmental, and external groups must help foster rational methods in education. Only by strengthening the profession can we increase the likelihood of effective practices being incorporated into early reading intervention as well as into other domains.

## SPECIFIC RECOMMENDATIONS

Early reading intervention is not a panacea for the education problems of students with LD. We also need look at content-area instruction, writing instruction, and transition services from school to work, for example. How do we go about strengthening the education profession to be able to help teachers meet these challenges? First, we must establish a mission statement for the profession that goes beyond beginning reading and professional preparation. For those of us concerned with LD, a good mission may be to increase cognitive access to the general education curriculum for students with LD. Physical access is important, but cognitive access must receive far more attention than it does. We may need a broader mission statement to create a broad, powerful coalition, possibly a mission statement that proposes to make education special for everyone.

Second, we must adopt criteria that rational schools can use to evaluate existing and potential educational, assessment, and administrative practices: 1) general effectiveness; 2) feasibility of teacher success with realistic expectations for what staff can accomplish; 3) the viability of the implementation process with an emphasis on effective professional development; 4) a quality assurance process that focuses on improvement and not on punishment; 5) attendance, participation, and contribution across a variety of outcomes for students with disabilities; and 6) cost.

Third, we need to convene consensus conferences. Such a conference is needed among researchers on how to improve the quality and usefulness of research. It should be noted, however, that research funded by the Office of Special Education Programs through the Division of Innovation and Development has been recognized in a national study for its excellence (McKenna, 1992). But improvement in special education research is still needed. Consensus conferences could establish 1) areas in which available knowledge justifies broad dissemination, such as early reading intervention; 2) suggested priorities for further research; and 3) research standards for grant proposals and papers submitted to journals.

We also need consensus conferences involving advocates, researchers, practitioners, funders, and policy makers to identify high-priority domains such as beginning reading and transition. If teachers are not successful in important domains, students cannot be successful. Just as we do not want to treat students as if they have a "won't-do" problem, we must not regard teachers as having a "won't-do" problem. Usually, it is the same for teachers and students—they have a "can't-do" problem. Teachers are overwhelmed by contradictory messages, and those of us who attended the summit are responsible for those contradictions.

NCITE is reaching out to work with other influential groups to build a coalition for strengthening the profession. Teachers' unions are slowly becoming aware that they need to take the professional interests of their members at heart; the six rational school criteria (Carnine, in press) are being incorporated in teacher contracts in some districts. In addition, rational school criteria are being used in some statewide education reform proposals and professional development activities (Oregon Education Association & NCITE, 1993).

NCITE is working with school boards to help them understand that they should not completely turn over their responsibility for ensuring quality education to school administrations (Farris, Carnine, & Silbert, 1993). Of course, we do not want boards to micromanage schools, but school boards have the responsibility to ensure that rational methods are used to make decisions about the education of the community's children.

Businesses, too, can use these rational school criteria in their funding decisions. NCITE is working with the Chicago White Sox, who are funding several schools in Chicago that replicate the successful school program in Houston that was mentioned earlier.

NCITE would also like to help look at how to bring rational methods into teacher education—possibly through the collaboration of several professions. One idea is for a national work group representing many professions to come together to help identify how the supports provided in other professions can be brought to education. Such information would then be taken back to colleges and universities and would serve as a basis, for example, for the law school, the engineering school, and the medical school to meet with the college of education. Peers from professional schools in the university could go to educators, based on the recommendations of the national work group, and propose, "We have reviewed these ideas and goals. Let's work on them together so that education can develop the supports and controls of other professions."

## CONCLUSIONS

Although the task of strengthening the education profession seems enormous, every profession has gone through what education is going through—every one. For example, Paré was one of the revolutionaries in the history of medicine (Haggard, 1929). In his time, physicians poured boiling oil on sword wounds as treatment. Paré ran out of boiling oil, so he used a salve. His extraordinary contribution was to look in on the patients who had received these two different treatments. And what did he find? He found those treated with boiling oil writhing in pain and those treated with salve sleeping restfully. He began the method of observing the effects of practice. Nevertheless, his finding was ignored because it deviated from the established practices of the time.

Every field has had to go through the developmental process of becoming a profession. It is hard, and it is time-consuming. But if we do not recognize the task and challenge and rise to it, we will not be able to help individuals with LD make the academic and social gains to which we are so fervently committed.

## REFERENCES

Alessi, G. (1988). Diagnosis diagnosed: A systemic reaction. *Professional School Psychology, 3*(2), 145–151.

Carnine, D. (in press). Systemic reform at the top: Standards for educational leaders. *Education Week.*

Farris, H., Carnine, D., & Silbert, J. (1993, December). Learning is our business. *American School Board Journal,* 31–33.

Haggard, H.W. (1929). *Devils, drugs, and doctors: The story of the science of healing from medicine-man to doctor.* New York: Harper & Bros.

McKenna, B. (1992). Special education research priorities focus on action. *Educational Researcher, 21,* 27–29.

Oregon Education Association & NCITE. (1993). *How site councils can help improve teaching and learning: A handbook for site councils and educational leaders on school improvement.* Eugene, OR: OEA Press.

Worrell, R.S., & Carnine, D. (1994). *Lack of professional support undermines teachers and reform: A contrasting perspective from health and engineering.* Eugene: National Center to Improve the Tools of Educators, University of Oregon.

# SECTION III

## LABOR

# Chapter 12

# Research Directions Leading Toward Inclusion, Diversity, and Leadership in the Global Economy

*Noel Gregg*

A transformation of philosophical, scientific, political, and economic mores is slowly occurring throughout our world. Some refer to this as a paradigm shift away from a Newtonian mechanistic model of thought toward a more holistic and constructivist model (Heshusius, 1989). Gregg and Ferri (1996) encouraged focusing on "this juncture of shifting paradigms as just the place where possibilities and promises of change and real reform begin to take focus within a changing lens" (p. 48). Although labeling or describing differences between paradigms often leads to a verbal exercise of wits, evidence of this search for change is demonstrated concretely in the call for school reform (Clark & Astuto, 1994), a "politics of meaning" (Lerner, in press), and the financial world's emphasis on a global economy. As Reich (1991) noted:

> Each nation's primary assets will be its citizens' skills and insights. Each nation's primary political task will be to cope with the centrifugal forces of the global economy which tear at the ties binding citizens together—bestowing ever greater wealth on the most skilled and insightful, while consigning the less skilled to a declining standard of living. (p. 3)

Those of us interested in ensuring that adolescents and adults with learning disabilities (LD) are prepared to meet the demands of the future must be careful not to over-rely on past directives that divert us from unique solutions for change. The key to empowering adolescents and adults with LD lies in the ability to help them gain access to tools and information so that they can add to the world knowledge and economy and thereby increase their own potential worth.

The direction of economic forces is moving from what Reich (1991) labeled a high-volume focus to a high-value focus. To meet the demands of this change, businesses are in search of individuals who demonstrate abilities in identifying and solving problems. "In the high-value enterprise, profits derive not from scale and volume but from continuous discovery of new linkages between solutions and needs" (Reich, 1991, p. 85). The Secretary of Labor's Commission on Achieving Necessary Skills (SCANS) (1991) clearly described the competencies and basic skills workers need for successful job performance in today's economy. According to the SCANS (1991) report, workers must be able to effectively utilize resources, interpersonal skills, information systems, and technology. The foundation for these competencies lies in the mastery of basic skills (i.e., reading, writing, mathematics), thinking skills (i.e., abstract and inferential problem solving), and personal qualities such as individual responsibility, self-esteem, self-management, and integrity. Acquisition of knowledge, either basic skills or thinking skills, has been linked to the widening income gap across the United States. From 1973 to 1987, for white males with a high school education, real earnings declined by 12%; for African Americans without a college education, real earnings declined by 44%; and for high school dropouts, inflation-adjusted earnings dropped by 18% (William T. Grant Foundation Commission on Work, Family, and Citizenship, 1988). Clearly, adults who dropped out or had difficulty completing high school have a harder time maintaining jobs that provide financial security and/or place them in leadership roles.

The profile of many adults with LD has been documented to include an early history of academic, social, and organizational problems as well as high unemployment (Malcolm, Polatajko, & Simons, 1990). It is interesting that researchers qualitatively studying the characteristics of successful adults with LD (Ginsberg, Gerber, & Reiff, 1994) have documented that success for such adults involved their taking control of their lives, learning creatively, matching their abilities to their job roles, and maintaining a pattern of personal support. These characteristics match the SCANS (1991) and Reich (1991) competencies for job success in a global economy. Unfortunately, the profile of the successful adult with LD is not the typical profile of the majority of adolescents and adults with LD attempting to find security in the work world (Gerber et al., 1990; Malcolm et al., 1990; Minskoff, Sautter, Sheldon, Steidle, & Baker, 1988).

## ISSUES AFFECTING ADULTS WITH LEARNING DISABILITIES

The terms *inclusion, diversity, leadership,* and *policy* appear to best encapsulate the issues facing adults with LD in the global economy. It is imperative, moreover, to keep in mind the advice of Bassett, Polloway, and Patton (1994) that it is "quite clear that adults with learning problems should not be viewed simply as children with disabilities, who have grown up" (p. 11). Future research and instructional agendas for adults with LD require a life-span and life-space perspective (Szymanski, 1994). A life-span approach to issues facing adults with LD stresses a longitudinal perspective in addressing solutions. A life-space perspective recognizes the many life roles that an adult assumes (i.e., student, citizen, worker, partner) and encourages an ecological approach to habilitation and rehabilitation (Szymanski, Dunn, & Parker, 1989).

The following section of this chapter briefly reviews the problems facing adults with LD in respect to education and employment. Following this section is a discussion of the research priorities needed to address the problems identified as critical for the adult population with LD.

## Inclusion Issues

A major obstacle for adolescents and adults with LD is inclusion in effective secondary school transitional programs, postsecondary schooling, vocational training, and employment. Unfortunately, each of these areas is often addressed in isolation by different services, and they are not examined as a continuum of life experiences with each building on the other. The result for many adults with LD is fragmented services from various agencies that have very little relevance in today's economy. Although transition-related legislation, policy statements, and professional organizations advocate for interagency collaboration, there is a greater need for service agencies to reassess the traditional roles and responsibilities of the personnel serving adolescents and adults with LD at the secondary and postsecondary level (DeFur & Reiff, 1994; Szymanski & Danek, 1985).

Despite federal and state dollars channeled into the development of secondary transitional programs since the 1980s, adolescents with LD are not gaining entry into either postsecondary education or the work force. Research on graduating secondary students with mild disabilities uncovered ineffective programming for adolescents that results in recurrent problems in adulthood (Edgar, 1987). The high dropout rates of adolescents with LD is certainly proof of a need to review service goals and objectives at the secondary level. The National Longitudinal Transition Study (NLTS) (Marder, 1992) reported a graduation rate of 61% for adolescents with LD, compared with 56% for all youth with disabilities and 71%–75% for the general population. Therefore, approximately 35% of individuals with LD are dropping out of school and thus are unprepared academically, socially, and vocationally for the world of work. Dropout rates for females with LD are just as high as those for males with LD, although females with LD were reported to have a higher grade-point average than males with LD (Wagner, 1992a). It is important to keep in mind that in 1980, male college graduates earned approximately 80% more than their high school counterparts and that by 1990, this figure had doubled. Therefore, a high school dropout is at a significant disadvantage in obtaining financially rewarding employment (Blackburn, Bloom, & Freeman, 1989).

Vocational and career development education usually confers substantial postsecondary outcomes for individuals with disabilities. According to the NLTS (Marder, 1992), approximately 40% of adolescents with LD maintained vocational concentrations throughout their 4 years of high school. Therefore, if adolescents with LD can be encouraged to stay in school and pursue a vocational concentration, it may result in greater probabilities of employment and higher wages following secondary school. Wagner's (1992a) research indicated, however, a gender bias in relation to enrollment and content in vocational classes. Females with LD were significantly less likely than males to be exposed to occupationally specific vocational training. If vocational education has a positive impact on later employment, women with LD are more at risk than males.

Postsecondary education figures for adolescents and adults with LD are extremely grim. According to NLTS (Marder, 1992) data, youth classified as having LD are less likely to attend and complete postsecondary degree programs than their peers with other types of disabilities. Wagner's (1989) figures documented that only 16.7% of individuals with LD participated in any type of postsecondary education, with fewer than 9% of them attending 2- or 4-year colleges. Approximately 50% of the general population attended some type of postsecondary education program (Wagner, 1989).

It appears, then, that the transition programming for the majority of adolescents with LD is not encouraging and is not preparing these youth for postsecondary training. According to Wagner (1992b), the low rate of involvement in postsecondary education "implies a lack of advancement in skills, they may reach a 'ceiling' in their progress toward independence" (p. 82).

Employment figures for adults with LD can appear somewhat misleading. The NLTS figures reported that 57.7% ($n$=429) of the high school graduates classified as demonstrating a learning disability were competitively employed (D'Amico & Blackorby, 1992). This compares with 45.9% of all individuals with disabilities and 61% of youth without disabilities. As Gerber et al. (1990) pointed out, however, this does not address the issue of unemployment. For example, if the figures from NLTS (Marder, 1992) related to lack of postsecondary options for adolescents with LD were compared with the above employment figures, it could be hypothesized that many of these individuals are underemployed. In addition, a significant percentage of individuals at risk for unemployment have not been encouraged to seek an eligibility assessment that would document appropriate accommodation and modification service needs.

Figures related to the population of adjudicated adolescents and adults document that a large percentage of these individuals demonstrate LD (Brier, 1994; Broder, Dunivant, Smith, & Sutton, 1981; Robbins, Beck, Pries, Cags, & Smith, 1983; Young, Pappenfort, & Marrow, 1983). The prevalence rates vary depending on the definition and eligibility criteria used by researchers. According to Brier (1989), approximately 30%–50% of the adjudicated adolescent and adult population demonstrated a specific learning disability. Support of such high incidence figures can be found, for example, in the research of Dunivant (1982), which found that juveniles with LD were 220 times more likely to commit delinquent offenses than their peers. In addition, Pearl and Bryan (1994) provided evidence that students with LD are significantly more likely than other students to choose the option of escaping from authorities after engaging in misconduct and are less likely to accept the consequences for their behavior.

Research findings have not been consistent with regard to the etiology for this high rate of delinquent behavior. Future research funds should be channeled toward exploring the factors, social and/or cognitive, that contribute to individuals with LD being at risk for delinquent behavior.

## Diversity Issues

Issues of diversity regarding the adult population with LD have not been well addressed. The risk and resilience research has addressed diversity in relation to type, number, severity, and age at identification of the learning disability (Hoy & Manglitz, 1996). Summarizing many of the studies in this area, adolescents with LD are at risk for dropping out of high school, being underemployed, demonstrating low self-esteem, and having high rates of dissatisfaction in their current life status (Spekman, Goldberg, & Herman, 1992). The factors enabling adults with LD to overcome many of these risk factors include self-understanding and acceptance of their LD, proactivity to advocate for themselves, realistic goal setting, perseverance, and effective support systems (Ginsberg et al., 1994). In addition, this research has identified the following as factors affecting stress in adults with LD: type of learning disability, number of learning disabilities, severity of learning disabilities; age at identification of learning disability, chronicity, and current developmental stages (Spekman et al., 1992). The results of this body of research must be integrated into secondary school transition curriculum and other educational opportunities for individuals with LD. Empirical research related to this issue is being conducted at the University of Georgia/Roosevelt Warm Springs Institute for Rehabilitation (UGA/RWSIR) Learning Disabilities Research and Training Center. More research funds need to be directed toward intervention studies addressing the issues raised in the risk and resilience literature.

Issues of gender, race, and culture have barely been addressed in the literature exploring the needs of adults with LD. Vogel (1990) was one of the first researchers to address the issue of gender bias in the LD literature. The NLTS has also provided extremely interesting data related to gender (Wagner, 1992a). Females with LD were less likely than males to be employed after graduation from secondary schools. Forty-four percent of women who had been out of secondary schools less than 2 years were employed, compared with 63% of men. When out of school 3–5 years, the lag is even greater—52% of the women were employed, compared with 77% of the men. This lag in employment for women with LD is counter to the pattern of change in employment for women in the general population (Center for Human Resource Research, 1988). The earned take-home salary of females with LD was also significantly lower than that of males. The NLTS also investigated factors related to gender differences in the postschool outcomes of youths with disabilities (Wagner, 1992a). It is interesting to note that more males were classified as having a learning disability and/or emotional disturbances, and more females were classified as having mental retardation. Female students with LD were significantly more likely to be from minority backgrounds (62%) than were male students (31%). Wagner (1992a) concluded that the greater incidence of mental retardation and the minority status of female students with disabilities relative to males suggest that females might be at greater risk for poor transition outcomes than males.

Marriage and parenting statistics for adults with LD also indicate a gender and minority bias. Women with LD were more likely to be married than were their male counterparts (Wagner, 1992a). Although information specific to LD is not available, according to NLTS research, marriage rates were significantly higher among Caucasian females with disabilities than among African American women. In addition, women with disabilities were significantly more likely to be mothers than were females in the general population, both groups having been out of secondary school for 3–5 years. Wagner (1992a) also found that single parenthood was more common among young women with disabilities than among women in the general population and that rates of single parenthood among men were similar, regardless of disability. Single mothers with disabilities were primarily from minority groups (55%), although minorities were represented by 35% of youth with disabilities as a whole (Wagner, 1992a). A 1988 study on the functional impairments of clients receiving Aid to Families with Dependent Children (AFDC) determined that nearly 1 in 4 women under the age of 45 receiving AFDC reported themselves as having a functional impairment, in contrast to 1 in 11 women not receiving AFDC (Office of the Inspector General, 1992). Along with this report, a study completed in 1992 evaluated AFDC mothers as potential employees. This study reported that most of the women had a limited education, scored below average on verbal and math skills tests, had little work experience, were long-term welfare recipients, and reported histories of LD and substance abuse.

Gender bias is apparent across the incidence figures related to rehabilitation services. Pilot data collected by the UGA/RWSIR Learning Disabilities Research and Training Center support research (Asch & Fine, 1992) that indicated that white males constituted the predominant category of clients receiving services through vocational rehabilitation agencies.

The issues of minority status and poverty have received minimal attention from the field of LD. The NLTS (Wagner, 1992a) general figures across all disabilities indicated that minority status and poverty may present additional obstacles to successful transition to employment and further education. Little research specific to LD is available to confirm these hypotheses, however. In addition, there has not been a concerted effort to examine how different minority populations construct the term *learning disabilities* and the types of services that are most appropriate given specific cultural mores. As Gregg and Ferri (1996) stated: "Diversity must go beyond a multi-cultural perspective and actually challenge hegemony; therefore, efforts toward reform must go beyond including the voices and perspectives of individuals with learning disabilities, and actually challenge the 'myth' of normal" (p. 43).

## Leadership and Policy Issues

There is a growing recognition that state governments, as well as the federal government, need to become proactive in developing policy for adults with LD. Issues related to definitions, appropriate accommodations and modifications, and eligibility criteria demand further investigation by researchers. Particular attention must be given to how states are complying with The Carl D. Perkins Vocational and Applied Technology Education Act of 1990 (PL 101-392), Job Training Partnership Act, the Rehabilitation Act of 1973 (PL 93-126) and Amendments of 1986 (PL 99-506) and 1992 (PL 102-569), the Individuals with Disabilities Education Act of 1990 (IDEA) (PL 101-476), and the Americans with Disabilities Act of 1990 (ADA) (PL 101-336) in relation to individuals with LD. State and federal agencies should clarify contradictory or confusing policies and mandates. In addition, there is a need for an examination of the financial investment of state governments with respect to providing services to adults with LD. A result of such research should be a scheme illustrating potential predictors of state fiscal efforts. Such research is being conducted by the University of Georgia Research and Training Center, a federally funded project of the National Institute on Disability and Rehabilitation Research (NIDRR).

Changes in federal legislation and policy since the 1980s have led to greater participation by consumers in all phases of research and services. The Constituency Oriented Research and Dissemination Policy (CORD) adopted by the NIDRR has been a way to integrate the expertise of consumers, researchers, and practitioners. All research pertaining to adults with LD should be CORD-driven and should use methodology that ensures validity in answers and solutions. CORD-driven research ensures that models arrived at through research can be applied to the real problems facing adults with LD and provide alternatives to current practices. Research and training projects funded by state and federal agencies (i.e., Department of Special Education, National Institute of Child Health and Human Development) should mandate the use of CORD policy.

## RESEARCH DIRECTIONS FOR ADULTS WITH LEARNING DISABILITIES

The research agenda for adults with LD needs to address the issues of inclusion, diversity, and leadership presented in this chapter. Five specific recommendations crucial for future research and funding pertaining to adults with LD are offered in this section.

First, the most pressing research need centers on issues pertaining to diversity and specifically those related to gender, class, and culture. Funding priorities should be directed toward the examination of the service needs (i.e., welfare, JOBS, literacy, adjudicated youth and adults) among populations currently at risk for unemployment in relation to the incidence of LD among these populations. Such an examination could foster the development of assessments, interventions, and priorities that are free of gender and cultural bias as well as shape sensitivity training for professionals working with such individuals.

A critical factor affecting the inclusion of adults with LD centers on the issue of diagnostic evaluation (G. Young, personal communication, September 1993). Access to accommodations and modifications requires thorough documentation of need. Many literacy teachers, adult educators, correctional personnel, and employers express concern that the individuals they work with often do not have the financial means to pay for such an evaluation. The LD/JOBS Project in the state of Washington is one of the first projects in which Medicaid is funding full-scale diagnostic testing at market rates (G. Young, personal communication, September 1993). More such creative collaborative ventures will help stimulate government and business interest in the issue of diagnostic evaluations of adults with LD.

The second pressing research directive concerning adults with LD centers on the issue of assistive technology. Adolescents and adults with LD attempting to integrate into the global economy must demonstrate mastery of basic academic and thinking skills (SCANS, 1991). For many of these individuals, lack of mastery is a barrier to further postsecondary education as well as to appropriate employment. Therefore, significant funds must be allocated to explore the application of assistive technology in helping with the development of literacy, organizational, thinking, and social skills in adults with LD. Researchers must explore the application of assistive technology across the range of the adult population with LD, with an emphasis on appropriate interventions for the postsecondary academic world as well as for employment.

The third research focus is on transitional programming for adolescents with LD and incorporates Szymanski's (1994) call for a life-span and life-space approach to transition. Research related to quality-of-life issues for adults with LD is of utmost priority. In addition, differential transitional programming addressing the range and types of individuals with LD is essential to success for these individuals in the work world. Greater focus on the transitional needs of adolescents for whom postsecondary education is appropriate, and greater effort at the secondary level to encourage many youths with LD, particularly females and individuals from minority backgrounds, to pursue postsecondary education are needed. Transitional programs must be encouraged by state and federal agencies to incorporate CORD policy directives into all educational and research activities. Transitional programs need to be certain that they are helping adolescents with LD obtain the competencies they need to function in a global society. Such competencies include being able to use resources, interpersonal skills, information systems, and technology.

A fourth area of research needs concerns employment and involves identifying both employee and employer issues related to the employment of adults with LD. Investigation of the impact of the ADA (PL 101-336) on individuals with LD leaving secondary institutions is critical for future program planning. The most pressing need in research related to ADA concerns eligibility and appropriate accommodations and modifications for postsecondary schooling and employment. Different types of job training programs need to be explored more fully in relation to their applicability to the heterogeneous adult population with LD. For example, Inge and Tilson (1994) discussed the advantages of a supported employment model for some adults with LD. Greater empirical research is required to explore employer perceptions and ability to work with adults with LD.

The fifth and final significant need concerns research pertaining to preparation of professionals who will work with adolescents and adults with LD, particularly the preparation of individuals concentrating in the area of rehabilitation counseling and special education. Greater emphasis across these educational programs on the specific needs of adults with LD is critical. Many professionals educated in traditional special education programs have learned only a child or adolescent focus, and professionals in rehabilitation counseling generally receive little to no direct training on the needs of adults with LD (Chetkovich, Toms-Barker, & Schlichman, 1989). It is imperative that cross-discipline education be provided at the postsecondary level to better prepare professionals to work with adolescents and adults with LD. It is recommended that such educational programs teach and evaluate competencies related to the ability to identify problems, to solve problems, and to link identification to solutions (Reich, 1991) rather than teach using only factual or historical information. According to Reich (1991), the focus of such a program should be the training of "symbolic-analytic" service providers by developing their competencies in abstraction, systems thinking, experimentation, and collaboration. Such professional preparation also needs to incorporate advanced assistive technology skills and sensitivity training related to issues of diversity. Postsecondary programs are clearly not preparing professionals who can serve adults with LD in the global economy.

## CONCLUSIONS

The fields of LD and rehabilitation are in the midst of significant changes that are leading toward the social and political construction of new solutions to the problems facing adolescents and adults with LD. "Thinking about individuals with learning disabilities as a minority group while recognizing the multiple and diverse contexts of culture presents a challenge to build coalitions about differences, as well as understand differences in new ways" (Gregg & Ferri, 1996, p. 42). The collaboration of consumers and professionals in the development of the research and educational agendas is the foundation for successful solutions for the success of all adolescents and adults with LD.

# REFERENCES

American with Disabilities Act of 1990 (ADA), PL 101-336. (July 26, 1990). Title 42, U.S.C. §§ 12101 et seq.: *U.S. Statutes at Large, 104*, 327–378.

Asch, A., & Fine, M. (1988). Beyond pedestals: Revisiting the lives of women with disabilities. In M. Fine (Ed.), *Disruptive voices: The possibilities of feminist research* (pp. 139–171). Ann Arbor: University of Michigan Press.

Bassett, D.S., Polloway, E.A., & Patton, J.R. (1994). Learning disabilities: Perspectives on adult development. In P.J. Gerber & H.B. Reiff (Eds.), *Learning disabilities in adulthood: Persisting problems and evolving issues* (pp. 10–19). Boston: Andover Medical Press.

Blackburn, M., Bloom, B., & Freeman, R. (1989). *Why has the economic position of less-skilled male workers deteriorated in the United States?* [Brookings discussion paper.] Washington, DC: Brookings Institution.

Brier, N. (1989). The relationship between learning disabilities and delinquency: A review and reappraisal. *Journal of Learning Disabilities, 22*, 546–553.

Brier, N. (1994). Targeted treatment for adjudicated youth with learning disabilities: Effects on recidivism. *Journal of Learning Disabilities, 27*(4), 215–222.

Carl D. Perkins Vocational and Applied Technology Education Act of 1990, PL 101-392. (September 25, 1990). Title 20, U.S.C. §§ 2301 et seq.: *U.S. Statutes at Large, 104*, 753–843.

Broder, P.K., Dunivant, N., Smith, E.C., & Sutton, L.P. (1981). Further observations on the link between learning disabilities and juvenile delinquency. *Journal of Educational Psychology, 73*, 838–850.

Center for Human Resource Research. (1988). *The National Longitudinal Surveys of Labor Market Experiences.* Columbus: Ohio State University Press.

Chetkovich, T., Toms-Barker, C., & Schlichman, M. (1989). *Evaluation of services provided for individuals with specific learning disabilities.* Washington, DC: Rehabilitation Services Administration, U.S. Department of Education.

Clark, D.L., & Astuto, T.A. (1994). Redirecting reform: Challenges to popular assumptions about teachers and students. *Phi Delta Kappan, 75*(7), 513–520

D'Amico, R., & Blackorby, J. (1992). Trends in employment among out-of-school youth with disabilities. *What Happens Next? Trends in Postschool Outcomes of Youth with Disabilities*, 41–46.

DeFur, S., & Reiff, H.B. (1994). Transition of youth with learning disabilities: The secondary education foundation. In P.J. Gerber & H.B. Reiff (Eds.), *Learning disabilities in adulthood: Persisting problems and evolving issues* (pp. 99–110). Boston: Andover Medical Press.

Dunivant, N. (1982). *The relationship between learning disabilities of juvenile delinquents.* Williamsburg, VA: National Center for State Courts.

Edgar, E. (1987). Secondary programs in special education: Are many of them justifiable? *Exceptional Children, 53*(6), 555–561.

Employment and Training Administration.(1991). *The learning disabled in employment and training programs.* Research and evaluation report series 91-C. Washington, DC: U.S. Department of Labor.

Gerber, P.J. (1994). The problem, the future, the challenge: The issue of employability for persons with learning disabilities In D. Brown, P.J. Gerber, & C. Dowdy (Eds.), *Pathways to employment for people with learning disabilities* (pp. 3–9). Washington, DC: President's Committee for the Employment of People with Disabilities.

Gerber, P.J., Schneider, C.A., Paradine, L.V., Reiff, H.B., Ginsberg, R.J., & Popp, P.A. (1990). Persisting problems of adults with learning disabilities: Self-reported comparisons from their school-age and adult years. *Journal of Learning Disabilities, 23,* 570–573.

Ginsberg, R., Gerber, P., & Reiff, H. (1994). Employment success for adults with learning disabilities. In P.J. Gerber & H.B. Reiff (Eds.), *Learning disabilities in adulthood: Persisting problems and evolving issues* (pp. 204–213). Boston: Andover Medical Press.

Gregg, N., & Ferri, B. (1996). Paradigms and theories: Changing and challenging. In N. Gregg, C. Hoy, & A. Gay (Eds.), *Adults with learning disabilities: Theoretical and practical perspectives* (pp. 21–54). New York: Guilford Press.

Heshusius, L. (1989). The Newtonian mechanistic paradigm, special education, and contours of alternatives: An overview. *Journal of Learning Disabilities, 22*(7), 403–415.

Hoy, C., & Manglitz, E. (1996). Social and affective adjustments of adults with learning disabilities: A life-span perspective. In N. Gregg, C. Hoy, & A. Gay (Eds.), *Adults with learning disabilities: Theoretical and practical perspectives* (pp. 208–231). New York: Guilford Press.

Individuals with Disabilities Education Act of 1990 (IDEA), PL 101-476. (October 30, 1990). Title 20, U.S.C. §§ 1400 et seq.: *U.S. Statutes at Large, 104,* 1103–1151.

Inge, K.J., & Tilson, G. (1994). Supported employment: Issues and applications for individuals with learning disabilities. In P.J. Gerber & H.B. Reiff (Eds.), *Learning disabilities in adulthood: Persisting problems and evolving issues* (pp. 179–193). Boston: Andover Medical Press.

Lerner, M. (in press). *The politics of meaning.* New York: Viking Press.

Malcolm, C.B., Polatajko, H.J., & Simons, J. (1990). A descriptive study of adults with suspected learning disabilities. *Journal of Learning Disabilities, 23,* 518–520.

Marder, C. (1992). Education after secondary school. *What Happens Next? Trends in Postschool Outcomes of Youth with Disabilities,* 32–39.

Minskoff, E.H., Sautter, S.W., Sheldon, K.L., Steidle, E.F., & Baker, D.P. (1988). A comparison of learning disabled adults and high school students. *Learning Disabilities Research, 3,* 115–123.

Office of the Inspector General. (1992). *Functional impairments of AFDC clients: Report to the Department of Health and Human Services.* Washington, DC: Author.

Pearl, R., & Bryan, T. (1994). Getting caught in misconduct: Conceptions of adolescents with and without learning disabilities. *Journal of Learning Disabilities, 27*(3), 193–197.

Rehabilitation Act of 1973, PL 93-112. (September 26, 1973). Title 29, U.S.C. §§701 et seq.: *U.S. Statutes at Large, 87,* 355–394.

Rehabilitation Act Amendments of 1986, PL 99-506. Title 29, U.S.C. §§701 et seq.: *U.S. Statutes at Large, 100,* 1807–1846.

Rehabilitation Act Amendments of 1992, PL 102-569. (October 29, 1992). Title 29, U.S.C. §§701 et seq.: *U.S. Statutes at Large, 100,* 4344–4488.

Reich, R.B. (1991). *The work of nations.* New York: Vintage Books.

Robbins, D.M., Beck, J.C., Pries, R., Cags, D.J., & Smith, C. (1983). Learning disability and neuropsychological impairments in adjudicated, unincarcerated male delinquents. *Journal of the American Academy of Child Psychiatry, 22,* 40–46.

Secretary's Commission on Achieving Necessary Skills (SCANS). (1991). *What work requires of schools: A SCANS report for America 2000.* Washington, DC: U.S. Department of Labor.

Spekman, N.J., Goldberg, R.J., & Herman, K.L. (1992). Learning disabled children grow up: A search for factors related to success in the young adult years. *Learning Disabilities Research and Practice, 7,* 161–170.

Szymanski, E.M. (1994). Transition: Life-span and life-space considerations for empowerment. *Exceptional Children, 60*(5), 402–410.

Szymanski, E.M., & Danek, M.M. (1985). School-to-work transition for students with disabilities: Historical, current and conceptual issues. *Rehabilitation Counseling Bulletin, 29,* 81–88.

Szymanski, E.M., Dunn, C., & Parker, R.M. (1989). Rehabilitation of persons with learning disabilities: An ecological framework. *Rehabilitation Counseling Bulletin, 33,* 38–53.

Vogel, S. (1990). Gender differences in intelligence, language, visual-motor abilities, and academic achievement in students with learning disabilities: A review of the literature. *Journal of Learning Disabilities, 23,* 44–52.

Wagner, M. (1989). *The transition experiences of youth with disabilities: A report from the national longitudinal study.* Palo Alto, CA: SRI International.

Wagner, M. (1992a). *Being female a secondary disability? Gender differences in the transition experiences of young people with disabilities.* Palo Alto, CA: SRI International.

Wagner, M. (1992b). Transition: Changes, challenges, cautions. *What Happens Next? Trends in Postschool Outcomes of Youth with Disabilities,* 41–46.

William T. Grant Foundation Commission on Work, Family, and Citizenship. (1988). *The forgotten half: Non-college youth in America.* Washington, DC: Author.

Young, T.M., Pappenfort, D.M., & Marrow, C.R. (1983). *Residential group care 1966–1981: Facilities for children and youth with special problem needs.* Chicago: University of Chicago, School of Social Service Administration.

# Chapter 13

# Accommodating Workers with Learning Disabilities

*Marcia B. Reback*

Constituting approximately 15% of the total population according to the National Center for Learning Disabilities (NCLD) (1995), individuals with learning disabilities (LD) represent a significant portion of the potential labor force in the United States. Their intellectual capacities make them capable of maintaining economic viability for themselves and their families and of contributing to the economic well-being of a company if they are assisted in performing their jobs. As reported in the National Longitudinal Transition Study of Special Education Students (Wagner, D'Amico, Marder, Newman, & Blackorby, 1992), however, adolescents and young adults with LD have very poor postsecondary outcomes and experience rates of unemployment, incarceration, and emotional illness well beyond their proportion in the general population. The loss of such a significant portion of potential workers is a great waste of talent in this nation.

## EMPLOYER RESPONSIBILITY

Although inadequate educational programs share some of the blame for these problems, employers also must accept responsibility for failing to recognize the special individual requirements of those with LD. By providing accommodations and nonthreatening, supportive employment environments, employers can become part of the solution for the serious problems that adults with LD experience, and tap into a potentially productive work force at the same time. Workers with LD must recog-

The author would like to acknowledge the assistance of Beth Bader of the American Federation of Teachers Educational Issues Department in the preparation of this chapter.

nize that they are expected to perform—to pull their weight in the workplace—but they must also be assured that their individual needs will be considered and supported.

The most important accommodation that employers must make is to have an Americans with Disabilities Act coordinator on site if there are more than 49 employees and to be sure that the coordinator is complying with all of the law's requirements. A second important accommodation that employers can make is to acknowledge that hidden LD create difficulties in effective job performance as real as disabilities that can be seen. Nevertheless, the difficulties often can be overcome with reasonable accommodations to the environment and to the job. Employers should also understand that once the difficulties have been resolved, individuals with LD have the potential to become valuable workers who make important contributions. By creating an environment where workers feel safe in discussing and addressing their problems, employers can avoid lost productivity, realize the full potential of valuable employees, and avoid needless employee turnover.

Although employers must understand that individuals with LD need assistance, accommodations, and support and must be committed to providing them, individuals with LD must also be committed to take responsibility, become partners with their employers, and give their best to their jobs. Employers must invest in workers who have the potential to contribute. Workers must invest in the organization that has given them an opportunity to succeed.

It is difficult and risky for people with LD to acknowledge their disabilities. Therefore, employers need to provide accommodations as a matter of course. Employers need to take stock of their organizations, from the mechanics of the employment application process through the types of positions available and the skills necessary to perform them to the kinds of support systems that can be provided, and develop systems of accommodations that are automatically there for those who need them. Much of what is done to assist workers with disabilities to perform to the best of their ability is also good practice for all workers. Many persons with minor learning problems or minor disorders of cognitive function perform much better on the job if accommodations are available as a matter of course.

Decisions about what kinds of accommodations and support systems to provide must also take into account the other workers. Accommodations should not be made that place undue burdens on them. Employers should also be careful not to make accommodations that violate collective bargaining agreements. Employers must involve the union in the planning and decision making about what is appropriate and what is feasible within the union contract and the workplace environment.

## THE APPLICATION PROCESS

Employers can accommodate potential workers with LD in the application process by giving more weight to positive references and work samples if test scores are low. Company job listings should be accompanied by complete descriptions of the skills and capabilities necessary to perform the job and what accommodations can be made available. Job descriptions should be written with the needs of people with LD clearly in mind.

Employers can provide application documents and information through a variety of media and thus make the application process less stressful and facilitate job applications from individuals with disabilities.

## ON THE JOB

Explanations of the Americans with Disabilities Act of 1990 (ADA) (PL 101-336) identify three categories of reasonable accommodations that employers should provide to allow individuals with disabilities to perform their jobs. The three categories of accommodations are:

1. Change in method: If, for example, a person with LD has difficulty recording information on printed forms, the employer can computerize the form in much the same way as the employment application can be computerized, which would allow the worker to enter information from a keyboard onto the form. An additional benefit of this is that data can be entered immediately into the company database for more efficient processing.
2. Orientation aids: When individuals cannot remember sequences of tasks or procedures, for example, a checklist of words or icons enables them to keep track of the procedures as they are performed.
3. Change in time: This change allows individuals more time to complete a task or allows them to perform tasks at times of the day when they are most efficient.

These accommodations are only the beginning. There are a number of resources that can be utilized to locate specific information on providing assistance for workers. Employers can work closely with the ADA coordinator to develop and provide necessary accommodations, such as

- Identifying skills necessary to perform essential functions
- Providing appropriate technology
- Explaining the sequence of events
- Using multiple methods and concrete examples
- Confirming comprehension

This list is *not* comprehensive. The ADA coordinator can obtain assistance from learning disability organizations, the Job Accommodation Network, the Office for Civil Rights of the Department of Justice, the AFL-CIO Human Rights Department, and other organizations about what accommodations are reasonable to provide to workers.

## PROVIDE WORKER SUPPORT SERVICES

One extremely effective support that employers can provide is the understanding that individuals with learning disabilities have real and significant learning problems. The willingness to invest in individuals as valued workers will go a long way in developing a partnership between workers with LD and employers. Additional supports that may be provided are:

- *Orientation and mentors:* Assigning mentors for new workers, particularly for those with LD, can minimize the difficulties that new workers feel.
- *Supervisor/worker problem solving:* Employers must encourage supervisors to be open to working with individuals with LD in problem solving on the job. This is actually good management practice for all workers. For workers with LD, however, this practice can make the difference between a successful employee and one who resigns or must be fired.
- *Literacy instruction:* A major accommodation that employers can provide to workers is research-based literacy training.
- *Worker counseling services:* This support service provides counseling to assist individuals who are having problems with their job or communicating with their supervisor. Support groups of other individuals with LD could be particularly valuable, although the employers' role in these would be to provide the use of company space for meetings. Individuals need to make these personal connections on their own and have a nonthreatening environment to talk about mutual problems they are experiencing.
- *Disability specialists:* It is valuable to have one staff person who is particularly knowledgeable about disabilities. The most likely person to fulfill this role is the ADA coordinator.

Above all, employers must treat workers with LD with dignity and respect. They should always consult these workers and not make choices or decisions about accommodations for them. They should keep workers with disabilities in mind when developing policy, changing the workplace, or organizing social events. Consulting with the ADA coordinator and with workers about what is successful and what is not helps workers to perform better and to maintain positive relationships with supervisors.

## UNIONS AND DISABILITY ADVOCACY GROUPS

Unions and disability advocacy groups can work together to open the workplace to workers with LD, ensure that accommodations are provided, inform workers about the laws and their rights, and monitor compliance with laws. The AFL-CIO (1992) has developed an excellent document that informs workers about their rights under law and specifies accommodations to assist workers in performing their jobs. Partnerships between the union and disability advocacy groups can be very important in realizing all of the benefits that ADA is capable of providing for workers with LD.

## REFERENCES

AFL-CIO. (1992). *The Americans with Disabilities Act of 1990: Instructor's guide for training representatives on application of the ADA.* Washington, DC: Author.

Americans with Disabilities Act of 1990 (ADA), PL 101-336. (July 26, 1990). Title 42, U.S.C. §§ 12101 et seq.: *U.S. Statutes at Large, 104,* 327–378.

National Center for Learning Disabilities. (1995). *Their world.* New York: Author.

Wagner, M., D'Amico, R., Marder, C., Newman, L., & Blackorby, J. (1992). *What happens next? Trends in postschool outcomes of youth with disabilities: The second comprehensive report from the National Longitudinal Transition Study of special education students.* (Prepared for the Office of Special Education Programs, U.S. Department of Education). Menlo Park, CA: SRI International.

# Chapter 14

# Center for Excellence

## Learning Disabilities in the Workplace

*Gary F. Beasley*

I am the Training Manager at one of Georgia-Pacific's sites in southeastern Arkansas, which represents about 1,800 employees. The entire corporation has approximately 60,000 employees.

There are five areas that we're working on concerning education, vocational education and learning disabilities (LD), and experiences in the workplace. First, I would like to put our efforts in context.

## SUCCESS IN TRAINING

We have an extensive technical training program throughout our organization that focuses on a "success in training" approach—training to successfully compete and progress through the jobs in the organization. We have a certification and qualification process whereby we do extensive training of all employees and prospective employees. We spend approximately $4 million–$5 million per year just on in-plant training for our work force.

## UPGRADING STANDARDS

In our overall training, we are continually upgrading the skills of our employees and examining how to upgrade standards for prospective employees. The global economy demands that we have the best-trained employees possible. It is problematic to determine what skills, capabilities, and prospective abilities employees need. At present, we are using a 12th-grade reading, writing, and math test, and an individual would not be employed by Georgia-Pacific without scoring a 12.9-grade equivalent on that test. In addition, every person has to spend 40 hours in training before coming into the plant, and this is done through our vocational division. All maintenance employees at our site have to complete 2 years of technical training in mechanical maintenance or electrical instrumentation programs. This is a joint program that Georgia-Pacific has developed at our site in cooperation with vocational schools and other businesses in the area.

In 1996–1997, the entry-level qualification for any job in our mill is completion of a 2-year postsecondary program, either pulp and paper or industrial processes, each of which includes chemistry, physics, and mathematics. When high standards are developed for employees and prospective employees, it causes some problems. What do you do with people who do not reach those levels? In addition to new employees, we also require the same standard in reading, writing, and math skills at the 12th-grade level for transferring employees. This requirement cannot be met by someone with only a high school diploma—we actually test reading, writing, and math levels.

## IDENTIFYING AND HELPING
## WORKERS WITH LEARNING DISABILITIES

When we began the program with our employees, we found significant problems. We found that 45% of them could not reach this level in reading, writing, and math. In terms of prospective employees, approximately 60% could not reach the 12th-grade standards. This is about our community, but there are similar statistics in workplaces across the country. We feel we have higher potential in the workplace than many other communities do.

We began our program in 1990, and by the end of 1993 approximately 78% of our employees reached a 12.9-grade equivalent in reading, writing, and math. We worked with adult education and literacy programs and also a workplace education program to provide the training. We would not require these tests until we had the systems in place to help our employees and prospective employees reach the desired educational level. We formed our workplace education program.

When approximately 20%–22% could not reach the 12th-grade level, something started happening. We questioned why they could not reach this level. We saw that people were studying longer and becoming frustrated. They could not quite get there. We set about trying to determine how we could help these employees. So in 1993, we set up a project to help those employees with LD. At the time, we checked on what had been done in the workplace for those with LD and we did not find any other companies with LD programs that addressed the work force actually on an industrial site. We then began using learning inventories and getting help from professionals in observation and diagnostics. Eventually, we started a statewide LD program to help other workplace efforts.

In 1994, we were at the end of the first year of this LD program, and we were making assessments about the tools and techniques that we had found helpful for employees in the workplace. We look forward to sharing our conclusions with other employers. From our experience, there are many things that cause problems for workers with LD. For example, we discovered that we have a $1 million inventory of parts that have been misordered. If you misplace $1 million worth of parts, you investigate. We found out that dyscalculia was the culprit. The problem was that these employees inverted, flipped, or misarranged the numbers, entered the information into the computer, and then the parts were delivered. It cost us $1 million in incorrectly ordered parts.

At Georgia-Pacific, we have a participatory management process in which decisions are made by employees at all levels. As you can imagine, more employees are responsible for decisions and 10%–15% of them have LD. You can imagine the problems that this management style could cause us in terms of bottom-line costs and profits. We are trying to set up programs so that we can start addressing these issues.

## LEARNING DISABILITIES IN THE WORKPLACE

There are some key points that need to be considered as far as workplace programs are concerned, and I want to identify some issues that should be addressed in the future. One of the key points that we need to examine is that most businesses and industries have no idea of the literacy levels of their employees, let alone the ramifications of LD. Most businesses and industries do not know how to go about measuring literacy levels. Industry and labor leaders need help with measuring literacy, and they need to understand LD and what opportunities exist for employees and prospective employees. Most businesses in Arkansas—and I cover the whole state as a vocational education board member—do not even recognize the terms when I talk about them. Cost control and profitability will suffer until we address the 10%–15% of our work force with LD.

Another consideration is that educators and workplace education programs need help in identifying workers with LD. We are trying to develop better identification processes. We need to help workers develop some self-awareness so that they can get help. This will also improve job performances.

Electronic media are great tools, but there are some problems with them. If you cannot read, or take the correct information off the paper, or the information changes in your mind before you speak it or enter it in that computer, electronic media are of no help.

## CONCLUSIONS

In terms of the future, we need to research, develop, and publish appropriate accommodations. When we used the Test of Adult Basic Education (TABE) (1987) and asked the publisher for appropriate accommodations, we were told they did not have any. We need to have lists of appropriate accommodations that will not compromise test integrity.

We also need to consider strategies for addressing LD in the private sector, and these strategies need to be formulated in a way that will minimize employers' exposure to lawsuits. We need public awareness so that the implications of LD are better understood.

We need linkages between professional diagnostic resources and educational practitioners. We can identify problems, but we need ways to help people. Whether through observation or assessment, we need to help students understand that they have LD and should not be afraid of it, so that they can go to their jobs and have employers who will help them perform in the workplace.

## REFERENCES

CTB/McGraw-Hill. (1987). *Test of Adult Basic Education*. Monterey, CA: Author.

# Chapter 15

# The Four R's

## Recognition, Remediation, Rehabilitation, and Reasonable Accommodation

*Glenn Young*

What do adults with learning disabilities (LD) want? This can be described by the four R's: recognition, remediation, rehabilitation, and reasonable accommodation. It seems that few adults with LD are fortunate enough to receive all four R's. I am among those who have. Throughout this chapter I point out the good luck, good fortune, or fate that has allowed me access to each of the R's and how that access has allowed me to dramatically change my life. It is clear that few adults with LD have been as fortunate as I. We must change how LD are addressed in this country so that all adults who have LD will be able to have the advantages that the four R's provide.

### RECOGNITION

The first R is *recognition*. Many adults are unaware that they have LD. Most adults went through school systems prior to the passage and implementation of the Education for All Handicapped Children Act of 1975 (PL 94-142). Even after that time, they often were not identified, not accepted, either not diagnosed or misdiagnosed, and not recognized. Most people with LD have gone through the process of education without knowing they have LD.

I was 30 years old before I was diagnosed, and I was initially diagnosed by accident. It was a spot diagnosis when my child was being tested to see if she was gifted. That day I was confirmed in the belief that my daughter was a genius, and for the first time I learned that I was not an idiot. Up until that point in my life, with my weaknesses in spelling and writing, and my reading problems, that is what I thought of myself. Here is where my first bit of good fortune was involved. If I had not commented on my difficulties with the standardized tests, and if my daughter's tester had not been aware of LD, I might never have been identified.

What was also true is that this finding of a reason for my dysfunction was a great emotional experience. Contrary to popular belief, it was not a burden to have a label. The recognition of the learning disability was a liberating experience for me. The identification of the issue provided me with a framework in which to start to understand the educational, social, and emotional issues that I had been confronted with my entire life. As with many other adults with LD who have shared with me that they felt this same sense of relief, the recognition of the LD was the key to allowing me to address the failures that I had refused to address. It allowed me to have a basis for believing in myself .

Part of the recognition of a learning disability is running into the issue of, "What next?" In other words, I may have a learning disability, but what do I do? The traditional answer that we receive is, "Go out and get tested." Testing? What does that mean? How much does that cost?

In the current market, testing costs can range from $350 to $2,000. Often adults who suspect that they have LD do not have resources and opportunities for proper diagnosis. Without testing, however, we cannot be classified as having a learning disability, and therefore we are not eligible for many programs and services, including accommodations. We have to get tested.

My response was, "But if I cannot support my family, how am I supposed to get at least $350 for a test?" Again, fortune was with me. At that point, I was a member of a health maintenance organization, which as part of their services provided diagnostic testing. I was therefore diagnosed for a $5 copayment fee. Most people are not so lucky.

One of the main sources for testing is a vocational rehabilitation program. In theory, anyone who suspects that he or she has a learning disability or has a background of receiving special educational services in schools can ask a vocational rehabilitation program to test him or her. Many anecdotal stories show that vocational rehabilitation is difficult and often nonresponsive to the needs of adults with LD. There are also many cases to the contrary. It did take me 8 years of effort before my vocational rehabilitation program agreed to provide me with support for college.

Once accepted as a vocational rehabilitation client, however, I did receive excellent services.

Another way of seeking testing is through Medicaid. The Social Security Administration and Medicaid have the ability under Health Care Financing Administration regulations to provide diagnostic testing for people suspected of having LD. So, technically, everyone who is qualified for Medicaid can receive diagnostic testing. Do they? No, they do not. Most states do not take advantage of the federal matching funds available for testing and the few states that do set the payment rate very far below market value, so diagnosticians cannot afford to take Medicaid clients. This failure to meet market rates has created a situation in which LD testing is available through Medicaid in only a few locations, either through major hospitals or in pilot projects.

Another source of testing is community colleges. In the 1990s, many of these schools have developed testing services as well as support services for their students who may have LD. After so many years of school failure, however, many adults with LD do not go near any educational settings such as a community college. In my case, I would literally have nightmares whenever I considered taking any type of course in a college or training program.

## REMEDIATION

The second R is *remediation*. It is extremely unfair to expect that a person who has experienced educational abuse for a number of years and who has been through a whole process of denial concerning literacy and other skills will be able to go immediately from recognition of a disability into job training or other education settings. It is a fundamental responsibility of educational leaders and employers to focus on that individual and to reconstitute the educational process as much as possible: to help persons with LD to help him or her learn how to learn. There is also a need to remediate the emotional scars resulting from years of failure and from feeling different without knowing why.

Again, in my case, I was very fortunate. I spent 2½ years with a Slingerland/Orton tutor learning phonics and reading. On more than one occasion, we spent our time together working on emotions rather than on phonics. I also had a great deal of support from family and friends. (An adult with LD once pointed out to me how many adults with LD do not have many friends, and the ones they do have are often as dysfunctional as they are. Again, I have the good fortune of having understanding friends.) My daughter, who was age 5 at the time of my diagnosis, was more phonetically advanced than I was and did flash cards with me, often correcting me.

The point is that adults with LD need to learn how to learn, and they need to learn the fundamentals of language. The functional impairments of an individual's learning disability may be so severe that he or she may never really master learning skills—after all, LD is a real disability. We need to strengthen the strengths and address the weaknesses as much as we can, though. This is necessary before an adult with LD can expect to go into a formal educational setting such as a training program or college.

## REHABILITATION

The third R is *rehabilitation*. How does the person with LD prepare for the world of work? Where do we receive services? Can we expect recognition and services in job training? Once again, I was fortunate in finding support in all these areas. It did not come easily, however.

Although I qualified as a person with a disability, I had an 8-year struggle with the vocational rehabilitation program in the state where I live over paying for my education. The first time I went to vocational rehabilitation, a counselor asked, "What do you do?" I said "I run up and down stairs at sporting events selling beer." He asked, "How much do you make?" I told him, and he said, "You make more than the counselors, get out of here."

The vocational rehabilitation counselor was happy to see that at least I was working, which is understandable. Persons with LD, given the proper support, are often capable of far more than, for example, being a fry cook. There is an ongoing struggle within vocational rehabilitation programs over getting people jobs, which is the main inclination of vocational rehabilitation counselors, or over helping people develop a career. For example, although it varies from state to state, in most cases, vocational rehabilitation programs do not pay for remediation services for adults with LD. The agency teaches individuals to accommodate themselves to being illiterate in the workplace, but, for the most part, it does not prepare the individual for higher education by addressing his or her literacy needs.

I was persistent, and they eventually agreed to pay for my college education. At age 37, I entered a college that understood that I am a person with a learning disability. In the community college and later at the University of Washington, I received services and support based on my having a disability. My state's vocational rehabilitation program paid for a laptop computer, as well as tuition and books. The colleges provided me with note takers, tutors, and the use of rooms for taking tests in isolation.

I was able to obtain an associate's degree, a bachelor's degree, and a master's degree in 3½ years. With the support of the college and the vocational rehabilitation program, I maintained honors-level grades throughout college and won the national competition for a fellowship called the Presidential Management Internship, which included an appointment to a federal government position.

Although I was fortunate, I am not alone. Many, if not most, adults with LD, if provided with the proper support, can achieve many things. Individuals with LD are often highly intelligent, and in many cases are gifted, but they need the opportunity to receive an education and job training as well as on-the-job training in an accommodated fashion, with support. They do not have to be channeled into low-level jobs.

## REASONABLE ACCOMMODATION

The fourth R is *reasonable accommodation.* This is the aspect that frequently is missing. Let me state this in a way that may sound redundant but expresses something most people fail to understand: Having a learning disability means that you have a disability. What this means is that individuals with LD are covered and protected by federal, state, and local civil rights laws.

What is fundamentally different between civil rights laws for persons with disabilities and all other civil rights laws is that all the other laws require only nondiscrimination. Civil rights for persons with disabilities mandate that there can be no discrimination on the basis of disability, and also that persons with disabilities are entitled to have access to reasonable accommodations in the performance of job duties or in educational settings.

My good fortune continued while in college and has continued in the workplace. I have had reasonable accommodations that enable me to show my abilities and thus do not let my disability prevent me from performing. My accommodations in the education system included taking tests in isolation, use of a computer on all tests, and waiving certain required courses (such as foreign language requirements) that were not germane to my field of study. I have continued to have reasonable accommodations in my employment setting, including not being required to provide any handwritten materials and having access to secretarial support.

Even today, with my education, employment history, and credentials, if I had to take a handwritten test using a blue book in a room filled with hundreds of people, I would fail every time, regardless of how well I knew the information. But given a test or assignment in an accommodated fashion as required under civil rights laws, I could show my knowledge and skills.

Many people with LD do not know that they are entitled to civil rights protections and reasonable accommodations. Few, if any, programs teach people with LD about their civil rights and how to go about requesting reasonable accommodations. The reasonable accommodations that I received should be available to all people with LD.

## CONCLUSIONS

The four R's are a framework on which an infinite number of lives can be designed. People with LD are individuals, and each needs to find his or her own way to a vocation and a happy life. With the four R's being met, the likelihood of success can be increased dramatically.

Let me also add that we need to concentrate on the social and emotional aspects of LD, using the four R's framework. There is tremendous trauma that goes with being an adult with LD. At a case-by-case level, we hear similar stories of the denial, anger, rage, and emotional trauma of being different and usually not knowing why. Adults with LD are labeled all their lives. They are labeled as stupid, dumb, incompetent, ignorant, rude, or crude—anything other than simply understanding them as people with LD. For many people I know with LD, much of their literacy instruction ends up being emotional instruction in gaining confidence in talking about the pain, anger, and trauma and in coming to terms with the denial and the anguish associated with LD.

What is also needed is clear leadership. LD in adults is an orphan disorder. No national organization or group has the adult with LD as their main focus. Without this type of group, developing and promoting ideas such as the four R's, adults with LD will continue to be without the support needed to gain access to such things as testing, appropriate education training, and reasonable accommodation at the job site. Without that leadership, the fundamental, dramatic change that is needed in how the United States addresses LD will not take place.

## REFERENCE

Education for All Handicapped Children Act of 1975, PL 94-142. (August 23, 1975). Title 20, U.S.C. §§ 1400 et seq.: *U.S. Statutes at Large, 89,* 773–796.

# Chapter 16

# Employment

## A Research Review and Agenda

*Susan A. Vogel*

The Summit on Learning Disabilities provided a unique opportunity to reflect on the state of knowledge regarding adults with learning disabilities (LD) and the influences of LD on functional literacy, economic status, and employment. These issues reflect concerns raised in the *Resolution on Adult Education for Persons with Learning Disabilities* (Learning Disabilities Association of America, 1994), which stated that more than 40% of students with LD drop out of high school, and that the educational needs of these adult learners are not being met. It may be helpful, however, to consider these concerns within the context of literacy skills and employment in the general work force.

## WORKPLACE LITERACY

In 1993, the U.S. Department of Labor (DOL) published the results of the 1990 workplace literacy assessment of unemployed workers. The study had a dual purpose: 1) to determine the relationship of workplace literacy skills to economic status and 2) to identify factors that contribute to developing workplace literacy skills, finding a job, and earning high wages. Workplace literacy skills that were thought to be most relevant to on-the-job performance were assessed. These skills included critical thinking and information-processing abilities (Kirsch, Jungeblut, & Campbell, 1992). Not surprisingly, a major finding was that workplace literacy is significantly correlated with hourly salary and the number of weeks worked per year. It was also reported that individuals with a high school diploma or general equivalency diploma (GED) were more successful in finding a job and in earning a good salary. The authors concluded that there was an urgent need for workplace literacy instruction to be integrated into job training as well as a need to assess job trainees' literacy periodically. Literacy assessment was recommended as a means of enhancing motivation, determining an individual's readiness for a specific job, and evaluating job training programs.

What is the effect on adults with LD in the workplace of this emphasis on critical thinking and information-processing abilities in workplace literacy training, combined with an increase in the complexity of specific job skills? An even more basic question concerns what percentage of adults in various job training and literacy programs have LD. What is known about their literacy skills, high school dropout rate, employment, economic status, the impact of learning disabilities on their jobs, and strategies to mitigate the effects of LD and to enhance success?

## INCIDENCE OF LD IN ADULTS

No one quite knows how many adults in adult basic education and/or in the work force have LD, and this proportion, no doubt, varies in different segments of the population. One of the earliest estimates of the incidence of LD in adults (Travis, 1979) was that 80% of students in Adult Basic Education programs had LD. More recently, the DOL reported that 15%–23% of all Job Training Partnership Act (JTPA) Title II-A recipients may have LD, and this percentage may increase to 50%–80% among those reading below a seventh-grade level. Not surprisingly, in a study of mothers receiving Aid to Families with Dependent Children (AFDC), the Office of the Inspector General of the Department of Health and Human Services reported that LD was one of the two most frequently reported functional impairments, according to AFDC clients (Kusserow, 1992).

A unique opportunity to determine the incidence and impact of LD in adults was provided by the National Adult Literacy Survey (NALS) (Kirsch, Jungeblut, Jenkins, & Kilstad, 1993). The impetus for the NALS came from the Adult Amendments of 1988, which charged the U.S. Department of Education Office of Educational Research and Improvement, National Center for Education Statistics, with the task of identifying the basic educational skills needed for literate functioning. The survey was administered to a national representative sample of 26,000 individuals ages 16 years and older. The survey included direct assessment of prose, document, and quantitative literacy, and scores were reported on five levels of difficulty, with 5 being the highest and 1 the lowest. Similar to the DOL 1993 study, the three scales involved critical thinking and problem solving. Although the focus of this chapter is on LD and employment, suffice it to say that the NALS findings shocked the nation when they were announced: 52% of the individuals who responded to the survey (representing 100 million of a total of 191 million adults in the United States) performed at the two lowest levels of literacy, that 21%–23% (or 40–44 million) scored at the lowest level, and that 66% did not complete high school (Kirsch et al., 1993). This study also reported that 41%–44% of the adults scoring at the lowest level were living in poverty. It came as no surprise that literacy was found to be inextricably linked to employment and economic status.

In addition to assessing literacy, interviewers asked the 26,000 individuals about their literacy skills and activities, language background, educational and work experiences, and health problems and disabilities. Specific questions included occupation, job maintenance, hourly wages, hours of work per week, and annual income. Participants were asked if they had a physical, mental, or other health condition such as visual or hearing difficulty or a learning disability that kept them from participating fully in work, school, housework, or other activities. Twelve percent reported that they had some physical, mental, or other health condition, and, even more astounding, this number increased to 26% among those who performed at the lowest level on all three scales. A series of follow-up questions provided a unique opportunity to determine the incidence of LD in a national sample of adults. When respondents were asked to specify their disabilities, 3% of the participants indicated that they had LD (Kirsch et al., 1993).

Although we must be cautious in interpreting these data because the adults were identified by self-report, there is strong evidence for the validity of self-report (Decker, Vogler, & DeFries, 1989). In an attempt to determine the usefulness of a family history of reading disability in predicting a child's risk of developing a reading disability, the reading ability of parents of children with LD in reading disabilities were compared with the reading ability of parents of matched controls (Decker et al., 1989). It was found that parents who indicated that they had experienced serious difficulty in learning to read scored significantly lower on a battery of reading measures than parents who did not report serious difficulty (Decker & DeFries, 1980). It is also interesting to note that both groups of parents of children with reading disabilities scored more than one standard deviation below the parents of controls on a battery of reading tests. The authors concluded that adults who self-reported serious difficulty in learning to read were indeed seriously impaired (Decker & DeFries, 1980). Because 80% or more of individuals with LD have reading disabilities (Blalock, 1981, 1982; Johnson & Blalock, 1987), adults who participated in the NALS may have equated LD with reading disability, especially in light of what we have learned from the NALS.

First, 60% of adults with self-reported LD scored at the lowest level (as compared with 21% among the general population) on the three literacy scales. Second, the lower the educational attainment, the higher the percentage of self-reported LD. When those who self-reported having LD were grouped by educational attainment, 10% (rather than 3%) of individuals completing 0–8 years of school reported having LD, whereas 2% who completed some college or had received a college degree reported having LD. In regard to economic well-being, having a learning disability puts an individual at significantly greater risk to be near or below the poverty level (Reder, 1995). The average income of adults with self-reported LD was $14,000, compared with $23,000 for the general population (Reder, 1995).

Moreover, 43% of adults in the general population with self-reported LD (compared with 18%) were at or below the poverty level (Reder, 1993, 1995). In summary, it seems clear that adults with self-reported LD were three times more likely than adults in the general population to have scored at the lowest literacy level, three times more likely to have completed 0–8 years of school, and almost three times more likely to be at or below the poverty level than adults in the general population.

More positive findings were obtained from the comprehensive research project of the National Longitudinal Transition Study (NLTS) based on a national sample of more than 8,000 youth ages 13–23 who were receiving special education services during the 1985–1986 school year (D'Amico, 1991; Wagner, 1991; Wagner, Blackorby, Cameto, & Newman, 1993). The sample included youths with disabilities who were receiving special education services in public secondary schools and in state-operated special schools. As a rule, students with LD who receive LD support services in high school have more significant disabilities than students with LD who are no longer receiving services in high school. Therefore, it was hypothesized that the NLTS results may not be generalizable to the general population of adults with LD (Adelman & Vogel, 1993). Nonetheless, the findings are noteworthy, especially in light of earlier studies.

Marder and D'Amico (1992) reported that the employment rate for 15- to 20-year-old secondary school exiters with LD (i.e., those who had graduated or dropped out) was 57%, which approached the employment rate of individuals without disabilities (60%). Other researchers using small samples had reported similar outcomes (Bruck, 1987; Preston & Yarington, 1967; Rawson, 1968; Rogan & Hartman, 1976, 1990; Shapiro & Lentz, 1991). For example, Bruck (1987) noted that the unemployment rate for students with LD was the same as that of their siblings without disabilities in the control group. She reported that individuals with LD found employment in a wide range of occupations, and only a few were employed in unskilled jobs. It is important to note, however, that subjects in these studies were of average or above-average intelligence, mostly from middle- and upper-middle-class backgrounds, and often attended private schools or colleges.

The encouraging NLTS outcomes (Wagner, 1991) were not consistent when the sample was divided by gender, which confirmed other studies (Wagner, 1992). Considerable evidence indicates that women with LD are unemployed at a significantly higher rate than men with LD (Buchanan & Wolf, 1986; Haring, Lovett, & Smith, 1990; Kranstover, Thurlow, & Bruininks, 1989; Scuccimarra & Speece, 1990) For example, Scuccimarra and Speece (1990) reported a 23.8% unemployment rate for women with LD and other disabilities compared with 6.8% for men with LD and other disabilities. Wagner (1992) reported that in the NLTS sample employment for men with LD approached the same percentage as that of men in the general population (63.5% and 68.2%), whereas the employment rate of women with LD was considerably lower than that of the general population of women (39.6% versus 53.7%).

The significant gap between the rates of LD in male and female employment (63.5% versus 39.6%) compared with the general population (68.2% versus 53.7%) may be related to differences in sample populations. In an extensive review of the literature, Vogel (1990) found that to be identified with LD by schools, females must 1) score significantly lower on intelligence tests, 2) have more severe impairments in their language abilities and/or academic achievement than males, and 3) have a greater aptitude–achievement discrepancy than their male counterparts. It is not surprising, then, to find less favorable outcomes for females with LD than for males in school-identified samples such as those in the NLTS study (Wagner, 1992). As a result, the differences favoring males that are found in longitudinal studies of school-identified males and females with LD may reflect a bias in identification and therefore must be interpreted with this in mind. The NALS data provide an opportunity to revisit the question of gender differences in employment of males and females with LD (Reder & Vogel, 1996).

## JOB SUCCESS

What factors have contributed to the success of adults with LD who have been successful in employment? Several series of the studies (Adelman & Vogel, 1990; Rogan & Hartman, 1976, 1990; Vogel & Adelman, 1990,

1992; Vogel, Hruby, & Adelman, 1993; Werner, 1993) followed adults with LD over a period of a decade or more (some from early childhood). These researchers identified intrinsic and extrinsic factors that seem to be related to success in postsecondary educational settings and in employment. Intrinsic factors included drive, motivation to succeed, willingness to work hard and persist over time, and willingness to seek help and use services or accommodations as appropriate. Some extrinsic factors that enhanced success were having a supportive family; one-to-one help as needed for educational, emotional, and psychological support; having work opportunities provided through family, friends, or teachers; and finding a teacher, friend, or mentor who had confidence in their ability to succeed, helped them solve problems when they had a setback, and helped them regain a balanced perspective, self-confidence, and renewed energy to persevere.

Many of these same factors were identified by Spekman, Herman, and Vogel (1993) and Gerber and Reiff (1992, 1993), and who incorporated them into a vocational success model, which was based on in-depth interviews with 71 adults with LD. According to this model, for adults to be effective self-advocates, to develop and use compensatory strategies, and to find the right job or career and setting (or to modify it) that allows them to perform at their highest level of abilities and minimize their disabilities, they must first decide that they are going to take control of their lives and acknowledge that they have a learning disability. Taking charge of one's life was a crucial first step to success and was accompanied by strong determination and desire, goal setting, and reframing, which consists of four stages: recognition of LD, acceptance of LD, self-understanding, and taking specific action.

In addition, successful adults were perseverant and willing to sacrifice to achieve their goals. They were resourceful in finding an environment that facilitated accomplishing their goals and that maximized their strengths. Finally, and most relevantly, they were highly creative in networking with supportive individuals, using technology, and participating in training programs (Gerber & Reiff, 1992, 1993).

## RESEARCH AGENDA

In order to understand how LD in adults affects the acquisition of literacy skills, educational attainments, and the ability to benefit from vocational or career preparation and advancement opportunities, many questions need to be addressed. These questions need to be divided into three areas: high school transition concerns, workplace concerns, and public policy issues. Following the discussion of these questions, recommendations for action are presented.

## High School Transition Questions

Questions that need to be addressed by research include:

1. How effective are present transition programs for high school students and how can the preparation of students with LD for postsecondary education and employment be improved?
2. How should elementary and junior high school vocational education curricula be revised to meet the specific needs of students with LD?
3. What vocational counseling and preparation are available to individuals with LD after they leave the school environment? How effective are they, and how can these programs be enhanced?
4. How effective are GED classes, literacy programs, adult education, vocational rehabilitation, and federal programs such as JOBS, JTPA, and AFDC in preparing adults with LD to be successful on the job? How can these programs be enhanced?

## Workplace Questions

Questions for research that specifically concern the workplace are:

1. What is the occupational, economic, and employment status of adults with LD?
2. How and why do men and women with LD differ in occupational, economic, and employment status as compared to the general population, and how can this trend be changed?
3. How can we design services and programs to enhance employment success for women with LD, with special attention being paid to their needs?
4. Many older adults who dropped out of high school may have LD that were never identified. How can such people be identified, and how can their needs for job training and literacy skills be identified and met?
5. What literature and educational programs about LD are available to employers, supervisors, workplace literacy instructors, and federal employment training program providers in order for them to comply with the mandates of the Americans with Disabilities Act of 1990 (ADA) (PL 101-336)?
6. How can incentives for employers to provide community-based vocational training and on-the-job educational opportunities for adults with LD be increased?
7. How often do job applicants and employed adults with LD disclose their disabilities, under what circumstances, for what reasons, and what has been their experience upon disclosure?

8. Why do individuals whose LD affects them on the job decide not to disclose this?
9. What are the reasons most commonly cited by adults with learning disabilities for disclosure?
10. In what ways, if any, are adults who disclose their LD different from those who do not disclose?
11. What accommodations are most commonly requested and provided, and what accommodations are most effective in enhancing job success?
12. What are the most commonly reported problems and strategies used on the job by adults with LD?

## Public Policy Questions

Because public policy determines much of the direction and funding of job training, adult education, and vocational rehabilitation services and programs, research in this area is critical. Some questions to be addressed are:

1. How can we coordinate efforts to enhance employment opportunities and job success for adults with LD among all service providers and at all entry points (e.g., Adult Basic Education, JOBS, JTPA, AFDC, vocational rehabilitation, public assistance)?
2. How can a seamless transition from one program to another or from one job to another be provided to adults with LD to avoid repeating at each program or job the process of intake, screening, referral, documentation of disability, and determination of eligibility for accommodations?
3. How can the Departments of Labor, Health and Human Services, Justice, and Education cooperate to identify and meet the needs of adults who may have LD?
4. How can conferences such as the Summit on Learning Disabilities have an impact on national health care reform so that universal screening and free assessment of adults with suspected LD can be provided in the same way it is for the school-age population and adults through the model statewide California community college system?

## RECOMMENDATIONS FOR ACTION

The following recommendations are based on the research reviewed in this chapter as well as on the recommendations of the President's Committee on Employment of People with Disabilities (Brown, Gerber, & Dowdy, 1990; Vogel, 1992).

1. We should continue to forge research collaborations among federal agencies, including the National Institutes of Health, other profes-

sional organizations, universities, formal and informal adult education providers, parents, and adults with LD.

2. We should renew our commitment to research to support follow-up, longitudinal, developmental, and neurobiological research on representative national samples of individuals with LD (not only school-identified or volunteer samples) so that we do not repeat the error of looking at the tail, the eye, or the eyelash of the elephant, so to speak, and erroneously generalize the results to the adult population as a whole.

3. We need to increase our funding of adult education and provide information, staff development, and education about LD to literacy providers, parent educators, adult educators, and vocational rehabilitation counselors. Often, the least well-trained (albeit very well-intentioned) individuals are assigned the task, as volunteers or as poorly paid staff, of teaching individuals with severe reading disabilities to improve their literacy skills.

4. Adults who have problems acquiring literacy and job skills because of unidentified LD need to be identified, taught, and provided with appropriate accommodations. Because these adults are often the least likely to be able to afford assessment and special tutoring, have the severest problems, and are the most likely to be unemployed, we need to provide inexpensive, validated screening and cost-effective assessment that will lead to effective instructional and compensatory strategies.

5. We need better and more effective transition programs targeted at all levels of occupation and not just for entry-level, poorly paid jobs.

6. We need to assist adults with LD through vocational career counseling, job searches, meaningful work experiences (through internships, job shadowing, and mentoring), and postsecondary education and employment settings to earn higher salaries in employment commensurate with their highest abilities rather than their disabilities.

7. We need to increase incentives through tax credits and other programs for employer involvement in community-based and on-the-job training programs.

8. We need to educate GED instructors so that they have a greater understanding of LD, and so that they can teach adults with LD and have a greater awareness of the mandates of the ADA, and learn how to assist clients in applying for reasonable accommodations in taking GED exams.

9. We need to assist workplace literacy providers (from top-level executives to on-the-line supervisors) to understand the nature of LD and how to modify their educational and supervisory practices to meet the needs of adults with LD.

10. We need to improve career counseling, rehabilitation, and vocational services for adults with LD, especially for women.

## CONCLUSIONS

What would be accomplished by answering these questions and implementing these recommendations? First, there would be a significant increase in full-time employment of adults with LD in jobs that are commensurate with their highest abilities, training, and preparation; in jobs that are satisfying; and in jobs in which they are successful. Moreover, the present cost of federal programs such as AFDC, public assistance, and Supplemental Security Income would be reduced as the number of employed women and men with LD increased. Price tags and economic considerations aside, however, the most important anticipated outcome is the effect on self-esteem for those hundreds and thousands of individuals with LD, now undereducated, unemployed, or underemployed, when they become successfully employed in satisfying jobs.

## REFERENCES

Adelman, P.B., & Vogel, S.A. (1990). College graduates with learning disabilities: Employment attainment and career patterns. *Learning Disability Quarterly, 13*(3), 154–166.

Adelman, P.B., & Vogel, S.A. (1993). Issues in the employment of adults with learning disabilities. *Learning Disability Quarterly, 16*(3), 219–232.

Americans with Disabilities Act of 1990 (ADA), PL 101-336. (July 26, 1990). Title 42, U.S.C. §§ 12101 et seq.: *U.S. Statutes at Large, 104,* 327–378.

Blalock, J.W. (1981). Persistent problems and concerns of young adults with learning disabilities. In W. Cruickshank & A. Silver (Eds.), *Bridges to tomorrow: The best of ACLD* (Vol. 2, pp. 35–55). Syracuse, NY: Syracuse University Press.

Blalock, J. (1982). Persistent auditory language deficits in adults with learning disabilities. *Journal of Learning Disabilities, 15,* 604–609.

Brown, D. (1984). Employment considerations for learning disabled adults. *Journal of Rehabilitation, 2,* 74–77, 88.

Brown, D., Gerber, P., & Dowdy, C. (1990). *Pathways to employment for people with learning disabilities.* Washington, DC: President's Committee on Employment of People with Disabilities.

Bruck, M. (1985). The adult functioning of children with specific learning disabilities: A follow-up study. In L. Siegel (Ed.), *Advances in applied developmental psychology* (pp. 91–129). Norwood, NJ: Ablex.

Bruck, M. (1987). The adult outcomes of children with learning disabilities. *Annals of Dyslexia, 37,* 252–263.

Buchanan, M., & Wolf, J.S. (1986). A comprehensive study of learning disabled adults. *Journal of Learning Disabilities, 19*(1), 34–38.

D'Amico, R. (1991). The working world awaits: Employment experiences during and shortly after secondary school. In M. Wagner, L. Newman, R. D'Amico, E.D. Jay, P. Butler-Nalin, C. Marder, & R. Cox, *Youth with disabilities: How are they doing? The first comprehensive report from the National Longitudinal Transition Study of special education students* (pp. 81–85). Menlo Park, CA: SRI International.

Decker, S.N., & DeFries, J.C. (1980). Cognitive abilities in families with reading disabled children. *Journal of Learning Disabilities, 13*, 517–522.

Decker, S.N., Vogler, G., & DeFries, J.C. (1989). Validity of self-reported reading disability by parents of reading-disabled and control children. *Reading and Writing: An Interdisciplinary Journal, 1*, 327–331.

Gerber, P.J., & Reiff, H.B. (1992). *Speaking for themselves: Ethnographic interviews with adults with learning disabilities.* Ann Arbor: University of Michigan Press.

Gerber, P.J., & Reiff, H.B. (Eds.). (1993). *Learning disabilities in adults.* Stoneham, MA: Butterworth-Heinemann.

Greenbaum, B.L. (1993). *A follow-up survey of students with learning disabilities after exiting a postsecondary institution.* Unpublished doctoral dissertation, University of Maryland, College Park.

Grossman, P. (1993). *Employment discrimination for the learning disabled community.* Northridge: California State University Press.

Haring, K.A., Lovett, D.L., & Smith, D.D. (1990). A follow-up study of recent special education graduates of learning disabilities programs. *Journal of Learning Disabilities, 23*(2), 108–113.

Johnson, D., & Blalock, J. (Eds.). (1987). *Young adults with learning disabilities.* Orlando, FL: Grune & Stratton.

Kirsch, I., Jungeblut, A., & Campbell, A. (1992). *Beyond the school doors.* Princeton, NJ: Educational Testing Services.

Kirsch, I.S., Jungeblut, A., Jenkins, L., & Kilstad, A. (1993) *Adult literacy in America: A first look at the results of the National Adult Literacy Survey.* Washington, DC: U.S. Department of Education, Office of Educational Research and Improvement, National Center for Education Statistics.

Kranstover, L.L., Thurlow, M.L., & Bruininks, R.H. (1989). Special education graduates: A longitudinal study of outcomes. *Career Development for Exceptional Individuals, 12*(2), 153–156.

Kusserow, R.P. (1992). *Functional impairments and AFDC clients.* Washington, DC: Department of Health and Human Services, Office of the Inspector General.

Learning Disabilities Association of America. (1994). Resolution on adult education for persons with learning disabilities. *Journal of Learning Disabilities, 27*(1), 4.

Marder, C., & D'Amico, R. (1992). *How well are youth with disabilities really doing? A comparison of youth with disabilities and youth in general.* Menlo Park, CA: SRI International.

Preston, R.C., & Yarington, D.J. (1967). Status of fifty retarded readers eight years after reading clinic diagnosis. *Journal of Reading, 11*, 122–129.

Rawson, M.R. (1968). *Developmental language disability: Adult accomplishments of dyslexic boys.* Baltimore: Johns Hopkins University Press.

Reder, S.M. (1993, November). *Literacy, learning disabilities, and education.* Paper presented at the 10th Work Now and in the Future Conference, Portland, OR.

Reder, S.M. (1995, March). National overview of the impact of learning disabilities on literacy, educational attainments, employment, and income level. In S. Vogel & S. Reder (Co-chairs), *Literacy and learning disabilities.* Symposium conducted at the meeting of the Third International Conference of the Learning Disabilities Association of America, Orlando, FL.

Reder, S.M., & Vogel, S.A. (1996). *Literacy, education, and learning disabilities.* Manuscript in preparation.

Rogan, L.L., & Hartman, L.D. (1976). *A follow-up study of learning disabled children as adults: Final report.* Evanston, IL: Cove School. (ERIC Document Reproduction Service No. ED 163 728)

Rogan, L.L., & Hartman, L.D. (1990). Adult outcomes of learning disabled students ten years after initial follow-up. *Learning Disabilities Focus, 5*(2), 91–102.

Sauter, D.L., & McPeek, D. (1993). Dyslexia in the workplace: Implications of the Americans with Disabilities Act. *Annals of Dyslexia, 43,* 271–278.

Scuccimarra, D.J., & Speece, D.L. (1990). Employment outcomes and social integration of students with mild handicaps: The quality of life two years after high school. *Journal of Learning Disabilities, 13*(4), 213–218.

Shapiro, E.S., & Lentz, F., Jr. (1991). Vocational-technical programs: Follow-up of students with learning disabilities. *Exceptional Children, 58*(1), 47–60.

Spekman, N.J., Herman, K.L., & Vogel, S.A. (1993). Risk and resilience in individuals with learning disabilities: A challenge to the field. *Learning Disabilities Research and Practice, 8*(1), 59–65.

Travis, G. (1979). An adult educator views learning disabilities. *Adult Literacy and Basic Education, 3,* 85–92.

U.S. Department of Labor. (1991). *The learning disabled in employment and training programs.* Washington, DC: Author.

U.S. Department of Labor. (1993). *Workplace literacy and the nation's unemployed workers* (Research and Evaluation Report Series 93-F). Washington, DC: Author.

Vogel, S.A. (1990). Gender differences in intelligence, language, visual-motor abilities, and academic achievement in students with learning disabilities: A review of the literature. *Journal of Learning Disabilities, 13*(1), 44–52.

Vogel, S. (1992). *Employment priorities for the '90s for people with disabilities.* Washington, DC: President's Committee on Employment of People with Disabilities.

Vogel, S.A., & Adelman, P.B. (1990). Extrinsic and intrinsic factors in graduation and academic failure among LD college students. *Annals of Dyslexia, 40,* 119–137.

Vogel, S.A., & Adelman, P.B. (1992). The success of college students with learning disabilities: Factors related to educational attainment. *Journal of Learning Disabilities, 15*(7), 430–441.

Vogel, S.A., Hruby, P., & Adelman, P.B. (1993). Educational and psychological factors in successful and unsuccessful college students with learning disabilities. *Learning Disabilities Research and Practice, 8*(1), 35–43.

Wagner, M. (1991). Introduction. In M. Wagner, L. Newman, R. D'Amico, E.D. Jay, P. Butler-Nalin, C. Marder, & R. Cox, *Youth with disabilities: How are they doing? The first comprehensive report from the National Longitudinal Transition Study of special education students* (pp. 1–15). Menlo Park, CA: SRI International.

Wagner, M. (1992, April). *Being female: A secondary disability? Gender differences in the transition experiences of young people with disabilities.* Paper presented at the annual meeting of the American Educational Research Association, San Francisco.

Wagner, M., Blackorby, J., Cameto, R., & Newman, L. (1993). *What makes a difference? Influences on postschool outcomes of youth with disabilities: The third comprehensive report from the National Longitudinal Transition Study of Special Education Students.* Menlo Park, CA: SRI International.

Werner, E. (1993). Risk and resilience in individuals with learning disabilities: Lessons learned from the Kauai longitudinal study. *Learning Disabilities Research and Practice, 8*(1), 28–34.

# Chapter 17

# Building Bridges

*Neil A. Sturomski*

Building a bridge involves teamwork. It involves working together toward the same goal. It involves building a solid foundation and structure. It involves connecting territory. It involves time, money, and commitment.

## THE TWO SHORES

But what does the bridge need to connect? On one shore is the fullest possible participation in American social and economic life: the ability to have a good job, to progress, and to gain new skills; the ability to figure sale prices in a store; the ability to read street signs; and the ability to order a meal in a restaurant. Literacy, which is fundamental to accomplishing these goals, no longer means just the ability to perform simple reading and writing skills. Literacy involves verbal communication, problem solving, reading, writing, and the ability to calculate. It involves an individual's ability to function on the job and in society and to develop one's knowledge and potential.

On the other shore are the estimated 30 million Americans who are functionally illiterate (National Literacy Act, 1991; Payne, 1992). This figure represents one in every five American adults. An additional 34% of Americans are considered marginally illiterate (Learning Disabilities Association of America, 1992). A large number of those individuals are believed to have learning disabilities (LD). Among adults who attend literacy or adult basic education programs, it has been estimated that as many as 50%–80% have a learning disability. Similarly, it has been estimated that 15%–30% of all Job Training Partnership Act participants and 25%–40% of all adults receiving Aid to Families with Dependent Children and those in Job Opportunities and Basic Skills programs have a learning disability (Nightengale, Yudd, Anderson, & Barnow, 1991).

The inability to successfully address the needs of adults with LD appears to have a significant cost. Many adults with LD fail to achieve the skills necessary to obtain satisfactory levels of employment, economic security, and self-esteem. All too often adults with LD are underemployed or are receiving public assistance. A productive part of our work force is lost when adults with LD are not successfully educated (Smith, 1991).

There are many who are trying to build a bridge between these two shores. Literacy, job training, and adult education programs are intended to help adults find their way to the other shore. Not all adults can profit from traditional programs, however. Teachers working in adult education and literacy programs are sometimes bewildered and frustrated by students who, although bright and articulate, do not seem to acquire needed skills (Klein, 1989). Unfortunately, few of the tutors in literacy programs, teachers in Adult Basic Education (ABE) classrooms, and instructors in job training programs have received adequate and ongoing training to successfully screen and instruct adults with LD (Herbert, 1988).

## FOUNDATIONS OF THE BRIDGE: TRAINING AND COLLABORATION

One of the main foundations of the bridge we are building is adequate training in LD for instructors in adult literacy, job training, and ABE programs. In a survey of practices in ABE, a majority of ABE directors recognized the need for regular in-service training in LD (Ryan & Price, 1993). In short, there has been a growing awareness by adult education, job training, and literacy professionals that LD are real and that they affect many of the individuals in their programs.

Another important foundation of this bridge-building effort is the need for the adult literacy and LD communities to work together. The adult literacy and LD communities for the most part have been operating in isolation from each other for many years. They do not always share a common language or philosophy regarding how to best meet the needs of adults who have LD. They do share, however, the common goal of helping adults who have LD acquire literacy skills. These groups need to coordinate their efforts and cannot become too protective of their territories. They need to build a bridge that remains stable. Only by supporting each other as professionals and sharing expertise can the adult literacy and LD communities build effective linkages.

By creating linkages between programs and agencies addressing adult literacy and LD, and by providing training and technical assistance to adult literacy providers, the ability of literacy practitioners to help adults with LD is strengthened. The National Adult Literacy and Learning Disabilities Center, which is funded by the National Institute for Literacy, has convened focus groups throughout the country. Eight focus group meetings were held in four cities: Washington, D.C.; Atlanta; Kansas City, Missouri; and San Francisco. Two meetings were held at each site, and approximately 10 individuals participated in each meeting. Participants were asked to share their opinions on the following issues:

- Screening processes used to determine the likelihood of the existence of LD
- Intervention methods used with adults who are suspected of having LD
- Staff training in the use of screening and intervention methods
- Dissemination of materials to adult literacy programs

These groups, which included individuals from the literacy, adult education, and LD communities, stated loudly and clearly that professionals in literacy, job training, and adult education programs need ongoing training in LD and that professionals in adult education and literacy need to work together with professionals in LD. Although the literacy and LD communities share a common goal of helping adults with LD to acquire literacy skills, there is disagreement between adult literacy and professionals in LD on the value of diagnosing LD.

## Screening for Learning Disabilities

Most literacy practitioners agree that some sort of basic screening is critical, even if only to eliminate the suspicion of LD. Therefore, various field-tested screening devices may be useful girders in the construction of this bridge.

Several screening instruments have been developed. For example, the University of Kansas Institute for Research in Learning Disabilities has completed 11 years of development, validation, and implementation research with the California community colleges to create and produce a screening battery for students with LD who are attending community colleges (Mellard, 1993). Other screening devices are also being developed for use by adult educators and literacy providers. To date, however, few field-based studies have examined screening and intervention techniques for adults with LD who attend literacy and adult education programs.

The National Adult Literacy and Learning Disabilities Center's focus group members suggested that screening batteries should include, among other things, the following:

- Interviews
- Reviews of medical, school, or employment histories
- Written answers to a few questions
- A brief test on academic skills

A screening battery can also include portfolios or other informal assessments that best express the uniqueness of each learner. In addition, several volunteer literacy groups, such as Literacy Volunteers of America and Laubach Literacy Action, are beginning to train volunteer tutors, not to be professional diagnosticians, but to detect the more obvious indicators of LD.

## Intervention Techniques

The bridge needs other girders—specifically, intervention techniques to be used with adults with LD. A model program for adults with LD that puts the needs of learners in the forefront has been created and designed by Sally Smith. This program, The Night School at the Lab School of Washington, D.C., is designed to individually instruct adults with LD in small classes of five or fewer individuals. Classes are taught by master teachers who are specialists in LD. The program involves an initial interview and, in many cases, an educational diagnostic evaluation. The intake procedure concludes with explicit recommendations for instruction. In this model program, it is clear that when adults are asked the right questions, they can provide information on their strengths and needs. Given the opportunity by an understanding instructor, these adult students can explain which techniques and types of instruction work and which do not. In this program, intervention techniques and strategies are tailored to adult needs; adults have different needs from children, and they must be involved in the development of their instruction.

Adult literacy programs that are utilizing information on LD are beginning to emphasize more flexibility and creativity in their teaching approaches and in their learning-style assessments. They are starting to focus literacy lessons on more practical and functional material. Instructors should be adept at modifying the pace of instruction; presenting a variety of approaches; locating and creating appropriate materials; and becoming familiar with an adult student's interests, strengths, and immediate needs. The aim of adult education and literacy programs should be to develop approaches based on learner strengths that focus on the individual and enhance his or her resources and abilities (Osher, Webb, & Koehler, 1993; Weisel, 1993). Collaborative efforts are also occurring with more frequency at the local level between adult literacy and LD programs (PLUS Outreach, 1992). Ongoing training for adult educators, job training instructors, and literacy providers in teaching adults with LD is necessary, however. In addition, continued collaboration between professionals in the adult literacy and LD communities is needed.

## Research

Training, collaboration, screening, and intervention techniques are supported by another important building component: research. Not only does a bridge need to be built between the adult literacy and LD communities, there needs to be more research on screening tools and intervention techniques that can be used by ABE teachers, literacy providers, and job training instructors who work with adults with LD. Research cannot stop at the door of the university, however. Practical applications of successful research interventions need to be delivered to educators and to adults with LD.

## CONCLUSIONS

Ultimately, what is a bridge for? A bridge enables individuals to move from one place to another or to get from one point in life to the next. From the statistical estimates, there are many adults who have low literacy skills and whose lives are hampered by these limited skills. Their job skills are few, their self-esteem is low, and their frustration is high. In addition, it is estimated that a large number of these individuals are adults with LD. Many of these individuals have tried to cross the bridge leading to full participation in American social and economic life but have been unsuccessful; they have tried to learn literacy skills but have failed.

To develop recommended practices for working with adults with LD in literacy and adult education programs, a solid structure of training and research is necessary and must include adequate screening devices and a variety of intervention techniques. This takes time, money, and commitment. Most important, the fields of adult literacy and LD must coordinate their efforts as both partners and collaborators to construct a firm, solid, unshakable bridge for adults with LD who seek support from adult education and literacy providers.

## REFERENCES

Herbert, J.P. (1988). *Working with adults who have learning disabilities* (Report No. Ce 053001). Topeka: Kansas State Department of Education, Manhattan Adult Learning and Resource Center. (ERIC Document Reproduction Service No. ED 310 237)

Klein, C. (1989). Specific learning difficulties. *Adult Literacy and Basic Skills Unit, 32*, 2–5.

Learning Disabilities Association of America. (1992). *Illiteracy in America.* Pittsburgh, PA: Author.

Mellard, D. (1993). *Academic attribute study—II: Screening for learning disabilities in the California community colleges.* Lawrence: Institute for Research in Learning Disabilities, University of Kansas.

National Literacy Act of 1991, PL 102-73. (July 25, 1991). Title 20, U.S.C. §§ 1201 et seq.: *U.S. Statutes at Large, 105,* 333–368.

Nightengale, D., Yudd, R., Anderson, S., & Barnow, B. (1991). *The learning disabled in employment and training programs* (Research and Evaluation Rep. Series 91-E). Washington, DC: Urban Institute.

Osher, D., Webb, L., & Koehler, S. (1993). *Study of ABE/ESL instructor training approaches: Learning disabilities: Learner-centered approaches.* Washington, DC: Pelavin Associates.

Payne, M. (1992). Teaching tips: Meeting the needs of adults with learning disabilities. *GED Items, 9*(4/5), 12–13.

PLUS Outreach. (1992). *Literacy learning disabilities collaboration project.* Pittsburgh, PA: Author.

Ryan, A., & Price, L. (1993). Learning disabilities in adult education: A survey of current practices. *Journal of Postsecondary Education and Disability, 10*(3), 31–40.

Smith, S.L. (1991). *Succeeding against the odds: Strategies and insight from the learning disabled.* Los Angeles: Jeremy P. Tarcher.

Weisel, L. (1993). *Strategies to support adults with learning differences in basic skills and literacy programs* (Teleconference workbook prepared for KET-TV). Columbus, OH: TLP Group.

# Chapter 18

# Dyslexia to Pluslexia

*Delos R. Smith*

I am a dyslexic, a person with a learning disability, and there are many phases that I have experienced in my life that are typical of those with this disability. I have divided these into three different stages—the first one is dyslexia, a learning disability. There is a second stage, which I refer to as "neutralexia," and the third stage is a complete turnaround. In this third stage, dyslexia, the disability, actually becomes an advantage that I call "pluslexia."

## STAGE 1

The first stage is a definite disability. Mildness is certainly a myth. You do not want to be "mild" in dyslexia. You want to be gross, absolutely gross, because if you are labeled "grossly disabled," no one labels you as lazy. Everyone knows you have some difficulties. In my case, I had a severe learning disability with speech problems, as well as the inability to read and write. I was a child who could not speak clearly. I did not read, and I wrote in a strange fashion. I never reversed my letters, but wrote in a perfectly mirrored way. It is vital to emphasize the important of parental support. If you are lucky enough to have supportive parents, you are truly blessed. I had parents who did not panic. They went out and got the help I needed.

This all happened in 1939, and there was not much help available at that time. But my parents found two people, Sam and June Orton, via our pediatrician. I was fortunate that the best experts available in 1939 were made available to me.

When I was 8 years old, they assigned me a day-by-day teacher, Katrina de Hirsh. She became very famous in this field, and at the age of 8 I started remediation for 15 months, 6 days per week. The results were that I could talk clearly and read and write very well. In fact, I read better than most normal students in my class, whatever *normal* means. In the dyslexic world, everyone who does not have dyslexia is normal.

## STAGE 2

So, that ends, in a sense, my dyslexia phase. I am a nice normal person now, correct? Ready to go. Not true! I now enter the stage that I refer to as my neutralexic stage, which lasted from age 9 to 41 and ended on December 9, 1976. What is a neutralexic? A neutralexic is a remediated dyslexic who still does not fit into society. At school, I strongly resisted the academic ways of doing things, and I did things in my own way. When I started working, I did not easily fit into the corporate environment. In other words, I marched to a different drummer.

So, in neutralexia, even after remediation and despite some very positive attributes, there were still many puzzling negatives that I did not understand at all. Neutralexia fits into Geshwind's thesis of strengths and needs in the individual with dyslexia. During this period, I experienced great strengths, but there were great needs that I did not understand.

I decided at age 35 to study music just because I was so awful at it. My whole family had problems with music, and my progress was painfully slow until December 9, 1976, at 9:30 P.M. when I played "Clementine" backward on the piano. I had just completed my first lesson in composition with retrograde devices, and I wanted to try out this composition technique. I was stunned at the ease with which I could play the piano by going from right to left. I literally had my first true musical experience. Also, I realized that the musical breakthrough I had just experienced and my early language difficulties were linked together. I did not have the slightest idea how or just what it all meant. I had not even heard of the term *dyslexia* or what it was. But I knew I had to investigate my early experiences with language remediation together with this musical experience and the ease with which I could play music backward. For 7 years leading up to my lesson in retrograde devices, I struggled to progress in reading music from left to right.

## STAGE 3

So, on December 9, 1976, I entered the world of pluslexia. In pluslexia, I understood all of the issues that went along with the original learning problems—so few people get to that stage of understanding. I read in the *Wall Street Journal*—as an economist, the *Wall Street Journal* is my bible—something about the Orton Society. I thought there had to be a connection to Dr. Orton, and there certainly was. I went to the New York Branch of the Orton Dyslexia Society and asked them if they had heard of my teacher, Katrina de Hirsh. This was like asking a baseball fan, "Have you ever heard of Joe DiMaggio?" Of course they knew her well.

Thus began the understanding of my problems. I could just feel my anger dissipate. Things started to make enormous sense to me. Through the Orton Society, I met neurologists such as Norman Geshwind and Dick Masland who explained so much to me and gave me an understanding of my situation. I became involved with the New York branch as its treasurer and then at the national level, where I met the experts in the Orton Dyslexia Society. Through my work with the Orton Dyslexia Society, I began to see and understand the biases of our society. An individual with dyslexia has to understand the biases. We are the minority, and we need that understanding to protect ourselves and to work within the system so that we may help others with this problem. That is what I mean by pluslexia.

## CONCLUSIONS

There are very few individuals with dyslexia who get to the stage of neutralexia. There are even fewer who reach the stage of pluslexia and who can actually think of the problem as an advantage in the final stage of complete self-acceptance. Remember that I know English literally forward and backward, and that happens to be an advantage. I now understand how the system works and have stopped fighting it. So many individuals with dyslexia are angry and bitter, and that bitterness sometimes turns to violence. By helping individuals with dyslexia to progress to the pluslexia stage and to experience and like themselves, we can succeed. Individuals with dyslexia will grow and society will benefit from rich, hidden resources.

# Chapter 19

# Information, Illustration, and Inspiration

*Richard C. Strauss*

My good friend Jamie Williams, who is involved in learning disabilities (LD) in Dallas, once told me that there should be three I's to every speech—information, illustration, and inspiration: information to help us know what is important to do, illustration to show us how and why it should be done, and inspiration to ensure that we have the will to do it.

## INFORMATION

There is some very important information about LD and their impact on the workplace. The Georgia-Pacific program is a good example of a fine program for the enhancement of employee literacy (see Chapter 14). We know that issues of adult literacy may in reality be related to unrecognized LD.

## ILLUSTRATION

I believe that personal stories best illustrate the impact of LD. I struggled with LD. School was the most frustrating experience of my entire life. From the earliest time I can remember, I had tutors. You can imagine that for a 16-, 17-, 18-year-old boy with dyslexia and hyperactivity, it was terrible to sit and go through flash cards over and over again with a tutor. This was not exactly how one would choose to spend afternoons and summers.

But I was fortunate. I had a supportive, understanding family, and, after a number of frustrating years, we were able to locate a tutor knowledgeable in LD. Today I have an excellent support staff, which includes an assistant who does all my reading and all my writing. Growing up, I coped, compensated, and overcame by acting out, and I was pretty good at it. That approach obviously does not work in the business environment or in any other kind of working environment.

Most workers with LD have not had my good fortune. There is a man I know who works for a midsize private university. He is a mover, and he moves furniture and books for the school. He does an excellent job and is the head of the moving crew. But he postponed his well-deserved promotion for a long time. It seems the head of the crew must write the work schedules, create the budgets, and update the pay records. This information must be precise and accurate, and it is an excruciating and painstaking task for him. To avoid mistakes and embarrassment, he takes work home. Late into the night, with his dictionary in hand, he goes through his work word-by-word, number-by-number, over and over again to make sure everything is correct. This is the happy part of the story.

In reality, this man is a gifted designer. He could have been a mechanical engineer or an inventor. There is no way possible to calculate the cost of lost potential and talent in our work force. In the early 1990s, after I spoke at an LD conference, a quiet young woman came up to me to privately tell me her story. She said her husband had been offered an important promotion. The promotion required a family move overseas. It would have been a great opportunity for both her and her husband. But this intelligent lady with LD was terrified of embarrassing herself and jeopardizing her husband's career if it were discovered that she was unable to read or write. Because of this, her husband turned the opportunity down. Just as significant as their loss of opportunity of advancement and experience was the company's loss of this young man's full talents.

These illustrations ask the question, What can we do? I have a few ideas. If we ask, and we should, that schools become more accountable to all learners; if we ask, and we should, that schools do more to recognize and address LD at the earliest possible time in a child's education, then it is time that we ask our companies to offer similar support so that people feel comfortable with their LD and have vehicles in place to maximize their abilities.

One such vehicle could be a support group, composed of both management and staff, to help both employees with LD and their companies reap the benefits of untapped potential. Every company should enthusiastically support and actively sponsor an LD awareness support campaign for all its employees. This campaign should be ongoing. For every child who is identified during his or her school years, there are countless others who have gone unidentified and unassisted throughout their school years. They enter our work force frustrated because their skills are far below their potential. A support campaign should be aimed at making employees without LD more supportive and understanding of their colleagues.

But equally important is that many employers are simply not aware of the lost potential and productivity in their companies. Awareness and support groups can help to provide answers and encouragement, but it is necessary also to have educational programs to provide solutions for employees with LD and the company.

One company that I know of has a job enhancement program with confidential opportunities for identification of LD and a wide selection of courses taught by special educators. All of the course materials not only strengthen the employees' learning skills but also use business language and company situations to teach the skills. Everybody wins.

## INSPIRATION

Now I come to the third I, inspiration. Inspiration for most of us comes through the influence of others who have perhaps struggled with the same problems and succeeded despite them. A perfect example of giving inspiration to other people with LD occurs at The Lab School of Washington, D.C.'s annual Outstanding Learning Disabled Achievers Award Gala. There The Lab School of Washington[1] recognizes people who have become outstanding in their fields of endeavor despite their LD. We are all inspired by Robert Rauschenberg, one of the great artists of our time; sports heroes Bruce Jenner, Magic Johnson, and Greg Louganis; the governors of West Virginia and New Jersey; and many others who have received awards.

## CONCLUSIONS

By publicly recognizing these people and other individuals who may never have believed they had even a chance of success, they become an inspiration for others to go on and do what it takes to reach their goals. I believe we cannot afford to waste the potential talent of 10%–15% of the American work force.

---

[1] The Lab of Washington, D.C., is a day school for children with severe LD (K–12), a night school for adults with LD, and a clinic to test and treat people of all ages with LD.

# Chapter 20

# The Emotional Toll

*Sally L. Smith*

I wish to address the issue of unexplained underachievement. There are so many subtleties to the hidden handicap of learning disabilities (LD): the disorder within an individual that craves incredible order from the outside world, the disorder in space and in time, and the disorder of not knowing left from right, forward from backward. Having no sense of time can profoundly affect a person's performance in school, on the job, and in social relationships.

The whole social area of LD is inextricably woven into a person's language. So many people with LD really struggle with language and cannot carry on a dialogue. Many of them are visual thinkers; they can draw anything, but when they have to use words, they do not see pictures in their minds that have words attached to them—they just see the pictures. This can affect what goes on in the workplace, and it affects social relations as well.

I do not know if we think enough about the emotional toll of learning disabilities—the devastation of feeling stupid, the devastation of feeling that you are so different that you are unable to meet standards. What this does to one's sense of self-worth is terrible. So many individuals with LD feel rotten about themselves. The biggest concerns of those with LD and those who work with them have is for their self-esteem. Parents as well as teachers must make this a prime concern. We have to find every possible way to build on competencies and to build self-confidence.

## REALITIES OF INCLUSION

Some parents and school personnel have a tendency to say that inclusion is wonderful and that separate institutions or special schools are not. Most people agree with the concept of inclusion and want to see everyone have access to the broadest possible education. But there are certain students who cannot get the educational experience they need in an inclusive environment, or at least unless the inclusive environment has only 10–15 children in a class and includes special services.

In some cases, the continuum of services mandated by the Individuals with Disabilities Education Act of 1990 (IDEA) (PL 101-476) is very much needed, so that all kinds of resources are available where students are taught. But we must also realize that some students need to be in a special school or a special class for a while where they can speak out without fear of ridicule. They can be on a student council, they can have the lead in a play, and they can head an expedition in a small class, none of which could happen for them in a general education setting. They can develop competence and confidence to return to the mainstream so that they *can* succeed.

## DEVELOP TALENTS

What adults tell professionals who deal with people with LD is what children cannot—how at school they felt they were total failures. They can also tell professionals some of the things they did. As one adult said, "I was a terrible child. I failed childhood. But, boy, I'm a great adult!" And it is true. Look at the most manipulative children you know. Very often they become astonishingly creative and excellent entrepreneurs: The tinkerer who tinkered all through school is now a terrific mechanical engineer; the doodler is now a graphic artist; the student who never did his work but had an eye for beauty is now an antiques dealer; and the most stubborn of all children later on in life show fierce determination in accomplishing what they wanted to accomplish.

Educators and parents need to look for those talents. Career awareness and career training start in childhood—early childhood. We need to concentrate on students in junior high schools. The statistics on dropouts do not include seventh and eighth graders who drop out. High schools need more job apprenticeship programs that are supervised by LD specialists who match the strengths and needs of the student to the job.

## THE BEST TEACHING

People with LD need the best teaching possible. We need to teach teachers the way we want them to teach children! People with LD have distinct kinds of intelligences and very different styles of learning. Some are very visual, some are very kinesthetic, some learn through music, some learn through interpersonal relations, and some learn best from experience. Howard Gardner (1983) wrote about multiple intelligences as a set of seven intelligences. Teachers must teach to different intelligences and different styles of learning. If we teach teachers this way, then they will surely pass it on to their students. More children will be reached and helped to feel successful in school.

Students need experiential education. We hear over and over again from adults with LD: "I need to see it," "I need to touch it," or "I need to do it, let me try it!" We need more hands-on education, along with research-based strategies for teaching.

What we see happening to adults with LD is the result of their feeling bad about themselves—quitting classes and jobs, giving up, starting a course and dropping it, starting a job and leaving it. A lot of people with LD are more prone to depression than the general population, and so the mental health aspects of LD are also of prime concern.

## PUBLIC AWARENESS

We need to conduct public awareness campaigns about LD for employers. We ought to be providing public awareness about LD through business councils and civic organizations such as the Kiwanis and the Shriners. We need videos to show how simple some employee accommodations are.

I work with adults with LD at the Night School of The Lab School of Washington.[1] Some adults with learning disabilities at the Lab School night school can tell you that they worked for a store where they were not allowed to tape their supervisor's instructions and that when they finally found an employer who would let them tape instructions, they were able to show how effective they were. Similarly, I know of a dentist who had a series of cards he showed to an employee who, because of her auditory processing problems, could not function when he talked to her when she felt pressured, but when he used the cards, she could function. I know of a secretary who worked for a research corporation and found she was very efficient when she color-coded her files. I also know a person who wanted to demonstrate a new procedure that his firm could use and made a video to show the procedure because he could not get the words out properly in front of a large group.

Businesses need to know about these simple strategies. My experience is that adults with LD are eager to become co-investigators and co-workers on their problems. They often can develop a strategy to help themselves become more productive, which in turn makes the entire

---

[1] The Lab School of Washington, D.C., is an institution devoted to serving those with LD. It has a day school for 270 children with severe LD, a night school for 80–90 adults with LD, and a clinic for adults and children to test, tutor, and treat all aspects of LD and attention-deficit/hyperactivity disorders.

company more productive. Often the vocational programs that exist are not appropriate for people with LD; they are at too low a level, usually, and many of these people can function at a much higher level, even though they have very distinct disabilities.

It is never too late to learn! Literacy councils and learning disability specialists must work together to make sure that we help all the people who need special techniques to learn. What is required is skilled teaching based on an in-depth knowledge of LD. Being a kind volunteer who wants to help is not enough; adults with LD need the best of educators.

## CONCLUSIONS

Critical thinking is a key for students with LD that enables them to explore new worlds. As the world of technology forges ahead, we need to train minds to question, to dare, to risk, to ask, and to work on problem solving. What we want is for people with LD to know themselves: to know what they can do, what they are interested in, what they cannot do, what works for them, and what does not work. Self-advocacy is needed for empowerment. It is our national responsibility to empower people with LD, which will then empower our society to become more productive. Unexplained underachievement in people, if diagnosed and treated correctly, can often lead to astonishing creativity and accomplishments.

## REFERENCES

Gardner, H. (1983). *Frames of mind: The theory of multiple intelligences.* New York: Basic Books.
Individuals with Disabilities Education Act of 1990 (IDEA), PL 101-476. (October 30, 1990). Title 20, U.S.C. 1400 et seq.: *U.S. Statutes at Large, 104,* 1103–1151.

# Chapter 21

# Employment Realities and Priorities

*Paul J. Gerber*

The field of learning disabilities (LD) has come a long way in its thinking since 1981, when a group of invited professionals gathered for the Learning Disabled Adult State-of-the-Art Conference. It was a time when little was known about what happened to individuals with LD in adulthood, and the field needed to generate an agenda in order to think about and respond to adults with LD. One of the primary issues that emerged from that conference, and one that was hotly debated, was how to prepare individuals with LD for employment. Moreover, the big question was what vocational training and employment meant for the diverse population of adults with LD.

That was a starting point. Then, sometime in 1982, the Rehabilitation Services Administration (RSA) organized a conference that I euphemistically called What Do We Do Now? That conference was held after individuals with LD became eligible for vocational rehabilitation services as a result of a change in RSA reauthorization legislation. From that point, the field gained momentum in the area of adults with LD. The decade culminated with a conference sponsored by the President's Committee for the Employment of People with Disabilities entitled Pathways to Employment—A Consensus Conference on the Employment of People with Learning Disabilities (Brown, Gerber, & Dowdy, 1990). All in all, the 1980s was a decade that was fraught with chaos and distinguished by valiant efforts to sort out what was going on with the myriad issues pertaining to adults with LD and employment.

---

This chapter represents the extemporaneous remarks delivered by the author in response to the presentations given by the labor panel during the learning disabilities summit.

One of the important items discussed at the President's Committee conference (1990) was a statement that concerned the paradigm shift in both the government's role and the role of personal responsibility in the lives of individuals with disabilities. The paradigm shift for individuals with disabilities necessitates movement from dependence to independence and from paternalism to empowerment. I think that this is quite significant because, in essence, what the field is trying to do is to enable individuals with LD to complete school, to experience a successful transition process, and to become gainfully employed. But again, one of the problems is that there are two different cultures that exist for individuals with disabilities—the culture of school and the culture of the broader society. The school culture is largely understanding of disability issues and the processes and procedures that are mandated by legislation. The broader society is largely ignorant of the numerous issues that affect individuals with disabilities and, more specifically, individuals with "the invisible disability"—learning disabilities.

## INDIVIDUALS WITH LEARNING DISABILITIES IN THE WORKPLACE

This understanding leads directly to the thought that individuals with LD who leave schools need to be very good self-advocates. They need to have a lot of experiences under their belts to compete in the workplace. They need to have the ability to reframe their understanding and acceptance of their LD, possess general knowledge about learning disabilities, utilize good social skills, and have a working knowledge of how they learn best. Individuals with LD move from a culture in which people generally understand what LD are to a culture in which people do not really understand what LD are. For example, it is not uncommon for an employer to say, "Well, tell me about learning disabilities, isn't that really mental retardation?" All of sudden, the individual with LD is thrown back to square 1, because he or she has to be able to define and explain what LD are all about and how LD might be manifested in the work environment.

More and more individuals with LD are confronted with situations in which they need to advocate for themselves. Put yourself in the place of someone with LD who is going for a job interview—a person who was not given the opportunity to develop any kind of self-advocacy skills in school. How does this individual answer these questions: What kind of learning disability do you have? Are you distracted all the time? What are your strengths and what are your needs? What kinds of accommodations do you need to do your job? Are they expensive? We train people in-house for various jobs. How do you learn best? In this particular business, we use total quality management. Do you work well with other colleagues in a group setting?

Then there are other questions such as, We have specific timelines because of productivity; can you get things done on time? The ultimate question, perhaps the most important one, is, Why should I hire someone like you who has a disability when I can hire someone with the same skills who does not have a disability? How do you advocate for yourself in an employment setting when you have not come to grips with these issues before?

In 1991, I was researching what was happening in the first year of the newly implemented Americans with Disabilities Act of 1990 (ADA) (PL 101-336), and I was reminded by a manager who worked for a Fortune 500 corporation that the company was not an equal employment opportunity office or a social service agency. The corporation was driven by productivity, and ultimately that was the bottom line. Management had to answer to a chief executive officer, a governing board, and stockholders. Corporations and businesses are not adverse to hiring people with LD, but these employees need to be able to perform, and they need to be able to articulate the dimensions of their learning disabilities. This is important if they are to become part of their company and part of their corporate family.

I came across the *Journal of Arthritis* (Young, 1994) in a doctor's waiting room, and I decided to peruse it to see what kinds of topics were discussed. There was an article that talked about the Americans with Disabilities Act and the Job Accommodation Network (JAN), which is an exceptional service headquartered at West Virginia University. You call an 800 number, and very knowledgeable people help you find ways to accommodate individuals with all kinds of disabilities in the workplace. It helps employers and employees in this ADA era.

In addition, in a small box on the second page of that article was a poll that indicated that 41% of the people in this country knew about the ADA. That is somewhat understandable. Information about ADA is getting to the general public slowly but surely. But then I was shocked to read that the poll found that only 29% of people with disabilities knew about the ADA. How do we get the word out faster to individuals with disabilities about the Americans with Disabilities Act? Individuals with disabilities and LD have a wonderful opportunity since the ADA to empower themselves and become gainfully employed. Obviously, there is a tremendous amount of work to be done to get the word out about the ADA. Time is a-wastin', as they say. The ADA was passed in 1990, partially implemented in 1992, and fully implemented in 1994. Full implementation of ADA is an issue that we have to address in order to evaluate its effectiveness and efficiency.

## EMPLOYMENT TRENDS OF
## INDIVIDUALS WITH LEARNING DISABILITIES

We have a data trend in the field of LD that shows underemployment and unemployment of people with LD (Gerber, 1990). If you examine individualized education programs (IEPs) of students with LD who are leaving school, you see some vocational goals that are astounding. They are depressingly low in terms of the expectations you would have for individuals with LD. They underestimate individual capabilities and focus on needs, not on strengths. I think that appropriate vocational goals are an interesting area of study and researchers in the field of LD should investigate that issue further.

In addition, there are other interesting data trends concerning employment of individuals with LD (Peraino, 1992). We now know, as a result of some preliminary studies, that some students who dropped out of school meet others in the same job setting who finished school. Can you see the irony here? At age 16, some students with LD are leaving school and getting jobs. A couple of years later students who have completed high school enter the work force in the same jobs as those who dropped out. So one of the things we must address is, What are professionals doing for students who are 16–18 years old to prepare them for the workplace? What kind of integrity is there in a program in which dropping out of and completing high school have equivalent outcomes in job status, pay, and satisfaction?

Also, we must bear in mind that economies expand and contract. In an expanding economy, there are more opportunities for all individuals, including individuals with LD. In a contracting economy, there is far more competition for jobs so that the ways in which employment trends at the macroeconomic level have an effect on people with LD must be examined. Moreover, given the structural employment (those who are permanently counted as unemployed in labor statistics) of approximately 7–8 million people in this country at any given time, you have to wonder what percentage of those individuals who are structurally unemployed have LD.

There is also a pattern of discouraging workplace experiences for some individuals with LD. It is a shame that some individuals with LD get jobs, fail at those jobs, get other jobs, fail at those jobs, and keep repeating the same mistakes. There are numerous implications not only for postsecondary instruction but also for vocational instruction in school programs. There is an important linkage of training, curriculum, and experience to the entire transition process and school-to-work programs.

## CONCLUSIONS

We need more basic research on adults with LD and studies of the implications of such research for employment and employability. It is not enough to adopt theories about childhood LD and to apply them to adults with LD. We have to approach the issue of education, vocational instruction, and employment from an adult development perspective. The research data are improving. From reading the research, you would think that adulthood ends somewhere around the age of 39. We must address adulthood through the entire continuum and realize that there are many life-span variables that mediate the many things that happen between the ages of 18 and 88. We must view adulthood as the longest and most extensive stage of human development, in which there are trials and tribulations, particularly in employment, from job entry to job advancement.

Dr. Mel Levine, a physician and LD expert at the University of North Carolina, has said something that all of us should keep in mind. To paraphrase his thoughts liberally, it is possible for a student in second grade to look like a total washout, but some second graders who are absolutely terrible become wonderful adults who do some terrific things. They struggle through school and then go off to explore their interests and opportunities and become entrepreneurs and do amazing things.

They may have been terrible second graders and not so great seventh graders, but they become extraordinary 35-year-olds, 55-year-olds, and 75-year-olds. His observations are illustrated beautifully in the findings of studies with highly successful adults with LD (Gerber, Ginsberg, & Reiff, 1992). We must take a broader perspective. Ultimately, the point is that we consider the issues of education and link them to labor and employment issues, beginning and ending with thinking that considers learning disabilities across the entire life span.

## REFERENCES

Americans with Disabilities Act of 1990 (ADA), PL 101-336. (July 26, 1990). Title 42, U.S.C. 12101 et seq.: *U.S. Statutes at Large, 104,* 327–378.

Brown, D.S., Gerber, P.J., & Dowdy, C. (Eds.). (1990). *Pathways to employment for people with learning disabilities.* Washington, DC: President's Committee for the Employment of People with Disabilities.

Gerber, P.J. (1990). The problem, the future, the challenge: The issue of employability for persons with learning disabilities. In D.S. Brown, P.J. Gerber, & C. Dowdy (Eds.), *Pathways to employment for people with learning disabilities* (pp. 3–9). Washington, DC: President's Committee for the Employment of People with Disabilities.

Gerber, P.J., Ginsberg, R., & Reiff, H.B. (1992). Identifying alterable patterns in employment success for highly successful adults with learning disabilities. *Journal of Learning Disabilities, 25,* 475–487.

Peraino, J.M. (1992). Post-21 follow-up studies: How do special education graduates fare? In P. Wehman, *Life beyond the classroom: Transition strategies for young people with disabilities* (pp. 21–70). Baltimore: Paul H. Brookes Publishing Co.

President's Committee on the Employment of People with Disabilities. (1990). *From paternalism to productivity—whatever it takes.* Washington, DC: Author.

Young, G. (1994). What people with disabilities know about the Americans with Disabilities Act. *Journal of Arthritis, 20,* 16–17.

# SECTION IV

## JUSTICE

# Chapter 22

# Shaping Public Policy

*Judith E. Heumann*

Researchers, parents, advocates, and other professionals—in fact, all of us—need to play a more active role in helping government formulate effective public policy and legislation in the area of education, particularly as such policy and legislation relate to individuals with learning disabilities (LD).

## IMPLEMENTATION

The development of appropriate legislation and public policy is undertaken to ensure that the needs of the population—in this case, children with LD—are more effectively addressed. We have many years of experience with the Individuals with Disabilities Education Act (IDEA) (PL 101-476) and, although the legislation has been in place since 1975, we have all too often seen a lack of consistent and aggressive implementation of the Act during the 1980s and early 1990s. One of the areas in which this lack of across-the-board and uniform implementation is evident is in the area of learning disabilities.

When we look at children with LD, we discover that many of them are not being identified early on and are not receiving appropriate services; that, in many cases, sufficient numbers of qualified personnel are not available to provide appropriate interventions; and that parents are not always being appropriately involved in the educational process. We also have a particular concern for parents from minority groups and parents whose first language is not English. The methods used for assessing children from these backgrounds and the methods by which information is provided to their parents are not always adequate. Consequently, these parents are not always assuming the roles that they should in ensuring that their children receive appropriate services.

For our part, one of the things we have been doing to help increase the effectiveness of our efforts is to review our monitoring process under IDEA in order to strengthen it. We firmly believe that monitoring that focuses on those elements most closely associated with positive results for students, in combination with effective technical assistance, is of the highest importance. Also, some advocacy-related changes are already underway, such as improved parent and advocate input into the special education process. In addition, we are continually exploring new and innovative ways of making our monitoring process better and more efficient.

The bottom line is that if we monitor with a focus on improved student results, then I believe that we will have a real and positive impact on overall educational results. If we truly can find creative and effective ways of increasing state and local education agency performance through the monitoring process, we will be going a long way toward increasing effective implementation of IDEA and producing better results, increased compliance, and identification of exemplary programs and services.

Another area in which we have a responsibility to play a key role is in helping to ensure that each state is examining its particular personnel-training needs and addressing those needs effectively. In preparing for the reauthorization of IDEA, personnel training was one of the key areas upon which the Office of Special Education and Rehabilitative Services (OSERS) focused. We know that, despite our best intentions, if there is not a qualified pool of trained professionals, then the problems experienced by all disabled students, including those with learning disabilities, will continue to exist or, in many cases, will be exacerbated.

In preparing for the reauthorization of IDEA, we sought input regarding methods of effective personnel development and the training models that are working well in states and local communities; we then used this information in developing our proposed legislation.

Whether we are talking about enhancing compliance, improving our monitoring capacity, increasing the availability of appropriate services, or training personnel, our ultimate goal is increasing positive results for students that will lead to these individuals living as independently as possible in the community. My own background is in the area of independent living, and, having had a disability for most of my life, I know from personal experience that if a disabled individual is not receiving appropriate services, he or she will experience many frustrations. These frustrations can have catastrophic effects on the ultimate education and employment outcomes for an individual. Therefore, it is acutely important that we all work to ensure that the education we provide disabled students, including LD students, is of the highest possible quality.

But education does not exist in a vacuum, and all too often we have seen that the lack of appropriate services experienced by many of these children in our school systems is compounded by the tendency for societal problems to be "scapegoated" onto individuals with disabilities and their families. For example, there has been increased media attention to violence and disruption in the nation's schools. Children who have not received appropriate services and then develop behavioral problems in school are too frequently and wrongfully blamed for any problems in the classroom environment and subsequently removed from the school. Too often the solution has been to provide services to these children outside of the general classroom, or to expel them and cease educational services altogether. We in OSERS believe that, with the right supports, these children can be taught effectively in the general classroom, to the benefit of disabled and nondisabled students alike.

## LONG-TERM CONSEQUENCES

From a public policy point of view, I think it really is incumbent upon all of us in the field of disability to play a much more focused role in helping the general population understand the long-term implications of the failure to provide appropriate services to children and their families, and the concomitant failure to provide appropriate training for teachers and administrators. We know, for example, that a few well spent hours of in-service training can provide staff with the valuable tools they need in order to help provide quality support services for many of these children. Neither effective staff training nor appropriate classroom support must of necessity involve large expenditures of dollars, and, if we can focus on providing that help, we can move toward an educational system for disabled students that is more results-driven and more oriented to improved quality of life.

Despite the fact that it has been hard for our society to understand the long-term implications of how it either nurtures or ignores public policy issues as they relate to disability, we must do our part to help enhance that understanding. If we can improve public policies by helping to reshape attitudes, we will go a long way toward improving the quality of services for all disabled students. The IDEA is a very strong piece of legislation. However, its effectiveness is directly linked to the degree that society as a whole actively supports its tenets and mandates, seeing it as a set of principles to be upheld, rather than as a set of mandates to be challenged.

## FAILURE TO PROVIDE SERVICES

In simple terms, we know that all children, disabled or not, who receive appropriate services early on have better results and are more likely to succeed in school. We know, however, that, in many cases, legislators are not attuned to this basic principle. For this to change, it is critical that we identify who the policy makers are—the people who determine the types of programs to be developed and where the dollars are going to be expended. We need to ensure that we live in a society where children can grow up to be well educated and productive. The key that can help to guide us in our efforts to shape effective public policy is the knowledge that policy makers are usually guided by the opinions, concerns, and fears of their constituents.

As an example, it is critically important to emphasize that delinquency is not a by-product of LD or any other disability category, but rather results from the impact of the failure of our system to provide appropriate services for these children. The negative and false perception that delinquency is synonymous with disability is having a deleterious effect on public policy, and it is up to us all to help bring about a positive change in this perception. Educators, administrators, legislators, and the general public need to know that the kinds of interventions that are successful in many cases are relatively simple.

Researchers, advocates, and concerned individuals in the area of LD need to work more actively with the media to get the message out in a clear way that allows people to understand that higher standards, quality services, parental involvement, and increased educational opportunities are all within our grasp.

## CONCLUSIONS

As advocates and experts, we are charged with the responsibility of working within both the educational system and the larger context of our society to change the negative misperceptions that exist about LD students, to emphasize the importance of quality services, and to emphasize the need for higher standards and better results. It is up to us to emphasize that it is not disability that is the problem in the classroom, but rather the lack of appropriate services and trained personnel. It is up to us to explain the simple truth that if every child with a disability were removed from the public schools (50% of whom are identified with learning disabilities), you would not see a markedly different classroom, full of peace and tranquility.

It is time for public policy and legislation to be shaped and developed by the average interested person. Those of us involved in disability and education issues need to see ourselves as people who understand the problems of the disabled population, who understand that empowerment for parents, empowerment for individuals with disabilities, and empowerment for teachers, superintendents, and principals can really improve the lives of so many students with learning disabilities. Greater accountability is needed from state school administrators to ensure that we are no longer allowing a population of children to be discarded, and that we no longer think that we can remedy the problem by conducting only the least activity required under the law. The power to empower the education community and the children it serves is in our hands.

## REFERENCES

Individuals with Disabilities Education Act of 1990 (IDEA), PL 101-476 (October 30, 1990). Title 20, U.S.C. §§ 1400 et seq.: *U.S. Statutes at Large, 104*, 1103–1151.

# Chapter 23

# The Justice System

*Carolyn R. Eggleston*

Characteristics associated with learning disabilities (LD) can create problems for a student in school, at home, and at work. Students with LD are often alienated, isolated, and misunderstood, which can lead to difficulties in personal relationships and life goal attainment. For the student with LD who comes in contact with the justice system, these characteristics can be life threatening. Yet, many times, the adjudication process does not even include information about an individual's learning disability. Many Americans consider the fact that a person has LD irrelevant once a crime has been committed. The United States no longer has the luxury of establishing a system of us against them, however, and we must consider all students as part of society. We are truly all part of "us."

Although we still do not know the exact numbers of individuals with LD in the justice system, we do know that students with disabilities are overrepresented in correctional facilities. The most accurate estimates suggest that at least 42% of the adults in correctional institutions are eligible for special education (Eggleston, 1983; Nelson, Rutherford, & Wolford, 1987). A large proportion of these individuals have LD. Most states have made strides in providing special education services in juvenile correctional systems, but much needs to be done in adult correctional systems.

## JUVENILE DELINQUENCY

There have been a number of theories proposed about the supposed link between LD and juvenile delinquency. The assumption has been that students with LD are somehow more likely than students without LD to become juvenile delinquents, particularly because males are overrepresented in both groups. Although this link has not been proved, there are several theories that suggest that there is at least a link between the two groups.

The first theory about this link is the susceptibility theory. This theory holds that the characteristics of an individual with LD make him or her more susceptible to committing a crime. These characteristics include impulsivity, suggestibility, and poor social perception skills, which may be present in both students with LD and juvenile delinquents.

The second theory, the school failure theory, suggests that an individual with LD who has failed and been failed by school may go looking for acceptance in another arena. Perhaps the most poignant example of this is the student who desecrates a school. Such a statement against the school speaks of rage and disappointment.

The third theory proposes that differential treatment exists and that an individual with LD is treated differently from an individual without LD when coming in contact with the justice system. Again, the very characteristics of an individual with LD may prompt an inappropriate response to an officer's first question and to the request for an accurate account of a crime. We know that individuals with LD are more likely to penetrate further into the justice system and to stay longer than their peers without LD (National Council of Juvenile and Family Court Judges, 1988; Nelson et al., 1987).

## EDUCATION OF INDIVIDUALS WITH LEARNING DISABILITIES IN CORRECTIONAL SYSTEMS

Whatever the link or cause, we know that individuals with LD are in both juvenile and adult correctional systems. State correctional systems have been making great strides in providing educational programming for individuals with LD, but there are some inherent problems. Legislation, including the Americans with Disabilities Act of 1990 (ADA) (PL 101-336) and the Individuals with Disabilities Education Act of 1990 (IDEA) (PL 101-476) may require some special interpretation in the correctional system. IDEA, especially, focuses on the special education needs of children in public schools. Some articulation is needed to make a better fit with correctional institutions. Cooperative agreements between state departments of education and correctional education agencies have been developed in a number of states, and these states are the most successful in working through problems. Unfortunately, one major source of implementation is still litigation.

## PROBLEMS OF IMPLEMENTATION

Most juvenile correctional agencies have some special education services available, but problems continue. Programs were developed to meet the guidelines of PL 94-142, the Education for All Handicapped Children Act of 1975, and are being adapted to meet the requirements of IDEA. Several states have established particularly interesting implementation plans, among them Virginia, Maryland, Connecticut, and Minnesota. Problems remain in implementing ADA, particularly in adult facilities, because programs for individuals with LD are not available in most adult systems.

Implementation difficulties can be found from the first court contact to the transition back into the community. Perhaps the overarching issue is that the agencies that adjudicate and incarcerate are not educational entities. Their purpose is the determination of guilt or innocence and the provision of security and custody.

Some areas covered by legislation are particularly difficult to implement in the justice system. One example is the problem that occurs with confidentiality and the transfer of records. Although PL 94-142 and later legislation were designed to correct inappropriate access and increase contact with parents, the result for the correctional system has been that records arrive from public schools much too late to be of use, if they arrive at all. Often special education records are not available at adjudication. The confidentiality and transfer requirements of correctional agencies can interact with special education requirements to that teachers in the facility sometimes never see the educational records.

Testing and assessment of LD presents particular problems for the justice system. Movement through the adjudication and reception process can be very rapid. In court, guilt or innocence is under scrutiny, not the presence of a disability. Once assigned to corrections, the evaluation and diagnostic process may be measured in days, not in weeks. A ward or inmate may be moved to a number of different facilities during this process, with not enough time being spent at any one facility to address real concerns. As a result, mandated time lines often are unmet and the individual does not have access to appropriate programming.

A special difficulty exists in providing qualified personnel—from security staff to evaluators to teachers. Security staff are not always aware of or trained in the requirements of ADA and IDEA. Specialized, ongoing training needs to be developed for personnel, ranging from the court service worker to the correctional officer on the block. There has not been a commitment on the part of most court and correctional systems to providing this training.

Educators in correctional school programs, although trained to teach, may not be credentialed special educators. Even when they are certified in special education, there are few training programs that focus on the needs of adjudicated students. It is extremely difficult to obtain and keep good, qualified educators. In some cases, the number of students with LD is so low in a particular institution that a certified teacher may have to travel between facilities or a student inmate may be placed in the one facility that has certified teachers. This then may conflict with the requirements of the least restrictive environment. More efforts must be made to train correctional system educators about students with LD.

We also know that there is a significant overrepresentation of individuals from minority groups in custody and in special education (California Department of Education, 1994; U.S. Department of Justice, 1992). Special problems exist for inmates with LD with limited English proficiency. Correctional systems are struggling to provide the most basic services in a second language. Testing, evaluation, and instruction may be conducted only in English. Agencies that are able to provide these services in another language most often provide them in Spanish. The many other languages represented in the institution may never be addressed.

The requirement of the least restrictive environment introduced in PL 94-142 has presented problems in correctional settings. Most states have interpreted the requirement to mean that students with disabilities in an institution must be housed and managed in a way that is no more restrictive than that of their peers in the institution. Although this interpretation has worked for most students with LD, problems continue in segregated units and during disciplinary actions.

Parental involvement for students ages 18 and younger has continued to be a major problem in some states. Although students with disabilities in custody are wards of the state, parents retain residual rights unless these have been legally terminated. The natural parent is therefore the appropriate contact person in the special education process. In many cases, however, the parent cannot be found. Greater efforts must be made by some states to involve parents. When parental rights have been terminated, surrogate parent procedures must be developed. Parental involvement creates difficulty for correctional systems, which traditionally have not accepted the idea of outsiders judging activities inside the institution.

## TRANSITION SERVICES

Transition services from the community and back to the community are required for students with LD in correctional institutions (IDEA, 1990). Although state systems often offer good programs within the structured environment of the institution, there is usually a significant breakdown at both transition points. Very little is done to provide an appropriate transition of a student into a correctional facility from the community. Attempts are being made to provide help with transition upon release from the facility, but this has been slow. Some states have legal prohibitions against contact with the ward or inmate once he or she has left state care. This makes transition impossible and must be changed.

Wards and inmates with LD have significant problems in an institutional setting, and some attention has been given to them. This cannot be said of the adult inmate with LD in a correctional facility. Limited attention exists despite the fact that IDEA is intended for students under the age of 22, and there are many inmates in adult correctional facilities under this age. ADA applies to all inmates in correctional facilities, juvenile and adult. There is much less awareness, however, of the needs of the adult offender with learning disabilities in the correctional system. Indeed, the focus has been on taking things away, not providing them.

## CONCLUSIONS

Strides have been made in providing appropriate programs for individuals with LD who are in contact with the justice system. Much more remains to be done. It is recommended that a task force be formed to study these issues, perhaps coordinated by the National Center for Learning Disabilities and the Correctional Education Association. The problems faced by students with LD in the justice system are relevant to all of us. These students remain part of our society; they are *us*.

## REFERENCES

Americans with Disabilities Act of 1990 (ADA), PL 101-336. (July 26, 1990). Title 42, U.S.C. §§ 12101 et seq.: *U.S. Statutes at Large, 104,* 327–378.

California Department of Education. (1994). *Ethnicity of California's teachers and students.* Sacramento, CA: Educational Demographics Unit, Research, Evaluation, and Technology.

Education for All Handicapped Children Act of 1975, PL 94-142. (August 23, 1977). Title 20, U.S.C. §§ 1401 et seq.: *U.S. Statutes at Large, 89,* 773–796.

Eggleston, C. (1983). *Results of a national correctional/special education survey.* Washington, DC: U.S. Department of Education.

Individuals with Disabilities Education Act of 1990 (IDEA), PL 101-476. (October 30, 1990). Title 20, U.S.C. §§ 1400 et seq.: *U.S. Statutes at Large, 104,* 1103–1151.

National Council of Juvenile and Family Court Judges. (1988). *Learning disabilities and the juvenile justice system.* Reno, NV: Author.

Nelson, C.M., Rutherford, R.B., & Wolford, B. (1987). *Special education in the criminal justice system.* Columbus, OH: Merrill.

U.S. Department of Justice, Bureau of Justice Statistics. (1992). *Prisoners in 1991.* Washington, DC: U.S. Government Printing Office

# Chapter 24

# Review of Research on Learning Disabilities and Juvenile Delinquency

*Dorothy Crawford*

> *Life must be understood backward. But. . . it must be lived forward.*
> Søren Kierkegaard (1843/1967)

The philosophy espoused by Kierkegaard serves as the basis for this chapter, which focuses on what we know about the link between learning disabilities (LD) and juvenile delinquency (JD). Important data and knowledge have been collected regarding the LD–JD link through a major research and demonstration project (Crawford, 1982). The magnitude, scope, and the lengthy process of validating the project give credence to the results gleaned from it.

## LOOKING BACKWARD

In 1976, under the sponsorship of the Learning Disabilities Association of America (LDA), a small group of parents of adolescents with LD (who were also professionals in the fields of education, juvenile corrections, and mental health), embarked on a plan to conduct a series of conferences, Youth in Trouble. The purpose of the conferences was to establish awareness of the possibility of an empirical relationship between LD and JD.

This same group approached the National Institute of Juvenile Justice and Delinquency Prevention (NIJJDP) of the U.S. Department of Justice to request an in-depth investigation regarding a relationship or connection between LD and JD. In 1975, NIJJDP commissioned a study by the American Institutes for Research (AIR) to review the literature, summarize the available data, and make policy recommendations. The AIR report (Murray, 1976) concluded that the existing literature clearly indicated that the learning problems of delinquents warranted further investigation. Thus, the report recommended that carefully controlled research be conducted to determine the incidence of LD among a few basic populations, including juvenile offenders and nondelinquents. Also, the report recommended conducting a project to assess the effectiveness of academic intervention in improving the educational achievements and in reducing the delinquency of juvenile delinquents with LD.

In light of these recommendations, NIJJDP funded a 12-year project beginning in the fall of 1976 through two grants. One grant was awarded to the Association for Children with Learning Disabilities (ACLD, now LDA) to 1) facilitate the conduct of the overall project, 2) design and conduct an intervention program, and 3) conduct 24 regional seminars over a period of 6 years to disseminate the data. The second grant was awarded to Creighton University (later moved to the National Center for State Courts) and assisted by the Educational Testing Service to 1) undertake large-scale studies of the relationship between LD and JD and 2) carry out an extensive evaluation of the effectiveness of the intervention program. Both cross-sectional and longitudinal studies of the relationship between LD and JD were conducted to obtain as much information as possible about the causal effects of LD.

The project and its participants were based in three metropolitan areas: Baltimore, Indianapolis, and Phoenix. The cross-sectional study consisted of 1,943 adolescent males: 973 from public schools who had not been adjudicated delinquent, and 970 who had been adjudicated delinquent by juvenile courts sampled from public schools, juvenile courts, and correctional facilities.

Of the delinquent sample, 34% were confined to youth correctional institutions, and 66% were on probation, parole, or in after-care supervision. The average age of the boys was 15 years. They came from varied ethnic backgrounds: 45% were Caucasian, 38% were African American, 6% were Hispanic, 4% were Native American, and 7% came from other ethnic groups. Of the delinquent youths who were classified as having LD, half were selected at random by the evaluators for inclusion in the intervention program, and the remainder were assigned to a control group.[1] The sample for the longitudinal study comprised 351 boys from the group of 973 official nondelinquents in the sample of the cross-sectional study.

---

[1]A longitudinal investigation (Dunivant, 1982) was conducted 4 years subsequent to the cross-sectional study. Its purpose was to assess the development of delinquency over a 2-year period.

Some highlights of the results of the study concerning research and intervention are presented below.

## Research Findings

Among the major research findings was that evidence for the existence of a relationship between LD and self-reported delinquent behavior was statistically significant; that is, the observed relationship was not likely to have been the product of chance events in sampling or measurement. Although the mean difference in seriousness of general delinquent behavior between the group with LD and the group without LD was not significant, the groups did differ significantly in frequency of violent acts (e.g., assault with a dangerous weapon and gang fighting), in marijuana and alcohol use, and in number of school discipline problems. LD was strongly related to official delinquency. The probability of being officially adjudicated (on a national measure) was 9 of every 100 adolescent males with LD compared with 4 of every 100 adolescent males without LD. To put it even more dramatically, the odds of being adjudicated delinquent were 220% greater for adolescents with LD than for their peers without LD. In addition, the same probability applied to being taken into custody by the police.

The incidence of LD in the adjudicated delinquent group was 36%. This indicates that a substantial proportion of official delinquents were individuals with LD. The greater delinquency of youths with LD could not be attributed to sociodemographic characteristics or a tendency to disclose socially disapproved behaviors. The data indicated that LD contributed to increases of delinquent behavior both directly and indirectly through school failure. In terms of the indirect contribution, there was not sufficient information available to determine which specific causal processes (e.g., frustration/aggression, economic incentives) were the bases of this effect. Results demonstrated that the effect of LD on delinquent behavior can occur without being mediated by school failure.

Furthermore, for comparable offenses, juveniles with LD had higher probabilities of arrest and adjudication than juveniles without LD. Among adjudicated delinquents, there was no difference between those with LD and those without LD in terms of incarceration. As nondelinquent boys advanced through their teens, those with LD experienced greater increases in delinquent activities than their peers without LD.

## Intervention Program Findings

The results of the intervention program showed that there was significant improvement in academic achievement (growth) in 1 school year with 55–65 hours of instruction per individual. In addition, there was a dramatic decrease in delinquency with at least 40–50 hours of instruction. The instruction was significantly effective in preventing or controlling delinquency. A major factor in preventing delinquency seemed to be not only academic skills improvement but also the nature of the relationship between the adolescents and the LD specialists in the program. Although the model of instruction did significantly foster academic and intellectual growth and reduce delinquent activity, it did not statistically change or improve school attitudes.

A program of remedial instruction was conducted to study its effects on academic achievement and to prevent or control future delinquency in the target population. The remediation program was based on an academic model that provided direct instruction in the youth's functional areas of greatest learning deficiency—for example, expressive language, reading, or arithmetic. Trained specialists in LD worked with participants individually or in small groups. Typically, remedial sessions that lasted approximately 50 minutes were held twice weekly in convenient locations, such as public schools, training schools, and community centers. The LD specialist and the youth worked to improve the youth's academic skills and his or her attitude toward school. A performance-based educational model was adopted in which clear learning goals were established individually for each participant, curriculum materials were carefully chosen to be compatible with the adolescent's strongest learning modality (visual, auditory, tactile, or motor), and teaching strategies and goals were constantly reevaluated on the basis of regular objective assessments of the child's progress.

## Implications of the Results

The results of the study carry a number of implications. These data alone indicate that youths with LD are a high-risk group of adolescents in need of special services. Youths with LD are a population at relatively higher risk for becoming trapped in the juvenile justice system than their peers without LD. This comparison should concern us because although only a relatively small proportion of the youth population is affected by LD, it appears to be one of the important causes of delinquency.

Intervention did reduce the likelihood of future delinquent behavior and official contacts with the juvenile justice system. The results implied that performance-based educational programs, which use direct instruction techniques, would help reduce the delinquency of adolescents with LD.

The great social and economic costs of crime and lost human potential can be avoided if intervention programs successfully prevent children and teenagers with nonadjudicated LD from becoming delinquent and rehabilitate those adolescents with LD who have already been adjudicated. Thus, the most significant implications of the project were in regard to public policy in education and juvenile justice.

## Data Dissemination

Dissemination of the project's results and data commenced in 1982. The 24 regional seminars were conducted with approximately 2,500 individuals attending between 1982 and 1989. The purpose of the regional seminars was to present and demonstrate to policy makers, program planners, and concerned individuals the results of the study to identify, discuss, and explore its implications at the state and local levels regarding continuing research, informed policy and program development, and funding issues.

Also, subsequent to the research and demonstration portion of the project, momentous events took place in relation to the study and dissemination of the data. The reauthorization of the Juvenile Justice and Delinquency Prevention Act Amendments of 1977 (PL 95-415) included sections that specifically set aside monies for instruction and programs about LD and the juvenile with LD. The National Council of Juvenile and Family Court Judges (NCJFCJ) and the American Bar Association (ABA) established a stand on LD for their training institutes and national conferences. The young attorneys' section of the ABA passed a resolution recognizing the special needs of the juvenile with LD. The Department of Education has funded numerous grants to conduct research and demonstration projects to broaden the database (e.g., Hazel, Schumaker, & Deshler, 1980). Within both the public and private sectors, there have been extensive policies and programs implemented. There have been hundreds of articles in journals publishing the results of many projects on the link between LD and JD (e.g., Ball et al., 1982–1983). There have been myriad direct service programs implemented for this at-risk group of adolescents.

The National Center for Learning Disabilities must be given additional credit for dramatically broadening awareness, knowledge, and understanding of the juvenile with LD who is at risk for penetrating the juvenile justice system. As early as 1986, the center established a major initiative providing funding for the NCJFCJ (National Council of Juvenile and Family Court Judges, 1986) and the ABA to produce benchmark journals (American Bar Association, 1983) on the connection between LD and JD and for the ACLD project to produce instruction manuals for probation and parole officers in the juvenile justice system (Crawford, 1985). In addition, the center produced a stream of articles on LD and JD in its publication and continues to view the issue as a priority (e.g., National Center for Learning Disabilities, 1989).

## LIVING FORWARD

Nevertheless, there continue to be profound gaps in knowledge of LD and services for the population with LD. Substance abuse, schools and delinquency, youth development, and intervention alternatives should be designated as priority issues for policy and decision makers to address the needs and treatment of youths with LD. An examination of available data indicates, for example, that the school environment is an influential factor with respect to delinquent behavior, and the schools are where adolescents experience success or failure and acceptance or alienation. Serious and violent crime in the education system and in the community continues to be a profound issue with corresponding problems. This phenomenon appears to occur particularly in adolescents with LD. Therefore, the following recommendations for what needs to be done, at minimum, to help close the gaps in knowledge, research, and intervention are presented.

## CONCLUSIONS

First, research should be conducted concerning LD as a high-risk factor in serious violent crime on the part of delinquents. Such research could 1) determine the specific causal processes in the links between LD and JD; 2) examine the cause of why youths with LD commit a disproportionate number of violent offenses, particularly in an educational environment; 3) determine the degree of severity of delinquent behavior patterns of juvenile offenders with LD and their propensity to become career criminals; 4) determine family characteristics that are involved in this correlation between LD and JD; and 5) examine the effects of substance abuse and gang involvement in relation to LD.

Second, the critical need for services for this high-risk population needs to be addressed by mandating a societal change in attitudes and understanding. This important societal change requires 1) an all-out public awareness campaign in public forum settings to guide the formulation of informed public and program policy, and 2) the dissemination of research and program development results to federal, state, and local organizations in the public and private sectors to garner interest and commitments at all levels.

In summary, we must have practical research, program development, education, technical assistance, and information dissemination. These efforts require the cooperation of every segment at every level of government, the identification of specific key players who are involved in changing the system and their responsibilities and roles, total commitment to this mission by designated entities in the private sector, and allocation of funds by both public and private sectors.

# REFERENCES

American Bar Association. (1983). *Learning disabilities and the juvenile justice system: What lawyers should know.* Washington, DC: National Legal Resource Center for Child Advocacy and Protection.

Ball, E.R., et al. (1982–1983, Winter). Incarceration and the rate of achievement of learning disabled juvenile delinquents. *Journal of Experimental Education, 51*(2), 54–57.

Crawford, D. (1982). *A study investigating the correlation between learning disabilities and juvenile delinquency.* Washington, DC: U.S. Government Printing Office.

Crawford, D. (1985). *Training manual on learning disabilities and juvenile delinquency.* Phoenix, AZ: Research and Development Training Institutes, Inc.

Dunivant, N. (1982). *The relationship between learning disabilities and juvenile delinquency: Brief summary of research findings.* Williamsburg, VA: National Center for State Courts.

Hazel, J.S., Schumaker, J.B., & Deshler, D.D. (1980). *Research approaches to studying the link between learning disabilities and juvenile delinquency.* Lawrence: University of Kansas, Institute for Research in Learning Disabilities.

Juvenile Justice and Delinquency Prevention Act and Amendments of 1977, PL 95-415.

Kierkegaard, S. (1967). *Journals and papers* (Vol. 1) (H.V. Hong & E.H. Hong, Trans.). Bloomington: Indiana University Press. (Original work published 1843)

Murray, C.A. (1976). *The link between learning disabilities and juvenile delinquency: Current theory and knowledge.* Washington, DC: U.S. Government Printing Office.

National Center for Learning Disabilities. (1989). *Their world.*

National Council of Juvenile and Family Court Judges. (1986). Learning disabilities and the juvenile justice system. *Juvenile and Family Courts Journal, 37*(3).

# Chapter 25

# The Americans with Disabilities Act of 1990

## Effects on Students with Learning Disabilities

*John L. Wodatch*

There is a good reason why someone from the Civil Rights Division of the U.S. Department of Justice is concerned about people with learning disabilities (LD): Individuals with LD are covered by the Americans with Disabilities Act of 1990 (ADA) (PL 101-336), and we in the Civil Rights Division are responsible for enforcing the rights of those individuals under the ADA.

In 1989, when the U.S. Senate was considering the ADA, one of the issues was the definition of *disability.* It was very clear from the beginning, if you look at the House and Senate reports, that individuals with LD were included in the definition of *disability.*

The ADA's definition of *disability* is a long one, but the key point is that it is an individual who has a physical or mental impairment that substantially limits a life activity. It is clear that individuals with LD have, in the words of the statute, a mental impairment and that learning is a major life activity. So, difficulty in achieving the major life activity of learning includes individuals with LD within the class of persons with disabilities under the ADA.

There is a little confusion about exactly what that means. One view is that if we just give some extra time for testing, individuals with LD compete at the same level as individuals without LD. Therefore, they are not individuals with a disability. That is not the position taken by the

Department of Justice or that the law itself takes. This position holds that an individual with a learning disability is similar to an individual who has diabetes and takes insulin. The fact that he or she takes insulin means that he or she can function in society, but it does not mean that the individual does not have a disability. Similarly, people with LD who are achieving at the same level as their peers because of accommodations such as double time and special services are still protected by the ADA.

## PROVISIONS OF THE ADA

The Americans with Disabilities Act is a very comprehensive statute. First, in the area of employment, the ADA covers all employers with 15 or more employees. The ADA covers every state and local government regardless of the number of employees in a state or governmental unit. Employment rights for individuals with LD are covered. Employers who dictate that they will not hire someone who has a learning disability are violating the law. Such action is illegal.

One interesting feature of the ADA is a preemployment inquiry prohibition. This means it is a violation of federal law for an employer to ask in a job interview or on a form if an individual has a learning disability. An employer can ask questions about job-related functions. An employer may say that reading, reading quickly, or reading under pressure is an essential function of the job, but it needs to be proved that it is an essential function. There are many professions and many jobs for which that skill is not necessary and can be accommodated reasonably. This is one avenue of protection for individuals with LD.

The most far-reaching aspect of the employment directives is the obligation to provide reasonable accommodation. Employers must make reasonable accommodation to individuals with disabilities unless it is an undue hardship, which is defined by very high standards. An employer has an obligation to provide accommodations such as readers, special computers, rest periods, job restructuring, or flexible time schedules as long as the accommodation is not an undue hardship on the operation of that employer's business.

All activities of state and local governments are covered by the ADA. Other services such as licensing processes and testing services are all protected and covered by the Americans with Disabilities Act of 1990.

The private sector is also covered by the ADA. Title 3 of the ADA covers places of public accommodation. The definition in Title 3 is very broad and covers private entities that provide goods and services to the public. The Department of Justice considers that the ADA covers everything from aquariums to zoos and from birthing centers to funeral parlors. Essentially, the ADA covers every part of the private sector.

At the Department of Justice, much of our work with the ADA has concerned adults with LD. Students at the college level with LD, regardless of whether they are admitted, have been a big issue for the department. Accommodations in testing for bar reviews, as well as accommodations for students in bar review courses, are all covered under the ADA.

In 1992, the Department of Justice filed a brief in a case in New York. (*Rosenthal v. New York State Board of Law Examiners*). This case illustrates many of the key issues of accommodation. Rosenthal had requested a separate room for taking the bar exam, twice the amount of time to take the exam, and a person to transcribe answers onto a multiple-choice grid. The issue that was joined in court was whether these accommodations were required. It was the position of the Department of Justice that they were required, and the case was eventually settled in Rosenthal's favor.

## PROVING THE EXISTENCE OF LEARNING DISABILITIES

The above case is instructive because it raises another difficult issue that may confront many concerned with LD. How do you prove that an individual has a learning disability? What kind of documentation is needed to prove this?

The Department of Justice holds that it is appropriate for a testing entity to require evidence that an individual has a learning disability and needs the accommodations that are being discussed. That requirement, however, must also be reasonable. Therefore, the position of the Department of Justice is that the state should accept, without further inquiry, documentation that represents the judgment of a qualified professional who has made an individualized assessment of the individual and who has expertise in the disability in question. When these criteria are met, there should be no reason to put a burden on the person with the disability to undergo further testing or to incur expenses in that regard.

## ACCOMMODATIONS FOR TESTS

Testing accommodations are really very simple. Such accommodations include extra time to take a test—double time is a very common accommodation. In addition, extra days may be needed to complete a test. For example, if a test is 6 hours long, just giving someone 12 hours in the course of a single day is not going to fairly test that individual, because of fatigue and other factors. Therefore, rest periods are often needed. A scribe to help write the answers for an individual, readers, large-print material, material on audiotape, and use of computer equipment are all types of accommodations that we have encountered.

It is the obligation of the Department of Justice to enforce the Americans with Disabilities Act, and we are very serious about doing this. We are very serious about ensuring that the rights of students with LD are protected according to law. Those of us at the Department of Justice really want to hear from the general public and from advocates about these issues.

## CONCLUSIONS

We have worked with the Office of Civil Rights, the U.S. Department of Education, the U.S. Department of Health and Human Services, and the other federal agencies concerned with civil rights efforts. Section 504 of the Rehabilitation Act of 1973 (PL 93-112) provides similar obligations of entities that receive federal funds. Together with those federal agencies, we are going to ensure that the rights of all students with LD and of all individuals with disabilities in this society are protected.

## REFERENCE

Americans with Disabilities Act of 1990 (ADA), PL 101-336. (July 26, 1990). Title 42, U.S.C. §§ 12101 et seq.: *U.S. Statutes at Large, 104,* 327–378.

# Chapter 26

# The Link Between Learning Disabilities and Behavior

*G. Emerson Dickman*

This chapter examines the link between learning disabilities (LD) and antisocial behavior. A hypothesis is offered that suggests that subtypes of LD vary significantly in the severity of risk or predisposition to the development of antisocial behavior and that such risk is enhanced in the presence of comorbidity and environmental factors such as school failure, low socioeconomic status, and adopted child status. It is argued herein that such risk is not properly addressed, because of fundamental weaknesses in the system of special education that preclude effective intervention.

## LINK BETWEEN LEARNING DISABILITIES AND DELINQUENT BEHAVIOR

Yes, no, maybe—these are the answers to be found in the research seeking to establish the existence of a link between LD and behavior. There are studies that support a strong correlation (Wilgosh & Paitich, 1982),[1] others that support a modest correlation (Lane, 1980), and still others that indicate that there is no correlation (Broder, Dunivant, Smith, & Sutton, 1981; Cornwell & Bawden, 1992; Spreen, 1981). Other studies indicate that people react differently to a child with LD than they do to a child without LD. Such studies indicate that individuals with LD receive differential treatment because of their inability to communicate effectively and are therefore more likely to be taken into custody by police (Thompson, 1985), to be found delinquent by a juvenile court (Broder et al., 1981), or to receive more severe penalties (Spreen, 1981). When indi-

---

[1]Many of the studies supporting a strong correlation are retrospective. They preselect a delinquent population and investigate for evidence of LD.

viduals with LD get in trouble, the same difficulties with language and pragmatics that lead to academic difficulty interfere with their ability to explain themselves and present a sympathetic posture. Many children with LD, in the face of an accusation, look guilty, act guilty, and cannot articulate satisfactory explanations.

The inconsistency found in these studies is more a result of a lack of comparable cohorts across studies than it is of poor methodologies within studies. To get consistent generalizable outcomes, research must be done with a similar population across studies. If research attempts to determine the link between balls and broken windows, it matters whether the study is limited to golf balls, basketballs, or baseballs. Rourke (1988) referred to such studies as addressing undifferentiated groups of learning disabilities. For example, studies that identified the LD population by indices of reading proficiency (Cornwell & Bawden, 1992) or by proficiency in content curriculum requiring reading proficiency (Rhodes & Reiss, 1969) identified an LD population that is psycholinguistically involved in terms of left hemisphere weaknesses (Pennington, 1991). Such an individual, with relative strength in visual–spatial skills and the ability to envisage different perspectives from a single vantage point (Masland, 1975; West, 1991), is not at significant risk for delinquent behavior (Rourke, 1988). Because of weak auditory processing skills (Harnadek & Rourke, 1994), however, such an individual may very well have difficulty meeting the communications demands of an apprehending officer or judge, which may help explain the differential treatment hypothesis of Broder et al. (1981), Spreen (1981), and Thompson (1985).

Studies of adjudicated youth who are identified as having LD by relying on evidence of previously recorded diagnosis (Broder et al., 1981) or that ruled out emotional disturbance (ED) (Broder et al., 1981) fail to recognize that the individual with a nonverbal learning disability (NLD) does not experience early academic failure sufficient for identification as being eligible for special education services (Semrud-Clikeman & Hynd, 1991).[2] In other words, because of strengths in psycholinguistic and rote verbal learning skills (Rourke, 1993), the young NLD pupil's academic achievement is not sufficiently discrepant from potential to demand the attention of school personnel. By the time the NLD child's deficits in visual–spatial–organizational and problem-solving skills (Rourke, 1993) begin to interfere sufficiently with academic achievement in the fourth or fifth grade, it is often too late to prevent the social and emotional conse-

---

[2]"One might also assume that this disability can be present early in development but may not necessarily be recognized until the child . . . moves into the age range in middle childhood where peers and peer relationships become more crucial" (Semrud-Clikeman & Hynd, 1990, p. 198).

quences of a negative peer environment burdened with unintelligible nonverbal language.

Emotional problems often develop as a result of the failure to identify the underlying LD. Studies that rely on previous school diagnosis or rule out ED also overidentify the LD population with left hemisphere, language-based disorders. Furthermore, studies that evaluate adjudicated individuals without reference to historical diagnosis rely primarily on the existence of a significant discrepancy in aptitude and achievement (Wilgosh & Paitich, 1982). The aptitude versus achievement formula for identification and diagnosis of LD has been universally discredited (Mather & Healy, 1990; Shaywitz, Fletcher, & Shaywitz, 1994). Any formula that utilizes a comparison of performance or achievement to a standardized norm identifies a result, not a cause. Using such a discrepancy to identify a cohort compounds the bias inherent in retrospective studies.

Commenting on the inconsistent results of studies addressing the co-occurrence of attention-deficit/hyperactivity disorder (ADHD) and LD, S.E. Shaywitz et al. (1994, p. 14) stated that

> Examination of both the methods and results of these studies are instructive. . . . [I]n fact each used a somewhat different definition—a methodological inconsistency that speaks to the current lack of a single universally accepted criterion for the diagnosis of either LD or ADD.

Consistent results are not obtainable across studies if one observes baseballs and another observes basketballs. Furthermore, such research cannot accurately predict how a golf ball will behave by studying baseballs and basketballs.

## SUBTYPES OF LD

The inconsistency observed in studies addressing the link between LD and delinquent behavior is of heuristic value in that it supports the existence of subtypes of LD, each of which has a different risk factor for delinquent behavior. In other words, if the inconsistent results are due to differences between the studies in the characteristics of the LD cohorts being researched, the conclusion is not that the studies are invalid, but that the characteristics of the particular cohorts being researched are a significant determinant in evaluating the link between LD and delinquent behavior. Thus, if nothing else, these studies prove that among the "ball" population there are different types, each with a unique set of characteristics. It is not surprising, therefore, that a study of the link between balls and broken windows finds no link when studying basketballs and a significant link when studying baseballs.

For the purpose of illustrating the hypothesis offered in this chapter, four possible subtypes of LD are briefly addressed: 1) nonverbal learning disability, 2) dyslexia, 3) attention-deficit/hyperactivity disorder, and 4) executive function deficit.[3]

## Nonverbal Learning Disability

As early as 1968, Myklebust (1968, 1975) suggested the possibility of a nonverbal LD subtype with deficits in interpersonal relationships or the ability to judge the emotion being expressed by other people.

Other researchers suggested that "the NLD syndrome leads to a distinct pattern of difficulty in socioemotional functioning" (Little, 1993, p. 653; Rourke, Young, & Leenaars, 1989). Furthermore,

> Children who are unable to acquire these skills because of difficulty in evaluating facial expressions, gestures, or prosody would be at high risk for the development of significant learning difficulties in, at the very least, the socioemotional arena of competence. (Semrud-Clikeman & Hynd, 1990, p. 198)

Although there appears to be a consensus among the many researchers and authors addressing the phenotype, there is no consensus regarding a name for the syndrome.[4] The most authoritative work in this field is that by Harnadek and Rourke (1994), which presents a comprehensive model of an NLD subtype. This research indicates that the NLD subtype evidences socioemotional and adaptive deficits, including compromised social competence and emotional stability.

## Dyslexia

Harnadek and Rourke (1994) convincingly distinguished the NLD subtype from the reading–spelling (R–S) subtype, which closely matches the LD construct often referred to as dyslexia.[5] Pennington (1991) indicated that the primary symptoms in dyslexia include problems in reading,

---

[3]The subtypes of LD discussed in this chapter are intended to be illustrative of the *concept* of subtyping. The author does not intend to indicate that the phenotypes chosen are either exhaustive of the LD subtypes that exist or valid subtypes in and of themselves (e.g., ADHD may consist of several subtypes that may or may not include components of the EF and NLD subtypes discussed).

[4]This author has reviewed articles that use 11 different names: 1) right hemisphere dysfunction, 2) nonverbal learning disability, 3) semantic-pragmatic learning disability, 4) nonverbal right hemisphere learning disability, 5) social communications spectrum disorder, 6) social perception disability, 7) nonverbal perceptual organization output disability, 8) left hemisyndrome, 9) right parietal lobe classification, 10) nonverbal social learning difficulties, and 11) social-emotional learning disability.

[5]This is the definition of *dyslexia* adopted by the Research Committee of the Orton Dyslexia Society in 1994 (Lyon, 1995):

> Dyslexia is one of several distinct learning disabilities. It is a specific language-based disorder of constitutional origin characterized by difficulties in single word decoding, usually reflecting insufficient phonological processing. These difficulties in single word decoding are often unexpected in relation to age and other cognitive and academic abilities; they are not the result of generalized developmental disability or sensory impairment. Dyslexia is manifest by variable difficulty with different forms of language, often including, in addition to problems reading, a conspicuous problem with acquiring proficiency in writing and spelling. (p. 9)

spelling, and the phonological coding of written language. Harnadek and Rourke (1994, p. 144) described the Group R–S as having "very poor reading and spelling skills" and "relatively poor psycholinguistic skills."[6] It is interesting to note that the literature is replete with indications that the learner with dyslexia may also exhibit unexpected strengths (Masland, 1975; West, 1991). Harnadek and Rourke (1994, p. 144) credited the Group R–S with "very well-developed abilities in visual-spatial-organizational, tactile-perceptual, psychomotor, and non-verbal problem solving areas."

## Attention–Deficit/Hyperactivity Disorder

The criteria for diagnosing ADHD have been revised and are presented in the *Diagnostic and Statistical Manual of Mental Disorders* (4th ed.) (DSM-IV) (American Psychiatric Association, 1994). Such criteria, all of which are observations of negative behavioral characteristics, may obviously impede the development of normal social relationships. Someone who fidgets, forgets, does not listen, is distractible, talks too much, does not wait his or her turn, and interrupts is clearly unlikely to have a large circle of good friends. S.E. Shaywitz et al. (1994) authoritatively challenged the predictive and communicative power of current methods for diagnosing ADHD. They convincingly argued that there is evidence for "at least two subtypes: (1) behavioral and (2) a cognitive type" (p. 7). The significance of this argument lies in the fact that each subtype presents a different socioemotional risk profile.[7] The inability to identify "the diverse populations now diagnosed as ADD represents a central problem in our ability to understand, to assess, and to treat affected individuals" (S.E. Shaywitz et al., 1994, p. 22).

## Executive Function Deficit

Bruce Pennington (1991) was most parsimonious in his description of *executive function* (EF), which he broadly defined "as the ability to maintain an appropriate problem-solving set for attainment of a future goal" (p. 13). Executive functions may include "organizational skills, planning, future-oriented behavior, set-maintenance, self-regulation, selective attention, maintenance of attention or vigilance, inhibition, and even creativity (Pennington, 1991, p. 13). Denckla (1994), a leader in exploring executive function, summed up the list of EF components by indicating simply "that executive function refers to attention not only to

[6]Ongoing authoritative research on this subtype is being conducted by Torgesen, Wagner, and Rashotte (1994).

[7]In this author's experience, there is significant overlap in the diagnosis of NLD and ADHD-behavioral subtype. Despite the significance of the distinction, it takes a discerning professional with extensive clinical experience to make an appropriate diagnosis.

the present but also to the future, as well as intention (preparedness to act)" (p. 118).[8]

Torgesen (1994) relates the term *executive function*, which reflects a neuropsychological perspective, to the term *metacognition*, which reflects an information-processing perspective. Torgesen's description of metacognition helps to clarify the extent of the difficulties that may be faced by an individual with a deficit in executive function:

> Metacognitive knowledge . . . includes information about one's own abilities, knowledge of what makes some tasks hard and others easy, and insights about what cognitive strategies are useful in achieving various goals. The more dynamic, behavioral side of metacognition includes the processes involving planning, organizing, coordinating, monitoring, and adapting various knowledge and strategic resources while a task is being performed. (p. 145)

## EXTRINSIC INFLUENCES

Factors that may be loosely referred to as environmental have also been shown by various studies to have a negative correlation to socioemotional development. Such factors, unrelated to neurobiological profiles, include low socioeconomic status (Grande, 1988), school failure (Grande, 1988; Rhodes & Reiss, 1969), and adopted child status (Brodzinsky & Steiger, 1991; Dickman, 1992). Many studies have hypothesized that school maladjustment and academic failure are causes of the disaffection that results in delinquent behavior (Bruck, 1985; Dunivant, 1982; Healy, 1933). In fact, LD can be a factor with a significant impact on academic and psychosocial development (Myklebust, 1968; Rourke, 1988; Rourke, Young, & Leenaars, 1989).

The hypothesis presented in this chapter would anticipate that future empirical research will support the finding that a neurobiological etiology is the primary precursor to the antisocial behavior exhibited by individuals with LD and that extrinsic influences such as socioeconomic status, adopted child status, and academic failure are secondary and not altogether necessary factors compounding the risk profile.

## COMORBIDITY

Denckla (1979) provided convincing evidence that the presence of various codiagnoses, including types of language disorder or ADD with hyperactivity, is meaningfully related to subtypes of childhood learning disabilities. More recent studies have provided further support for the idea that learning

---

[8]In this author's experience, there is significant overlap in the diagnosis of EF and ADHD, cognitive subtype. Appropriate diagnosis requires (as with the NLD/ADHD confusion) a discerning professional with extensive clinical experience.

disabilities frequently co-occur with other psychiatric disorders. (Semrud-Clikeman & Hynd, 1990, p. 199)

Clearly, one or more of the intrinsic and extrinsic conditions heretofore discussed may co-occur, creating the specter of complicated diagnostic profiles unique to the individuals, such as a child who has dyslexia, ADHD cognitive subtype, is adopted, and suffers school failure. The fashion of sorting children into separate and distinct diagnostic pigeonholes is a bureaucratic convenience with no scientific or pedagogic merit.

## PROSOCIAL DEVELOPMENT

Researchers interested in the mechanics of normal psychosocial development have determined that prosocial behavior is intimately involved with cognitive growth and the development of perspective-taking and role-taking abilities (Moore & Underwood, 1981).

> Although the ability to anticipate the cognition of another may be a more complex cognitive feat than the ability to recognize different visual perspectives, they are usually assumed to generate from a common basis.
> This basic construct was examined in a study (Underwood, Froming, & Guarijuata, 1980) using the "three-mountain task." In this task, a child is placed before a model of a mountain scene and is asked to imagine what he or she would see if placed in some other position. The child is asked to choose which of several photographs accurately represents the view from an alternative position.
> The . . . children . . . were given 25 pennies when they entered the experimental room, ostensibly for helping the experimenters with their work. Following completion of the three-mountain task, the children were given an opportunity to donate some of their pennies anonymously to a fund for children who wouldn't get a chance to earn pennies. Perspective-taking scores were significantly correlated with the number of pennies donated. (Moore & Underwood, 1981, p. 78)

Although this study was intended to investigate the correlation between the development of altruism and perspective taking in typical children, the following conclusions can be related to individuals in whom perspective-taking and role-taking skills do not develop, owing to neurobiological deficits. "Empathetic reaction is an internal response to cues about the affective states of someone else; the empathetic reaction must depend heavily on the actor's cognitive sense of the other as distinct from himself" (Moore & Underwood, 1981, p. 86).

Using the NLD model (Harnadek & Rourke, 1994) discussed earlier as an example, the individual with NLD who has difficulty with visual attention, visual memory, prosody, semantics, and pragmatics has a significantly impaired ability to interpret the paralinguistic cues (e.g., body language, expression, tone of voice) necessary to develop a "cognitive sense of others" (Hoffman, 1975, p. 610). Therefore, the individual with NLD has an impairment of neurobiological etiology in both perspective taking and role taking, which have been found to have a significant correlation to the development of normal prosocial behavior.

## INTERIM CONCLUSIONS

There appears to be robust support for the following conclusions:

1. LD consist of various subtypes.
2. Each LD subtype poses a unique and variable risk of predisposing a child to anomalous development of prosocial behavior.
3. Co-occurrence of LD subtypes enhances the risk of evidencing anomalous development of prosocial behavior.
4. Environmental factors such as school failure, low socioeconomic status, and adopted child status also enhance the risk of evidencing anomalous development of prosocial behavior.

Table 1 demonstrates the possible relationship of various LD subtypes and codiagnoses to a hypothetical risk factor predisposing a child to experiencing anomalous development of prosocial behavior.[9] This table is intended only as a visual representation of an example of what this author would expect if consistent and generalizable studies were to be conducted addressing the link between intrinsic and extrinsic influences to a predisposition for the anomalous development of prosocial behavior.

Table 1 anticipates that each LD subtype predisposes a child to a quantitatively different risk for the development of behavior problems. For example, the research surveyed supports the finding that dyslexia (R–S) poses a very low risk, EF deficits present a slightly higher risk, ADHD poses an even higher risk, and NLD poses the greatest risk of all for the development of behavior problems.

If children with NLD display relative proficiencies in reading and spelling (Harnadek & Rourke, 1994) as compared with children with dyslexia who have problems with reading and spelling (B.A. Shaywitz, Fletcher, & Shaywitz, 1994), it is logical that prospective studies of individuals with dyslexia find little or no link to delinquent behavior and that retrospective studies of delinquent populations find a significant link between delinquent behavior and LD. Obviously, the prospective

---

[9]The values presented in Table 1 are intended to structure the order in which the author feels that different profiles of disability and comorbidity would appear on a continuum of least problematic to most problematic. Such values are not intended to quantify the actual risk that a particular profile or comorbidity may have for the anomalous development of prosocial behavior.

Table 1. Possible relationship of LD subtypes and codiagnoses to a hypothetical risk factor for the anomalous development of prosocial behavior

| Disability profile | Enhanced risk predisposition for antisocial behavior | School failure | Low socioeco-nomic status | Adopted child |
|---|---|---|---|---|
| No LD profile | 0[a] | 1 | +2 | +1 |
| R–S[b] | 2 | +1 | +2 | +1 |
| EF[c] | 3 | +1 | +2 | +1 |
| R–S/EF | 4 | +1 | +2 | +1 |
| AD/HD[d] | 5 | +1 | +2 | +1 |
| R–S/ADHD | 6 | +1 | +2 | +1 |
| ADHD/EF | 7 | +1 | +2 | +1 |
| R–S/ADHD/EF | 8 | +1 | +2 | +1 |
| NLD[e] | 9 | +1 | +2 | +1 |
| NLD/R–S | 10 | +1 | +2 | +1 |
| NLD/EF | 11 | +1 | +2 | +1 |
| NLD/EF/R–S | 12 | +1 | +2 | +1 |
| NLD/ADHD | 13 | +1 | +2 | +1 |
| NLD/ADHD/R–S | 14 | +1 | +2 | +1 |
| NLD/EF/ADHD | 15 | +1 | +2 | +1 |
| NLD/EF/ADHD/R–S | 16 | +1 | +2 | +1 |

[a] Scale = 0–20, with 0 being normal risk.
[b] R–S = Reading-spelling (dyslexia) profile.
[c] EF = Executive function profile.
[d] ADHD = attention-deficit/hyperactivity profile.
[e] NLD = Nonverbal learning disability profile.

study observed individuals with one LD subtype and the retrospective study observed individuals with a different LD subtype. Rourke's research involving 750 children with LD supported his conclusion that "the better the reading the more serious the psychopathology" (Rourke, 1993). The inference is clear: A significant risk for anomalous prosocial development is not common to all LD subtypes. Rourke (1993) also described children with NLD as having a "modality specific attention deficit" in that they do not pay attention to visual and tactile stimulation, whereas dyslexics do not pay attention to auditory stimulation.

The individual with NLD responds best to auditory stimulation and worst to visual and tactile stimulation, whereas the person with dyslexia is the reverse, responding best to visual and tactile stimulation as compared to auditory stimulation. Nevertheless, both are often labeled simply as LD and receive a generic approach to intervention that does not recognize their differences.

Could there be a better argument for the need to subtype individuals with learning disabilities and individualize intervention and remediation?

One wonders if the real progress will not come from disentangling groups of children from this huge conglomerate mass, rigorously specifying the nature of their difficulties, and systematically exploring appropriate educational interventions for these subgroups. (Doris, 1993, p. 112)

## SYSTEMATIC WEAKNESSES

If we know so much about risk for LD individuals developing antisocial behavior, why is more not being done to avoid the process of risk becoming reality? In large measure, the fault appears to lie in the system of education, which evidences intrinsic weaknesses that interfere with the appropriate delivery of services. Three of these intrinsic weaknesses require specific mention.

First, schools are required to quantify or establish concrete, measurable growth in pupil achievement. Pretesting and post-testing is applied to virtually every increment of the educational experience to quantify measurable growth. This quantitative accountability causes administrators and teachers to deemphasize efforts promoting skills that are not readily quantifiable (e.g., morality, ethics, problem solving, decision making) as well as strategies for the acquisition of social competencies and nonverbal literacy.

Second, a related weakness is the slice of time perspective adopted by educational evaluators. Current procedures of multidisciplinary evaluation focus on what *is*, with no concern for prognosis. Such evaluations are motivated by a desire to establish concrete baselines to quantify the success of remediation. Possible interventions are overlooked because prognosis is ignored.

Third, the aptitude–achievement discrepancy formula used to determine eligibility for special education services is predicated on school failure. This threshold of failure must be crossed before services can be delivered (Mather & Roberts, 1994).

This combination of weaknesses has established a dynamic that ignores the evaluation of risk. A problem must exist, not merely be possible or even probable, before resources can be devoted to intervention or remediation. Our system of education has greater regard for those who cure than for those who prevent, reversing Franklin's axiom that an ounce of prevention is worth a pound of cure. Our educational system is a hostage to accountability and a slave to outmoded paradigms.

## WHAT WILL HELP?

An 11-year-old child died while being restrained. A review of this child's records indicated a profile that placed him among those with the highest risk of developing anomalous prosocial behavior (NLD/EF/ADHD). He was not properly diagnosed, and his needs were not properly evaluated. Care providers in his environment overlooked the neurobiological etiology of his behavior, thereby missing opportunities for intervention, and instead implemented a punitive as well as self-protective response.[10] Society can better protect itself by delivering efficacious intervention. Society must understand the character of the threat. For many children with LD who lack the ability to interact and communicate effectively with others, the classroom, the hall, the playground, the candy store, and even their own homes are arenas for misunderstanding and conflict. Without appropriate intervention, this relatively innocuous constitutional disorder can cause the child with LD to experience an alien and hostile environment that results in anger and disaffection.

This particular example is used to indicate the seriousness of the issues involved. An educational system that does not respond to the needs of our children does not merely compromise their potential to benefit themselves, their families, and society, but risks making them burdens to their families and society and even risks their lives. What can be done?

First, in the area of research, studies are needed to identify and define learning disabilities subtypes. Second, teachers need preservice and in-service instruction to recognize children at risk and to appropriately respond to their needs. Third, parents should be provided with or directed to instruction and education that will enable them to effectively respond to their child's needs. Parents must meaningfully participate in development of their child's individualized education program (IEP) and must be part of a comprehensive home–school service delivery package. Fourth, the IEP should address risk and prognosis as well as diagnosis and current status. The IEP should also address the need for intervention strategies and should evaluate household and peer relationships in terms of service delivery potential. Fifth, successful educational policies require the commitment of administrative personnel. Top-down support is necessary for successful implementation of innovative service delivery strategies. Sixth, interventions must redirect dysfunctional patterns in the home and in peer groups and avoid problematic social situations. Interventions should model, in the home and at school, ethics, problem solving, decision making, conflict resolution, social skills, and nonverbal competency. Seventh, the legal community of attorneys, courts, police, and correctional facilities must be educated and enlightened about the reasons behind the behaviors they observe. Law enforce-

---

[10]Among many other indicators, this young man had a verbal IQ of 140, a performance IQ of 102, a relative weakness in math, and poor visuospatial skills and was distractible, hyperactive, and impulsive.

ment personnel must take steps to overcome the inadvertent bias that results in individuals with LD being more likely to be taken into custody, to be found guilty, and to get more severe penalties than their peers without LD. It must also be recognized that a key to modifying behavior is understanding the causes for the behavior.

Our children suffer from the isolationist perspective of school systems that define their responsibility within the parameters of a wall that they build between themselves and the communities they serve. The failure to recognize and respond to the social and emotional needs of individuals with particular LD subtypes is an example of this head-in-the-sand attitude, which encourages schools to avoid addressing a cause when they do not have to address the effect.

## CONCLUSIONS

There are factors both intrinsic (e.g., dyslexia, NLD, ADHD, EF) and extrinsic (e.g., school failure, socioeconomic status, adopted child status) that predispose an individual to anomalous prosocial development. For this observation to have meaning, LD subtypes must be appropriately defined, and the research inconsistency that has been discussed must be addressed. S.E. Shaywitz et al. (1994) put it best: "The development of a unitary, empirically derived nosology . . . should increase the consistency and generalizability of findings across investigations and across disciplines" (p. 22).

To accomplish such consistency, S.E. Shaywitz et al. (1994) proposed a "systematic classification study" (p. 22). Such a study is essential if we are to understand the unique needs of individuals with LD subtypes, the comorbidities involved, and the complex correlation of subtypes with social and emotional development. This call to arms is perhaps the single most important movement occurring in the field of LD. We must "disentangle this huge conglomerate mass" (Doris, 1993, p. 112) if we are to develop truly efficacious methodology and service delivery. The system of education must recognize the false promise of quantitative evaluation of pedagogy and curriculum and embrace a less Newtonian and more holistic paradigm (Dickman, 1990; Heshusius, 1989) aimed at identifying risk and preventing failure.

## REFERENCES

American Psychiatric Association. (1994). *Diagnostic and statistical manual of mental disorders* (4th ed., DSM-IV). Washington, DC: Author.

Broder, P.K., Dunivant, N., Smith, E.C., & Sutton, L.P. (1981). Further observations on the link between learning disabilities and juvenile delinquency. *Journal of Educational Psychology, 73*(6), 838–850.

Brodzinsky, D.M., & Steiger, C. (1991). Prevalence of adoptees among special education populations. *Journal of Learning Disabilities, 24,* 484–488.

Bruck, M. (1985). The adult functioning of children with specific learning disabilities: A follow-up study. In L. Siegal (Ed.), *Advances in applied developmental psychology* (pp. 91–129). Norwood, NJ: Ablex.

Cornwell, A., & Bawden, H.N. (1992). Read disabilities and aggression: A critical review. *Journal of Learning Disabilities, 25*(5), 281–288.

Denckla, M.B. (1979). Childhood learning disabilities. In K.M. Heilman & E. Valenstein (Eds.), *Clinical neuropsychology* (pp. 535–573). New York: Oxford University Press.

Denckla, M.B. (1994). Measurement of executive function. In G.R. Lyon (Ed.), *Frames of reference for the assessment of learning disabilities: New views on measurement issues* (pp. 117–142). Baltimore: Paul H. Brookes Publishing Co.

Dickman, G.E. (1990). Comments on Heshusius (1989): The Newtonian mechanistic paradigm and quantitative accountability as the source of systemic weaknesses affecting education of individuals with learning disorders. *Journal of Learning Disabilities, 23,* 138–140.

Dickman, G.E. (1992). Adoptees among students with disabilities. *Journal of Learning Disabilities, 25*(8), 529–531.

Doris, J.L. (1993). Defining learning disabilities: A history of the search for consensus. In G.R. Lyon, D.B. Gray, J.F. Kavanagh, & N.A. Krasnegor (Eds.), *Better understanding learning disabilities: New views from research and their implications for education and public policies* (pp. 97–115). Baltimore: Paul H. Brookes Publishing Co.

Dunivant, N. (1982). *The relationship between learning disabilities and juvenile delinquency.* Williamsburg, VA: National Center for State Courts.

Grande, C.G. (1988). Delinquency: The learning-disabled student's reaction to academic school failure? *Adolescence, 23,* 209–219.

Harnadek, M.C.S., & Rourke, B.P. (1994). Principal identifying features of the syndrome of nonverbal learning disabilities in children. *Journal of Learning Disabilities, 27*(3), 144–154.

Healy, W. (1933). The prevention of delinquency and criminality. *Journal of Criminal Law and Criminology, 24,* 74–87.

Heshusius, L. (1989). The Newtonian mechanistic paradigm, special education, and contours of alternatives: An overview. *Journal of Learning Disabilities, 22,* 403–415.

Hoffman, M.L. (1975). Developmental synthesis of affect and cognition and its implications for altruistic motivation. *Developmental Psychology, 11*(5), 607–622.

Lane, A.L. (1980). The relationship of learning disabilities to juvenile delinquency: Current status. *Journal of Learning Disabilities, 13*(8), 20–29.

Little, S.S. (1993). Nonverbal learning disabilities and socioemotional functioning: A review of recent literature. *Journal of Learning Disabilities, 26*(10), 653–665.

Lyon, G.R. (1995). Toward a definition of dyslexia. *Annals of Dyslexia: An Interdisciplinary Journal of the Orton Dyslexia Society, XLV,* 3–27.

Masland, R.L. (1975, November). *The advantages of being dyslexic.* Paper presented at the annual conference of the Orton Dyslexic Society, Santa Barbara, CA.

Mather, N., & Healey, W.C. (1990). Deposing the aptitude–achievement discrepancy as the imperial criterion for learning disabilities. *Learning Disabilities: A Multidisciplinary Journal, 1*(2), 40–48.

Mather, N., & Roberts, R. (1994). Learning disabilities: A field in danger of extinction. *Learning Disabilities Research and Practice, 9*(1), 49–58.

Moore, B., & Underwood, B. (1981). The development of prosocial behavior. In S. Brehm, S. Kassin, & F. Gibbons (Eds.), *Developmental social psychology theory and research* (pp. 72–95). New York: Oxford University Press.

Myklebust, H.R. (1968). Learning disabilities: Definition and overview. In H.R. Myklebust (Ed.), *Progress in learning disabilities* (Vol. 1, pp. 1–15). New York: Grune & Stratton.

Myklebust, H.R. (1975). Nonverbal learning disabilities: Assessment and intervention. In H.R. Myklebust (Ed.), *Progress in learning disabilities* (Vol. 3, pp. 85–122). New York: Grune & Stratton.

Pennington, B.F. (1991). *Diagnosing learning disorders: A neuropsychological framework*. New York: Guilford Press.

Rhodes, A.L., & Reiss, A.J., Jr. (1969). Apathy, truancy, and delinquency as adaptations to school failure. *Social Forces, 48,* 12–22.

Rourke, B.P. (1988). Socioemotional disturbances of learning disabled children. *Journal of Consulting and Clinical Psychology, 56*(6), 801–810.

Rourke, B.P. (1993, November). *Syndrome of nonverbal learning disabilities: Developmental manifestations in neurological disease, disorder and dysfunction.* Paper presented at the 44th annual conference of the Orton Dyslexia Society, New Orleans, LA.

Rourke, B.P., Young, G.C., & Leenaars, A.A. (1989). A childhood learning disability that predisposes those afflicted to adolescent and adult depression and suicide risk. *Journal of Learning Disabilities, 22*(3), 169–175.

Semrud-Clikeman, M., & Hynd, G.W. (1990). Right hemisphere dysfunction in nonverbal learning disabilities: Social, academic, and adaptive functioning in adults and children. *Psychological Bulletin, 107*(2), 196–209.

Semrud-Clikeman, M., & Hynd, G.W. (1991). Specific nonverbal and social skills deficits in children with learning disabilities. In J.E. Obrzut & G.W. Hynd (Eds.), *Neuropsychological foundations of learning disabilities: A handbook of issues, methods and practice* (pp. 603–629). San Diego, CA: Academic Press.

Shaywitz, B.A., Fletcher, J.M., & Shaywitz, S.E. (1994). A conceptual framework for learning disabilities and attention-deficit/hyperactivity disorder. *Canadian Journal of Special Education, 9*(3), 1–32.

Shaywitz, S.E., Fletcher, J.M., & Shaywitz, B.A. (1994). Issues in the definition and classification of attention deficit disorder. *Topics in Language Disorders, 14*(4), 1–25.

Spreen, O. (1981). The relationship between learning disability, neurological impairment, and delinquency: Results of a follow-up study. *Journal of Nervous and Mental Disease, 169*(12), 791–799.

Thompson, O.M. (1985). The nonverbal dilemma. *Journal of Learning Disabilities, 18,* 400–402.

Torgesen, J.K. (1994). Issues in the assessment of executive function: An information-processing perspective. In G.R. Lyon (Ed.), *Frames of reference for the assessment of learning disabilities: New views on measurement issues* (pp. 143–162). Baltimore: Paul H. Brookes Publishing Co.

Torgesen, J.K., Wagner, R.K., & Rashotte, C.A. (1994). Longitudinal studies of phonological processing and reading. *Journal of Learning Disabilities, 27*(5), 276–286.

West, T.G. (1991). *In the mind's eye.* Buffalo, NY: Prometheus Books.

Wilgosh, L., & Paitich, D. (1982). Delinquency and learning disabilities: More evidence. *Journal of Learning Disabilities, 15*(5), 278–279.

# Chapter 27

# Reducing School Failure and Preventing Criminal Behavior

*Thomas P. McGee*

With serious juvenile crime escalating at an alarming rate, the Summit on Learning Disabilities filled a vital function. As a juvenile judge in a major metropolitan area, I see a clear and strong correlation between school failure and criminal behavior. I believe statistics bear this out.

It is not that individuals with learning disabilities (LD) have any inherent criminal propensities. Adolescents with LD are involved with the juvenile justice system more frequently because their disabilities are undiagnosed and unremediated, which results in school failure. School failure can lead students to drop out of school and to be involved with substance abuse and violence.

## DELINQUENCY AND SCHOOL FAILURE

The Federal Bureau of Justice Statistics reported the federal and state jail population in the United States as approximately 950,000 in 1993, a figure that does not include the tens of thousands of inmates who are confined in local facilities (Pace Publications, 1994). The Correctional Education Association reported that an estimated 75% of all inmates are illiterate; that is, their reading, writing, and mathematical skills are insufficient for employment (Correctional Education Association, personal communication, 1994). The Adult Literacy Survey in 1992 stated that the "prisoner tended to be both younger and less educated than adults in the nation as a whole" (p. 48) and confirmed the significantly disproportionate rate of illiteracy among prisoners (U.S. Department of Education, 1992).

With regard to juvenile offenders, the Office of Juvenile Justice Delinquency and Prevention reported a daily average population of

65,000 juveniles in secure facilities in 1991 (U.S. Department of Justice, 1994). A multitude of studies conducted since the 1960s have clearly shown that delinquent juvenile behavior is linked to school failure.

A report of the President's Commission on Law Enforcement and the Administration of Justice identified a connection between delinquent commitments and adverse or negative school experiences (Schafer & Polk, 1967). Critchley (1968) found school failure to be more closely correlated with delinquency than poverty, broken homes, physical and mental disabilities, or psychopathic conditions. Since the late 1960s, the results of many additional studies have supported the relationship between school failure and delinquency. Definitive evidence has been provided that school failure resulting from undiagnosed and unremediated LD is a major factor in delinquency (Dunivant, 1981, 1982). In 1994, the National Governors' Association again identified school failure as a significant risk factor for violent behavior (Thornberry, Garnett, & Steinhart, 1994).

Of course, academic failure is not the *only* factor that contributes to criminal behavior. My personal experience (and many studies bear this out) is that family dysfunction, by itself and as a cause of academic failure, probably accounts for the majority of the incarcerated population. The Office of Juvenile Justice Delinquency and Prevention (U.S. Department of Justice, 1993), a component of the Office of Justice Program under the U.S. Department of Justice, in its *Program Summary on Comprehensive Strategy for Serious, Violent, and Chronic Juvenile Offenders,* concluded: "The family is the most important influence in the lives of children and the first line of defense against delinquency.... Outside the family, the school has the greatest influence in the lives of children and adolescents" (pp. 15, 16). The National Governors' Association report (Thornberry et al., 1994) also identified the critical role that families play in the development of violent behavior. Secretary of Education Richard Riley and Waldemar Rojas, superintendent of schools of the San Francisco Unified School District, said that parents have an enormous impact on their children's education. But delinquency is not all that we see. Many abused and neglected children also have LD.

Almost all of the children we see in the juvenile justice system have several things in common: 1) a dysfunctional, chaotic, and unsupportive family; 2) a history of educational failure; and 3) a poor self-image. Lack of positive self-image typically leads to other social and medical problems, such as drug and alcohol abuse and an inability to acquire employable skills.

Parents must be encouraged to be actively involved with their children in the school process, and fathers should be specifically targeted. If investment in the child's educational welfare from the parents is not feasible, then at least financial commitment should be required of parents. Financial support enforcement programs can and should be instituted on a local level so that child support is actively pursued and at least part of this support is earmarked to benefit the child's education.

Historically, public policy with regard to crime has been reactive. We have toughened laws, expanded jails, and provided more and more social and mental health services to little avail. But we cannot continue to simply react, because the problem is growing more rapidly than society can react to it. Instead, we need to focus on stemming the tide of crime by decreasing the number of children at risk.

## PREVENTION

How can such a policy be implemented? There is no simple answer or a single solution. Intervention must be multidimensional. From my experience, the key is to develop early childhood intervention strategies.

Parental education concerning child care is necessary to encourage parents to have wanted and healthy babies. We need to protect the health of babies born to drug abusers.

Preschool development, such as that offered by Head Start, is crucial to academic success. Child development from infancy on must be encouraged by making available a varied array of good, differential educational services. Although Americans believe that all people are born with equal rights, in truth and in fact, all are born with differing capabilities and capacities. We cannot educate everybody in the same way. We need to provide what the law requires: free, appropriate public education. Free, appropriate public education can be accomplished through the early identification of strengths and needs of individuals and through effective programmatic and teaching strategies. We must identify and intervene with children with LD early!

Limiting the size of schools and classroom population is also necessary. Economies of scale do not work in education. The size of classes is particularly important with young and at-risk children.

Teachers in the elementary school grades must be taught to identify and appropriately instruct children at risk for and with LD. The typical school system must be reevaluated, and teacher preparation must be improved.

Perhaps we do not need many more laws. The Individuals with Disabilities Education Act of 1990 (IDEA) (PL 101-476) and its amendments (PL 102-119) provide most of the mandates necessary for providing good quality public education. It has been my experience, however, that, nationwide, the provisions of IDEA are not being fully, fairly, and appropriately implemented. The public school systems are not providing early identification and evaluation of all children (including those with LD). Labels are used and misused as resources are available or lacking. *Emotionally disturbed* is an increasingly popular label for children with LD.

Public schools are not providing the individualized education that IDEA requires. We have a public education system that does not accept variation in abilities or learning styles. There is very little diversity of approaches in the public education system. Public education is oriented to serve the university-qualified student, which in reality may be, in my opinion, only 20% of our nation's students. What about all the other students, including students with special needs, such as those with LD?

As a result of the failure of our public education systems to truly implement IDEA, we have more than a 40% dropout rate of students before high school graduation. We in the juvenile justice system see this more than 40% every day. In other words, we see a business (the public education system) operating at a questionable 60% efficiency. Of the 60% who are estimated to graduate, it is estimated that only 20% can read and write at a college level. A private business operating at that rate would have to fold. There must be some accountability.

The sad part of this is that most public school educators are very dedicated, knowledgeable, and frustrated people. Their voices simply do not seem to be heard. If we do not reduce school failure and parental failure, the problem of crime will continue to grow, even more jails will be built, and the criminal justice system will become even more inundated and ineffectual. With the current cost of a juvenile's incarceration between $35,000 and $60,000 annually, the impact of such an increase on the economy would be immeasurable (Jones & Krisberg, 1994). We cannot afford the economic loss to our society, and we as a civilized nation should not tolerate the human misery that school failure produces.

## CONCLUSIONS

Perhaps we can only react to the present generation of delinquents and adult criminals to protect the public as best we can, but we must begin investing in the next generation now by promoting and funding good quality, sensible early childhood development programs and good quality, differential educational programs for individuals of all abilities.

Successful systematic changes are made when private and broadly based public education efforts combine to awaken the public. Statistics on the reduction in cigarette smoking over the past 30 years bear this out. We have come from a nation in which 52% of the population were smokers to a nation in which 26% of the population smokes, but it took more than 30 years of effective public education sponsored by public and private endeavors to achieve this. Good prenatal care and early childhood development programs and education will go a long way to reducing the problems we have to address in the juvenile and adult criminal justice systems. As the saying goes, you pay me now or you pay me later.

## REFERENCES

Critchley, E.M. (1968). Reading retardation, dyslexia, and delinquency. *British Journal of Psychiatry, 114*(517), 1537–1547.

Dunivant, N. (1981). *The relationship between learning disabilities and juvenile delinquency: Executive summary.* Williamsburg, VA: National Center for State Courts.

Dunivant, N. (1982). *The relationship between learning disabilities and juvenile delinquency: Brief summary of research findings.* Williamsburg, VA: National Center for State Courts.

Individuals with Disabilities Education Act of 1990 (IDEA), PL 101-476. (October 30, 1990). Title 20, U.S.C. §§ 1400 et seq.: *U.S. Statutes at Large, 104*(Part 2), 1103–1151.

Individuals with Disabilities Education Act Amendments of 1991, PL 101-119. (October 7, 1991). Title 20, U.S.C. §§ 1400 et seq.: *U.S. Statutes at Large, 105*, 587–608.

Jones, M., & Krisberg, B. (1994). *Images and reality: Juvenile crime, youth violence and public policy.* San Francisco: National Council on Crime and Delinquency.

Pace Publications. (1994, June). *Criminal Justice Newsletter, 25*(11), 6.

Schafer, W., & Polk, K. (1967). *Delinquency and the schools* (Task Force Report of the President's Commission on Law Enforcement and the Administration of Justice: Juvenile Delinquency and Youth Crime). Washington, DC: U.S. Government Printing Office.

Thornberry, T., Garnett, D., & Steinhart, D. (1994, March/April). Kids and violence. *Youth Law News*, 16.

U.S. Department of Education. (1992). *National Adult Literacy Survey, 1992.* Washington, DC: Author/National Center for Education Statistics.

U.S. Department of Justice. (1993). *Comprehensive strategy for serious, violent and chronic juvenile offenders: Program summary.* Washington, DC: U.S. Government Printing Office.

U.S. Department of Justice. (1994). *1991 children in custody census. Conditions of confinement: Juvenile delinquency and youth crime.* Washington, DC: U.S. Government Printing Office.

# Chapter 28

# Academic Performance and Its Relationship to Delinquency

*Eugene Maguin*
*Rolf Loeber*

Poor academic performance is frequently mentioned as an important cause of delinquent offending, and, at the same time, it is also believed that a worsening of academic performance is a consequence of offending. Reasoning from these premises, improving academic performance—whether through school-based educational or social–behavioral programs—is seen to lead to a reduction of offending among youth who are already offending as well as to prevent the onset of offending among youth. But to what extent are these beliefs—and the hopes they engender—justified?

## STRENGTH OF THE ASSOCIATION BETWEEN ACADEMIC PERFORMANCE AND DELINQUENCY

To address these questions, we present data from a study in which the authors reviewed the published studies of academic performance and delinquency (Maguin & Loeber, 1996). *Academic performance* was defined broadly as any measure of achievement such as grades, achievement test scores, being held back, or having a learning disability label. *Delinquency*

This chapter was adapted from Maguin and Loeber (1996) with the permission of the University of Chicago Press and was prepared under the following grants: Grant No. 86-JN-CX-0009 from the Office of Juvenile Justice and Delinquency Prevention, Office of Justice Programs, U.S. Department of Justice and Grant No. 1RO1 MH48890-01 from the National Institute of Mental Health. Points of view or opinions expressed in this document are those of the authors and do not necessarily represent the official position or policies of the U.S. Department of Justice or the National Institute of Mental Health.

The authors wish to acknowledge the contributions of several readers of prior drafts. Also, we wish to thank the researchers who were willing to look for old unpublished reports, as well as those who provided supplementary data or clarified questions.

was defined simply as any self-reported or officially recorded violation of law. From each study reviewed, we abstracted information on the strength of the association between academic performance and delinquency. We then used meta-analytic techniques to derive a quantitative measure of the strength of the association between academic performance and delinquency. Meta-analysis is a method for quantitatively summarizing a body of literature (Hunter & Schmidt, 1990).

We found a total of 40 studies representing 28,552 male and female subjects that measured both academic performance and delinquency at the same point in time (i.e., cross-sectionally). The meta-analysis of these 40 studies yielded a correlation between academic performance and delinquency of −.149. To put our results into a more concrete and familiar metric, consider one group of children with average grades of D and F and another group with average grades of A, B, or C. The results of the meta-analysis showed that children and youths with average grades of D or F are 2.07 times more likely to be delinquent than children or youths with average grades of C or better when both variables were measured simultaneously.

In addition to cross-sectional studies, 30 studies were found representing 24,361 male and female subjects that measured academic performance 1 or more years before the delinquency measure was collected (i.e., longitudinally). The meta-analysis of these 30 studies yielded a correlation of −.153. In terms of the two previously defined groups of children with D or F and with C or better, this result shows that the lower grade point average (GPA) group is 2.11 times more likely to be delinquent. The particular significance of this finding is that children who performed poorly in school were more likely to be delinquent some years later.

## CAUSES OF ACADEMIC FAILURE AND DELINQUENCY

The finding that poor academic performance predicts delinquency in adolescence should not obscure the possibility that both poor academic performance and delinquency are the result of the same antecedent cause or common cause. Furthermore, there is no reason why there would be only one common cause; there may be several such causes. One way to identify potential common causes for both academic failure and delinquency is to compare theories of learning and theories of delinquency. Variables that are identified in both theories of learning and delinquency are very good candidates for potential common causes. Three such variables were examined: socioeconomic status (SES), intelligence, and attention problems or hyperactivity. If one of these variables actually is a common cause of both academic performance and delinquency, then one would expect that academic performance and delinquency would no longer be related to each other when the common cause variable was statistically controlled.

Once again, meta-analysis was used to derive the average association between each of the three potential common cause variables and both academic performance and delinquency. We excluded data from studies of females because few of these studies also measured intelligence, attention problems or hyperactivity, or SES. Our analysis for males showed the following results.

After controlling for attention problems, academic performance and delinquency were just barely related to each other. The partial association was −.029 for cross-sectional studies. Again, in terms of the two groups of male children, low academically performing males were approximately 1.2 times more likely to be delinquent than high academically performing males. Because controlling for attention problems reduced the association between academic performance and delinquency to near zero or, equivalently, the likelihood of delinquency, given low academic performance, to near 1.0, attention problems appeared to function as a common cause of both academic failure and delinquency.

Turning to intelligence, academic performance and delinquency were just barely related to each other when the effect of intelligence was controlled: The partial association was −.018 cross-sectionally. In terms of the two groups of male children, low-performing males were about 1.1 times more likely to be delinquent than high-performing males. Thus, intelligence appears to function as a common cause of both poor academic performance and delinquency.

The situation was different for SES. After controlling for SES, academic performance and delinquency remained related to each other, with a partial association of −.138 for cross-sectional studies and −.157 for longitudinal studies. The results imply that low academically performing children were about 2.0 times more likely to be delinquent than high academically performing children based on cross-sectional studies, and 2.2 times more likely to be delinquent based on longitudinal studies. Because controlling for SES did not materially reduce the association between academic performance and delinquency, SES did not function as a common cause variable.

In summary, both intelligence and attention problems appear to function as common cause variables, but SES does not. Why are common cause variables particularly important? Changing a child's standing on a common cause variable, in principle, directly affects his or her likelihood of both low academic performance and delinquency. For example, if an intervention were successful at reducing the level of attention problems of a group of children or in teaching such children compensating strategies, then we would expect that those children would simultaneously do better in school and have a lower likelihood of delinquent offending.

The findings described so far were based on studies in which none of the variables was systematically manipulated. Therefore, these studies cannot inform us about whether we actually can improve academic performance or decrease delinquency. To answer these questions, intervention studies must be examined, because only they reveal whether improving children's standing on a putative common cause variable *actually* leads to higher academic performance and a lower likelihood of delinquency.

## INTERVENTION STUDIES TO IMPROVE ACADEMIC PERFORMANCE AND REDUCE DELINQUENCY

We reviewed intervention studies that reported measures of both academic performance and delinquency. From the many studies that evaluated interventions to reduce delinquency or to improve academic performance, only 12 reported data on both academic performance and delinquency. Of these 12 studies, only 2 studies targeted variables that were identified as possible common causes.

The first study, the Perry Preschool Project, sought to improve intellectual and social development through a comprehensive 2-year intervention program during the preschool years for children from a low-income area (Berrueta-Clement, Schweinhart, Barnett, Epstein, & Weikart, 1984). Subsequent testing revealed that children receiving the intervention scored higher on intelligence tests at school entry than children not receiving the intervention. At age 19, the results showed that children who had received the intervention had a higher high school GPA and lower prevalence of arrest than children who had not received the intervention. These findings show that intelligence scores are not completely fixed, immutable values. Rather, intelligence scores may, within limits, be improved by a focused intervention program, and the benefits of such a program are reflected in both improved academic performance and decreased delinquency.

In the second study, Tremblay et al. (1992) provided a 2-year school-based program of self-control and social skills instruction to first-grade boys with high levels of disruptive behavior, including attention problems and hyperactivity, and a parent instruction program for their parents. Compared with a similar group of boys not receiving the intervention, boys receiving the intervention displayed some evidence of reduced involvement in delinquency at age 12 and an increased likelihood of not having been held back at grades 4 and 6. This study showed that children can be taught to better regulate their own behaviors and to interact in a more cooperative and less coercive manner with other children. Children displaying relatively more of these skills appear to derive more benefit from academic instruction. Moreover, it is unlikely that the acquisition of these skills depends on intellectual ability.

## CONCLUSIONS

The results of the meta-analysis and review of intervention studies indicated the following conclusions. Academic performance and delinquency are related to each other in both cross-sectional and longitudinal studies. It appears, however, that they are related primarily because both are related to the common variables of attention problems or intelligence. Two intervention studies that targeted either low intelligence or high disruptive behavior were found to lead to both improved academic performance and reduced delinquency. Although replication of these studies is needed, the results thus far support the value of targeting common cause variables when designing interventions.

In conclusion, we offer the following thoughts on directions for research. First, intervention programs for children and youths that have either educational or criminal justice goals should be encouraged to collect both behavioral and educational data. Because interventions are complex and expensive enterprises, it is incumbent on both investigators and funding agencies to derive the maximum practical amount of data for the investment even if those data are not of direct concern to that agency. To the extent that it is possible and methodologically valid, the collection of measures of both self-reported and officially recorded delinquency for existing and recently completed educational interventions should be supported. It is equally important that educational performance and attainment data be collected as a part of delinquency intervention studies.

Second, it is critically important for investigators to describe how their intervention program is expected to work. For example, through what processes does improving intelligence lead to lower delinquency? But the quest should not stop there—that these processes actually worked as anticipated also needs to be demonstrated. Only then can knowledge be improved.

Third, further work is needed to identify other possible common-cause variables and to test those variables with interventions. Although new studies are needed, efforts also should be made to extract the maximum yield from the literature. To that end, investigators should be encouraged to retain their data sets when their study ends and consider depositing them with data archives.

Fourth, the emergence of intelligence and attention problems as common-cause variables should give impetus to efforts to understand the structural and functional meanings of these constructs at the neurological level. From these efforts may come the possibility of early detection and treatment. Equally important is research directed at ascertaining how children with low intelligence or attention problems process stimuli, learn from experience, and regulate their behavior. Efforts such as these will produce more effective teaching strategies and more effective social interventions.

## REFERENCES

Berrueta-Clement, J.R., Schweinhart, L.J., Barnett, W.S., Epstein, A.S., & Weikart, D.P. (1984). *Changed lives: The effect of the Perry Preschool Program on youths through age 19* (Monograph No. 8). Ypsilanti, MI: High/Scope Educational Research Foundation.

Hunter, J.E., & Schmidt, F.L. (1990). *Methods of meta-analysis.* Beverly Hills, CA: Sage Publications.

Maguin, E., & Loeber, R. (1996). Academic performance and delinquency. In M. Tonry & N. Morris (Eds.), *Crime and justice: A review of research* (Vol. 20.). Chicago: University of Chicago Press.

Tremblay, R.E., Vitaro, F., Betrand, L., Le Blanc, M., Buauchesne, H., Boileau, H., & David, L. (1992). Parent and child training to prevent early onset of delinquency: The Montreal Longitudinal-Experimental Study. In J. McCord & R.E. Tremblay (Eds.), *Preventing deviant behavior from birth to adolescence: Experimental approaches* (pp. 117–138). New York: Guilford Press.

# Chapter 29

# Learning Disabilities and the Juvenile Justice System: A Perspective

*Mark J. Griffin*

When you work with children who have disappointed a lot of people, including themselves, parents, and professionals, you have to find a way to see the good and work from there. Despite all that seems to be problematic for children and adults with learning disabilities (LD) who are involved with the justice system, I have, happily, found some positive possibilities within the justice system.

But first, I would like to recount my suburban juvenile delinquency tale. In Greenwich, Connecticut, you do not find a lot of youngsters who end up in the juvenile justice system, because they have a lot of resources and tend to be well behaved most of the time. Several years ago, we had a parent come to us who wanted to have her youngster enrolled in our school. During the admissions process, the parent related that her son had experienced a brush with the law. This was a youngster who was 11 years old. I wondered what this transgression might have been. In Scarsdale, New York, this youngster and four of his friends got together and decided that they would like to set off a fire alarm. They found a fire alarm box, pulled the alarm, and as soon as the alarm went off, the others scurried away; but her son, a youngster with LD, stayed there. He waited for the fire trucks to come, and when they arrived, they snagged him. Later on, when they took him to the juvenile police officer, the officer asked him why he had not run away like the others. The child told him that last year, when his class went to visit the fire station, he had to stay back because he was making up some work that he did not do very well the day before. One of the youngsters came back and said there was a "really cool Dalmatian" at the fire station, and he was hoping that when the fire trucks came, they would bring the Dalmatian, because he had not had a chance to see the dog.

## LINK BETWEEN LEARNING
## DISABILITIES AND JUVENILE DELINQUENCY

My point is that the learning disability–juvenile delinquency link should not come as a great surprise to any of us. When we talk about children who do not organize well, do not read well, do not see cause and effect, tend to be a little more impulsive than other children, and generally have poor judgment, they simply are not good at being bad—they get caught. So, some youngsters with LD tend to become involved with some facet of the justice system early. Many of the attributes that allow some individuals to be reasonably successful criminals (e.g., good problem-solving skills, organizational skills) are not there for a lot of these young people.

There have been many good points made by the authors in this section. Wodatch (see Chapter 25) writes that the U.S. Department of Justice is going to be very militant about the implementation of the Americans with Disabilities Act of 1990 (ADA) (PL 101-336). Although this is good news, it is disturbing to note that in this country only 29% among people with disabilities even know about ADA. So, even if we are going to be militant about the implementation of ADA, we need to find a way to get that other 71% involved with the Act and to understand the importance of its implementation. The same levels of militancy promised in the implementation process should be applied to the awareness process, so that those people who really need the protection and entitlements of ADA can avail themselves of this strong legislation.

We know quite a bit about young people with LD. Crawford's study (1982) demonstrated clearly that with 45–50 hours of academic help, there were marked changes in children, not only in their ability to read but also in their ability to stay out of the juvenile justice system. The study reported that they did not change their attitudes toward school at the level hypothesized; I cannot help but think, however, that better outcomes would occur in that arena, too, with more time devoted to intervention. Children with LD abound in the justice system. Professionals in the field should employ a wide variety of strategies aimed at educating children with LD more effectively to prevent such large numbers of these children being incarcerated.

Many children who run afoul of the law tend to lack social competence and self-esteem. Given the fact that we have spoken frequently about social skills and the development of social competence in children with LD, if we took good academic intervention and coupled it with a proven, effective social skills program, just think of some of the things that we could change for young people.

## FOCUSED INVOLVEMENT

The authors in this book have argued persuasively for good practical research in the area of individuals with LD and the juvenile justice system. We are finally addressing the need for practical research. The authors have not discussed measuring eye blinks or the number of individualized education program objectives that were reached in a particular resource room. Authors *have* discussed topics such as phonological awareness and intervention early on with students so that we might prevent involvement in the justice system rather than react to youngsters who end up in courtrooms.

We have also heard extensively about collaborations. The National Institutes of Health (NIH) and the U.S. Department of Education are actually working on projects together! We have talked about collaboration between the Department of Justice and the juvenile justice practitioners, another necessary but overdue relationship that has developed in the mid-1990s. Such collaborations among agencies that design and implement policies are a critical part of the provision of better services and better lives for people with LD. Researchers in the LD field have quantified and qualified what we do not know and mapped out a plan outlining how we are going to go about systematic inquiry that will give us good information in those areas.

Authors have also discussed the need for a thematic approach. There are data-driven reasons to believe that it is much more productive to be analytic in the diagnosis of LD instead of using discrepancy formulas of achievement versus potential. We need to rethink, based on documented need, not on discrepancy, how we determine who is eligible for special education services in the justice system. This change would be a major accomplishment.

## THE MYTH OF MILDNESS

We continue to struggle, however, with the "myth of mildness" (Martin, 1993) in connection with individuals with LD. If you are in the juvenile justice system, nobody is particularly concerned that you have a learning disability, because the myth of mildness of your disability exists at some level within that system. If they were worried that you were going to hang yourself overnight because your file said you were suicidal, you can be sure that corrections officials would take away your belt and your shoelaces. But the fact that you cannot read and you do not do particularly well in school are not necessarily factors that carry immediacy. The efficiency of the juvenile justice system has been emphasized—it moves you through a number of buildings and a number of processes very quickly. These are children and young adults whom people do not want on the streets. People want them out of circulation and in a place that is safe and secure so that they can walk around feeling safe. There is something inherently bad about this system for youngsters in trouble, which is not reflective of the good people who work in that system. We must help promote changes that reflect the thinking of those who provide daily services and those who know the children best.

We live in a society in which people still worry about whether they should tell their employers that they have LD. I am concerned about the 16-year-old whose parole officer gets him a job at McDonald's and who has real trouble with the operation of his cash register. He likes his job, and he is making some money for a change. He is not doing it by selling drugs or doing something else that is inappropriate or illegal, and he is very proud of his accomplishments. He does not disclose his difficulty to his shift manager, however, because he is afraid that if someone finds out he does not know what to do, he will lose his job. So, it comes down to understanding what ADA means for 16-year-olds and that they, as well as older Americans with disabilities, are protected in those situations.

We are also still fighting the issues of biases regarding gender, class, and culture. In Judge McGee's court (see Chapter 27), juveniles represent what is the most disturbing part of diversity for us—the poor, both Caucasian children and those from minority groups. It is not just youths from minority groups who end up in the court, but any child from a family of limited socioeconomic status.

## THE FAMILY AND THE JUVENILE JUSTICE SYSTEM

Families are overburdened by their youngsters who end up in the juvenile justice system and have LD. These children with special needs often seem overwhelming to these two very different but intertwined systems of the family and the juvenile justice system.

The juvenile justice system has limited resources and a tremendous job. We who are special educators think our job is tough, and we are simply trying to address some of the intervention issues. We are not trying to design and implement effective rehabilitative systems for youngsters with LD who have been incarcerated. It is an overworked, underfunded system that we are asking to do an almost impossible job.

We are also asking the impossible of the already burdened family structure. The dysfunctional family is one of the three key elements, along with school failure and low self-esteem, that contribute to juvenile delinquency in this country. We are, in effect, asking families with few resources, families with the least capability, to take on the burden of raising and parenting a youngster who does not learn easily, does not act appropriately, and does not respond socially the way other youngsters do. Without a significant increase in the help available from many agencies for these families, the outcomes for these children and their families will continue to be miserable.

We know of a family with many resources that has experienced a personal struggle with the juvenile justice system. The family spent between $250,000 and $300,000 in an attempt, over a period of years, to have a son with LD treated fairly and effectively by the local school and juvenile justice systems. The family finally achieved an outcome in which the son is still incarcerated but with a lesser sentence, and the system has begun to provide some appropriate educational services.

The juvenile justice system must initiate some fundamental changes to ensure that young offenders receive appropriate educational intervention while incarcerated. These services should address their learning problems while helping them to avoid the justice system in the future through effective intervention and prevention.

## CONCLUSIONS

There are potentially wonderful outcomes from the Summit on Learning Disabilities for the field of LD and for the approximately 15% of the population who have LD. There *is* a national responsibility to provide the best possible services for people who need our expertise and help to achieve their considerable potential. Clearly, we have been challenged to achieve this lofty goal. There appear to be three components that need to be in place to effectively meet the needs of individuals with LD: the field of LD must respond, the federal government must respond, and external agencies must respond to this challenge.

The field has responded, and the government has responded. External agencies must be the vehicle of change—the National Center for Learning Disabilities, the Learning Disabilities Association of America, the Orton Dyslexia Society, the Council for Exceptional Children, and others interested in individuals with LD need to work together. NIH has certainly committed itself to the issue of LD.

I am encouraged for the first time in a long time that children and adults with LD will actually come closer to the outcomes we all desire for them. The research being done and completed, the collaboration efforts, and the commitment of the federal government to support this issue are truly exciting.

## REFERENCES

Americans with Disabilities Act of 1990 (ADA), PL 101-336. (July 26, 1990). Title 42, U.S.C. §§ 12101 et seq.: *U.S. Statutes at Large, 104*, 327–378.

Crawford, D. (1982). *A study investigating the correlation between learning disabilities and juvenile delinquency.* Williamsburg, VA: National Center for State Courts.

Martin, E.W. (1993). Learning disabilities and public policy: Myths and outcomes. In G.R. Lyon, D.B. Gray, J.F. Kavanagh, & N.A. Krasnegor (Eds.), *Better understanding learning disabilities: New views from research and their implications for education and public policies* (pp. 325–342). Baltimore: Paul H. Brookes Publishing Co.

# SECTION V

# HEALTH AND HUMAN SERVICES

# Chapter 30

# Learning Disabilities as a Public Health Concern

*Duane Alexander*

Learning disabilities (LD) include a wide range of disorders in learning and speaking and in reading, writing, and mathematics that put children and adults at substantial risk for failure, whether it be in the classroom or in the workplace. We know the most frequently occurring type of learning disability involves learning to read, and we also know that the skill of reading is absolutely essential for success in school or in work. Those working in the field of LD now know from our longitudinal studies that one in five children and adults will experience reading-based learning disabilities unless early and appropriate interventions are provided (Lyon, 1994, 1995; Shaywitz, Fletcher, & Shaywitz, 1994).

## EFFECTS AND CONSEQUENCES OF LEARNING DISABILITIES

In addition, we now understand that the effects and consequences of learning disabilities extend far beyond school and work. For example, a child or adult with LD is much more likely than a typical peer to have difficulties in forming friendships and maintaining social relationships. In turn, these difficulties result in significant decrements in self-esteem, which is a consequence that is debilitating to the individual no matter what age. Moreover, when a child or adult with LD also has difficulties attending to tasks or is impulsive, that individual is at a much higher risk for developing disruptive and aggressive behaviors and much more likely to demonstrate severe problems with learning to read, learning mathematics, learning computer skills, and completing school.

In fact, recent information tells us that children with learning disabilities are dropping out of school at a much greater rate than the typical population. Providing exact numbers is difficult because schools, cities, and states all define dropouts differently and often do not analyze dropout data by type of disability. But the data that do exist suggest that more than half of students with learning disabilities leave school before graduation compared with our already bad national dropout rate of 27% (Shaywitz & Shaywitz, 1994).

In addition, the employment rates for individuals with learning disabilities are significantly lower than for the overall population. Then, if you ask employers how their employees with LD are faring, the supervisor is likely to report that individuals with LD have a harder time keeping a job, learning new occupational skills that require reading or computer literacy, and getting along effectively with co-workers.

These academic and occupational outcomes for individuals with LD are certainly bleak and clearly constitute a significant public health concern. Given these outcomes, a critical question that has to be asked is whether the lives of individuals with learning disabilities have to be so traumatic and tainted with negative experiences. I do not think they do.

## RESEARCH FINDINGS

We at the National Institute of Child Health and Human Development, and in our learning disabilities research centers in particular, have made tremendous strides in understanding learning disabilities that can help to alleviate the educational and occupational barriers confronted by those with learning disabilities. We have come a long way since the *Report to Congress on Learning Disabilities* (Kavanagh & Truss, 1988), because we tried very seriously to implement the recommendations in that report and because the learning disabilities advocacy community went to bat and got Congress to appropriate some of the resources that we needed such as those for the learning disabilities research centers.

From the research that was called for in that report, conducted to meet the higher standards also called for in that report, here are some of the things that we have learned.

The major causes of learning disabilities are centered around a lack of development of the particular linguistic skill termed *phonological awareness*. Given this discovery, we know how to measure whether a child has the requisite language skill before he or she enters school, and we can predict reliably from these measurements whether a student will have difficulty learning to read once he or she is in school (Lyon, 1995).

We also know that adults with reading-based learning disabilities display this linguistic deficiency in phonology. This deficiency can be measured reliably and remediated in intervention programs. We have preliminary data informing us that some teaching and intervention methods are better than others for particular individuals with learning disabilities.

We know that girls are just as likely as boys to manifest dyslexia. This replicated finding stands in contrast to the previous incorrect view that boys were more likely than girls to manifest dyslexia and has alerted parents and teachers to be vigilant in their observations of language and reading development in both boys and girls (Alexander, Gray, & Lyon, 1993; Lyon, 1995).

Through neuroimaging techniques, we can identify some of the neurobiological correlates of dyslexia and map the neurophysiological systems for oral and written language disorders including reading disability. This information is particularly useful in helping us understand the neurobiological foundations of both typical and atypical brain development and function in children and adults (Lyon, 1995; Lyon & Rumsey, 1996).

These findings are indeed exciting and demonstrate some of the substantial strides that have been made since the report to Congress (Kavanagh & Truss, 1988) stressed the need to develop a classification system for learning disabilities that would more clearly define them, the need to develop information to help in the identification of causes in the developmental course of learning disabilities, the need to develop early predictors of learning disabilities and valid diagnostic measures for children and adults, and the need to develop methods of intervention to reduce the negative impact of learning disabilities.

## RESEARCH IMPERATIVES

Nevertheless, more research remains to be accomplished if we are to advance our understanding of the causes and effects of LD throughout the life span. For example, although much has been learned in the 1980s and 1990s about the effects and developmental course of learning disabilities in children, we must begin to study systematically the effects of learning disabilities in adulthood, particularly with respect to how such disabilities influence occupational success, mental health, family life, employability, social skills, and career development.

In this context, we must learn whether the diagnostic and intervention methodologies developed for children are equally efficacious and relevant for adults. We must develop better ways to measure the unexpected underachievement that is manifested by individuals with LD.

We know that use of IQ–achievement discrepancies, the traditional measure, is problematic. Now we have to identify more valid means to assess underachievement in learning disabilities. We are on the threshold of some of the most exciting discoveries in the neurobiology of learning, which have been made possible through technology that allows us to see clearly the structure and functions of the brain as children and adults pay attention, listen, speak, read, write, and carry out mathematical tasks. We have to continue our work in this area because an understanding of the neurobiology of learning and learning disabilities will ultimately lead us to optimal preventive strategies.

Likewise, our behavioral genetics studies have advanced knowledge to the point that we now know that reading disabilities are largely inherited. In turn, this information helps us to predict and intervene early with children from affected families. In addition, we must continue the search for the genetic loci responsible for these patterns of heritability.

It is imperative that we continue our longitudinal developmental studies so that we can clearly understand how early in a child's life we can predict the possibility of a learning disability and develop predictive diagnostic tools for this purpose.

Early identification is critical because early intervention relies upon it. As such, we must continue our research on the effects of different teaching and intervention methods and styles at different ages to better understand how to achieve the most favorable outcomes for youngsters with learning disabilities. The importance of early intervention for reading disabilities and other disabilities is underscored when one considers that unless these children are provided appropriate intervention by the third grade, their chances for improvement in reading are minimal (Francis, Shaywitz, Steubing, Shaywitz, & Fletcher, 1994).

Finally, we need to better understand how having a learning disability affects the range of physical, emotional, and social health issues of children and adults. We need to know whether individuals with learning disabilities are more likely to engage in behaviors such as substance abuse, to become delinquent or commit crimes as adults, or to have higher rates of suicide or mental illness and, if so, whether these are intrinsic to the learning disability or are consequences of the frustration and failure these individuals so often experience.

Seeking answers to these questions is part of our ongoing effort for child health and for human development throughout adulthood. Our research programs will continue to be designed and conducted with a clear eye toward excellence, discovery, and the application of these discoveries to the welfare of our children and our adult citizens.

## REFERENCES

Alexander, D., Gray, D.B., & Lyon, G.R. (1993). Conclusions and future directions. In G.R. Lyon, D.B. Gray, J.F. Kavanagh, & N.A. Krasnegor (Eds.), *Better understanding learning disabilities: New views from research and their implications for education and public policies* (pp. 343–350). Baltimore: Paul H. Brookes Publishing Co.

Francis, D.H., Shaywitz, S.E., Steubing, K.K., Shaywitz, B.A., & Fletcher, J.M. (1994). The measurement of change: Assessing behavior over time and within a developmental context. In G.R. Lyon (Ed.), *Frames of reference for the assessment of learning disabilities: New views on measurement issues* (pp. 29–58). Baltimore: Paul H. Brookes Publishing Co.

Kavanagh, J.F., & Truss, T.J. (Eds.). (1988). *Learning disabilities: Proceedings of the national conference.* Parkton, MD: York Press.

Lyon, G.R. (1994). *Research in learning disabilities at the NICHD* (Tech. Rep.). Bethesda, MD: National Institute of Child Health and Human Development.

Lyon, G.R. (1995). Research initiatives in learning disabilities: Contributions from scientists supported by the National Institute of Child Health and Human Development. *Journal of Child Neurology, 10,* 120–126.

Lyon, G.R., & Rumsey, J. (Eds.). (1996). *Neuroimaging: A window to the neurological foundations of learning and behavior in children.* Baltimore: Paul H. Brookes Publishing Co.

Shaywitz, S.E., Fletcher, J.M., & Shaywitz, B.A. (1994). Issues in the definition and classification of attention deficit disorder. *Topics in Language Disorders, 14,* 1–25.

Shaywitz, S.E., & Shaywitz, B.A. (1994, March 11). *Unlocking learning disabilities.* Paper presented at Understanding and Healing the Human Brain: Neuroscience and Behavior Research for Improving the Public Health, a Capitol Hill public forum sponsored by the NIH Reunion Task Force, Senator Edward M. Kennedy, and Congressman Henry A. Waxman, Washington, DC.

# Chapter 31

# Unlocking Learning Disabilities

## The Neurological Basis

*Sally E. Shaywitz*
*Bennett A. Shaywitz*

Children are our most precious resource; they epitomize our hopes and our dreams for ourselves and for the future of our country—hopes and dreams that come to an abrupt halt for millions of children who, despite often Herculean efforts, cannot learn to read, because of a learning disability (LD). There is not a family in this country that has not been touched by a learning disability in some way. For millions of American children, a learning disability has extinguished the light of childhood.

But learning disabilities and, in particular, reading disabilities, have consequences beyond school and beyond childhood. The eager third graders experiencing reading difficulties become, in turn, the frustrated ninth graders who drop out of school, the barely literate 25-year-olds who read at a fourth- or fifth-grade level, the thirty-something generation who are unemployed, and the defeated adults now raising families and needing public assistance.

Simply put, the goal of research is to stop this terrible cycle and to do so at the earliest possible moment. By uncovering the very basis of reading disability and the core deficit responsible for reading failure, research discoveries have brought us, for the very first time in history, to the threshold of stopping the cycle that begins with reading failure and ends with illiteracy, unemployment, and, often, incarceration. Such progress is remarkable—for our country in terms of lost resources regained, and for each child in terms of a life reclaimed.

These remarkable discoveries have come about through a targeted program of research initiated by the National Institute of Child Health and Human Development (NICHD). This story of the journey of LD from a vaguely defined and often poorly understood entity to a disorder on the cutting edge of neurobiological research represents the best example of what can be accomplished when parents and policy makers, government, and science work together for a common societal goal. It is the true story of science serving the public interest.

## FOCUSED RESEARCH ON LEARNING DISABILITIES

In 1988, NICHD, under the leadership of Duane Alexander, instituted a systematic program of research embracing program projects, learning disability research centers, and, most recently, intervention effectiveness projects. What have we learned? How far have we come? Tremendously exciting discoveries have emerged from a sharply focused program of research designed to address three critical questions concerning 1) epidemiology and developmental course, 2) cognitive mechanisms, and 3) neurobiological mechanisms. The three critical questions are, first, from the broadest perspective. What is the epidemiology and developmental course of LD? How many children are affected, and what happens to these children over the course of development? Once we are able to identify exactly who these children are, scientists can then focus on the next level of inquiry, which is, What is the basic or core deficit responsible for the learning disability; that is, what is the specific cognitive deficit that is preventing learning from occurring? Third, at the most basic level, can we identify the underlying brain mechanisms themselves, the specific neural systems that are responsible for a particular learning disability? This question, the most fundamental question of all, addresses the most abstract and yet most compelling question facing researchers: How does the mind work, and what is the relationship between mind and matter or between thinking or reading and brain function and structure? It is very exciting to be able to report that substantial progress has been made in addressing each of these questions.

## LONGITUDINAL STUDY OF READING DEVELOPMENT

Extraordinary changes take place across the period of childhood, and one of the most extraordinary is that children learn to read! Before the NICHD initiatives, the unfolding of this process, the developmental course of reading from early childhood through adolescence, had never been systematically studied in the United States. The Connecticut Longitudinal Study was initiated in 1983 to chart the course of development in a large, randomly selected group of kindergarteners. This cohort of 445 schoolchildren has been carefully monitored for the entire span of their schooling. In 1996, the children are 18 years old, seniors in high school, and continue to participate, although they now live in 26 states.

Results of this study provided the first indication of the scope of the problem, of how many children in grades one through nine are reading disabled. The data indicate that reading disability is a very common disorder affecting at least 10 million children, or approximately one child in five.

Although schools tend to identify four times as many boys as having reading disability as girls, data from the Connecticut study indicated that, when tested individually, as many girls as boys are affected by reading disability (Shaywitz, Shaywitz, Fletcher, & Escobar, 1990). These data suggest that in the classroom, the naturally more active and rowdy behavior of boys leads to their identification as reading disabled whereas girls, who are equally reading disabled, but who tend to be quieter, are often overlooked because of the mistaken notion that disruptive behaviors are an indicator of a reading difficulty.

Data from the longitudinal study indicate that not only is reading disability common, it is also persistent. For example, we now know that of the children who have reading disability in third grade, 74% still have reading disability in ninth grade; reading disability does not go away, but represents an enduring deficit that remains with a child from the beginning of school through high school and, most likely, beyond.

## CORE DEFICIT RESPONSIBLE FOR READING DISABILITY

We now know not only that reading disability persists but also what it is that remains with the child and prevents him or her from learning to read. We are learning *why* some children cannot learn to read. Scientists have now isolated the specific cognitive deficit responsible for reading disability.

For many years, it was thought that reading was a visual problem and that children with reading disability tended to read words backward. Converging evidence from many different lines of investigation, however, clearly indicates that it is not the visual system, but the language system, that is responsible for reading. Reading reflects language. Furthermore, we now know that the core deficit responsible for reading disability is at the most basic level of the language system, the level of the *phoneme*.

The phoneme is the basic unit of language. Defined as the smallest unit of discernible sound, the phoneme represents the common building block of all spoken and written words. Just as proteins must be broken down into their constituent amino acids before they can be digested, words must be broken down into phonemes before they can be processed by neural systems in the brain.

Children and adults with reading disability have difficulties with this most basic step in the reading pathway: breaking down the written word into simpler phonological units. As a result of this deficit, children cannot break the reading code. The discovery of the phonological basis of reading disability allows us to understand why even some very bright individuals cannot learn to read. Thus, although other components of the language system, such as the higher-order language processes involved in reading comprehension and meaning are generally not impaired in reading disability, individuals with reading disability cannot access or use these higher-order skills until they have translated words into their phonological forms. The phonological model crystallizes exactly what a reading disability involves: children with good intelligence who cannot use their often excellent higher-order neurolinguistic and cognitive skills, because of a block in the first step of the reading pathway.

## A NEW ERA IN READING DISABILITY

We are now poised to enter a new and extraordinary era in the study of reading disability. Until the mid-1990s, scientists have been limited in their ability to study the basic neural mechanisms serving reading. Reading can be studied only in people; there can be no animal models of reading. Previously, our understanding of such complex brain functions was limited to studies of individuals with brain injuries or to the examination of the brains of deceased individuals. Clearly, neither of these approaches is appropriate to study reading disability in children, in whom the disorder is not the result of injury, but represents a subtle developmental disorder. Consequently, in order to study and understand reading disability, we must be able to measure brain function in the intact individual as reading is taking place.

In 1994 and 1995, a powerful and revolutionary new technology emerged, one that now allows scientists to image the working brain. This remarkable technology, termed *functional magnetic resonance imaging,* captures the physiological changes that take place when brain activation occurs. In more direct terms, functional magnetic resonance imaging allows us to directly visualize the inner workings of the human brain. It is as if the vast system of neural networks in the brain had suddenly lit up and become visible, thus allowing scientists to actually peer into and view the working brain. Using standard magnetic resonance imaging techniques, functional imaging is painless, noninvasive, and involves no harmful radiation. Some of our findings using this remarkable technology are discussed below.

## NEW DATA FROM FUNCTIONAL IMAGING

Data from our laboratory indicate that it is now possible to study reading in children and adults using functional imaging. In a series of experiments in which the subject is asked to read, we can now clearly demonstrate where in the brain phonological processing (the basis of reading) takes place. Furthermore, we have now demonstrated that the functional organization of the brain for phonological processing differs in men and in women; men are highly lateralized to the left inferior frontal gyrus, whereas women demonstrate activation bilaterally. With this demonstration, we have taken a giant step forward in our quest to understand the underlying neural basis of reading disability. This remarkable technology allows scientists, for the first time, to identify and to isolate with surgical precision those brain regions activated while the child is actually reading a word.

With this achievement, the ability to pinpoint the specific neural networks serving reading, our quest to understand, to treat, and even to prevent LD has taken a quantum leap forward. Now that we have identified the particular neural networks engaged by reading, they can be mapped and quantified. We can map their specific locations within the brain, their size, their composition, and the specific intensity of their activation when reading takes place. Then we can use these as potential markers for studying and better understanding why some children and adults cannot learn to read.

In addition, we can now begin to analyze in a precise and quantitative manner how brain function and learning are affected by important biological events that affect every child, such as puberty, and events such as menopause that eventually affect every adult woman. For example, one NICHD-funded study at the Yale Center for Learning and Attention is using functional imaging to examine hormonal influences on both neural function and the development of reading skills in children as they mature and go through puberty. There is reason to believe that these reading skills may change over the course of maturation; for example, as mentioned, an earlier study demonstrated that equal numbers of boys and girls were affected by reading disability. This equal prevalence of reading disability in boys and girls combined with reports that women tend to compensate more as adults converges with the newly demonstrated differences between men and women (with women having bilateral representation) in organizational patterns for reading. These epidemiological data join with the new biological data to provide a possible basis for the greater ability of women, compared with men, to compensate for reading disability. A new study will examine specific cognitive, hormonal, and brain organizational changes in males and females across the entire span of pubertal development (7–17 years).

Because adults, too, and particularly older women, experience significant hormonal changes, the Office of Research on Women's Health of the National Institutes of Health, in conjunction with NICHD, funded an exciting study at the Yale Center for Learning and Attention that is applying our newfound knowledge to investigate hormonal influences on cognition and brain function in postmenopausal women.

## CONCLUSIONS

In summary, we are in the process of harnessing the extraordinary power of neurobiology to improve the lives of children and adults with LD. We are at the cusp of a true revolution in our ability to use science to inform public policy, one in which biological discoveries serve the health and education of our children. Children and adults with LD no longer need to be at the mercy of vague impressions or misguided notions of LD. We no longer have to grope in the dark—for scientific discoveries illuminate our paths.

The child with a reading disability is, in a sense, locked away from the joys and privileges of the American dream, with his or her potential contributions lost to the child, his or her family, and to society as a whole. To be able to unlock that potential, to allow that child to contribute to and participate in society, represents the ultimate goal of this research, a goal that represents not only a remarkable achievement for us as a society but also a goal that lies within our grasp.

## REFERENCE

Shaywitz, S.E., Shaywitz, B.A., Fletcher, J.M., & Escobar, M.D. (1990). Prevalence of reading disability in boys and girls: Results of the Connecticut Longitudinal Study. *Journal of the American Medical Association, 264*(8), 998–1002.

# Chapter 32

# Advocacy

*Patricia Glatz*

The achievements since the 1970s in the area of learning disabilities (LD) are impressive. We now have the protections of such legislation as the Individuals with Disabilities Education Act of 1990 (IDEA) (PL 101-476) and the Americans with Disabilities Act of 1990 (ADA) (PL 101-336). What is more impressive, however, is the tenacity and persistence of the parents and professionals who fought relentlessly for the passage of these laws. These parents and professionals were masters of networking and interfacing before the terms even existed. They became politically astute and adept in their endeavors to persuade legislators to sponsor bills. That is why the Learning Disabilities Association of America (LDA) exists today, with many of the same people still actively involved. They continue to fight for the rights of the very same group of children of the 1960s and 1970s who are the parents of young adults today.

In the 1980s, it was still virtually impossible for individuals with LD to receive services through their state departments of rehabilitation. LD were invisible. Now high school seniors are being certified by state departments of rehabilitation to receive services. Nevertheless, parents and professionals continue to struggle to document students' LD, and students continue to flounder.

## NEEDS OF INDIVIDUALS WITH LEARNING DISABILITIES

Vocational services need to be increased considerably so that education results in the acquisition of job-related skills, especially for individuals with severe LD. Transition services need to be intensified, be directly tied to the student's program, and become a part of the curriculum. At the secondary school level, students who lack organizational, time management, and goal-setting skills and information-processing abilities have difficulty in school unless there is a consistent attempt to make a connection between these skills and abilities and the world in which the students must function.

Social skills instruction also needs to be directly linked to transition services for many adolescents with LD. If these needs are not addressed, young adults with disabilities are at risk for dropping out, contact with the justice system, unemployment or underemployment, and problems in personal relationships and marriage. There simply are not enough success stories.

Accommodations and adaptations for students with LD have resulted in more and more high school graduates who are continuing with postsecondary education. Students are now able to take college aptitude and achievement tests with accommodations. If students self-advocate, then the chances of their success increase accordingly. A tremendous amount of dedication on the part of special education teachers is necessary to manage, plan, invent, maneuver, bolster, and support the student, parents, general education teachers, administrators, and outside sources of assistance. It is almost like being the owner, coach, player, and referee of a professional football team all at the same time.

The inclusion programs with which I am familiar all require much planning and cooperation. The individualized education program (IEP) must be based on individual needs without shortchanging anyone or anything. I have heard too many horror stories of plans gone awry because services were not in place or because the general education teacher was not accepting of the child or the program. Laws can mandate services, but they cannot mandate attitudes or acceptance. If the classroom environment is not appropriate, the program will not succeed. It is an extremely difficult task to accommodate a problem that cannot be seen.

All educators need to be special. The range of concerns that students bring into the educational setting is ever-increasing. Some students are already parents, some have been thrown out by their parents, others carry weapons, some deal drugs, some abuse alcohol, and some students test positive for human immunodeficiency virus (HIV).

A 1987 study by the Illinois Health Care Cost Containment Council reported that teenage boys were hospitalized for treatment of psychological problems more than for any other cause. The leading cause of hospitalization for teenage girls was childbirth and the second cause was psychological problems. Youth with LD are often susceptible to these very same conditions. All children need to know that adults care and have realistic expectations of them.

Just as all teachers need to be sensitive to the needs of all students, special educators need to be sensitive to the needs of general education teachers. They need to be won over gently by experiencing the successes of their students that result from collaboration. Gradually, success will carry over to all students in all classes. This is especially true because Goals 2000: Educate America Act of 1994 (PL 103-227) has begun to be implemented in local schools. The learning outcomes need to be clearly communicated to parents. Their input concerning individual needs is crucial.

## PARENT AND PUBLIC AWARENESS NEEDS

LDA of Illinois and its local chapters regularly sponsor sessions for parents at conferences and seminars. The Chicago Board of Education has developed a parent education program and sponsors the Friends of Special Education, a parent advocacy group. This group has developed a procedures manual for parents to become involved in their child's education. There can be no gearing down in respect to parent participation in their children's education.

In fact, the education of all citizens about LD needs to be an ongoing process. The Museum of Science and Industry in Chicago has a marvelous permanent exhibit on the brain and how it functions. It is accompanied by hands-on activities of how the brain processes information. There are videos featuring children, youths, and adults with LD. Computer monitors display answers to questions and provide sources for further information. It is an amazing "must see" exhibit that is the direct result of the brain research done during the 1980s and 1990s.

One other area of concern involves eligibility criteria. If a student's family relocates, the new school district often reinterprets the IEP or the evaluation data and does not provide the same level of services that were previously provided. This has occurred regardless of the distance of the move. Again, advocacy is vital in this regard.

## CONCLUSIONS

Our achievements are many, and the list continues to grow. These issues of the causes, diagnosis, intervention, and prevention of LD, which were the focus of the 1987 Interagency Committee on Learning Disabilities Report to Congress, continue to be issues for further research. Transition services and improved models of inclusion based on individual needs are slowly being developed. Adult services vary from city to city and from state to state. There is a need for consistent standards for services that are not under the direct supervision of the state departments of education. We continue to need the protections of both federal and state law as well as increased funding from both federal and state agencies, and we need the continued support of parent and professional organizations to keep all of us focused on the important issues in the field of LD.

## REFERENCES

Americans with Disabilities Act of 1990 (ADA), PL 101-336. (July 26, 1990). Title 42, U.S.C. §§ 12101 et seq.: *U.S. Statutes at Large, 104*, 327–378.

Goals 2000: Educate America Act of 1995, PL 103-227. (March, 1994). Title 20, U.S.C. §§ 5801 et seq.: *U.S. Statutes at Large, 108*, 125–180.

Individuals with Disabilities Education Act of 1990 (IDEA), PL 101-476. (October 30, 1990). Title 20, U.S.C. §§ 1400 et seq.: *U.S. Statutes at Large, 104*, 1103–1151.

Interagency Committee on Learning Disabilities 1987. (1987). *Learning disabilities: A report to the U.S. Congress.* Washington, DC: Author.

# Chapter 33

# Attention-Deficit/ Hyperactivity Disorder

*Jack M. Fletcher*
*Bennett A. Shaywitz*

Attention-deficit/hyperactivity disorder (ADHD) is a common disorder of children and adults. Depending on the sample and the approach used for diagnosis, early studies found that the prevalence rate in children ranged from less than 1% to 14% of the school-age population (Szatmari, Offord, & Boyle, 1989). Subsequent studies that employed more sophisticated epidemiological methods obtained prevalence rates of 6.7%–9.5% (Shaywitz & Shaywitz, 1994). Of particular importance is the relationship of ADHD and learning disabilities. Depending on whether children are identified in a school or in a clinical setting, it has been estimated that 30%–50% of children with a formally diagnosed learning disability meet diagnostic criteria for ADHD; 10%–25% of children identified with ADHD have a diagnosed learning disability; and more than 50% of children with ADHD underachieve in school (Barkley, 1990; B.A. Shaywitz & Shaywitz, 1988; Shaywitz, Fletcher, & Shaywitz, 1994; S.E. Shaywitz & Shaywitz, 1988).

Disorders of learning and attention commonly co-occur in a child, but they are not the same disability and one disorder does not cause the other. ADHD is not a *learning* disability, it is a *behavioral* disorder. Unlike learning disabilities, ADHD is not (and should not) be identified on the basis of psychometric or cognitive tests of learning, achievement, or attention (Barkley, 1994). Rather, ADHD is identified on the basis of

This chapter was supported in part by National Institute of Child Health and Human Development Grant No. P01 HD21888, Psycholinguistic and Biological Mechanism in Dyslexia and by Grant No. P50 HD25802, Center for Learning and Attention Disorders. Although the views expressed in this chapter are the authors', the thoughtful reviews and suggestions of Russell Barkley and James Swanson are gratefully acknowledged.

behavioral criteria. Many children with learning disabilities have attention problems, but this does not mean that they have ADHD. The psychological construct of attention and the behavioral construct of ADHD are not synonymous (Barkley, 1994; Fletcher, Shaywitz, & Shaywitz, 1994). Hence, disorders of learning and attention may co-occur in the same child, but the mechanisms of inheritance, biological underpinnings, and treatment needs are very different. Nonetheless, virtually all the concerns and recommendations expressed for children with ADHD in this chapter apply—with different twists—to children with learning disabilities.

## EVOLUTION OF THE CONCEPT OF ADHD

Contrary to recent media reports, ADHD is neither a fad nor the disease of the hour. Described contemporarily since the early 20th century, the concept of ADHD as an organically based behavioral disorder is inherently intertwined with issues concerning school achievement and learning disabilities (Doris, 1993). This relationship can be seen in Figure 1, which provides a schematic overview of the evolution of the concepts of ADHD and learning disabilities as classification hypotheses.

Figure 1 shows that both disorders have their roots in early conceptions of the relationship of brain injury and behavioral disorders (Rutter, 1981). Over time, these conceptualizations evolved into the notion of minimal brain dysfunction (MBD), representing a syndrome of children with learning and/or behavioral problems stemming from some form of common, but unknown, cerebral dysfunction (Satz & Fletcher, 1980). The first formal federal definitions of learning disabilities were derived in the 1960s from earlier federal definitions of MBD (Doris, 1993; Satz & Fletcher, 1980). Conceptualizations now clearly separate a disorder of learning involving reading, arithmetic, and writing skills from a behavioral disorder involving hyperactivity, inattention, and impulsivity (see Figure 1). This separation has proven invaluable and essential in guiding neurobehavioral research into the heritability, neurological underpinnings, and intervention with both disorders.

## CLINICAL DESCRIPTION

ADHD represents at least two types of disorders. The most widely recognized manifestation, the hyperactive/impulsive subtype, is a *behavioral* disorder characterized by problems with self-regulation, including impulsivity, overactivity, and inattention. Less widely recognized is the inattentive subtype, which is a *cognitive* disorder characterized by prob-

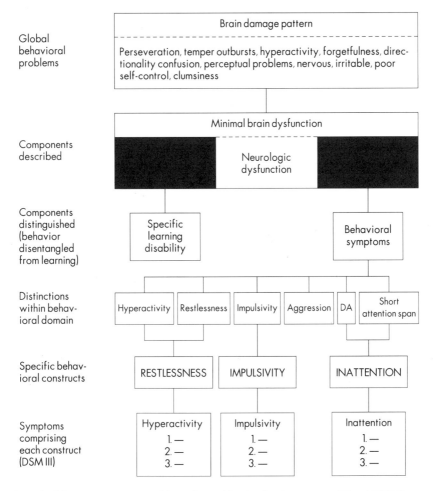

Figure 1.    Schematic representation of the evolution of the classification concepts of LD and ADHD. (From Shaywitz, S.E., & Shaywitz, B.A. [1994]. Learning disabilities and attention disorders. In K.F. Swaiman [Ed.]. *Pediatric neurology: Principles and practice* [2nd ed.] [Vol. 2, p. 1121]. St. Louis: Mosby; reprinted by permission.)

lems with concentration, initiation, and organizational skills (Lahey & Carlson, 1992). Both subtypes are identified by the presence of the relevant behavioral features in several contexts (home, school, community). The existence of these disorders is widely accepted in the professional community with extensive research support for potential biological mechanisms and treatment (Barkley, 1990). It is clear that the symptoms of ADHD persist into adulthood and lead to major problems with behavioral control, achievement, and adjustment (Satterfield, Swanson, Schell, & Lee, 1994).

Table 1 lists criteria for different types of ADHD published in the *Diagnostic and Statistical Manual of Mental Disorders,* Fourth Edition (DSM-IV) (American Psychiatric Association, 1994). However, an unresolved research issue involves the best criteria for identifying children with ADHD, particularly in relationship to intervention and the different settings in which children with ADHD are expected to perform (school, home, community). In some settings, application of behavioral criteria alone leads to high identification rates. Accurate identification of ADHD requires consideration of other explanations for the child's behavior and the application of multiple exclusionary criteria (Barkley, 1990; B.A. Shaywitz & Shaywitz, 1994; Swanson, Cantwell, Lerner, McBurnett, & Hanna, 1991). In particular, age-of-onset and exclusionary criteria in DSM-IV must be met, and the behaviors must be seen in multiple settings with significant impact on adaptive functioning. It is possible to take the criteria listed in DSM-IV (American Psychiatric Association, 1994) and convert them to a scale. The scale can be normed relative to age-based expectations. Under this approach, children are identified if their score exceeds a certain cutoff-point (e.g., top 7% of the population, consistent with the prevalence data). Even with this approach, however, criteria B–E in Table 1 must be met (Barkley, 1990).

## CURRENT STATUS OF RESEARCH

When evaluating what is known about ADHD, progress has been made in areas involving classification, treatment, and biological mechanisms of ADHD. When identified and intervened with early and persistently, the prognosis of children with ADHD is quite good. As described above, valid, objective criteria are available for identifying ADHD. However, identification can be a problem in part because of the need for research addressing the best set of criteria for identifying children with ADHD in different settings and in relation to treatment. Like disorders such as obesity, hypertension, and dyslexia, ADHD is a variation on normal development. It represents a continuum and is not a disorder that represents a qualitative departure from normality. All of us could be said to manifest characteristics of ADHD at times—the issue is how frequently, how severely, and in what context. Severe ADHD leads to behavioral problems at home, school, and work and contributes to school failure, crime, and unemployment. For disorders such as ADHD, obesity, dyslexia, and hypertension, the issue is determining the level of severity that indicates a need to begin intervention, particularly in relationship to setting and the different objective criteria available for identifying ADHD.

Table 1. Diagnostic criteria for attention-deficit/hyperactivity disorder

**A.** Either (1) or (2)

    (1) Inattention: Six (or more) of the following symptoms of inattention have persisted for at least 6 months to a degree that is maladaptive and inconsistent with developmental level:

        (a) Often fails to give close attention to details or makes careless mistakes in schoolwork, work, or other activities

        (b) Often has difficulty sustaining attention in tasks or play activities

        (c) Often does not seem to listen when spoken to directly

        (d) Often does not follow through on instructions and fails to finish schoolwork, chores, or duties in the workplace (not due to oppositional behavior or failure to understand instructions)

        (e) Often has difficulty organizing tasks and activities

        (f) Often avoids, dislikes, or is reluctant to engage in tasks that require sustained mental effort (such as schoolwork or homework)

        (g) Often loses things necessary for tasks or activities (e. g., toys, school assignments, pencils, books, or tools)

        (h) Is often easily distracted by extraneous stimuli

        (i) Is often forgetful in daily activities

    (2) Hyperactivity-impulsivity: Six (or more) of the following symptoms of hyperactivity-impulsivity have persisted for at least 6 months to a degree that is maladaptive and inconsistent with developmental level:

      *Hyperactivity*

        (a) Often fidgets with hands or feet or squirms in seat

        (b) Often leaves seat in classroom or in other situations in which remaining seated is expected

        (c) Often runs about or climbs excessively in situations in which it is inappropriate (in adolescents or adults, this may be limited to subjective feelings of restlessness)

        (d) Often has difficulty playing or engaging in leisure activities quietly

        (e) Is often "on the go" or often acts as if "driven by a motor"

        (f) Often talks excessively

      *Impulsivity*

        (g) Often blurts out answers before questions have been completed

        (h) Often has difficulty awaiting turn

        (i) Often interrupts or intrudes on others (e. g., butts into conversations or games)

**B.** Some hyperactive-impulsive or inattentive symptoms that caused impairment were present before age 7.

**C.** Some impairment from the symptoms is present in two or more settings (e. g., at school [or at work] and at home).

**D.** There must be clear evidence of clinically significant impairment in social, academic, or occupational functioning.

**E.** The symptoms do not occur exclusively during the course of a pervasive developmental disorder, schizophrenia, or other psychotic disorder, and are not better accounted for by another mental disorder (e.g., mood disorder, anxiety disorder, dissociative disorder, or a personality disorder).

*(continued)*

Table 1. *(continued)*

Code based on type:

*314.01* Attention-Deficit/Hyperactivity Disorder, Combined Type: Both Criteria A1 and A2 are met for the past 6 months

*314.00* Attention-Deficit/Hyperactivity Disorder, Predominantly Inattentive Type: Criterion A1 is met, but Criterion A2 is not met, for the past 6 months

*314.01* Attention-Deficit/Hyperactivity Disorder, Predominantly Hyperactive-Impulsive Type: Criterion A2 is met, but Criterion A1 is not met, for the past 6 months

The issue of setting is particularly important. ADHD has only recently been recognized as a disorder that represents a potential obstacle to a child's education. With the passage of the Individuals with Disabilities Education Act of 1990 (IDEA) (PL 101-476), children with ADHD became eligible for modified educational programs. Much progress has been made in the design of home environments that are appropriate for the child with ADHD, which, often in conjunction with pharmacological interventions, lead to good outcomes. However, intervention with the child with ADHD in the educational setting is an area in need of research (Swanson, 1992).

The development of school environments may present some difficulties. Education typically approaches children according to their needs to develop certain skills. When children have difficulties learning these skills, such as reading, interventions are based on teaching the lacking skills. However, ADHD is a disorder of performance, not of skill; that is, of not doing what you know, not of not knowing what to do (R.A. Barkley, personal communication, 1994). Skill-based intervention programs are demonstrably ineffective for children with ADHD (Barkley, 1990). One cannot send a child with ADHD to an "ADHD therapist" or "ADHD teacher" for two 30-minute sessions weekly and expect to see improvement. Rather, intervention with the child with ADHD requires helping the child to cope with the environment and altering the environment to help the child regulate impulsivity and focus of attention.

The Office of Special Education Programs of the Department of Education has become increasingly aware of the need to approach ADHD as an educational problem. Several model school-based programs for ADHD have emerged (Burcham & Carlson, 1993), but additional research on the types of school-based environmental modifications required for the child with ADHD is needed (Swanson, 1992). General education teachers are not trained or well prepared to manage children with this highly prevalent disorder in an inclusive educational environment. Identification of the disorder is often delayed until the child fails or develops severe behavior problems. Research on teacher characteristics that facilitate learning in children with ADHD is essential.

More generally, the incorporation of children with ADHD-related behaviors into general education environments should be a major research priority, with specific attention to the influence of current common, popular educational practices such as inclusion, multi-age classrooms, holistic teaching methods (e.g., whole language), early pressures to pass standardized tests, no pass–no play, and so forth. We state flatly our belief that the widely publicized increase in the number of prescriptions written for stimulant medication over the past 3 years reflects *in part* an attempt to prevent problems with school failure, poor self-esteem, and the development of aggressive behavior patterns associated in part with implementation of these types of educational practices. There are also other factors in this increase (Swanson, McBurnett, Christian, & Wigal, 1995). Nonetheless, implementation has occurred despite a lack of support for the efficacy of these practices in general and specifically for children with ADHD and learning disabilities. The need to examine the relationship of educational environments to the behavior and achievement of children with ADHD, particularly when it co-occurs with a learning disability, should be a major research priority.

There are several additional priorities for research on children with ADHD. These can be divided into the areas of classification, intervention, and biological mechanisms.

## Classification

In the area of classification, the National Institute of Child Health and Human Development has led efforts addressing the diagnosis and classification of learning and attention disorders (Lyon, Gray, Kavanagh, & Krasnegor, 1993). At this point, there are several competing and viable models for the diagnosis of ADHD. The intervention implications of these models in different settings requires more research, particularly in relation to the severity of the disorder. For example, in hypertension, large-scale clinical trials eventually helped indicate the severity of hypertension needing intervention to prevent strokes and other problems associated with high blood pressure. This type of research has not been attempted for ADHD or for learning disabilities. More research is needed on how comorbid disorders, such as conduct disorders or learning disabilities, influence the diagnosis of ADHD. For example, are some children with learning disabilities being diagnosed with ADHD because available instruments include items such as "poor school performance"? The manner in which schools identify children with ADHD is a particularly urgent problem. Different approaches vary in terms of which child is identified with ADHD, particularly in mild or borderline cases. With the implementation of IDEA, schools are required to develop educational plans for children with ADHD, but they have not been given the tools to identify these children. There is a great danger that diagnostic criteria will be loosely applied, which will make biological and intervention research more difficult. Hence, research on methods for diagnosis, the influence of characteristics of the environment and the child that lead to diagnosis, and the degree of severity warranting different interventions is sorely needed.

### Intervention

There is a major need for research on intervention programs that are embedded in the natural contexts in which children with ADHD learn and develop. Clinic-based, short-term, skill-oriented interventions are not effective. New approaches are needed that address the development of prosthetic environments, particularly in schools, that permit children with ADHD to do what they know. Those who work with individuals with ADHD, particularly teachers, must be better instructed in designing environments that help the child with ADHD. This emphasis is no different from a research emphasis on the types of school and family modifications that must be made to help the child with brain injury (Barkley, 1990).

Stimulant medications are clearly very effective in intervention with children with ADHD. It is apparent that short-term normalization of behavior may occur in 50%–60% of cases, with 70%–90% of children with the hyperactive/impulsive subtype showing a positive response (Barkley, 1990). The literature indicates that the efficacy of these intervention persists only for 2–3 years and has little influence on achievement (Swanson et al., 1993). However, this may reflect earlier misconceptions supporting the need for drug holidays, elimination of medication at puberty, the absence of research on long-term intervention, and the failure to identify children with ADHD who also have learning disabilities. Table 2 summarizes what should and should not be expected when stimulants are used for intervention with ADHD. The fact that not all clinicians and researchers would agree with the summary in Table 2 indicates the need for more research on this common clinical practice.

The National Institute of Mental Health recently initiated the first multimodality intervention trial examining long-term interventions. This study was motivated in part because of concerns that difficulties with long-term use of medications may be more common than is presently believed and that psychosocial intervention may be more effective than indicated by the literature (J.M. Swanson, personal communication, 1994). More research is needed on the long-term intervention with ADHD with explicit incorporation of school-based interventions and examinations of the effectiveness of stimulants on behavior

Table 2.  Expectations for responses to stimulant medication in children with ADHD

### What Should Be Expected

1. Temporary Management of Diagnostic Symptoms, due to decreased:
   a. hyperactivity (increased ability to modulate motor behavior)
   b. inattention (increased concentration or effort)
   c. impulsivity (improved self-regulation)
2. Temporary Improvement of Associated Features, due to decreased:
   a. defiance (increased compliance)
   b. aggression (less physical and verbal hostility)
   c. negative social skills (improved peer interactions)

### What Should Not Be Expected

1. Paradoxical Response does not characterize ADHD, because:
   a. most responses of normal children are in the same direction
   b. some responses of normal adults are in the same direction
   c. adults and children with ADHD have similar clinical responses
2. Prediction of Response has not been shown for nonsymptom variables such as:
   a. neurological signs
   b. physiological measures
   c. biochemical markers
3. Absence of Side Effects in clinical treatment is rare because:
   a. frequently there are problems with eating and sleeping
   b. sometimes negative effects on cognition and attribution occur
   c. infrequent motor or verbal tics appear or increase
4. Large Effects on most complex skills are considered unusual because controlled studies show:
   a. no significant improvement of reading skills
   b. no significant improvement of basic athletic skills
   c. no significant improvement of positive social skills
5. Improvement in Long-Term Adjustment is considered unlikely, because most studies show:
   a. no improvement in academic outcome
   b. no reduction in antisocial behavior or arrest rate
   c. small effects on learning and achievement

From Swanson, J.M., McBurnett, K., Christian, D.L., & Wigal, T. (1995). Stimulant medications and the treatment of children with ADHD. In T.H. Ollendick & R.J. Primz (Eds.), *Advances in clinical child psychology* (Vol. 17, p. 305). New York: Plenum Press; reprinted by permission.

and learning. This is particularly important because it has become apparent that ADHD can be a lifelong disorder persisting into adulthood (Barkley, 1990).

To summarize, intervention with children with ADHD who have other co-occurring disorders (learning disabilities, conduct disorder) needs to be emphasized to establish the degree to which interventions for ADHD are efficacious in children with co-occurring disorders. Research on the use of stimulants as a component of long-term intervention, particularly in relation to possible side effects and lack of long-term efficacy, is urgently needed. The bottom line is that aggressive and scientifically based intervention with ADHD may have a significant impact on school failure, juvenile delinquency, and crime as well as on a host of problems of adult adjustment (Satterfield et al., 1993).

## Biological Mechanisms

Research on the neurobiological basis of ADHD should proceed in three directions. The first direction is heritability. Several prominent geneticists have described ADHD as the most heritable of all childhood behavioral disorders, with genetic heritability coefficients averaging .80 and a shared environmental contribution of approximately .10 (R.A. Barkley, personal communication, 1994). There is a major need for studies of the heritability of ADHD to parallel the remarkable strides made in the understanding of the heritability of dyslexia. We need to know more about the genetic mechanisms of inheritance and what gene(s) may be involved with ADHD.

The second direction is for more research on the brain basis of ADHD. Studies using functional neuroimaging methods, although preliminary, have highlighted the role of different brain structures in mediating cognitive functioning in children with ADHD (B.A. Shaywitz & Shaywitz, 1994). This technology continues to evolve, and newer methods for fast magnetic resonance imaging and quantitative electrophysiological measurement show particular promise. The application of these methods to children with ADHD and other developmental disorders should be a priority.

The third research direction involves the use of molecular biology techniques to isolate potential genetic mechanisms and to examine individual variations in neurotransmitter responses to pharmacological challenges. These techniques are just beginning to be used to study ADHD but have great promise. Altogether, these three research directions could lead to the development of biological markers for different types of ADHD, which would facilitate resolution of some of the issues concerning classification and intervention.

## CONCLUSIONS

To return to the issue of the relationship of ADHD and learning disabilities, it should be apparent that many of the recommendations and concerns discussed in this chapter pertain directly to children with learning disabilities (see Chapter 2). Like learning disabilities, ADHD has been the subject of intensive investigation since the 1980s. Major strides have been made in classification, intervention, and identification of possible biological mechanisms. Research must continue to be supported. Like many other professionals, we believe that these disorders are at the heart of many problems faced by our society. Early identification and intervention may have significant effects on achievement, employment, juvenile delinquency, and many other problems that can be associated with these common disorders of childhood.

# REFERENCES

American Psychiatric Association. (1994). *Diagnosis and statistical manual of mental disorders* (4th ed. rev., DSM-IV). Washington, DC: Author.

Barkley, R.A. (1990). *Attention deficit hyperactivity disorder: A handbook for diagnosis and treatment.* New York: Guilford Press.

Barkley, R.A. (1994). The assessment of attention in children. In G.R. Lyon (Ed.), *Frames of reference for the assessment of learning disabilities: New views on measurement issues* (pp. 69–102). Baltimore: Paul H. Brookes Publishing Co.

Burcham, B., & Carlson, L. (1993). *Promising practices in identifying children with attention deficit disorder.* Washington, DC: U.S. Department of Education.

Doris, J.L. (1993). Defining learning disabilities: A history of the search for consensus. In G.R. Lyon, D.B. Gray, J.F. Kavanagh, & N.A. Krasnegor (Eds.), *Better understanding learning disabilities: New views from research and their implications for education and public policies* (pp. 97–115). Baltimore: Paul H. Brookes Publishing Co.

Fletcher, J.M., Shaywitz, B.A., & Shaywitz, S.E. (1994). Attention as a process and as a disorder. In G.R. Lyon (Ed.), *Frames of reference for the assessment of learning disabilities: New views on measurement issues* (pp. 103–106). Baltimore: Paul H. Brookes Publishing Co.

Individuals with Disabilities Education Act of 1990 (IDEA), PL 101-476. (October 30, 1990). Title 20, U.S.C. 1400 et eq: *U.S. Statutes at Large, 104,* 1103–1151.

Lahey, B.B., & Carlson, C.L. (1992). Validity of the diagnostic category of attention deficit disorder without hyperactivity: A review of the literature. In S.E. Shaywitz & B.A. Shaywitz (Eds.), *Attention deficit disorder comes of age: Towards the twenty-first century* (pp. 119–144). Austin, TX: PRO-ED.

Lyon, G.R., Gray, D.B., Kavanagh, J.F., & Krasnegor, N.A. (Eds.). (1993). *Better understanding learning disabilities: New views from research and their implications for education and public policies.* Baltimore: Paul H. Brookes Publishing Co.

Rutter, M. (1981). Psychiatric sequelae of brain damage in children. *American Journal of Psychiatry, 138,* 1533–1543.

Satterfield, J., Swanson, J., Schell, A., & Lee, F. (1993). Prediction of antisocial behavior in attention-deficit hyperactivity disorder boys from aggression/defiance scores. *Journal of the American Academy of Child and Adolescent Psychiatry, 33,* 185–190.

Satz, P., & Fletcher, J. (1980). Minimal brain dysfunctions: An appraisal of research concepts and methods. In H.E. Rie & E.D. Rie (Eds.), *Handbook of minimal brain dysfunction: A critical review* (pp. 669–714). New York: John Wiley & Sons.

Shaywitz, B.A., & Shaywitz, S.E. (1994). Learning disabilities and attention disorders. In K.F. Swaiman (Ed.). *Pediatric neurology: Principles and practice* (2nd ed.) (Vol. 2, pp. 1119–1151). St. Louis: Mosby.

Shaywitz, S.E., Fletcher, J.M., & Shaywitz, B.A. (1994). A conceptual model for learning disabilities and attention-deficit/hyperactivity disorder. *Canadian Journal of Special Education, 9,* 1–32.

Shaywitz, S.E., & Shaywitz, B.A. (1988). Attention deficit disorder: Current perspectives. In J.F. Kavanagh & T.S. Truss (Eds.), *Learning disabilities: Proceedings of the national conference* (pp. 369–523). Timonium, MD: York Press.

Swanson, J.M. (1992). *School-based assessments and interventions for ADD students.* Irvine, CA: K.C. Publishing.

Swanson, J.M., Cantwell, D., Lerner, M., McBurnett, K., & Hanna, G. (1991). Effects of stimulant medication on learning in children with ADHD. *Journal of Learning Disabilities, 24,* 219–227.

Swanson, J.M., McBurnett, K., Christian, D.L., & Wigal, T. (1995). Stimulant medications and the treatment of children with ADHD. In T.H. Ollendick & R.J. Primz (Eds.), *Advances in clinical child psychology* (Vol. 17, pp. 265–322). New York: Plenum Press.

Swanson, J.M., et al. (1993). Effect of stimulant medications on children with attention deficit disorder: A "review of reviews." *Exceptional Children, 60,* 154–162.

Szatmari, P., Offord, D.R., & Boyle, M.H. (1989). Ontario child health study: Prevalence of attention deficit-disorder with hyperactivity. *Journal of Child Psychology and Psychiatry, 30,* 219–230.

Chapter 34

# Research Implications for Health and Human Services

*Melinda Parrill*

In an ideal world, all people would be created equal. Realistically, opportunities and needs vary. Those who need assistance cannot always afford to pay for, or to have access to, quality services. People with knowledge, resources, and influence have a responsibility to actively support and assist people by designing and making available quality service, regardless of financial status, age, and type of disability.

Considering some of the statistics available, we know that, within the disability category, the highest occurrence is learning disabilities (LD). This category includes an estimated 10% of the school population, and, with our knowledge of genetics, there is strong evidence of the heritability of LD (Lyon, 1995a). Of individuals with disabilities, those with LD have the highest levels of self-care skills (95.5%), high functional mental skills (66.0%), and high community living skills (74.2%) (SRI International, 1993). The only group of individuals with disabilities that had more arrests within 3–5 years of leaving school than individuals with LD (31%) was the group with emotional disturbances (57.6%). The employment rate for those with LD (48%) was lower than the national average (68%). Individuals with LD have a higher dropout rate from high school (58%) than the national average (27%) (SRI International, 1993). Of those entering an adult literacy program, 70% of those with LD drop out after the first 6 weeks (see Chapter 15).

Efforts described by authors and proposed in this book provide legitimate ways of beginning to change those statistics. These efforts span age, situation, and daily and occupational expectations. Information can be used to an even greater extent to create better research, legislation and regulations, programs, and partnerships and to establish funding priorities. In this chapter, implications from knowledge about

LD are drawn to address specific issues related to health and human services. Emphasis is placed on *prevention, identification, intervention,* and *preparation.* The topics of research and selected service programs for children, youth, families, and adults provide the structure for this discussion.

## RESEARCH

Care must be taken to address what we know with the appreciation that it is easier to acquire new information than it is to change people's minds, prejudices, emotions, and misconceptions (W.B. Perry, personal communication, September 19, 1994). There are plausible research projects and programs deserving continued and increased funding. Research efforts involving partnership and collaboration are also in progress. These initiatives reflect new knowledge and offer opportunities for change. This is not to negate the importance of the gaps in our knowledge, but a solid foundation is forming on which to base research that will help to predict, anticipate, intervene with, and lessen the impact of LD.

The research programs and centers of the National Institute for Child Health and Human Development (NICHD) have placed us in a better position to more effectively address cause, prevention, and early intervention through application of these discoveries (see Chapter 30). Applications have included collaboration by investigators across and within research projects and studies, requirements for replication, continued investigation of questions regarding medical and behavioral correlates (DeFries, Olson, Pennington, & Smith, 1991), and inclusion of investigations of recommended practices for intervention of basic reading skill within the broader context of medical, behavioral, and cognitive variables already under study (Torgesen, Wagner, & Rashotte, 1994). Major findings from the NICHD research programs are detailed in Lyon (1995a), and interested readers are referred to this work.

Applications of these NICHD findings should be reflected in funding priorities, identification and eligibility procedures, interventions, partnerships, and policies. Some of the areas from which to draw these implications are summarized briefly in the following sections: genetics, identification and assessment, intervention, prevention, and partnerships.

### Genetics

There is documentation of a genetic basis for at least some disorders under study (e.g., reading, language disorders ) (DeFries et al., 1991). Relevant findings related to etiology and identification are that different disorders have different biological and neurological correlates, the determination of differential diagnosis and comorbidity among disorders, and the discovery of patterns of heredity in LD (Lyon, 1995a). Furthermore, if certain learning disabilities are indeed inherited, knowledge of etiology can eventually lead to prevention and recognition of LD at early stages of development. With adults, persistence of LD can affect daily life functioning and outcomes. It is important to specify developmental markers and track and evaluate the development of other family members with respect to those skills and their consequences and persistence.

There is increased knowledge concerning the comorbidity of LD with other disorders (Fletcher, Shaywitz, & Shaywitz, 1994). The estimates of the co-occurrence of LD and attention-deficit/hyperactivity disorder range from 26% to 80%. In addition, a strong pattern of heredity for both disorders has been demonstrated (Gilger, Pennington, & DeFries, 1992). This information may be most useful in identifying and delineating variables associated with success in many different activities as well as eligibility for services and benefits. Included in such a study should be variables associated with life success and problems (e.g., juvenile delinquency; school dropout; unemployment; family, peer, co-worker problems). Although being able to anticipate and alter the course of negative life outcomes do not necessarily prevent the occurrence of LD within this group, intervening early can provide an avenue for minimizing such problems.

## Identification/Assessment

Frequently used tests are inadequate in identifying and delineating LD and in determining and differentiating the occurrence of LD with other disorders. Tests seldom measure the quality of a skill or the integration and application of complex skills. Such measurements are desirable. Assessing variables associated with ease, efficiency, and automaticity across a variety of ages and situations and for a variety of learning disabilities is indicated.

Tests are also used to diagnose and determine eligibility, and test score differences are often used to calculate discrepancy between measured achievement and intellectual functioning. Discrepancy as an operational formula for determining LD is invalid (see, e.g., Chapter 32; Shaywitz, Fletcher, & Shaywitz, 1994). "Unexpected underachievement" is now part of the operational definition of *dyslexia* (of the Orton Dyslexia Society) (Lyon, 1995b). Another application of the unexpected underachievement model has been proposed for use with adolescents and young adults and bright individuals (see Shaywitz et al., 1994). A broader application of the unexpected underachievement model would be used across age, type of disability, or comorbidity (Lyon, 1994). Somewhat different from this proposed application is the need to address 1) those who show discrepancies among and within domains not necessarily manifested in below-average or grade-level performance; 2) lack of validity in assessment tools and tests in evaluating actual situational demands, such as reading job manuals and taking notes; and 3) the occurrence and consequences of comorbidity (Parrill, 1994). Some researchers have suggested that adults with LD may well have compensated for early and basic deficits, which are not apparent when achievement is measured. Developmental and academic histories are relevant to the identification of reading disabilities (Shaywitz et al., 1994).

## Intervention

Implications for intervention involve prevention, anticipation, accommodation, and remediation. Intervention should be studied with the same care and rigor as LD. This includes NICHD studies of longitudinal intervention studies with children with LD by Torgesen (1993) and by Foorman (1993). Studying intervention issues in the context of medical, behavioral, and cognitive factors provides benefits not available from narrower research. For example, addressing the effectiveness of the intervention approach as a function of the relationship to the identified core disability allows the determination of recommended practices and enables faster generalization. Intervention and research are needed beyond the basic academic deficit level (e.g., phonology in reading single words). Research consideration should be given to situation, history and persistence, complex application, and the differential effects of learner characteristics that are not necessarily primary concerns in designing interventions for basic academic deficits.

## Prevention

Intervention can be successful in preventing and lessening the impact of learning problems, before as well as after identification. Although research in genetics and cognitive and behavioral manifestations should eventually lead to earlier identification and intervention of LD, learning problems can be anticipated or avoided through educational intervention. Intervention aimed at prevention can take at least three forms: 1) intervention incorporating recommended teaching practices before identification or within the general educational curriculum, 2) intervention addressing the needs of family members, and 3) intervention to address characteristics associated with disorders and to maximize successes during development.

## Partnerships

Partnerships among researchers across agencies, within projects and centers in the same institutions, and with service providers and advocacy groups are essential. Part of these partnership efforts should involve

1) imparting and employing knowledge of recommended practices (e.g., how and what skills required for success to explicitly teach); 2) obtaining precise analysis of necessary skills; 3) establishing guidelines and standards for conducting research; 4) creating legislation, regulations, and funding priorities and sources; 5) taking advantage of existing opportunities for partnerships (e.g., Head Start, National Institute for Literacy); 6) collaborating with others with similar interests, including government agencies (e.g., Office of Special Education Programs, U.S. Department of Education) and researchers (see Chesapeake Institute, 1993); and 7) developing valid assessment procedures and eligibility criteria.

NICHD's longitudinal research must continue to be supported, but cross-sectional research must also be conducted. Cross-sectional research should be incorporated into longitudinal research. This type of research should focus on the impact of LD at a specific time and on the immediate environmental consequences. Research in applied settings using knowledge of recommended practices must be included. Such research should involve careful and systematic study of the effects of intervention, access to service, organizational strategies, and use of available resources.

## SERVICE PROGRAMS

Research findings in the field of LD have broad and far-reaching possibilities concerning identification of learning problems, eligibility for services due to appropriate diagnosis of LD, intervention of service providers, and design and implementation of service programs.

Intervention can take the form of prevention, early intervention, accommodations, remediation, and financial support. The knowledge and the role of families, communities, and local involvement should not be underestimated in the success of interventions. Preparation of those involved in service design and delivery must take into account age, situation, provider, the individual with LD, environmental expectations, and social acceptance. Knowledge and preparation should be reflected in program development and implementation, and should ensure quality of service, accountability of the provider, and receipt of service by all who are eligible. Quality of service, accountability of the provider, and receipt by all who are eligible can be maximized through partnerships and collaborations. Partnerships and collaborations must reflect the diverse needs and interests of individuals with LD.

### Child, Youth, and Family Programs

Two programs are discussed that are designed to provide assistance to those with limited financial resources. Although poverty does not create LD, many of the statistics for adults with LD and individuals living in poverty are similar when considering school achievements and life outcomes. Common needs of individuals with LD and individuals living in poverty can be addressed through available research findings specific to individuals with LD. To demonstrate these possibilities, within this section the Head Start program and Supplemental Security Income (SSI) are discussed.

First, statistics associated with poverty are reviewed. Poverty, or low income, is often a requirement for eligibility for the children's programs discussed. Poverty and literacy are often linked to outcomes of adults with LD without successful intervention. Circumstances associated with poverty affect identification of eligibility for and accessibility to appropriate service. Furthermore, children living in poverty, even with identified LD, do not always have access to needed services. Family members with significant learning problems do not have access to needed service, owing to lack of identification of LD.

**Head Start**   Head Start grew out of the War on Poverty and was reauthorized through the Human Services Reauthorization Act of 1994. The basic tenet of Head Start programs was to provide help to low-income children ages 3–5 years, of which at least 10% were to be children with disabilities. Families' needs were also to be assessed and addressed. Help was to be provided through 1) early childhood education; 2) health screening and referral; 3) mental health programs to assist in the child's emotional, cognitive, and social development; 4) nutritional services and hot meals; 5) social services for children and families; and 6) parent educators (Zigler & Styfco, 1993). When reauthorized in 1994, a number of significant changes were mandated. These reflected three priorities: 1) to improve the quality of the Head Start programs (e.g., staff development, federal oversight); 2) to be more responsive to the needs of children, their families, and communities; and 3) to encourage and form working relationships and partnerships and to plan and support service programs at all levels of government (see Chapter 5).

To address program improvements, 25% of the reauthorized funds were to be used to update performance measures, establish outcome measures, promote staff development and adequate wages, and provide technical assistance and monitoring. In response to family needs, a family needs assessment included comprehensive evaluation of the educational, health, and social services needed. Adult literacy needs were to be identified and addressed; services were expanded to include children below the age of 3 and children within the program with disabilities. If needs were determined to exist, the provision of services was required. These included parent education; referral for adult education (including literacy instruction); employment and job training; and assistance in securing adequate income, health care, and housing (S. Rep. No. 251, 1994).

In 1992, the number of children served by Head Start was 621,000 (Zigler & Styfco, 1993). This was fewer children than were served in the 1960s, but the number represents a 35% increase from 1989. In 1992, 90% of the Head Start children were living below the poverty level; 13% had disabilities; and 92%–94% of the enrolled families received support, including the hiring of 35% of the parents to work in the Head Start programs (Zigler & Styfco, 1993). In 1994, concerns were expressed in U.S. Senate reports that children were not receiving needed and available services, that children with disabilities were undeserved; and that longitudinal research was limited. The Secretary of Health and Human Services also was urged by the Advisory Committee on Head Start Quality and Expansion (appointed by the secretary in 1993) to research recommended family and child practices, including practices related to community integration and participation.

Piotrkowski, Collins, Knitzer, and Robinson (1994) discuss the Head Start program performance standards. These performance standards outlined the services that must be provided to children and their families. Among the performance standards (U.S. Department of Health and Human Services, Administration for Children and Families [DHHS/ACF], 1992) was the requirement that children with disabilities be identified, evaluated, and provided with intervention. Federal regulations provide a listing of recognized disabilities to be addressed through Head Start programs. These include emotional–behavioral disorders (previously termed severely emotionally disturbed) and attention-deficit/hyperactivity disorder for those age 4 and 5 years (45 C.F.R. § 304). Learning disabilities was not included as a disability in the Head Start performance standards. Even for those with listed disabilities, there were concerns expressed regarding both identification and receipt of appropriate service (S. Rep. No. 414, 1994; Piotrkowski et al., 1994; Taylor, 1994).

Taylor (see Chapter 5) estimated that very few of the 20% of Head Start children requiring some type of mental health service received those services. Furthermore, Taylor (see Chapter 5) noted that of the children with disabilities, 66% were identified as having speech and language problems and 6% were identified as having LD. Although no longitudinal data were available, Taylor reported anecdotal evidence suggesting that speech and language problems persisted into early elementary school and that many of these children were later identified as having LD. In addition to not recognizing learning disabilities in Head Start performance standards, hesitancy was reported regarding the negative effects of labeling these preschool children (see Chapter 5).

Issues regarding identification, service, and early labeling have developed in the context of 1) knowledge of the relationship between basic reading ability and language processing (Lyon, 1995a), 2) the persistent effects of reading disorders (e.g., Shaywitz et al., 1994), 3) the positive effects of early intervention through Head Start programs (Torgesen et al., 1994; Zigler & Styfco, 1994), 4) the requirement to provide transition services for Head Start children into preschool and elementary school in coordination with local education agencies, 5) the greater than expected occurrence of LD in families, 6) Head Start's commitment and mandate to early intervention and family assistance, and 7) the appreciation that children living in poverty are at risk for academic problems (Huston, 1994).

Even if Head Start were functioning at an optimal level, gaps exist in meeting the needs of poor children and their families before, during, and after the preschool years. Part of this gap is financial. SSI offers additional financial support and access to other federally funded programs for eligible poor children and their families.

**SSI for Children with Disabilities** SSI for children is not the same as SSI for adults. For adults, SSI is considered by many to be the end of the line and the acceptance that the individual cannot and will not be able to work, regardless of his or her efforts or support. For children below the age of 18 years, SSI can assist in the move from dysfunctional to functional. In 1993, 720,000 children received SSI benefits. These included children with the following disorders: 43% with mental retardation, 20% with psychiatric disabilities, approximately 15% with neurological or sensory disabilities (including blindness), and approximately 5% with congenital abnormalities. The remaining approximately 17% had disabilities such as diseases of endocrine, respiratory, circulatory, or musculoskeletal systems (Manes, 1994; Schulzinger, 1994).

Even with all of the avenues available through SSI, there are two far-reaching concerns: 1) lack of awareness that children with LD who are from low-income families can qualify for benefits, and 2) lack of appreciation that those with LD should be considered. The importance of advocating on the behalf of eligible children with LD must be stressed.

**Joint Considerations of Learning Disabilities and Child, Youth, and Family Programs** It has been documented that LD, with the most common type of learning disability being reading disability (Shaywitz, Fletcher, & Shaywitz, 1995), are the most frequently occurring disability. There is increasing evidence that a reading disability has genetic and neurologic associations, often occurs within families, persists into adulthood, occurs with other disabilities, and frequently reflects a core deficit in language (phonetic) processing (Lyon, 1995a). The most frequent disability identified in Head Start programs is language disorder, which might later be diagnosed as a learning disability (latter, H. Taylor anecdotal report). Comorbidity between ADHD and LD occurs, and ADHD is a disability eligible for SSI. Furthermore, evidence of a medical etiology for reading disability is increasing, and developmental delays are often apparent (both criteria for SSI eligibility).

Given that LD are the most frequently occurring disability, this category should be listed as an eligible disability for both Head Start and SSI. LD can and should be identified early to prevent or lessen school and life failures. Identification of preschool disabilities is complex if LD are present and is compounded by the influence of poverty. An unexpected underachievement model using schedules of expected development can be useful in tracking, screening, and evaluating response to intervention. Difference between same-age peers and among domains (e.g., language, motor, academic) must both be considered when applying the unexpected underachievement model.

It is possible to use developmental schedules to screen for unexpected underachievement within and among domains. Although thorough evaluation is required in order to understand reasons for unexpected underachievement, skills can be initially screened using developmental markers and differences from expected development detailed during more thorough assessments by specialists. Initial screenings are inexpensive, require limited training for use, and can be quickly administered. A note of caution: Regardless of the type of measure used, only what is screened is evaluated and often only severe problems are identified during screenings. Observation of actual functioning in a particular setting (e.g., home, school) and detailed developmental and medical histories are essential components of any screening. Screenings and thorough assessments should extend to family members as well, with care to take into account information about changes in expectations as a function of age and situation, developmental and medical histories, and information about present functioning. To accomplish screenings or thorough assessments, mandates are in place, and monies have been set aside with the reauthorization of Head Start to screen Head Start children and family members, train staff to conduct the screenings, and coordinate with experts and community resources to provide this type of service.

Once individuals have been determined to be eligible, services often are not forthcoming. Three problems regarding preparation of service administrators and providers are shared by Head Start and SSI: lack of awareness of eligibility criteria; lack of awareness of services available, and lack of assistance to the individuals with disabilities in obtaining eligibility for and access to services. Preparation of service administrators and providers and partnership and collaboration among agencies and advocates for those with disabilities offer solutions to eligibility for and accessibility of service. An example of a program that is available but that people do not use is Early and Periodic Screening, Diagnosis and Treatment (EPSDT). The EPSDT is available to Head Start recipients and to those receiving Medicaid (eligibility is provided through SSI in 38 states). Yet, few who are eligible receive this service. Children who are not healthy, physically or psychologically, cannot learn effectively, and many children living in poverty demonstrate early and progressive delays in school achievement. A wealth of knowledge is available about developmental markers associated with physical, psychological, and learning factors. Furthermore, knowledge is available about expected development, unexpected development, consequences and outcomes, poverty, and successful interventions.

As mentioned previously, child and family assessments (screenings, and thorough evaluations when indicated) and interventions are mandated in Head Start programs. Funds have been designated for instructing parents and staff to conduct these evaluations and interventions, and to coordinate with other resources to actually conduct or train staff to follow through efficiently and effectively. Successful models of collaboration are in place in several Head Start programs, and also in the private and public sectors that conduct large-scale screenings. Public and private resources should be identified and contracts should be made to train staff and implement mandated programs. It is the responsibility of local, state, and federal leadership, as well as the service providers within Head Start, and government agencies to ensure that this occurs.

Longitudinal and cross-sectional research should be conducted to assess long- and short-term effects of Head Start programs and other available services. Applied research should consider child and family characteristics (e.g., functional skills, developmental histories, financial security), intervention needs and the effects of addressing those needs, poverty, the developmental effects of LD on children (including the effects of transitioning) and family members (e.g., job training, employment), and efforts to obtain and provide quality services. In addition, within SSI, it would be relevant to study the characteristics of children receiving benefits, their outcomes and those of their families, uses of financial assistance, and functioning over time. Attempts to compare the outcomes of those in similar situations who do not receive benefits should be made.

Leadership, vision, and foresight are needed in order to maximize the benefits of legislation (Kassebaum, 1994). Federal involvement to ensure program and agency accountability is essential, as are support and enforcement. Federal involvement does not negate the importance of state and local responsibility and commitment, but rather enforces the need for large-scale oversight to monitor the effectiveness of Head Start programs in different locations and to assist in the awareness and implementation of recommended practices. Monitoring should include assurance that providers are aware of eligibility criteria, and actively identify, inform, and enforce SSI and other available programs.

**Programs for Adults**  In the mid-1980s, the largest advocacy group for individuals with LD changed its name from the Association for Children with Learning Disabilities to the Learning Disabilities Association of America. The reason for the change was that children with LD grew up to be adults with LD, and an increasing number of parents began to recognize or recall their own learning problems. The persistence of LD into adulthood is multifaceted. Consequences and outcomes place demands on adults that are not experienced by children; however, careful study of the developmental course of LD and effective interventions will help to lessen their impact on adults. Rigorous research stressing ecological validity with standards in subject selection, research design (including use of cohorts), and outcomes is limited at best. To better understand adult consequences and needed support, outcomes, availability of literacy programs, proper identification of LD and eligibility for and access to appropriate service, interventions, and partnerships are discussed next.

*Outcomes*  Gottesman (1994) summarized the results of 30 studies reporting on the outcomes of adults identified as having LD as children. There were considerable differences in the reports of specific outcomes, as well as a lack of consistency in subject selection, outcome measures, and use of controls and cohorts (Gottesman, 1994). In general, IQ scores, family situation, and severity and onset of LD were relevant to outcomes. Primary academic disabilities in reading, frequently reflecting a history of language and auditory processing disorders, were reported. This review of information was consistent with results obtained by other researchers in which a core deficit in phonology was identified (Shaywitz et al., 1994).

The summarized results presented should be interpreted as trends because of the lack of careful studies over time, lack of consistency in who was studied, methods used, and details available (Gottesman, 1994). Nevertheless, reports of outcomes were consistent with those reported elsewhere (SRI International, 1993) and with disorders noted by researchers working with children (e.g., reading, language, persistence) (Lyon, 1995a). Best adult outcomes were associated with high socioeconomic status (SES), average or above-average IQ scores, and mild LD. Poorest outcomes were associated with lower SES, low or below-average IQ scores, and moderate to severe LD. When comparisons were made with same-age peers or siblings, individuals with LD had less positive outcomes as adults. Of individuals completing college, career selections were overrepresented in business and underrepresented in math and science. Less success was associated with adults with more severe LD, who were also more likely to experience chronic unemployment, poor interpersonal skills, and difficulties in independent living (Gottesman, 1994). The role of modifications and accommodations is a relevant variable for those in the college setting (see Chapter 7). This type of support has increased dramatically.

Although specific outcomes for adults with LD were reported, less information was available regarding what about intervention and context were positive influential variables. A variable associated with more positive outcome was the educational setting of the intervention (Finucci, Gottfredson, & Childs, 1985). Although these data were limited to one location, adults who had been enrolled in the private school as children fared better as adults than those enrolled in public schools; however, the characteristics of the children and their families and the severity of the learning disability were probable considerations in private school placement (Gottesman, 1994). This finding did emphasize the need to further investigate the influences of the severity of the learning disability, the quality of the LD service provided, the availability of financial resources, and family support on adult outcomes, and adult education programs. When designing adult education programs aimed at literacy, the recognition and identification of learning disabilities and the preparation for addressing learning disabilities are essential components (Johnson, 1994).

*Literacy Programs*    Adult literacy programs have been funded at both federal and state levels since the 1960s. By 1965, all states had adult education programs. These programs now provide assistance to adults in the workplace, to those for whom English is a second language, to those who are homeless, and to those who are incarcerated (Newman, 1994). In a few programs, both children and their parents have been provided with support. Success has been demonstrated in literacy programs, but the appropriateness of this support, without taking into account the presence of LD, has been of concern. Two-and-one-half million adults have been enrolled in Adult Basic Education and General Education Development programs (Bursuck, Rose, Cowens, & Yamaya, 1989). Within those programs, estimates of adults with LD have ranged from 20% to 89% (Bursuck et al., 1989). Lack of recognition of and preparation for addressing LD have been interpreted as being reflected in the dropout rate, for example, in programs such as Literacy Action (see Chapter 15).

Two needs basic to the success of adults with LD in literacy programs are to establish a working definition of LD and to implement appropriate intervention (Gottesman, 1994). Partnerships and collaboration are essential. One effort aimed at increasing recognition and inclusion of appropriate curriculum has been undertaken by the National

Institute for Literacy through formation of the Learning Disabilities Center. This effort is designed to provide support to children and family members by forming a link between selected Head Start programs and Literacy Action programs.

*Identification*    Appropriate identification of LD precedes access to service. When disabilities are encountered, by the adult, assessment procedures for identifying LD and eligibility requirements for access to service must be valid and take into account adult history (previous speech, language, educational problems), present functioning, and environment. The nature and extent of the learning disability must be determined; however, a number of problems regarding children with LD have implications for adult identification and eligibility. These problems include measurement and diagnosis of LD (Shaywitz et al., 1994). We also have a better understanding of the significance of ease, efficiency, and automaticity in how children acquire and apply basic reading skills (Torgesen et al., 1994). Through clinical studies, detailed information is available about the delineation of basic reading disability and other LD (Hagin, Kugler, & Ellsworth, 1994; Johnson, 1994). Efficiency, ease, and automaticity in acquisition and application of basic reading skills are critical to the understanding of LD manifested in adulthood. For example, it has been suggested that excessive time completing tasks in relation to high level of competencies achieved by adults is relevant to the diagnosis of adult LD (Shaywitz et al., 1994).

Most measures do not, but should, evaluate variables or markers associated with adult histories or skills (Hagin et al., 1994). These variables include those considered critical to basic reading skill and ability (e.g., ease, efficiency, phonetic awareness) and to other academic skills. Lack of validity of measurement is more pronounced when complex skills, actual functioning, and compensation are considered (e.g., response to lecture formats, outlining skills, foreign language learning. Knowledge of college, employment, and daily skills requirements must be carefully analyzed as part of the assessment process. Tasks need to be developed to assess competencies required within different environments. The quality of performance must be part of this assessment. Eligibility criteria should be based on performance in situations relevant to adult functioning rather than on an IQ–achievement discrepancy model. The lack of validity of this model for identifying children with LD is even more pronounced with adults. It is well documented that IQ scores change as a function of age, educational achievement, and years in school (Kaufman, Penney, & Jaixen, 1990), and problems occur when this model is used with adults with LD (Hagin et al., 1994).

Study of the validity of the unexpected underachievement model for adults has merit. The model can be used to consider actual functioning in response to environmental demands and also to previous histories and intervention procedures employed. An adult's history and recognized compensation have been considered relevant in the diagnosis of dyslexia (Shaywitz et al., 1994). Social competence, family dynamics, affective style, and determination of comorbidity are also essential to broadening use of the unexpected underachievement model with adults. The influences on adult outcomes of academic preparation and experiences during childhood, adolescence, and adulthood, including variables associated with previous service, must be carefully researched. Interventions for adults with LD should be structured to reflect the same validity that is required in measurement. Intervention must consider the variety of needs, approaches, and resources available to that adult. Services should include education, financial assistance and management, mental health, and medical support.

*Interventions* Adult education interventions should offer a continuum and combination of options, and also a variety of educational approaches and practices (Johnson, 1994). These options should incorporate intervention, accommodation, and transition. Intervention should be a first consideration, and accommodations should not be made in place of remediating a basic or more severe learning disability (see Chapter 15). Interventions can be conducted in or outside of the environment requiring a specific skill. Services can be provided in a class, an individual session, or a particular situation. Models of such interventions are to be found in both higher education and work settings.

In labor, major changes have occurred in response to legislation, regulations, and an increase in sensitivity toward the needs of adults with LD. These changes have ranged from providing accommodations to establishing training centers (see Chapter 14). Successful models should be identified across settings, studied carefully, and, when appropriate, applied to other environments.

*Partnerships* Partnerships and collaborations are being undertaken by the National Institute for Literacy (NIFL) and Head Start. The National Literacy Act of 1991 included a mandate for the creation of the NIFL. The NIFL, an independent federal agency, is governed through coordinated and joint efforts of the Secretaries of Labor, of Education, and of Health and Human Services. In 1993, the NIFL formed the Learning Disabilities Center (LDC) to respond to the needs of adults with LD. The coordination among federal agencies and the formation of LDC provide a model of federal partnership and leadership.

A different type of partnership collaboration between Head Start and adult literacy programs considers the needs of low-income families with preschool children and adult members with literacy needs. Although trends are available only from outcome research for adults, low SES, coupled with LD, adversely affected adult functioning (Gottesman, 1994). Head Start and Literacy Action have formed partnerships in locations such as Atlanta. It is, however, critical that the nature of the literacy, learning disability, generalized delay, or lack of education, must be determined, and intervention must be based on that determination. As part of the intervention, the impact of literacy on adult and family functioning must be addressed appropriately.

In addition to interventions addressing literacy, Head Start's commitment and mandate to families encompass medical, mental health, and employment and training services. Although children with disabilities in Head Start may be eligible for SSI, adults are not provided the same benefits. This is particularly problematic considering the high rate of unemployment and limited financial resources listed as an outcome for a large group of adults with LD. SSI for children emphasizes movement from nonfunctioning to functioning. Adults should be provided with the same type of support if they meet criteria similar to that constructed for children with LD. Financial support is needed to gain access to quality service, which may or may not be provided in the public sector. Medical and other benefits should be extended as well. SSI provides one avenue for gaining access to, and expanding available service for, Head Start families.

## CONCLUSIONS

Much has been gained since the early legislation was passed in the 1960s to confront problems in education, literacy, and poverty. Rights, protections, and opportunities now are available that never were before. Also available are knowledge and understanding of needs, needs not met, and the means of closing the gap between what is needed and what exists for individuals with LD. Barriers still exist, however. Problems with identification procedures, eligibility criteria, and quality of and access to appropriate services are discussed in this chapter. Solutions are proposed through the use of the unexpected underachievement model that would reoperationalize the concept of discrepancy underlying LD and establish eligibility criteria consistent with that application. Diagnosis of LD based on quality of performance associated with basic skills and application of those skills in response to environmental demands and developmental changes are emphasized. Ways of anticipating, lessening, and intervening are all considered parts of the service model.

Services must extend beyond the individual. Financial, health, and social assistance must be provided as needed. In order to accomplish such multifaceted services, partnerships and collaborations must be formed. New knowledge must be incorporated and further study is required. Research should be carefully designed and directed toward the continued study of the nature, manifestation, and developmental course of LD. If possible, these should be studied simultaneously. Academic and nonacademic skills and use of these skills in actual functioning must be part of these studies. The influences of income, family needs and support, and intervention also must be included in studies. Standards must be established in order to achieve both validity and replicability. Benefits and successes of program structures, organizations, and actual services should be determined through longitudinal and cross-sectional study.

Without adequate funding, coordination, enforcement, and accountability, needs cannot be met and programs and research cannot be cost-effective. Accountability is central to the issue of program development, implementation, and evaluation and should be ensured by monitoring procedures both external and internal to the programs. Again, leadership and collaboration are essential to ensure accountability. Although we must consider and work within political, social, and economic constraints, we must not be deterred from supporting research, and from creating, implementing, and making accessible quality service programs to all in need. We must move forward not only with the enthusiasm, energy, and commitment of the idealist but also with the wisdom of the pragmatist.

## REFERENCES

Bursuck, W.D., Rose, E., Cowen, S., & Yamaya, M.A. (1989). Nationwide survey of postsecondary education services for students with learning disabilities. *Exceptional Children, 56*, 236–245.

Chesapeake Institute. (1993). *Proceedings of the forum on the education of children with attention deficit disorder.* Washington, DC: Author.

DeFries, J.C., Olson, R.K., Pennington, B.F., & Smith, S.D. (1991). Colorado Reading Project: Past, present, and future. *Learning Disabilities: A Multidisciplinary Journal, 2*, 37–46.

Finucci, J.M., Gottfredson, L.S., & Childs, B. (1985). A follow-up study of dyslexic boys. *Annals of Dyslexia, 35*, 117–136.

Fletcher, J.M., Shaywitz, B.A., & Shaywitz, S.E. (1994). Attention as a process and as a disorder. In G.R. Lyon (Ed.), *Frames of reference for the assessment of learning disabilities: New views on measurement issues* (pp. 103–116). Baltimore: Paul H. Brookes Publishing Co.

Foorman, B.R. (1993). *Early interventions for children with reading disabilities.* Bethesda, MD: National Institute of Child Health and Human Development.

Gilger, J.W., Pennington, B.F., & DeFries, J.C. (1992). A twin study of the etiology of comorbidity: Attention-deficit hyperactivity disorder and dyslexia. *Journal of the American Academy of Child and Adolescent Psychiatry, 31*, 343–348.

Gottesman, R.L. (1994). The adult with learning disabilities: An overview. *Learning Disabilities: A Multidisciplinary Journal, 5*(1), 1–14.

Hagin, R.A., Kugler, J., & Ellsworth, N.J. (1994). Assessment with adults with severe learning disabilities. *Learning Disabilities: A Multidisciplinary Journal, 5*(1), 35–41.

Head Start Program: Final Rule, 45 C.F.R. Pt. 1304, 1305, and 1308 (January 21, 1993).

Head Start Program Performance Standards, 45 C.F.R. § 304 (1992).

Human Services Reauthorization Act of 1994, PL 103-252. (May 18, 1994). Title 42, U.S.C. §§ 9801 et seq.: *U.S. Statutes at Large, 108.*

Huston, A.C. (1994). Children in poverty: Designing research to affect policy. *Social Policy Report, 8*(2), 1–12.

Johnson, D.J. (1994). Clinical study of adults with severe learning disabilities. *Learning Disabilities: A Multidisciplinary Journal, 5*(1), 43–50.

Kassebaum, N.L. (1994). Head Start: Only the best for America's children. *American Psychologist, 49*(2), 123–126.

Kaufman, A.S., Penney, J., & Jaixen, M. (Eds.). (1990). *Assessing adolescent and adult intelligence.* Boston: Allyn & Bacon.

Lyon, G.R. (1994). *An operational definition of learning disabilities: Application of the unexpected under-achievement model.* Bethesda, MD: National Institute of Child Health and Human Development.

Lyon, G.R. (1995a). Research initiatives in learning disabilities: Contributions from scientists supported by the National Institute of Child Health and Human Development. *Journal of Child Neurology, 10*(Suppl. 1), S120–S126.

Lyon, G.R. (1995b). Toward a definition of dyslexia. *Annals of Dyslexia, 45,* 3–20.

Manes, J. (1994). *SSI new opportunities for children with disabilities* [Brochure]. Judge David L. Bazelon Center for Mental Health.

National Literacy Act of 1991, PL 102-73. (July 25, 1991). Title 20, U.S.C. §§ 1201 et seq.: *U.S. Statutes at Large, 105,* 333–368.

Newman, A.P. (1994). Adult literacy programs: An overview. *Learning Disabilities: A Multidisciplinary Journal, 5*(1), 51–61.

Parrill, M.N. (1994). *An operational definition of learning disabilities: Application of the unexpected under-achievement model using dimensions.* Bethesda, MD: National Institute of Child Health and Human Development.

Piotrkowski, C.S., Collins, R.C., Knitzer, J., & Robinson, R. (1994). Strengthening mental health services in Head Start. A challenge for the 1990's. *American Psychologist, 49*(2), 133–139.

Schulzinger, R. (1994, March). Basic facts about SSI for children. *Children's SSI Campaign Alert,* 2–3.

Shaywitz, B.A., Fletcher, J.M., & Shaywitz, S.E. (1994). A conceptual framework for learning disabilities and attention-deficit/hyperactivity disorder. *Canadian Journal of Special Education, 9,* 1–32.

Shaywitz, B.A., Fletcher, J.M., & Shaywitz, S.E. (1995). Defining and classifying learning disabilities. *Journal of Child Neurology, 10*(Suppl. 1), S50–S57.

S. Rep. No. 251, 103rd Cong., 2nd Sess. (1994).

SRI International. (1993). *The transition experiences of young people with disabilities: A summary of findings from the National Longitudinal Transition Study of Special Education Students.* Menlo Park, CA. (Prepared for U.S. Department of Education)

Torgesen, J.K. (1993). *Prevention and remediation of reading disabilities.* Bethesda, MD: National Institute of Child Health and Human Development.

Torgesen, J.K., Wagner, R.K., & Rashotte, C.A. (1994). Longitudinal studies of phonological processing and reading. *Journal of Learning Disabilities, 27*(5), 276–286.

Zigler, E., & Styfco, S.J. (1993). Using research and theory to justify and inform Head Start expansion. *Social Policy Report, 7*(2), 1–17.

Zigler, E., & Styfco, S.J. (1994). Head Start: Criticisms in a constructive context. *American Psychologist, 49*(2), 127–132.

# SECTION VI

## COMMENTARY

# Chapter 35

# Looking to the Future

*Shirley C. Cramer*

A major goal of the Summit on Learning Disabilities was to inform and motivate the federal government to improve policies for children and adults with learning disabilities (LD), to place the issue of LD on the national agenda, and to underline the substantial agreement on the problems and solutions by experts from varying disciplines, parents, and advocacy groups. It was critical that correct information be presented in a clear and concise fashion, as was done in the summit presentations, to those with the authority and responsibility to effect change. It was also vital that members of the Clinton administration and Congress present their views as leaders of government agencies, the general administration, or as chairs or members of relevant House or Senate subcommittees. In one sense, being invited and accepting the invitation to speak at the summit focused the attention of government leaders on the issue of LD and on developing priorities.

At the onset, the summit organizers, the National Center for Learning Disabilities (NCLD), did not have any preconceived idea of how many government leaders and congressional representatives would accept the invitation to be involved with the summit. We also did not know how aligned their views and interpretations of the situation for individuals with LD would be. The high level of acceptance of NCLD's invitation to speak was due in no small part to Senator Christopher J. Dodd. The high level of acceptance was also a realization that more needed to be done to help individuals of all ages with LD and that the time was right to begin a dialogue on what could be done to improve outcomes.

After congressional staff members listened to presentations at the summit and took back to their senators and representatives the key issues raised at the summit, many members of Congress asked for copies of specific presentations and for the summit report, *Learning Disabilities:*

*A National Responsibility* (Cramer & Ellis, 1995), which was published 4 months after the summit. NCLD summit organizers were honored and gratified by the active participation of so many leading national political figures, who had substantive and proactive comments to make regarding the future of individuals with learning disabilities. This chapter outlines the common themes discussed by government leaders and points to the level of concern by those in positions to effect change. The issues broached by many of the speakers serve to underline the changes that need to be made in policy and practice.

## EARLY INTERVENTION AND PREVENTIVE STRATEGIES

Senator Dodd, co-chair of the summit and a leading advocate in the Senate for children's issues, has often said that early intervention is a matter of simple logic. This statement relates to many situations, but is particularly relevant to children with LD. The negative outcomes for so many adults with LD are the result of the lack of help in their early years. The gradual erosion of their self-esteem can be prevented by intervention when it matters most—at the youngest possible age. Secretary of Labor Robert Reich expanded on this by stating that the more that is invested in the early years, the more that is saved in the long term, not only in hard financial terms but also in the capacities of individuals to lead full and productive lives.

The importance of early intervention for individuals with LD was emphasized again and again by government leaders. Secretary of Health and Human Services Donna Shalala pointed to growing consensus in the country on the need to invest in early prevention programs. Secretary of Education Richard Riley noted that, in studying students with LD who do well in school and those who do not, a major factor is how early their disabilities are identified and helped. Although difficulties are often first experienced in the primary grades, especially in learning to read, a student often does not receive help until the fourth or fifth grade. By this time, the student has already tuned out the education system. Secretary Riley stated that good educational practice provides assistance to children when they are experiencing initial difficulties and does not wait 2 or 3 years to provide services, which is a common situation in the United States today.

Lowering of self-esteem can begin at a very early age, as was attested to by Secretary Reich, whose 7-year-old nephew had exhibited frustration, anger, and behavior that was not understood until his LD was diagnosed. Fortunately, because he received the help he needed, he is now sociable and open to learning. The negative effects of LD begin at a very early age, and the longer failure and low self-esteem continue, the harder they are to reverse.

First Lady Hillary Rodham Clinton pointed out that most good teachers can recognize a child with problems in kindergarten or first grade, but many education systems do not begin to address problems even though they have been identified. She indicated that this is a major flaw in the education system and one that needs to be rectified immediately.

Former Representative Marjorie Margolies-Mezvinsky cited her experience as a journalist and mother of 11 to highlight the importance of early intervention. She pointed out that having access to written information is vitally important to a child growing up in today's world, and for so many children with LD, the way they process information is often distorted and incorrect. A small problem grows into a bigger problem and then into traumatic adult problems.

The majority of government speakers alluded to personal and familial experiences in emphasizing the importance of early identification, and they noted the pain and misery attached to delayed identification and intervention. If one were to underline one single theme from their comments, it would be to take action with preventive strategies and early intervention for children with LD.

## TEACHER PREPARATION AND PARENTAL INVOLVEMENT

A key element in the success of individuals with LD is that parents and teachers recognize the signs of LD. For too many children, the warning signs are misinterpreted and the wrong conclusions are drawn.

Secretary Riley pointed out that parents and educators need to work together more closely and to listen to and understand each other to ensure the best outcomes for a child. He commented that students with LD often do not get the support they need from general education teachers and that, in turn, general education teachers themselves often do not have access to support services.

Secretary Shalala echoed Secretary Riley's call for more parental involvement in their children's education and development. She illustrated how a caring adult, whether a parent, teacher, relative, or friend, is critical to a child's moving ahead successfully. She emphasized the need for every educator in America to be made aware of the new findings about LD. Secretary Shalala commented on the need for athletic coaches also to understand the nature of LD. In her career as an educator, she had met many brilliant athletes who were not doing well in school and who were subsequently found to have LD. Many of those students were not diagnosed until they reached college.

First Lady Hillary Rodham Clinton focused on the important aspect of catering to individual needs and of not lumping children with disabilities together in segregated environments. She indicated that changes in

the educational bureaucracy would help in delivering more individualized services to many students.

## FUNDING AND MINORITY ISSUES

Aspects of funding was an area raised by both Senator James Jeffords
and Representative Major Owens. In any discussion of public policy, the
issue of funding always looms large and is frequently cited as a reason
for not taking action on pressing concerns.

Senator Jeffords put education funding in its wider context by point-
ing out that only 2% of the federal budget is currently being spent on
education. In 1995, Senators Jeffords, Dodd, and Simon were all advocating an increase in the amount spent on education at the federal level.
Their initiative is entitled "The One Percent Solution for Education," with
the goal of shifting 1% of current federal dollars each year for 10 years
from other programs to education. The overall aim of the initiative is that
in 10 years, education would have 10% of the entire federal budget, not
by increasing taxes, but rather by reallocating funds. The federal contribution would then match that of the state and local governments so that
each source would be responsible for one third of total education costs.

Senator Jeffords compared the commitment to education after
World War II, which was 9.2% of the federal budget, to the meager 2% at
this time. He contrasted this lack of funding, resulting in 30–80 million
Americans being either illiterate or functionally illiterate, to the great
need for an educated work force. He pointed out that Congress has yet to
match resources to good intentions. Only 8% out of the 40% of the dollars
pledged by Congress in 1975 under PL 94-142, and later under the Individuals with Disabilities Education Act of 1990 (IDEA), has been appro-
priated at the state and local levels. He stressed the need for a national
campaign to start a revolution in the way education is funded.

Representative Owens commented that financial considerations
are often the reason for advocating change and pointed to "inclusion"
(where all children are served in the general education classroom) as an
example. This innovation was regarded by many as less costly than
maintaining separate educational systems. Owens argued for substantial
investment in education in general and, echoing Senator Jeffords, he
commented that the money can be found by reallocating federal dollars
rather than by increasing taxes.

There was agreement that the special education system needs to
change, particularly in respect to its treatment of children from minority
groups. Representative Owens pointed out the high incidence of children from minority groups, especially males, inappropriately placed in
special education classrooms. First Lady Hillary Rodham Clinton also

stressed the disproportionate number of students from minority groups in segregated environments and suggested that more advocacy is needed on their behalf. Secretary Riley was even more forceful in his analysis of the negative implications of inappropriate placements and of some special education practices. He underlined the need for regular assessments of students in special education classes because too many are tracked into these segregated classes and then forgotten. Secretary Riley emphasized that many students get the message that they are not important and then drop out of school. They can become disconnected and disinterested, as he put it, leading to more serious difficulties later.

## COLLABORATION

A thread running through all the comments from governmental leaders was the issue of collaboration. There was general acknowledgment that there had been little collaboration between departments and agencies concerning LD.

Secretary Riley discussed the importance of federal departments working together to better serve people with LD. He was especially committed to collaborating with the Department of Labor to assist school-to-work transitions for students with LD and collaborating with the Department of Health and Human Services to disseminate and put into practice the research findings of the National Institutes of Health.

First Lady Hillary Rodham Clinton described her early experiences as an advocate on behalf of children at the federal level and being sent from one agency to another trying to stimulate a coherent approach to an issue and being told that the issue was not in the jurisdiction of the agency she was visiting, but in the one she had just left. She stressed the importance of a common mission that would lead to a cooperative approach. If the impact of LD on the lives of individuals and families in terms of lost productivity and lost academic achievement is understood and appreciated, then a united effort can be developed that brings together the resources of the public and private sectors. Promoting a coherent strategy on LD at the national level was seen to be necessary to improve the lives of all individuals with LD.

## CONCLUSIONS

The views expressed by these government leaders and their recognition of the essential issues in LD offer substantial hope that action will be taken sooner, rather than later, on some of the serious issues articulated at the Summit on Learning Disabilities. General consensus about what needs to be done and the importance of LD as an issue as stated by these government leaders allows for some optimism that improved policies and strategies can be developed. There is clearly no cause for complacency in the field of LD, and consistent advocacy and grass roots pressure will help to ensure that words are translated into actions to help all individuals with LD.

An overriding goal of the summit was to develop a blueprint for looking to the future for those with LD, to agree on priority actions that need to be taken to improve the lives of both children and adults with LD, and to develop a plan to implement those actions. The summit report, entitled *Learning Disabilities: A National Responsibility*, published by NCLD in 1995, highlighted several actions that would make significant positive changes in attitudes, public policy, training, and the delivery of services to those with LD. So what, if anything, has happened since the contributors to this book made their suggestions and recommendations for the future? Have the good intentions expressed by those in positions to influence policy been matched by any decisive actions?

Collaboration at many levels was deemed to be an essential component for progress in the field of learning disabilities, and it is a consistent theme throughout these chapters. The report recommended that an interagency committee on learning disabilities be created to coordinate research activities, practice efficacy, and public policy initiatives on the issue. It was envisioned that this committee would include senior representatives from the U.S. Departments of Labor, Education, Health and Human Services, and Justice and that this coordinated activity would generate a sharing of information and a national cohesion on policy, programs, and practices.

Shortly following the summit, Secretary Shalala convened a meeting of her senior staff at the department to discuss with NCLD representatives the recommendations from the summit. The department wished to consider the priority recommendations and act upon them if appropriate to do so. Consequently, the Department of Health and Human Services agreed to take the lead role in one of the major recommendations, that of developing an interagency committee on learning disabilities.

In the fall of 1995, a working group on learning disabilities was created at the federal level. The working group involves all the government agencies previously mentioned and the White House Domestic Policy Council. The implications for progress from this initiative are far-reaching. For the first time, each department knows exactly what its counterparts in other agencies are doing in the area of LD, and everyone has access to research findings and validated practices that help to standardize effective intervention strategies.

Bridging the information gap between scientific knowledge and educational practices is another common element in this book and is crucial to the priority of early identification and intervention as well as improved teaching practices. In 1995, a number of new initiatives surfaced to address this issue. Specifically, the Office of Special Education Programs (OSEP) at the Department of Education began a collaborative dissemination initiative entitled "Learning to Read/Reading to Learn: Helping Children with Learning Disabilities To Succeed." The material developed in this venture highlights what parents can do to encourage better reading in their children and translates the research findings into user-friendly teaching strategies for educators. The department has involved many membership nonprofit organizations to increase the program's outreach.

The American Federation of Teachers (AFT) devoted an entire edition of their journal, *American Educator*, to the subject of reading, heavily emphasizing the research findings and examining best practices related to the findings. This collection of articles does much to educate teachers on ways to help children with LD, particularly in the reading and language areas. State departments of education, too, have been paying closer attention to the nonreaders and poor readers in their classrooms and considering solutions to what has become an epidemic of illiteracy in some states. California began to examine why its reading scores had dropped so dramatically in the 1990s and concluded that the mandated whole language method of teaching reading to which it had subscribed was not conducive to teaching all children to read. The subsequent change in state policy in California to include different methods of teaching reading, which are based on validated research, should dramatically improve reading scores there over the next few years. There are doubtless many other initiatives in other states that are slowly but surely helping to inform parents and educators about how children and adults with LD learn best.

An underlying element of many of the chapters in this book has been the poor knowledge and understanding of LD by the general public. Without a common understanding of the issue—its importance, relevance, and urgency—it is difficult to change public attitudes and create the demand and recognition needed to improve services. In short, a national public awareness campaign on LD needs to be launched as a backdrop to all the other recommendations represented in these chapters. During 1995, a critical first step was taken toward the launch of such a campaign.

The Emily Hall Tremaine Foundation, a family foundation based in Connecticut, commissioned independent research and analysis into public awareness and attitudes about LD. Through a series of focus groups and a Roper Starch Public Opinion Poll, they discovered that the public was confused and misinformed about LD and that many professionals designated to help were similarly misinformed. They concluded that the information available to the public was often inconsistent as well as inaccurate, with no clear simple message. As a consequence of this objective information, the foundation decided to fund a coordinated effort to combat these deficiencies in public awareness. At the end of 1995, the National Coordinated Campaign for Learning Disabilities was formed and for the first time brought together all the national LD groups and experienced media and communication professionals to develop a long-term communications strategy for the field of LD. This collaborative effort is devising simple, clear, and consistent messages about LD for public consumption. With the launch of this national public awareness campaign, major changes in public attitudes toward the issue of LD are anticipated by the late 1990s.

This book is filled with thoughtful, well-argued analyses of the state of the field of LD and with creative ideas about a better future. It is uplifting to know that so many new and important initiatives are under way, with the goal of improving the quality of life of those with LD. Some of the constructive suggestions contained in these chapters are already being acted upon with positive effect. It is particularly pleasing that there is a greater spirit of cooperation than ever before around the issue of LD and a commitment to finding solutions. The overwhelming agreement around the areas of priority in the field ensures that our actions are focused in the key areas. With a measure of political will, a collaborative strategy, commitment, and energy we shall attain our goals.

## REFERENCES

Cramer, S.C., & Ellis, W. (1995, February). *Learning disabilities: A national responsibility*. Report of the Summit on Learning Disabilities, Washington, DC. New York: National Center for Learning Disabilities.

Education for All Handicapped Children Act of 1975, PL 94-142. (August 23, 1975). Title 20, U.S.C. §§ 1400 et seq.: *U.S. Statutes at Large, 89*, 773–796.

Individuals with Disabilities Education Act, PL 101-476. (October 30, 1990). Title 20, U.S.C. §§ 1400 et seq.: *U.S. Statutes at Large, 104* (Part 2), 1103–1151.

McPike, L. (Ed.). (1995/Summer). *American Educator* [Special issue], *19*(2).

# Index

*Page numbers followed by "t" indicate tables.*

stimulant medications for, 272, 273*t*
Attention problems, academic failure, delinquency and, 237
Attitude, performance and, 104–105

Behavior, 215–226
ADHD, 265–274
antisocial, 215–216, 220–226
comorbidity, 220–221
conduct disorder, 107
criminal, school failure and, 229–233
extrinsic influences on, 220
learning disabilities and, 215–226
prosocial development issues, 220–221
subtypes and, 217–220, 222–224
*see also* Criminal behavior; Juvenile delinquency
Brain
dysfunction, reading disabilities and, 32–33
functional magnetic resonance imaging of, 258–259
Brown v. Board of Education, 109

Career development education, 124
Carl D. Perkins Vocational and Applied Technology Education Act of 1990 (PL 101-392), 127
Chicago Board of Education, 263
Chicago White Sox, 117
Child abuse, nonunderstanding of special needs as, 106–107
Child-centered approach, 99–102
Children with learning disabilities
accommodation requirements for, 212–213
ADA and, 211–214
differential treatment of, 215–216
identification of, 191
incidence, xxx
juvenile delinquency and, 197–198
labeling, 232
needs of, 261–262
self-esteem of, 298
services for, 281–287

teaching methods for, 180–181
*see also* Learning disabilities; Students
Children, youth and family programs, 281–287
Civil Rights Division, U.S. Justice Department, 211
Classification systems, problems with, 6–9
*see also* Subtypes
Clinical (rational) subtyping, of reading disabilities, 28–29
Coarticulation, 15
Cognition, attention-deficit/hyperactivity disorder, 266–268
Collaboration, 243, 290–291
need for, 301, 302
*see also* Partnerships
Communication disorders, 12
differential treatment and, 215–216
*see also* Oral language disabilities
Comorbidities, xxx, 220–221, 279
ADHD, 35, 279, 285
behavior, 220–221
emotional disturbances, 35
mathematics learning disabilities, 45–46
nonverbal learning disabilities, 46
oral and written language learning disabilities, 39
with phonological disorders, 18–19
reading disabilities, 33, 39
social skills deficits, 35
Comprehension, in reading, 26–27, 29
Conduct disorder, 107
Connecticut Longitudinal Study, 256–257
Consensus conferences, 116
Constituency Oriented Research and Dissemination Policy (CORD), 128
CORD, *see* Constituency Oriented Research and Dissemination Policy
Correctional Education Association, 201, 229
Correctional systems
education of individuals with learning disabilities in, 198–201